W9-BBK-437

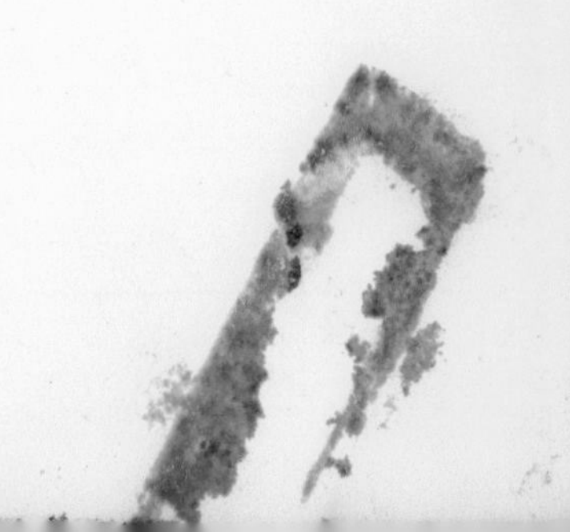

# ADENAUER

*His Authorized Biography*

*Karsh, Ottaw*

Konrad Adenauer

# *ADENAUER*

**HIS AUTHORIZED BIOGRAPHY**

*by*

*PAUL WEYMAR*

ILLUSTRATED

*Translated from the German by*
*Peter De Mendelssohn*

---

E. P. Dutton & Company, Inc.
New York
1957

FIRST EDITION





LIBRARY OF CONGRESS CATALOG CARD NUMBER: 56-6313

# LIST OF ILLUSTRATIONS

ILLUSTRATIONS

# ADENAUER

*His Authorized Biography*

"My wish is that sometime in the future, when mankind looks beyond the clouds and dust of our times, it can be said of me that I have done my duty."

KONRAD ADENAUER

# PROLOGUE

"So you're planning to write the story of my life? Let me tell you, it's been a very simple and straightforward life. I can't see that there is much to write about."

It was my first interview with the German Federal Chancellor, in the summer of 1953, in his office at the Palais Schaumburg, at Bonn.

When I entered the long, bright room, Dr. Adenauer was sitting at the far end behind a large desk. He rose and came forward to greet me. My first impression was: a man of simple and very conscious dignity which was enhanced by his erect bearing, his measured movements, and the solemn black of his clothes. With a brief and courteous gesture he invited me to sit down, and took a chair opposite me. I glanced at him. His face, with its wide cheekbones under a high and well-modeled forehead, seemed strangely rigid, and his narrow, gray-blue eyes looked at me coolly and deliberately.

"Well, how are you planning to go about it?"

Dr. Adenauer's question went straight to the heart of the matter. Here indeed was my difficulty.

When I had first come to Bonn, a few weeks earlier, to collect material for this biography, the task had seemed easy. For several decades now Konrad Adenauer had occupied a position of eminence in German politics, plainly visible and familiar to all. The number of people who knew him well was legion. I felt certain that there must be an almost embarrassing wealth of material enabling a biographer to build from the fullness of a rich and varied life covering the span of almost three generations and measuring, like few others, in victory and in defeat, all the heights and depths of our time. That is how it seemed to me when I first came to Bonn, in May, 1953.

I soon discovered that it was not so.

Adenauer's life seemed as impenetrable and inscrutable as his face. Certainly, there was no lack of people well acquainted with him. But all they had to offer, on the whole, were small and trifling incidents, anecdotes, this or that characteristic utterance, and at best disconnected scraps of information on some short and isolated period or other in his long life.

Besides, I found that opinions differed very sharply. There are those among his colleagues and associates who call Adenauer the "grandfather of foxes," and there are others who admire him as the "prototype of a Christian statesman."

There are those who regard him as a true Renaissance type, cunning, wily, ambitious, incapable of any warmth of feeling, a man who considers his fellow men merely as means toward his ends and will drop in cold blood anyone who has served his purpose. There are others who will declare indignantly that only people who don't know Adenauer at all could possibly talk like this, people unaware of the profound goodness and kindliness which lie behind the marble coolness of his outward appearance. Not sentimental kindliness, it is true, but a severe and strict goodness of heart which tries to do justice to others and springs from true Christian charity. These friends of the Chancellor will dwell on the slavery of work to which Adenauer, in great old age, submits day after day in the service of his people, to the point of utter physical exhaustion.

Where was the truth in all this? Was he either, both, or neither? The answer, I felt, must be somewhere in the story of his life. Probably the story of his life was the answer.

But one thing had become clear to me. A biography of Konrad Adenauer written without his assistance could never hope to be accurate, truthful, or complete. Therefore I had written to him and asked for an interview. It was the first of many which took place mostly at his home in the village of Rhöndorf, in his study, in his garden, and on the terrace of his house overlooking the Rhine Valley.

"Well, how are you planning to go about it?"

Unhurriedly Adenauer waited for my answer to his question. I noticed then, for the first time, his capacity for listening patiently for which he is reputed and which makes him so attractive a partner in conversation. I knew this to be the decisive question. My answer could make or break the enterprise. I felt that, if this man could be induced at all to reveal his life to the world at large, personal considerations would never do the trick. Only political motives could persuade him.

"I wish to try to write the life of a Christian statesman," I answered with some hesitation. I explained that in my view there was need for this at the present time. A wealth of new literature was once again extolling soldierly virtues and holding them up to German youth as a guide to life. It seemed desirable to balance this tendency and create a counterweight. That was, I said, how I understood my purpose.

Adenauer smiled.

"Professional politics," he said, "are not exactly favorable to a Christian. It is as though you were putting a staff into a pool of water. The deflection of the light rays will cause a perfectly straight staff to appear crooked and distorted."

"But can the spirit of the Gospel be translated at all into terms of political practice?" I asked. "Hasn't Christ himself said: 'My kingdom is not of this world'?"

Adenauer gave me a brief glance. Then he said:

"We have reason, and we have a conscience, and both are the gift of God. In using them, as a politician, I make my contribution toward the establishment of the order willed by God even here, in this world." He paused, then added, "There is a most deplorable misunderstanding on the part of many evangelical Christians who believe that with us Roman Catholics highest and ultimate authority is vested in the Church. This is not so. With us, too, our own individual conscience makes the final decision. I should always, in any conflict, act according to what my own conscience tells me. That is the attitude which the Church expressly demands of us."

Two maxims, he said, had always guided him. He quoted them to me in Latin. One was St. Augustine's "Thou hast created us for Thyself, and our heart cannot be quieted till it may find repose in Thee," and the other, Terence's "I am a man, I count nothing human indifferent to me."

"These two sentences have accompanied me throughout my life," Adenauer said. Somewhat thoughtfully he continued, "Come to think of it, I have lived not one, but three lives. The first leads up to the year 1917. The second comprises my period as Chief Mayor of Cologne. And the third—well, it began after the German collapse in 1945. . . ."

So he seemed willing, after all, to tell his story. After the rather discouraging understatement of his opening words, I now felt more hopeful. But his very next sentence damped my enthusiasm.

"I'm afraid I simply haven't time to tell you the whole story myself," he said. "But you are free to approach my family, my relatives, my friends, colleagues, and associates. I will arrange for you to have access, as far as possible, to official files and archives, and wherever there remain gaps I shall be glad to help fill them in."

That is how this book came to be written.

It is a mosaic composed of a large number of individual and separate narratives. Putting them together and fitting them into the frame of a homogeneous portrait was a long and difficult job—a task which the Chancellor supervised with unvaried interest and sympathy. Some parts of the story he has told himself in his own words—far more, in fact, than I had originally dared to hope for. Elsewhere he has in many instances completed the stories of others with details they had overlooked or forgotten, and which his astounding memory had preserved. The very large, though outwardly invisible, share which the Chancellor has taken in the shaping of this work permits this book, in many parts, to be regarded as an autobiography.

Konrad Adenauer was born on January 5, 1876, in Cologne.

There was no one left to tell me of his childhood and early youth. His parents and brothers and sisters are dead, and of his early playmates none has survived. The story began with a gap which no one except himself could now fill in. At the very outset I had to ask him for the help he had promised, and went to see him at his house in Rhöndorf.

Apart from the policeman guarding the gate, the house gives the impression of being the residence of some well-to-do private gentleman. Its situation, it is true, is exceptionally beautiful. On the western slope of the Siebengebirge a lavishly flowering rock garden spreads up the steep mountainside, and from its height one has a wide and unhindered view across the entire Rhine Valley as far as the Rolandsbogen, behind which the crests of the Eifel mountains, like giant green waves, extend as far as the horizon.

"I am fond of the wide sweep of this view," said the Chancellor. "At times I feel it clears the mind and widens the heart to take a look into the far-off distance."

Later we sat in his study. It was a medium-sized room furnished with a bookcase, a writing desk, a few low easy chairs, and a couch with a green cover. In the bookcase I noticed rows of identical book spines, the collected works of Joseph Conrad, Jack London, Fritz Reuter, the great North German humorist, volumes of art history. On the Chancellor's desk was a well-thumbed copy of Eichendorff's poems. "For my dear father—from Paul," I read on the flyleaf.

Even more instructive were the pictures. There were some early Italians, Dutch masters, and some German primitives, showing mostly religious subjects, with deep, ardent feeling. Between them hung two modern portraits painted in the smooth technique of the Düsseldorf school: a gentleman with a pointed beard, serious, dignified and commanding respect, and a motherly lady, her kindly face crowned by a towering coiffure.

"My parents," said the Chancellor.

After this introduction he began, and his first sentence was, characteristically, as magisterial as an incontrovertible axiom:

"A man's life is determined by the first impressions received in the home of his parents."

# CHAPTER I

"MY FATHER was a secretary at the District Court of Cologne. We lived in a house in Balduinstrasse where two of my brothers, my sister, and I were born. It was a small, two-storied house with a narrow front of only three windows and very small rooms, nine or ten feet across. As we had rented half of the first and the whole of the second floor to various tenants, we had little space left to ourselves and were rather crowded. We were three boys then, all sleeping together in one room, and until the age of seventeen I had to share my bed with one of my brothers."

Thus begins Konrad Adenauer's own account of his childhood and early youth.

"Behind the house was a garden. It was small, but to me it meant a great deal. There were a tree, two vines, and in the center a plot of lawn which my mother used for bleaching her linen. Later, my father planted a plum tree, and I remember well the loving care with which he spread out its roots before placing the slender stem in the earth. In this garden I was allotted two small beds for my own purposes. I sowed flowers in one, and radishes in the other. From day to day I watched the growth of my plants. But one day, in my impatience, I pulled up the radishes to see how fat their red tubers were, and of course the next morning they had all withered. 'One must be patient and give things time to grow,' said my father.

"This was the first lesson the earth taught me, and, as I have remained faithful to my love of gardening, many others were to follow. Some years later I tried to cross pansies and geraniums. It was my ambition to grow creeper pansies, and I dreamed of making a name for myself in horticulture with my own creation, '*Viola tricolor Adenaueriensis*.' Naturally my attempt failed, and my father summed up the result of my endeavors, 'One must never try to interfere with the work of God,' a warning I have remembered in many a political situation. Indeed, it is not too much to say that the wisdom of the earth and the basic rules given to me by my father have helped me, time and again, in mastering difficult situations in private and public life."

The Adenauer parents were devout Roman Catholics, and their children were brought up on strictly Christian principles. Every morning and evening the family said prayers together; twice every Sunday the family would go to the Apostelkirche in Cologne, to attend Mass in the morning, and evening prayers in the afternoon.

"My father's rules and principles were very simple. Besides religious devotion, they were: a sense of duty, honesty, industry, and a straightforward, matter-of-fact ambition to master any given task by using to the full all one's powers and abilities. I well remember my father reprimanding my brother August because he had deserted his homework to watch a large fire which was raging in the city. 'Even if they fire guns beside you, you have to stay with your work!' he would say angrily. There was one further rule which was sternly enforced at home—economy. But mentioning it would mean making a virtue of what was but necessity. My father's salary was modest, amounting to just over 300 marks a month, and, since he sent four of his children to secondary school and, later, three of his sons to the university, it was obvious that we had to do without many things. My mother had a difficult time keeping house. Our way of life was very simple. I remember one year, at the approach of Christmas, when we children agreed to go without meat on Sundays for several weeks to enable our parents to buy a Christmas tree and candles. Later on when we boys went to the Gymnasium and earned some extra money by coaching and giving private lessons, it was understood that every penny of it went into Mother's housekeeping fund.

"If we scarcely felt these privations, it was above all due to my mother. She was sixteen years younger than my father, a native of the Rhineland, and gifted with unusual energy and a happy, serene temperament. She used to sing all day long while doing her housework. She was a good cook, kept house and children faultlessly tidy, looking after not only her own family but also our various tenants, and had besides an ambition to earn some extra money as well. She took in needlework, and in the evening she would sit by the dim light of the kerosine lamp sewing oilcloth aprons. I helped her by pulling out the basting threads, and in this way earned my first money at the age of five. I was paid one pfennig for each apron."

To some, Adenauer feels, this description may appear rather rose-colored. But looking back on his early childhood he is sure that life in his parents' home differed in no way from that of any average, normal family.

"My father was a man of few words who spoke but seldom of himself. It was only from occasional hints and from what our mother told us that we children knew about his early life. He was the child of poor people—my grandfather owned a small bakery at Bonn—and his education had been limited to elementary school. For a time, as a youth, he worked as a farm hand on an estate and at the brickworks owned by a relative. Eventually he joined the army and became a regular soldier, in order, as was then the practice, to qualify for a post in the civil service.

"He certainly wasn't a passionate soldier. But his devotion to duty, which in every situation demanded of him the utmost his strength would give, drove him to unusual feats. He was seriously wounded in the Battle of Königgrätz, and when he was finally rescued from under a pile of dead and wounded, his fist clutched a captured Austrian flag. Although we children would have loved to hear more of such heroic deeds, he never gave us more than this brief hint. However, his bearing during the Battle of Königgrätz did not go unnoticed. For his bravery in the face of the enemy he was promoted to an officer, an honor most unusual in the Prussian Army at that time. Besides my father, it was bestowed on only one other private soldier during the 1866 war.

"I'm sure my father would have used his chance and pursued the career now open before him had he not, at that moment, met my mother. She was Helen Scharfenberg, daughter of a bank clerk in Cologne and one of a very numerous family. It was out of the question for Scharfenberg, the small bank clerk, to provide the bond then required for the bride of an officer. Lieutenant Adenauer would have been refused permission to marry. He decided to leave the army and become a court clerk, first at Keleve, and later in Cologne. I know this from my mother. My father never mentioned it. It was his silent sacrifice, tacitly built into the foundations of our domestic happiness.

"I suppose," said Adenauer, "one has to reach maturity to appreciate fully such an attitude. In the same way I have understood only much later what it meant for my father to teach all his children himself, between the ages of five and six, every evening of the week. He sacrificed his short hours of leisure, but he made sure that on entering school we were able to skip the whole of the first year and start with a considerable advantage."

Life was not without its tragedy in the Adenauer family. One experience impressed itself indelibly on the mind of the small boy. He was six years old when his youngest sister, Elisabeth, fell seriously ill. Dr. Lohmer, the old family doctor, was summoned.

"It was toward evening, and my father was already home from the office. In our small world Dr. Lohmer's arrival was always a sensational event. He disappeared with my parents into the sickroom. We remained outside and tried to catch something of what went on behind the door. But we heard only vague murmurings and could not understand what was being said. Eventually the doctor came out again, accompanied only by my father. 'An inflammation of the brain, *Herr Kanzleirat*,' he said gravely. 'The dreaded meningitis. I'm not sure she'll pull through.' He hesitated for a moment, then added hastily, 'And frankly, I'm not sure that one should wish for it, because it is most unlikely that she would ever regain complete mental health.' This conversation took place in the dark, narrow hall of our little house. I sat waiting in the kitchen. The door was ajar. I could hear every word.

"My father saw the doctor to his carriage. When he returned his face was pale as death. As usual the family gathered around the large table for supper. We said our prayers, as always, but thereafter remained quiet and oppressed. When supper was finished my father said suddenly, 'And now let us pray for our little Elisabeth.' He went down on his knees at the table, my mother knelt beside him, we children followed, and then my father with a clear voice said his prayer which we repeated after him: 'O Lord God, take this child with you! Spare her the cruel fate of having to live in this world without mind and reason. Lord God, have mercy on her!' We children repeated the words. 'Lord God, have mercy on her!' Suddenly my mother rose. Her face buried in her hands and sobbing loudly, she rushed from the room.

"Two days later Elisabeth died, at the age of six months. My mother refused to attend the funeral. She locked herself in her room and cried day and night. It only became clear to me much later what she must have felt in those moments of prayer. We had asked God for the death of the child, and God had fulfilled our wish. This experience taught me to understand the profound wisdom of the third request in the Lord's Prayer, 'Thy will be done!' We should ask the Lord for this, and nothing else. . . ."

On the old family doctor, Konrad apparently made an uncommonly favorable impression. He was the same age as the doctor's own son, and later the two boys were schoolmates at the Apostel-Gymnasium at Cologne, where they were in the same grade. Young Lohmer became a doctor like his father and, living in retirement today, is the only surviving member of Adenauer's class at high school.

"I knew him well even before I had ever met him," old Dr. Lohmer says. "In a way he was the bogeyman of my youth. Each time my father returned from one of his visits to the Adenauers we were made to listen to his long accounts of praise about their harmonious family life and their well-behaved and splendidly brought-up children. 'Chiefly their third son, Konrad,' my father would say. 'That's the sort of boy I should have liked to have myself. What a tough and obstinate little fellow he is when he's bent on getting his way! I shouldn't be at all surprised if that boy were to go far in life!'

"When I finally met this model boy in the lowest grade of the Apostel-Gymnasium, I was pleasantly surprised. He was just as naughty as the rest of us, and his work wasn't nearly as brilliant as I had been led to believe. It is true, he was always very good at his work, especially in Latin and German, and he was always among the first six in class, but as far as I can remember he was never top of the form. The only truly spectacular thing about him was his physical height. Until the very end of our schooldays he was invariably the tallest boy in class, and each time we changed classrooms he was sent ahead to make a 'sitting test' and find out if the new desks were large enough for us.

"Among his classmates he was well liked. He was always ready to prompt people and allowed anyone to crib from his own copybooks. But I believe there was only one among us with whom he was on really intimate terms. That was Ildefons Herwegen, who later became Abbot of the Monastery of Maria Laach and played an important part at a critical moment in Adenauer's life. After Ildefons had left our school, quite early, Adenauer never developed a closer friendship with any of us.

"My impression of him," Dr. Lohmer says, looking back over almost seventy years which have passed since those schooldays, "was always that of a lone wolf who kept to himself. The reason for this may have been that he began to read at a very early age. He read with truly amazing speed, and rather indiscriminately devoured an immense number of books on every sort of subject. His favorites were Cooper's Leatherstocking tales and the utopian novels of Jules Verne. But some great works of literature, too, caught his imagination and held him in their spell. I remember he once told me on our way home from school that he had read *David Copperfield* four times running."

Having graduated from the Apostel-Gymnasium with his high-school diploma, Adenauer hoped to go straight on to university. He was just eighteen. But there was a hitch, and an interlude.

He tells the story himself.

"Shortly before my final examinations my father asked me one evening whether I had yet given any thought to what I would like to do after leaving school. I answered that I wanted to study law. My father remained silent for a while. Then he explained, with an unhappy undertone in his voice, that the meager savings of the family had been exhausted by sending August and Hans, my two elder brothers, to the university. I tried to hide my disappointment while he hastily went on: 'Since you're obviously gifted for business, I thought . . . there's going to be a place available on April first for an apprentice at Seligmann's, the bankers . . . they're an old established firm of very high standing, and I imagine that a talented young man should have good prospects in banking. . . !'

"He gave me an encouraging smile, but I felt that it was forced. I sensed only too well what went on inside him. Probably he suffered even more than I at the idea that I should not be able to study. At length he asked, 'Well, what do you think of my suggestion?' I answered, 'Yes, Father, I will take the job at the bank.' So on April 1, 1894, I joined the Cologne banking firm of Seligmann as an apprentice. I had a poor time there. I was required to be first at the office in the morning, take the ledgers from the safe and place them on the desks, pour the clerks their breakfast coffee, and run errands to the post office. My immediate superior was a former schoolmate of mine who had left school with a general certificate and without doing the advanced courses. He behaved fairly decently toward me, but all the same there were occasions when he gave me to understand that he had done better than I, with my superior education. I wrote to a Cologne newspaper inquiring how long it would take in the banking profession to work one's way up to a leading position. The answer I received was not encouraging.

"My father soon became aware of my depressed mood. I had been at the bank for about two weeks when, one Sunday, he asked me to go for a walk with him. As soon as we were alone, he said, 'I can no longer bear to watch you torturing yourself. Your mother and I have been thinking what we could do, and in any case we will try to let you study. If you do your best to be as economical as possible, and we do the same at home, it must be possible. I have made an application to the Kraemer Foundation, and perhaps you can get a grant from them to help you along.

"The Kraemer Foundation was a local Cologne institution administering a special scholarship fund to assist talented sons of Cologne middle-class families. I was so touched that I reached for my father's hand and pressed it silently. Shortly afterward I was informed that the application had been granted, and, with the help of this subsidy and the money my parents were able to raise, I went to the university.

"However, the short interlude at the bank had one good point. During this fortnight at Seligmann's I came to realize what it means to a young man to be compelled to adopt an unloved profession. I shall never cease to be grateful to my father for having, from the goodness of his kind heart, spared me this fate."

Konrad Adenauer's student days are strangely shrouded in obscurity. Enough people survive, it is true, who knew him in those days, doctors and lawyers who were his fellow students at the universities of Freiburg, Munich, and Bonn, and almost every one of them can supply some anecdote or other, more or less interesting, about the present Federal Chancellor. But all this is slight and superficial stuff. It tells us little or nothing about the young man during these decisive years of his development.

Adenauer himself is markedly reserved regarding this period in his life, possibly because he considers these student years, compared with events of his later life, relatively unimportant. It is more probable that an inborn reticence prevents him, quite automatically, from speaking of personal things about which he feels deeply. One of his fellow students said of him, "He gave the impression of someone living by himself, separated from the rest of us by an invisible layer of insulation." He has not changed since his schooldays.

Adenauer began his studies at Freiburg University where he registered as a law student in the spring of 1894, and joined the Catholic students' association, Brisgovia. This may seem surprising, since his means of support were less than modest. He had no fixed monthly allowance. His father had asked him to live as economically as possible, and he complied strictly with the parental wish. He never spent more than ninety marks per month (in those days about $21.50), and frequently managed with less.

These very limited means would have made things difficult for him in other students' associations where he would have been made conscious of his inferior station. But the members of the Catholic students' clubs were almost without exception the sons of civil servants, officials, and small tradespeople whose parents lived in straitened circumstances and, as in the case of Adenauer, often sacrificed their last comforts to enable their sons to study. Here Adenauer was, and remained, among his equals, and his ability to save and adhere strictly to his "financial dispositions" even won him admiring recognition from his fellow students.

"In this respect he was truly a phenomenon," one of his Freiburg colleagues said. "He never visibly seemed to stint himself on excursions or when drinking and carousing with the rest of us, and yet he always managed to make both ends meet. I could swear that he never borrowed so much as a penny from any of us." Indeed, he acquired such a reputation for good husbandry that others became anxious to profit by it. One student, somewhat older than he and hopelessly incapable of making his allowance last until the end of the month, entrusted the much younger Adenauer with the administration of his funds, and found himself subjected to severe and pitiless discipline. Each day Adenauer would hand him his allotted sum and remain totally unmoved by his "ward's" pleadings to let him have a few extra pennies for a glass of beer or some cigarettes.

"His industry and his sense of duty could on occasion get on one's nerves," one of his fellow students said. "But secretly we were all most impressed, especially as we knew that his physical stamina was not due to natural strength but to sheer mental energy and toughness."

However, the "insulating layer" remained, and there was only one human being who was really close to Adenauer in his student years. It is deeply moving to hear the Chancellor say even today, "Schlüter was my one and only true and real friend."

Adenauer met Raimund Schlüter during his first term at Freiburg. Like him, Schlüter was studying law and had joined the Brisgovia at about the same time. He was the son of Westphalian peasants, honest, sincere, and straightforward, but by nature so reserved that it was almost impossible to approach him. His youth had been clouded by a whole series of family misfortunes, and as a result things were very tight at the Schlüter home. Of all the Brisgovians, Schlüter and Adenauer probably had to make do with the scantiest allowances. Schlüter never mentioned his domestic circumstances in the company of his fellow students, and even Adenauer learned details of them only after years of close acquaintance.

The two young men found that in character and temperament, intellectual interests, and material circumstances they had much in common, and it is very likely that this reticence and respect for the private life of others was the strongest tie binding these two self-willed and uncommunicative youths together. They attended their lectures together, they went together for walks and excursions through the Black Forest, and when Adenauer left Freiburg after his first term and transferred to the University of Munich, Schlüter went with him.

The two terms at Munich which followed seem to have been the happiest and most carefree period in Adenauer's student life. Examinations were still a long way off, and Adenauer and Schlüter, not yet twenty, were able to enjoy their academic freedom to the full. They would spend whole afternoons studying the magnificent collection of paintings in the famous Alte Pinakothek museum, and several times a week visited the opera or the theater, standing through even the longest performances. (Wagner's operas were then the general rage, a preference which Adenauer in later life abandoned completely.) During their holidays they traveled together through Switzerland, Bohemia, and Italy, visiting Venice and Florence, Ravenna and Assisi, mostly on foot, spending their nights in the haylofts of hospitable farms or in small country inns, accepting hospitality where it was offered, and when none was offered sleeping in the waiting rooms of railway stations. It was a happy time.

After his third term (the German university year being divided into two half-year terms), Adenauer once more changed his university and, again accompanied by Schlüter, went to Bonn to start working in earnest for his examinations. From the very first he had been an assiduous, hard-working, and conscientious student, but with the approach of the examinations his work gathered such speed and intensity that his mother became worried and pleaded with him not to overdo it. One of his fellow students at Bonn has told of Adenauer burning the midnight oil over his law books; as soon as tiredness threatened to overcome him he would take off his shoes and socks and put his feet in a pail of ice-cold water.

There was no such thing, with young Adenauer, as a student's love affair or even a lighthearted flirtation. Money was short, and therefore time was short. He took his first examination after only six terms (three years), the minimum period allowed, and, having passed it, was qualified as a *Referendar*—a barrister admitted to practice at court without emolument—with the mark "good."

In the autumn of 1901, at the age of twenty-four, Adenauer took his second law examination in Berlin and became an *Assessor* or assistant judge. But this time he achieved only a modest "satisfactory," and this was a heavy blow to the ambition of the young and able lawyer. The poor result was bound to have an unwelcome effect upon his career, since only those with a "good" could count on early admission to the Bar. Adenauer, however, could not wait; he had to earn his living without further delay. He applied for a commission with the Office of the State Prosecutor at Cologne, received the appointment, and remained in it for two years.

It was at this time that he finally had to part company with his friend Schlüter. They had lived and worked together during their four years' training at various Cologne courts, but after his second examination Schlüter obtained a position at the district court of Gmünd, a small town in the Eifel mountains, and they had to take leave of each other. They promised to keep in touch, and a few weeks later Schlüter wrote that he was engaged to be married to the daughter of the local doctor. Adenauer congratulated his friend, and they exchanged a few more letters. Then came the appalling news that Schlüter was dead. Tuberculosis had been prevalent in his family; it had already claimed his mother and several brothers and sisters, and now, a fortnight before his wedding, a sudden hemorrhage had put an end to his own life.

Adenauer traveled to Gmünd to attend the funeral of his only friend. Schlüter's prospective father-in-law had to struggle against his tears as he told him what had happened. A former fellow student who had made the journey with him said, "Adenauer was utterly composed. He stood at the grave, stiff and erect, and without a tear."

Adenauer did not feel happy in the State Prosecutor's Office, and when, one day, he was offered a position in the law office of Justizrat Kausen, he decided for the change and accepted gladly. Kausen had the reputation of being the best civil lawyer at the Cologne High Court of Justice, and, as the leader of the Catholic Center Party in the Cologne City Council, wielded considerable political influence. Adenauer never regretted his decision. Now, as a practicing lawyer, he had full scope for the development of his abilities, and even today the Federal Chancellor gratefully acknowledges, "It was from Kausen that I learned how to present even the most involved case in a clear and simple manner."

He loved his work, and his keenness was soon rewarded by recognition of his ability. There was high praise from old Dr. Trimborn who was, next to Kausen, Cologne's most outstanding barrister. One day, after a case in court in which Adenauer had represented the opposing party, he was heard to say, "This fellow Adenauer is running rings around all of us; he's almost as good as Kausen." Another Cologne lawyer who knew Adenauer in those days remembers him thus: "He had no brilliant oratory but instead an enormously effective way of convincing people with the sheer weight of his sober and factual arguments. Upon the Judge's Bench this peculiar eloquence of his worked like quiet and persistent rain which gently and stubbornly soaked every objection and counterargument until they simply disintegrated."

In the spring of 1902 when he was just twenty-six and well launched on a promising career, Adenauer became engaged to be married.

His bride, Emma Weyer, came from one of the old established Cologne families who used to form a closely knit society where nearly everyone was somehow or other related to everyone else. Her mother was a Wallraf, and her mother in turn came from the Berghaus family who for decades played a leading part in Cologne life. The Weyers belonged to the solid Rhenish upper middle class of the early nineteenth century which lived securely and placidly on its inherited wealth, hospitable, charitable, and devoted to the arts. Emma Weyer's grandfather, Peter Weyer, the city architect, owned a private art gallery of more than 600 paintings, known throughout the world.

Max Weyer, Emma's elder brother by seven years, a former district Judge and today, at well over eighty, living in quiet retirement, still remembers very vividly the day when young Adenauer entered the Weyer family circle.

"A special characteristic of this circle of closely related old Cologne families," he says, "was their profound and strict devotion to religion, and this was also true of my parental home. In my mother this took the form of an almost other-worldly seclusion. There was a special reason for this. Our father had died very early, and after his death she lived only for his memory and in the hope of reunion with him beyond. In a house thus shrouded in perpetual mourning, life was not always easy for my two sisters, Mia and Emma. It was especially hard on Emma, who had a gay temperament and an exuberant love of life.

"Emma tried hard to escape this oppressive atmosphere and one day surprised our mother with the announcement that she had joined a local tennis club where three times a week young professional men of academic background met with the daughters of the well-to-do upper-class families. It was not very long before we heard that a member of this club, Assessor Adenauer, was showing an interest in Emma, and my mother charged me with making some discreet inquiries about this gentleman. The information received was distinctly favorable. Assessor Adenauer, I learned, was employed in Kausen's law office and was reputed to be an industrious, able, and ambitious young man. My mother was particularly reassured when she heard that Adenauer took his religious duties very seriously.

"Eventually, on a Sunday morning, Assessor Adenauer, in a dark suit and wearing a high starched collar, called on my mother. She received him stiffly and solemnly in the drawing room. Outwardly most majestic but inwardly most unsure of herself, she asked him, 'And how, Herr Assessor, do you intend to support my daughter?' Soberly and with great seriousness Adenauer explained his prospects. He intended to take over a notary's practice and was confident of earning shortly something in the neighborhood of 6,000 marks a year. My mother considered this satisfactory, and in the spring of 1902 their engagement was announced.

"During this time," the old gentleman's account continues, "my sister changed out of all recognition. Frankly, I had never considered Emma a beauty. She was certainly pretty and always very attractive, but now the shy and timid girl grew into a radiant bride who simply adored her future husband. Adenauer, on the other hand, always maintained his restraint and self-control. Smilingly he put up with her excessive exuberance, and only occasionally damped it a little with some slightly ironical remark. As I noticed later, he often uses this faintly ironical undertone when speaking to women. I used to see a good deal of him in those days. Frequently we went for long walks together, and I became aware how deeply devoted he was to nature. He knew every flower, its origin, its relation to other flowers, and the special conditions particularly favorable to its growth. He told me that he would have liked to become a gardener, and in all seriousness explained to me his plan to acquire a notary's practice in some small county town and devote himself, in peaceful seclusion, to his true passions—gardening, his little inventions, and his family."

Max Weyer thought this an illusion, and told Adenauer so. But Adenauer soon proved that he meant it seriously. He relinquished his position in Kausen's law firm and accepted an appointment as Assistant Judge at the district court of Cologne, hoping that this would be a steppingstone and make it easier for him to obtain a notary's practice as soon as one fell vacant.

Nothing came of this idyllic plan. Events took a different turn. Konrad Adenauer and Emma Weyer were married in January, 1904, when he was just twenty-eight years old. They moved into a flat in Lindenthal, a suburb of Cologne. Not long afterward, in 1906, Adenauer's career in local government began. Later he was Chief Mayor of his native city.

## CHAPTER II

EARLY in 1906 the position of an Adjunct became vacant in the Cologne city administration. Dr. Kausen, who, as the leader of the local Catholic Center Party, practically dominated the municipal parliament, had intended to appoint a young judge from Saarbrücken to the post. Hearing of this, Adenauer walked into the office of his former principal and asked, "Why not take me, *Herr Justizrat?* I'm sure I'm just as good as the other fellow." The straightforward question and the self-assurance of the young man, supported as it was by manifest ability, so pleased old Kausen that he agreed to put Adenauer up as a candidate.

The administration of a large city like Cologne was based then, as it is today, on the *Stadtverordneten-Versammlung,* or Municipal Council. The members of this council were the elected representatives of the various political parties, and they in turn elected the *Oberbürgermeister,* or Chief Mayor, and his adjuncts or assistants in charge of the different administrative departments. In those days, however, the Municipal Council was still elected according to the old Prussian three-class electoral system, and the election was contested by only two political parties, the Liberals and the Center Party. The Liberals had a firm hold on the first class of the electorate, in which only a few very wealthy taxpayers were entitled to vote. The third class, comprising the great mass of the "small people," was the uncontested domain of the Center Party. The second class, made up largely of the well-to-do upper middle class, represented more or less the "floating vote" which both parties endeavored to capture.

It was Adenauer's good fortune that through his marriage he was related to the influential Wallraf family and through them well connected also with the Liberals. He could thus rely on the support of both major parties in the Municipal Council, and on March 7, 1906, he was duly elected Junior Adjunct, in the first poll, with thirty-five votes out of a total of thirty-seven. His new post carried a salary of 6,000 marks a year.

This success was one of the last happy things old *Kanzleirat* Adenauer lived to see. When told of his son's election, he said to him, "Now, Konrad, you must aim at becoming Chief Mayor of Cologne!" Three days later he suffered a stroke. Adenauer received the news during a hearing at the Criminal Court. He left hurriedly for his parents' house, but arrived too late.

After his father's death Adenauer gave up his small apartment in Klosterstrasse, in the suburb of Lindenthal, and took a house in Friedrich-Schmitt-Strasse large enough to provide a home for his mother and sister as well. Reserving the second floor for them, he lived with his wife on the first floor and in the attic, a thoroughly inconvenient arrangement for young Frau Adenauer. But, knowing how deeply attached her husband was to his mother, she put up with it without a murmur and never complained about the awkwardness of having to live in a divided home.

In the autumn of 1906 their first child, a son, was born. He was christened Konrad, like his father, but his parents called him "Koko." It was a difficult birth, and for a long time Emma Adenauer could not regain her strength. She complained of all sorts of ills, but the true cause of her ailments eluded the doctors. Adenauer grew very worried, consulted a number of well-known specialists, and eventually had her transferred to a sanatorium for observation. Here it was found that a slight curvature of the spine was impeding the normal functioning of the kidneys, and it became necessary for her to keep to a very strict diet and avoid all excessive strain. Although her husband did everything conceivable to make life easier for her, she recovered very slowly. In 1910 the second son, Max, was born, and fortunately this time there were no complications. But after the birth of Ria, her third child and only daughter, in 1912, her health suddenly took a turn for the worse. From now on Emma Adenauer was, and looked like, someone gravely ill.

It was just at this time, in 1912, that Adenauer's star began to rise. When in 1909 the First Adjunct, Wilhelm Farwick, relinquished his post to take over an appointment in industry, Adenauer was elected in his place with a large majority. He had then spent a bare three years in municipal government and was not quite thirty-five years old. His new office meant a multiplication of his duties and a great increase in his work. He was now in charge of the Finance and

Personnel branches of the municipality, and as Chief Mayor Wallraf, owing to his many political commitments, was frequently absent in Berlin, Adenauer had to deputize for him on many occasions. Soon the entire administration of the city was more or less concentrated in his hands.

He now began to arrange his life according to a strict timetable. His day was divided up and organized with mathematical precision. He would be at his office at nine in the morning, return home for lunch at one-thirty, resume work after a brief nap at three-thirty, and continue at his desk until eight in the evening. Whenever the municipal council was in session, his working day would extend far into the night. Any other man in his place would presumably have tried to make life a little easier for himself by shifting part of the burden onto other shoulders. Not so Adenauer; on the contrary. He was a fanatic for work, always looking out for new and additional duties to seize and concentrate in his hands. On the outbreak of the 1914 war he asked the Municipal Council to transfer the Food Department to him, and upon taking it over assumed responsibility for feeding and supplying a population of 600,000.

"In those days," his brother-in-law, Max Weyer, says, "Adenauer displayed remarkable initiative and bold enterprise. He concluded a series of agreements with the farmers of the surrounding districts which secured adequate food deliveries for the city. The farmers were supplied by the city with seeds and fertilizers and in return undertook to hand over their harvests in bulk. Cattle were bought in large numbers for the account of the city and boarded out to the peasants of the neighborhood. Considerable tracts of land owned by the city were put into cultivation. In this way Adenauer succeeded in making Cologne, the largest of all German fortress towns, the best supplied city of Germany."

The people of Cologne soon became aware of Adenauer's services to the community and were generous enough to express their appreciation in terms of hard cash. As a Junior Adjunct Adenauer had started, in 1906, with a salary of 6,000 marks a year (approximately $1428). Three years later, when he advanced to First Adjunct, it was raised to 15,000 marks, and soon afterward the Municipal Council "in recognition of his achievements" raised it voluntarily by another 3,000 marks, thus giving him an income of approximately $4284 a year.

Konrad Adenauer (*left*) with his sister Lilli and his brothers August and Hans

Young Adenauer at the time of his first communion

As a student in 1897, Konrad Adenauer poses with friends on vacation in the Aggertal

At a fancy dress party of the Arminia student society at Bonn, young Adenauer (*center*) wore Bavarian costume

Konrad Adenauer (*top, center*) in 1900 with members of his tennis club. At its gatherings he courted Emma Weyer, whom he married in 1904

The family's material foundations were now secure, and Adenauer, who even as a father of a growing family had remained faithful to the principles of strict economy of his student days, was now in a position to make the dream of his youth come true—building a house of his own. Thus, in 1911, No. 6 Max-Bruch-Strasse was built. It was a beautiful and spaciously planned house. But unfortunately, as the Adenauer family moved in, illness, anxiety, and sorrow moved in with them.

Emma Adenauer's health deteriorated steadily, and gradually the family became convinced that she must be suffering from some incurable disease.

"Despite her diminishing strength," her brother recalls, "she never ceased, until her very last days, to look after her husband and children. Adenauer never spoke to his wife about the gravity of her illness. The doctor had warned him; she was so sensitive that even the slightest hint was liable to have serious consequences. My sister, however, was well aware of the gravity of her condition. Again and again she talked to her husband about the future of their children.

"Adenauer's own bearing during this period commanded great admiration. Outwardly he displayed utter composure, and even serenity, always concerned to conceal his knowledge of her true condition from the patient and the children. During the last years of her life Emma had grown rather shy of people. She would not allow anyone to nurse her, and only Konrad was permitted, during his lunch hour at home, to renew her poultices and do all the little jobs and ministrations required for the patient. In the evening it was the same. Having returned dead tired from his work, he would first look after his wife, then eat a hasty supper, and spend the rest of the evening at her bedside, holding her hand and trying to divert her mind with little jokes and stories.

"I'm not easily impressed by outward success," said Max Weyer, "but in those days I came to recognize the human stature of my brother-in-law, and, although I'm by no means blind to his faults, he has had a secure place in my affections ever since. The way this man, overburdened with work as he was, stood by my sister during her illness was in my view a greater achievement than anything he's ever done in politics."

Only once did his iron self-control break down. That was when, after yet another examination of the patient, the doctor had a long heart-to-heart conversation with him. After the doctor had left, Adenauer's little son, nine-year-old Koko, saw his father standing in the hall, staring in front of him with somberly knit brows, and murmuring to himself, "So she has to die, after all!"

The Christian name of Konrad has become a tradition in the Adenauer family; it has now been established through four generations. Konrad was the first name of the Federal Chancellor's father, it is his own name, it is the name of his eldest son, and his grandson, the first child of his first-born, makes no exception. However, in order to avoid misunderstandings and mistaken identities during family gatherings, the youngest Konrad Adenauer is generally called "Konradin," and his father, for the same reason, has remained "Koko."

This Dr. Konrad Adenauer junior, Doctor of Law, born on September 21, 1906, who today occupies a leading position in public life, resembles his father in many ways. There is the same skeptical intelligence, the same sharp eye for the inadequacies of the world around him, and the same dry humor in dealing with the weaknesses of his fellow humans. Toward his famous father Konrad Adenauer the younger, despite his genuine love and devotion, maintains a decidedly critical attitude.

"Of course," he said in recalling his early childhood under the shadow of his mother's tragic illness, "my father made great demands upon himself, but he demanded even more of his children, or so at least it seemed to us. At school we were required to be 'good,' and a 'satisfactory' report was acknowledged with a severe frown. My father had a masterly way of persuading others to his view, and he exercised his skill even in the family circle. Since all his measures were always supported by a well-reasoned argument, he contrived to maintain with us children a fiction of complete liberty, although in actual fact his rule was as absolute as that of a biblical patriarch. The entire course of our daily life at home was adapted strictly to the requirements of his official duties, and, as soon as he entered the house on his return from the office, everyone literally stood at attention.

"He was at that time First Adjunct of the municipal administration, but our standard of life was as modest as that of a small official. My father never drank and never smoked, and his clothes were always of the simplest. For instance, he would wear his shoes until their tips began to turn upward and my mother implored him to discard this medieval footwear in favor of a new pair. With us children, too, little value was placed on outward appearance as long as we were clean and tidy. Once a fortnight a municipal employee who had formerly owned a barber shop, would come to the house and give my father and his two sons a 'close crop' which left our heads spotlessly bald. 'It's hygienic and cheap,' Father would declare. Protests on aesthetic grounds were thus firmly nipped in the bud.

"He had only one passion, and to this he never grudged any money. It was his inventions. He was always inventing something. At one time it was a new type of streamlined body for automobiles designed to reduce air resistance; at another it was a new type of oddly curved hairpin which allegedly it was impossible to lose; and during the war he surprised us with the invention of a new type of sausage, containing soya flour and called 'Cologne Sausage,' and a new variety of corn bread known as 'Cologne Bread.' The entire family was immediately pressed into the service of these inventions, my mother had to wear the new hairpins, and all of us had to eat the 'Cologne Sausage' and 'Cologne Bread,' although my father remained in a minority of one in recommending its pleasant flavor. He was always hoping one day to make a lot of money with these inventions, and even took out a patent for his 'Cologne Bread,' but once the war was over no one was very keen about it, and the only financial result from it, as far as I remember, was the fee payable to the patent office.

"But I was immensely proud of my father, even as a small boy, and I liked him best when he told us stories of his own childhood and youth. Often he would tell us what it meant for a child to have to grow up in a big city, far away from nature, without a garden, trees, or flowers. He would then show us a favorite newspaper item of his: in 1912 an inquiry made in a Cologne elementary school had revealed the fact that 60 per cent of the children had never seen a wheat field. 'You see, Konrad,' my father would say to me, 'bringing the joys of nature to such children would be something really worth doing.'

"Conversations of this kind took place mostly on Sundays. During the week my father had little time to spare for his children. He spent practically his entire leisure time with my mother, who was then already a permanent invalid. But on Sundays—every Sunday without fail, weather permitting—he would take me on an excursion into the Siebengebirge. All day long we would walk through the woods, and out there, surrounded by nature, he was a changed man. It is true, even then he remained the thrifty family man; we took our food along in a rucksack, and if we did stop for refreshments no innkeeper was likely to grow rich on us. All the same, the seriousness and severity which he displayed at home were suddenly shaken off. He laughed a great deal and talked to me animatedly as he would to a grown-up friend.

"Small things like these created a bond of quiet and deep affection between us. But there was something else which deepened my feelings for him. Somehow we children were all convinced that he would die early. In 1914 he was struck down by thrombosis. He would spend his afternoons lying on the terrace, his leg fixed in an outstretched and elevated position. Trembling, we would tiptoe past him. 'If the blood clot in my leg begins to move,' he told us, 'I shall fall down dead.' We were terrified lest this should happen.

"It didn't happen. Father's thrombosis was cured. But Mother died."

Emma Adenauer finally succumbed to her mortal illness on October 16, 1916, at the early age of thirty-six, after a long struggle borne with great bravery.

"Her death changed everything for us," her eldest son recalls. "We no longer went for walks together. Instead my father would spend his Sundays at home, sitting by the fireplace and plunged in long conversations with Uncle Hans, his brother, who later became Dean of Cologne Cathedral. In my memory this whole period is shrouded in dark veils. For one year and six weeks we all wore deep mourning, and even my small sister, four-year-old Ria, was put into a black dress.

"Later my father told us that the time immediately after my mother's death had been 'absolute hell.' Everything, he said, had been in disorder, with the servants quarreling constantly and stealing like magpies. We children noticed little of this. We clung to our Grandmother Adenauer, whose warmhearted kindliness helped us over the sadness of those months. After a few weeks my father began again to take more interest in his children. He now made a point of coming home for all his meals, talking to us at table, and listening willingly to all our little troubles and worries."

But one day Adenauer failed to return home from the City Hall during the lunch hour. In vain the family waited for him. At long last—it was nearly three o'clock—there was a telephone call from Trinity Hospital. Dr. Adenauer had had an automobile accident. He was seriously injured, and had been operated upon immediately. The driver of the car was only slightly hurt.

Throughout the afternoon old Frau Adenauer telephoned frantically, to the police, the doctors, the witnesses of the accident who had been named to her by the police. Gradually it emerged what had happened. Apparently the driver had fallen asleep at the wheel, and the car had crashed with full force into a streetcar. The car was a wreck, and in the streetcar every single window was shattered by the impact. Adenauer, who was sitting at the back of the car, was thrown through the glass partition. His face was flattened, cheekbones and nose were broken, his lower jaw was crushed, several teeth were knocked out, and his upper lip was torn. Besides this, he had suffered injuries on his hands, knees, and feet. The worst was, however, as the surgeons admitted reluctantly, that there was reason to fear for his eyesight.

"Toward evening," his eldest son recalls, "Grandmother and I went to the place where the accident had occurred. The fire department had already cleared away the wreckage. There was nothing to be seen except, in one place, a large dark patch of blood among a few scattered splinters of glass. But the owner of a nearby shop told us in great excitement how it had happened: 'There was a fearful crash as though a shell had hit the pavement and exploded. The car was just a mass of torn and twisted metal. I should never have believed that even a mouse could still be alive inside that wreckage. But then slowly a man came crawling out from under it, straightened himself up, and, streaming with blood, just walked away, stiff like a puppet. That was Herr Adenauer. The driver himself, who was only slightly injured, had himself carried away on a stretcher.'"

At the hospital the family were told that, indeed, Adenauer had arrived there on foot. Apart from all his other injuries he had suffered several deep cuts in his head. Owing to the heavy loss of blood, the surgeon had been compelled to stitch him up without an anesthetic. Only after the operation was over, Adenauer had fainted and fallen into deep unconsciousness. When his family were allowed to visit him for the first time, three days later, they felt deeply shocked. A total stranger was looking at them from his pillows. The accident had given Adenauer a new and entirely different face. It was the face which, in later years, sometimes reminded American newspaper reporters of the distinguished features of an old Indian chieftain, the face the world knows today.

Adenauer had to spend over four months in hospital. During his first week he complained frequently about his disturbed eyesight. He saw everything double and oddly contorted, he said, and it took a long time for his vision to right itself. Severe attacks of headache which first appeared soon after the accident have been with him ever since.

In the summer of 1917 Max Wallraf, then Chief Mayor of Cologne, was appointed Undersecretary of State in the Ministry of the Interior in Berlin. The post of Chief Mayor thus became vacant, and the City Council decided unanimously to offer it to Adenauer.

He was at that time convalescing at St. Blasien, in the Black Forest. One day, two City Councilors, Hugo Mönnig and Johann Rings, called on him at the sanatorium. For two hours they talked to him about this and that, the weather, the prospects of the war, city finances, mutual acquaintances in Cologne, and so forth. Eventually Adenauer cut the pointless conversation short by declaring firmly, "Gentlemen, it's only outwardly that my head isn't quite right." The two emissaries broke into laughter and proceeded to offer him the appointment of Chief Mayor. Mönnig later confided to Adenauer that in view of his severe head injuries they had been instructed to involve him in a long conversation to test his mental faculties. It had not taken Adenauer very long to see through this stratagem.

On October 18, 1917, he was solemnly introduced into his new office. Old Frau Adenauer took her elder grandson along to witness the ceremony of investiture in the Hansa-Saal of the City Hall. Konrad Adenauer the younger was then eleven years old, and he remembers the occasion well:

"My father mounted the rostrum. As he stood there, tall, slim, clad in solemn black, reading his speech with a clear, ringing voice, I felt very proud of him. I still remember one passage of his speech:

" 'There is nothing better life can offer than to allow a man to expend himself fully with all the strength of his mind and soul, and to devote his entire being to creative ability. This field you have opened up for me by electing me Chief Mayor of the City of Cologne, and for this I thank you from the bottom of my heart.' "

Konrad Adenauer was forty-one years old. The first of his "three lives" lay behind him. The second had begun.

## CHAPTER III

ADENAUER had foreseen Germany's defeat in World War I. Early in 1918 he had remarked to his predecessor, Max Wallraf, that the war would be lost, and that meant the end also of the Monarchy. But he had not anticipated that the upheaval would take the form it did. Like many others he did not believe the German people, with their inborn patience and submission to authority, capable of violent political outbursts. It was a Russian who had said, "When German revolutionaries plan to storm a railway station, they start by buying platform tickets." This observation was generally felt to be true; the very idea of a revolution in Germany seemed absurd.

Therefore, when serious unrest flared up, in November, 1918, Adenauer was resolved to counter this rebellion with every means at his disposal.

On November 6, 1918, he received confidential information that mutinous sailors were on their way to the Rhineland from the naval base at Kiel. The mutineers, the message said, had occupied several carriages of a railway train and were due to reach Cologne station in the afternoon. Adenauer went at once to see the Military Governor and general officer commanding the Cologne fortress district. He found a man who, in the face of a crisis, had clearly lost his resolution and sat slumped apathetically behind his desk. Adenauer reported the message just received, and urged, "Your Excellency, I advise you to have the train stopped in open country before it reaches Cologne, and to have the mutineers arrested!"

The Governor hesitated, his lips tight, his pencil nervously drumming his desk. Eventually he called the President of the State Railways on the telephone. Adenauer remained present during the conversation. The railway chief, at the other end of the line, talked at great length while the Governor gave but monosyllabic answers. Putting down the telephone, he gave Adenauer an empty stare. "I'm afraid the railway people refuse to cooperate," he said. "The train must reach Cologne main station on schedule."

"And what do you propose to do in this situation?"

The Governor gave a shrug. "I shall reinforce the sentries at the station and give orders that no one wearing a red rosette is to be allowed past the barriers."

"And that is all?"

"All I can do at the moment."

Adenauer gave the man one piercing look. Then he said, "Your Excellency, I have no more business with you," and left, his face white with anger.

In the afternoon the sailors were all over town. They had simply taken off their red badges and passed through the barriers without the slightest difficulty. Twenty-four hours later the Republic was proclaimed in Cologne. The city resembled a disturbed anthill. Waving red flags and yelling their slogans, the revolutionaries marched through the main streets. Trucks with armed detachments pushed their way through the crowds, and military buildings were beleaguered by an infuriated mob demanding the surrender of the officers.

Once more Adenauer made an attempt to stem the tide. He telephoned the Governor and informed him that a battery of field artillery, with adequate ammunition, was standing in readiness in the courtyard of the Apostel-Gymnasium—Adenauer's old school—awaiting marching orders. The Military Governor thanked the Chief Mayor for his message, adding, "There's nothing further I can do; you'll have to see how you can manage yourself." Several weeks later Adenauer by chance met the officer commanding the battery, an artillery captain, and asked him what happened in the end. The captain told him: "The Governor sent me word that in a situation like this a Prussian officer must know himself what to do. So I ordered my men back to the barracks."

Adenauer had wanted to fight it out with all the means at the disposal of the State, so long as prospects were still favorable. But when the military authorities capitulated and gave in to the mob ruling the streets, he resolutely changed his ground and accepted the new situation in order to protect the city and its inhabitants, as far as he could, against looting and violence. When the representatives of the revolutionary committee, the "Workers' and Soldiers' Council," called on him at the City Hall, proud of their victory and very self-assured, he was reserved but not unfriendly.

He remained in conference with them the whole afternoon. Unperturbed by interruptions and heckling, he explained to them that it was in their common interest to restore calm and order in the city as soon as possible. Pointing out the chaos which was likely to arise as soon as the armies returning from the front passed through Cologne, he appealed to their comradely feeling of sympathy and solidarity with the front-line soldiers, and their civic sense as citizens of Cologne. Patiently he made it clear to them that one couldn't govern a great city while holding a rifle in each fist, and that an administration needed such things as offices, telephones, typewriters, and official rubber stamps. Having said all this he made offices available to them in the City Hall.

In return, he asked for concessions. He achieved what no one had thought possible: the "Workers' and Soldiers' Council" did not insist on hoisting the Red Flag on the City Hall, and the Military Governor, who was under siege in his office, was allowed to withdraw unmolested. Toward evening this Commander in Chief of Cologne fortress quietly slipped out of town. "I forget what his name was," the Federal Chancellor says. Two days later his successor arrived in Cologne. He was Captain Otto Schwink, appointed by General Headquarters at Spa.

"Schwink is one of the bravest men I have ever known," Adenauer had said of him. It was amusing to find that Captain Schwink, who is today a successful businessman in Munich, used almost identical words in giving his own account of Adenauer's role during the days of revolution in Cologne when the two men worked closely together.

"Konrad Adenauer is one of the bravest men I've come across," Schwink said. "I went to call on the Chief Mayor as soon as I arrived. I found the City Hall beleaguered by a crowd of thousands, mostly women, children, and old people, clamoring in furious chorus for bread. Inside it was the same. All the corridors and passages were filled with people. Adenauer's office resembled a front-line operational headquarters on the day of battle. Messengers and deputations came and went unceasingly, almost invariably bringing bad news: in the suburbs the crowds were looting the shops, an army depot where 300 liters of alcohol were stored was in danger of falling into the hands of the rebels, in one working-class district hunger revolts had broken out. . . .

"Amid all this excitement Adenauer remained absolutely calm and unruffled. He ordered the alcohol to be quietly poured into the Rhine as soon as it grew dark; he gave instructions to feed the hungry population from army field kitchens; he discussed the organization of a Civil Guard composed of civilian volunteers which a few days later took over responsibility for safeguarding life and property in the city. That was the first impression I received of Cologne and its Chief Mayor. During the following months when I saw him almost daily, it was confirmed, and more than confirmed. This man, I felt, was a true Commander in Chief.

"They were tough and exhausting months," Captain Schwink recalls. "Often, for several days running, we had no more than two or three hours' sleep. Four German army corps were passing through Cologne on their way back from the front. They had to be fed, they had to receive their back pay, and—this was Adenauer's explicit order—they had to be disarmed before receiving their demobilization papers. Adenauer felt, and he told me so, that hundreds of thousands of armed men roaming the big cities without work and adequate food were an acute social danger. As a result, army field kitchens were installed everywhere in the streets, and officers worked in two or three shifts making out papers. Only soldiers who had surrendered their arms were entitled to receive their discharge papers, railway tickets, pay, and rations for the journey to their home towns.

"Cologne resembled a huge army camp. At the army depots mountains of surrendered arms were piling up. Field kitchens were steaming day and night, and before long fed not only the returning soldiers but a large part of the hungry population as well. Our main difficulty was how to finance this operation. The city was unable to raise the several millions needed every day, and no help could be expected from the government, at any rate during the first few weeks. Adenauer had a way out. He gave me orders to sell every available piece of army property, horses, cars, trucks, everything. I knew the people rushing up to buy this stuff were mostly rather shady customers who felt no compunction at profiting from Germany's bankruptcy—but they had the cash! And ready cash was what we needed most urgently.

"We earned little thanks for our efforts. On the contrary. People would loudly call Adenauer all sorts of uncomplimentary names whenever he drove through the streets. Once, on a Sunday, walking in the Municipal Park, we came across a freshly made grave. There was a wooden cross on the mound, and it bore the inscription: 'Here lies Konrad Adenauer.' The gazing crowd silently stepped aside as we approached, and Adenauer stood looking at it for a little while. Then he walked on, without saying a word.

"He hardly ever spoke about things which moved him deeply. I remember only one occasion when he very nearly lost his composure. That was on the day the last German regiment marched through Cologne. We stood in front of the cathedral as the men filed past their commanding officer, their uniforms tattered, their faces gray and hollow, showing every mark of the strain of the past weeks, yet bearing themselves with faultless discipline. A large crowd had gathered for this spectacle, and as the last company disappeared across the Rhine bridge, they spontaneously began to sing the 'Thanksgiving Hymn.' I looked across to where Adenauer stood. His lips were firmly pressed together, and there was a moist glint in his eyes."

Three days later the British Army entered Cologne, and within the hour of their arrival their commanding officer, accompanied by his staff, called on the Chief Mayor. The welcome was, on both sides, short-clipped but correct. The British general was an energetic and forceful man. His first request to Adenauer was to have an official proclamation by the occupation authorities posted everywhere in the city. A staff officer had brought several hundred printed copies of it, and the General handed Adenauer a specimen.

It was a lengthy document, comprising fifteen separate articles and setting out the orders of the British military authorities to the civil population of the occupied city: a general curfew was imposed, bicycling in the streets was forbidden, telephone and telegraph services must not be used except by permission, all lights must be turned off in private houses at nine-thirty in the evening, and, most awkward of all, Article Thirteen, which required all male Germans to demonstrate their respect by raising their hats to British officers whenever encountering them in public.

"As Adenauer read through this proclamation," Captain Schwink recalls, "his face grew steadily more somber. When he had finished he looked the General straight in the face and said: 'I cannot imagine that a British gentleman would wish to humiliate a vanquished people in this manner.' The General looked somewhat perplexed. Then he answered, 'My orders are to hand you this proclamation. What you do with it is your own affair.' Thereupon Adenauer silently accepted the parcel and carried it to the corner of his room, where he put it down on the floor. Straightening himself again, he said, 'I shall carry out your order as far as my conscience permits.' The General replied, 'We shall treat you correctly as is our duty.' "

The proclamation was never posted. One night some unknown person stuck a copy to one of the piers of the Rhine bridge. Adenauer called the General on the telephone, and the poster was removed within an hour.

There are more than a few people in Germany even today who, while giving Adenauer full credit for his dignified bearing toward the occupation authorities, yet have one important reservation regarding his patriotic attitude during the immediate postwar years. This concerns the part Konrad Adenauer played—or is alleged to have played —in the Rhenish Separatist Movement, which early in 1919 endeavored to detach the Rhineland from Prussia and establish it as a separate Rhenish State.

On February 1, 1919, these critics point out, Chief Mayor Adenauer called a representative meeting of Rhenish politicians at Cologne City Hall where, in a widely publicized speech, he not only identified himself with the separatist movement but was also elected chairman of a committee charged by the assembly with the preparatory work for the establishment of a Rhenish State. In the view of many this amounted to high treason, and they feel that "All the waters of the Rhine will never be able to wash this blemish from his reputation."

There is no doubt that this affair has dogged Adenauer's steps ever since. His opponents never tire of reviving this old charge against him. What did in fact happen? What substance is there in this accusation? No one denies that the meeting of February 1, 1919, took place, that it was Adenauer who called it, that its purpose was to discuss the establishment of a new West German State, and that Adenauer made the main speech. All this is confirmed by one who was present, who heard Adenauer speak, and who preserved a shorthand record of this speech.

This witness is none other than Captain Schwink.

"From the very start," he recalls, "there was high tension in the atmosphere of the meeting. Everyone present—the mayors of all the principal Rhenish cities, councilors, deputies, and leading personalities of public life—was conscious that a subject of fateful significance to the existence of Germany was about to be discussed. Two groups, or schools of thought, were represented in the meeting. There were the uncompromising separatists advocating a radical solution, namely, a complete detachment of the Rhineland from the body of the German Reich and the establishment of an independent Rhenish State. And there were the moderates who were in favor of detaching the Rhineland from Prussia but insisting that such a Federal Rhenish State must remain within the framework of the German Reich.

"No one knew precisely where Adenauer stood regarding these two propositions. But it was known that he was not in sympathy with the radical separatists. This movement was led by Dr. Dorten, a lawyer from Wiesbaden, who was widely credited with the intention of eventually placing the separate Rhenish Republic under French suzerainty. Dorten had made a number of attempts to establish contact with Adenauer, but Adenauer had consistently refused to meet him and declared indignantly that 'he wouldn't even speak to such people.' In view of this, he had caused much surprise by apparently taking the initiative in having the entire, highly explosive matter brought into the open, and discussed."

What then was Adenauer's position? What did he, in fact, say?

He opened the meeting with a speech which must certainly rank among the longest he has ever made. It lasted more than three hours. The shorthand record in Captain Schwink's possession makes it possible to reconstruct its main argument.

He began by warning his hearers that he was going to disregard all emotional aspects of the matter, even patriotic considerations. "It is my opinion that this problem of ours should be probed and discussed only on soberly rational grounds." What, he asked, was the actual political situation? "It is necessary for us to put ourselves in the place of our opponents and, first of all, try to follow their thoughts and reasoning. Considerations of foreign policy quite generally will lead to reasonable conclusions only if one tries to think with the other fellow's mind, if one asks himself the question: how would I act if I were, at this moment, in the position of France, Britain, or the United States?"

His first point, then, was to look at Germany with the eyes of a Frenchman. Sketching the development both countries had made during the five decades since 1870, he pointed out that Germany had pulled ahead of France, that her population had increased to sixty-five million, and her economy had greatly increased in strength, while during the same period the population of France had decreased to forty million. Yet France had succeeded, with the help of a unique combination of powers, in crushing Germany utterly and completely.

"But Germany will recover," Adenauer said, "and in the same way as France revenged herself fifty years after her defeat in 1870, a resurgent Germany will eventually try to take her revenge in turn. Inevitably France concludes from this that it is vitally necessary for her to obtain such guarantees as will safeguard her national existence and make it impossible for Germany, within the foreseeable future, to revenge herself." One of these safeguards, Adenauer said, was the proposed League of Nations and general disarmament. "I do not believe, however, that even among the powers of the Entente there is anyone fully convinced that in the long run disarmament will win through.

"Any responsible French statesman must endeavor, therefore, to get hold of real and tangible guarantees. For him, by far the most desirable guarantee would undoubtedly consist in making the Rhine France's strategic frontier against Germany. That is how France really feels. Differences of opinion exist only with regard to the best way of carrying out this plan. While the chauvinists would like to make the Rhine the political frontier between France and Germany, the moderates aim at turning the Rhineland into a buffer state under French influence."

There was nothing very new or very surprising in this policy, Adenauer declared. Not so very long ago Germany herself had thought along very similar lines, and there was, therefore, no case for moral indignation on her part. "There was a time," Adenauer reminded his hearers, "when people in Germany, believing victory to be within their grasp, declared we must have safeguards against France and England. These safeguards were to be provided by Belgium. There were those who wanted to incorporate Belgium into Germany and annex her altogether, and there were the moderates who proposed to keep Belgium under German domination by maintaining military garrisons there and placing her railways under German management."

It was a reminder which, undoubtedly, made many among Adenauer's audience feel distinctly uncomfortable, and it was certainly not the sort of argument a rabble-rousing demagogue would care to use.

So this was the French point of view. Next Adenauer put the question: Is Germany in a position to resist these French plans? The answer, he said, was an unqualified no. "Is there any solution available," he asked next, "which could satisfy the claims of France and yet avoid such damage to Germany as would necessarily be caused by a cession of the left bank of the Rhine?"

In his view, there was. He had the solution ready. It was the creation of a West German Republic within the constitutional framework of the German Reich. This federal state, what was more, was to comprise not only the left bank of the Rhine and the Rhineland Province but also adjacent counties on the right bank of the river. "This," Adenauer declared, "is the only way out I can see. If it isn't practicable, it is my firm conviction that in the long run we Rhinelanders shall be lost. But the answer to the question whether it is practicable or not depends neither on Germany nor on France. The decision lies with England, and with England alone."

It was necessary, therefore, at this stage, to try to think with the mind of an Englishman. Seen with British eyes, what did the situation look like? Nothing need in the future be feared from Germany, but the strength of France had become all the more threatening. If Britain consented to France establishing herself on the left bank of the Rhine, Adenauer argued, and possibly agreed to her maintaining bridgeheads on the right bank, France would at once become overwhelmingly powerful on the European continent. Traditional policy of a European balance of power demanded therefore that Britain should place herself on the side of the weaker Continental power, that is, on the side of Germany.

On the other hand, Adenauer continued, England was bound to recognize France's justified desire for safeguards against German lust for revenge. In the light of all this, did the suggested creation of a West German Republic within the constitutional framework of the German Reich furnish France with the security she so urgently demanded? Adenauer thought it did. In his view the effect which a partition of Prussia was bound to have abroad, and particularly in France, would be decisive.

Prussia, he declared emphatically, was the crux of the matter.

"In the opinion of our former enemies," Adenauer said, "it was Prussia who drove the world into this war. They believe that Prussia is dominated by a military and Junker caste, and that Prussia in turn dominates the rest of Germany, including the peoples of Western and Southern Germany with whose general outlook and temperament the Entente nations are basically in sympathy. Public opinion abroad therefore demands: Prussia must be partitioned.

"Now, if this were done," Adenauer argued, "if the western provinces of Germany were joined together in a federal state, it would no longer be possible for Prussia, in the opinion of other countries, to dominate Germany. Owing to its size—and it must be large in order to exercise adequate influence—and its economic importance, this West German Republic would play a very considerable part in the affairs of the new German Reich, and correspondingly it would be able to guide Germany's foreign policy along peaceful and conciliatory lines. This could, and should, satisfy France."

This, then, was Adenauer's concept, based on his analysis of the international situation and evolved, it seemed, with convincing logic. It remained for him to deal with criticism raised by his political opponents.

"There were two main objections," Captain Schwink recalls. "The first was to the effect that the eastern parts of Prussia would be unable to subsist once they were detached from their western counterparts, since both were complementary. Adenauer denied this. 'The West is impoverished,' he said, 'and the traditional slogan of the rich West and the poor East has become devoid of all meaning.' But, be that as it might, what was the alternative? 'Which is the lesser evil for Germany?' he asked. 'The complete detachment of the left bank of the Rhine from Germany and its total loss, or some possible economic disadvantage which the East may have to shoulder?'

"The second objection was much more weighty. It insinuated that the advocates of a West German Republic were lacking in patriotic sense of responsibility. They were reproached with playing straight into the enemy's hands. Foreign countries, especially France, would interpret such a move as nothing less than a first step on the part of the Rhineland to break away from the German Reich altogether. With passionate indignation Adenauer refuted this allegation, asking the meeting to register publicly its emphatic protest against all foreign moves aiming at the annexation of German territory, and to declare solemnly that the Rhineland would remain with Germany, the aim being a West German federal state within the framework of the German Reich and nothing else.

"Adenauer's speech was an overwhelming success," Captain Schwink asserts. "His achievement may be measured by what resulted from this meeting of February 1, 1919—the resolution which was adopted unanimously."

This historic resolution reads:

"We, the undersigned representatives of the Rhenish people in occupied Prussian territory, register our emphatic and solemn protest against all plans and efforts, now discernible in the press of foreign countries, aiming at the detachment of the left bank of the Rhine, or parts of it, from Germany. We claim for ourselves the right of self-determination of the nations which is accepted and recognized throughout the world, and demand that we should remain united with our fellow nationals in the Reich. In view of the fact that a partition of Prussia is now being seriously considered, we charge a special committee, elected by ourselves, with the task of preparing plans for the establishment of a West German Republic within the constitutional framework of the German Reich and based on the Reich Constitution to be drafted by the German National Assembly."

Chairman of this committee was Konrad Adenauer, who was elected unanimously—the same Adenauer who until now had brusquely refused to take part in any discussion about the establishment of a Rhenish Republic. Now, it seemed, on the strength of a single speech, the Chief Mayor of Cologne had emerged as the leading figure of the Rhenish separatist movement. What was the explanation of this puzzle? It took a little time before Adenauer's game became clear, but then it turned out to be simple enough: Adenauer never called a single meeting of the committee whose chairman he was. His entire purpose in creating this committee was to ensure its speedy, if unobtrusive death. His sole aim had been to lay his hands on the separatist movement which was growing to dangerous underground dimensions, get control of it, and, once control was gained, strangle it. In this he succeeded.

It took people a long time to grasp this. One man, however, immediately saw through this stratagem: Georges Clemenceau. In his memoirs, *Grandeur and Misery of Victory,** the great French statesman writes: ". . . several weeks passed. The Mayor of Cologne, Adenauer, had taken over the leadership of the 'movement.' On February 1, 1919, all the Rhenish deputies who had been elected members of the National Assembly, as well as the mayors of the Rhenish cities, were called to a meeting at Cologne. The purpose of the meeting was the solemn proclamation of the foundation of the Rhenish Republic. But what happened? Under the influence of Adenauer the meeting contented itself with electing a committee charged with preparing plans for the establishment of a self-contained Rhineland within the constitutional frame of the German Reich. And how often did this committee meet? Not once!"

Adenauer, however, was not content with merely exercising passive resistance. His position as chairman of the "Rhenish Committee" lent him special political authority, and he used this authority to impress upon the occupying British that the Rhenish people felt and thought as loyal Germans and had no thought of breaking away from the fatherland. Having in this way pledged his word, Adenauer found his stand put to an unexpectedly acid test a few months later.

On June 1, 1919, Dr. Dorten, the extreme separatist leader, suddenly sprang a surprise on the world, and in particular on Adenauer. Hoping to create an accomplished fact and to carry the wavering population with him, he announced the establishment of a "Rhenish Republic" by simultaneous proclamation at Mainz and Wiesbaden. June 1 was a Sunday. There were no newspapers, and radio did not then exist. Adenauer was in complete ignorance of events when at midday he received a telephone call from British Headquarters. General Sir Sidney Clive, Political Adviser to the Commander in Chief, asked him to come and see him at once. On arrival Adenauer learned from the General what had happened. The General was most upset and pointedly reproachful; had not the Chief Mayor assured him time and time again that the Rhinelanders were loyal citizens of the Reich and would never dream of setting up a state of their own against the will of the Reich Government?

"What am I to do now?" Clive asked indignantly.

Adenauer thought for a moment. Then he answered:

* Harcourt, Brace & Company, Inc. © 1930.

"Your Excellency, my advice is that you issue an order forthwith to the effect that constitutional changes in British-occupied territory are prohibited unless prior permission has been obtained from the occupation authorities."

General Clive saw the point, and accepted the advice without hesitation. At his request Adenauer, there and then, drafted the text of the prohibiting order, and it was posted the same day all over the British area of occupation. That broke the back of Dorten's *Putsch.* Without Cologne, no Rhenish State could hope to live or survive. A few days later Dorten's enterprise collapsed. The separatists, however, knew very well to whom they owed the frustration of their plans. A "revolutionary tribunal" at Koblenz passed a sentence of death on the Chief Mayor of Cologne in his absence.

"This verdict," Adenauer remarked later, "is worth more to me than a decoration."

But still the legend of Adenauer's "high treason" in 1919 refused to die. A quarter of a century later, during the election campaign of August, 1953, a pamphlet written by an unnamed author and widely distributed in the Federal Republic revived the old charges and sought to prove that the Federal Chancellor "was a separatist and will always remain one." This time Adenauer felt deeply offended, and spoke of it in bitter tones.

"One is almost tempted to despair of divine justice," he said, "seeing that God has set such narrow limits to wisdom, and no limits at all to stupidity. The slanderous lie that, in 1919, I worked for the detachment of the Rhineland from Germany has been refuted and disproved a hundred times over, and yet at every election it crops up again. But the fact that the Reich Government themselves tried to detach the Rhineland and parts of Westphalia is never mentioned by anyone!"

This historic event took place in November, 1923. Adenauer played a prominent part in it. It never became very widely known, and today is totally forgotten.

The following is the Federal Chancellor's own authentic account of it.

"On November 13, 1923, representatives of the Rhineland population were invited to attend a meeting in the Reich Chancellery at Berlin. The meeting was to begin at ten o'clock in the morning. I remember arriving a little ahead of time, and as I was about to enter the conference room Undersecretary of State Schmidt took me aside and asked to have a word with me in private. We withdrew into a corner of the corridor, and Schmidt said in great agitation, 'I feel I must warn you! There's a sinister game afoot. The Cabinet decided yesterday to give up the provinces of Rhineland and Westphalia. They're costing the Reich too much money. The government fear they will not be able to maintain the stability of the *Rentenmark* (the provisional currency newly introduced by Dr. Schacht and designed to overcome the inflation) if they have to go on paying subsidies to these occupied areas. Therefore, the Rhinelanders will be asked to agree to the *de facto* establishment of a state of their own. The matter has been decided, and the press has already been warned to stand by. At six o'clock this evening Stresemann intends to announce the Cabinet's decision, together with the formal agreement of the occupied territories.'

"This news took me completely by surprise. But there was no reason to doubt it. Schmidt was Undersecretary in the Ministry for Occupied Territories, and he should know. He told me he could not bring himself to watch the sacrifice of a piece of German territory for purely financial reasons. I thanked him for the information and told him that he had done us Rhinelanders a great service. As I walked into the conference room I noticed, among a group of people, the Prime Minister of Prussia, Otto Braun. I went straight up to him and asked him point-blank, 'How can you, as head of the Government of Prussia, take the responsibility for surrendering two Prussian provinces to the French?' Braun denied nothing. He shrugged his shoulders and said, 'You may be sure that I, too, found this a very hard decision to take. But, believe me, there is no other way. The cover for the currency is so weak that, financially, we can no longer carry Rhineland-Westphalia.'

"At this moment members of the Reich Government entered the room, headed by Reich Chancellor Dr. Gustav Stresemann. He was accompanied by Reich Ministers Jarres and Luther, and several undersecretaries. Stresemann asked us to take our seats at the conference table, and, after a few noncommittal words of welcome which betrayed his nervous agitation, went straight to the heart of the matter. He said; 'Gentlemen, we are faced with the necessity of discontinuing our policy of subsidies for the occupied territories. If we continue to pay this subsidy at its present rate, we shall not be able to maintain the currency, and there is no need for me to explain to any of you what this would mean for Germany as a whole.'

"The Rhinelanders were horrified. Although I had been prepared by Schmidt, I was nevertheless stunned by Stresemann's revelation. None of us stirred, and there was a breathless silence as Stresemann continued. He sought to convince us that there was but one way out of the dilemma, and that was the establishment of an independent Rhenish State, detached *de facto*, although not *de jure*, from the body of the Reich. He tried to persuade us to agree to this solution by pointing out that it was merely provisional and temporary and imposed entirely by dire necessity, and ended by asking us, 'Gentlemen, you must go and see Monsieur Tirard, the President of the Inter-Allied Commission, at Koblenz tomorrow! You must ask him to grant you the right to levy your own taxes in the occupied territories. And then you'll just have to see how you can get along!'

"I was the first to speak. 'And how soon, in your opinion, Herr Reich Chancellor,' I asked, 'will this state be able to return to the Reich?' Stresemann hesitated. Then he said, 'As things are at present, it is impossible to say.' We men from the Rhineland glanced at each other, and without exchanging a word we all knew our future was at stake. Eventually I said, 'We feel we must refuse most emphatically to agree to this detachment. I believe we are all quite clear in our minds about one thing: once this step has been taken we shall remain separated from the Reich for a very long time.'

"In the course of the discussion which followed Stresemann sent for Dr. Hjalmar Schacht, the then Reich Currency Commissar, to support him. Meanwhile Reich Finance Minister Dr. Hans Luther gave detailed reasons for the government's stand. He gave representatives of the occupied territories a lengthy account of the cost incurred by the Reich for the 'Ruhr Struggle,' and told them of the subsidies devoured even now day after day by a West German economy shattered and undermined by the effects of passive resistance. 'Since the first of November alone,' he said, 'we have pumped credits into the Rhineland to the tune of one hundred million *Rentenmark*, in order to maintain unemployment benefits in the occupied territories. And still we were told by you, gentlemen, that it was merely a drop in the ocean. But as Minister of Finance I must now tell you: we cannot undergo further bleedings! Our supreme objective must be to maintain the stability of the currency. Let us be clear about this. If we are compelled to resort once again to unrestricted note-printing, Germany will sink into an economic morass from which there will be no hope of salvation.'

"Meanwhile Dr. Schacht had joined the conference, but he did not speak. I declared, 'In my opinion the policy proposed by the Cabinet is wrong. The Reich is under an obligation to support the occupied territories in any circumstances. No government can take the responsibility before history for sacrificing a vital part of the German territory purely for reasons of financial policy.' Those who spoke after me were less restrained. One delegate exclaimed, 'We will not be hoodwinked by all this and have the wool pulled over our eyes. We've seen right through the government's dastardly intentions. We Rhinelanders are meant to be the price with which the government plan to buy themselves free of their reparations obligations. But don't you believe that we shall allow ourselves to be sacrificed like calves on the altar of currency!'

"For several hours the debate continued backward and forward without interruption. The only man showing understanding for our position and lending us his support was Reich Minister Jarres, who went against the Cabinet decision by agreeing with the arguments of the Rhenish representatives. It was getting dark, the lights were turned on, and still we were struggling. Stresemann's face was moist with perspiration. Suddenly with a groan he felt for his heart and slumped back in his chair. Two of his assistants helped him stagger from the room. He had suffered one of the heart attacks which even then undermined his health and to which he succumbed a few years later.

"We were all deeply shocked, but the argument continued. Toward seven o'clock representatives of the press inquired how soon the anticipated important communiqué might be expected. They were told no agreement had yet been reached, and they should not go on waiting for it.

"Late in the evening the meeting was adjourned. No agreement had been reached, but a provisional compromise formula was finally knocked together after much haggling: the Rhenish representatives undertook to plead with Tirard for a reduction of the payments due from the Reich, while the Reich government undertook meanwhile to go on paying. In the meantime both parties agreed to consider once more their respective points of view. As for myself, no such consideration was needed. I always held the view that there could never be any question of separating the Rhineland from the Reich. When immediately after the collapse I advocated the creation of a Rhenish Federal State, it was for one purpose only—to take the wind out of the sails of the separatists who aimed at detaching the left bank of the Rhine from the Reich. This decision of the Reich Government, however, was an entirely different matter. To grant the occupied territory financial sovereignty and the right to raise its own taxes would have meant the severance of all ties with the Reich, and that would have finished the Reich, too. For the territory which was meant to form a state of its own, '*de facto* but not *de jure*,' as they said, comprised not only the left bank of the Rhine but also the whole of the industrial area of the Ruhr then occupied by the French.

"When ten days after our conference in Berlin the Stresemann government fell, I felt certain that this was also the end of our quarrel. I was astonished, therefore, to receive an invitation from Stresemann's successor, Reich Chancellor Dr. Wilhelm Marx, to come to Berlin for a continuation of the discussion. From Undersecretary Schmidt I learned this time that the Minister of Finance, Dr. Hans Luther, had renewed his demand to discontinue, once and for all, the financial subsidies to the occupied territories. In support of this demand the Ministry of Finance had gotten out figures which gave the impression that a continuance of the subsidies to the Rhineland must inevitably lead to the collapse of the currency. Schmidt warned me that the figures in this balance sheet were misleading and gave no true picture of the position. He gave me a draft paper of his own which was much less disquieting.

"When the new meeting opened under the chairmanship of Reich Chancellor Marx, the Minister of Finance was not present but had sent one of his permanent officials, Dr. Alexander von Brandt, as his deputy. I declared at once that I must refuse to discuss so vital a matter without the Minister of Finance, and requested Dr. Luther's personal attendance. Reich Chancellor Marx thereupon adjourned the meeting, and Dr. Luther was summoned. When he arrived I proved to him, on the basis of Schmidt's paper, that the particulars on which the Cabinet had taken their stand were not correct. Again there was an agitated discussion lasting several hours.

"In the end Reich Chancellor Marx declared that, if it had been necessary for him to come to a decision the day before, he would have taken the same stand as the late government. The discussion which had just taken place had convinced him, however, that the matter required further, thorough consideration. And that was the last we ever heard of the detachment of the occupied territories."

## CHAPTER IV

ADENAUER'S next-door neighbors in Max-Bruch-Strasse were the Zinsser family. Professor Zinsser, a noted dermatologist at Cologne University, was a gay, cheerful man, hospitable and of cosmopolitan outlook, who was fond of music and good talk. Almost every night he would have a party of guests at his house, colleagues and fellow lecturers from the university, students, musicians, artists; and often music and lively conversation would last until the small hours. The professor was especially fond of children, not only his own but all children who came his way. He would play with them for hours and entertain them with conjuring tricks, and the older ones, stuck with their homework, would come to him for help.

The Adenauer children too, Koko, Max, and Ria, were frequent visitors. If the professor was out, his two daughters, Lotte and Gussi, sixteen and seventeen years old, would look after them, and often Frau Zinsser would ask them to stay for dinner. The Zinssers were well aware that their mother's illness overhung the Adenauer household like a dark cloud, and they tried to give the children a few cheerful hours whenever they could.

Gradually this grew into a friendly and neighborly relationship between the two houses and families. When Frau Adenauer heard that the Zinsser children were having small musical parties at their house—Gussi played the violin, Lotte the piano, and their brother Ernst the cello—she invited the three musicians over, and soon these small house concerts became a permanent institution in the Adenauer home as well. Often Adenauer asked the two girls to sing for him. He was particularly fond of simple, tuneful melodies, especially two-part folk songs.

This idyll was abruptly ended by Frau Adenauer's death. Adenauer, for a time, completely withdrew from all contact with his friends and the outside world. The children remained in the care of a governess and their grandmother, but before long they found their way back to the hospitable Zinsser home. It was they who maintained contact between the two neighboring families. Through them the Zinssers learned of events in the Adenauer household, comforting the terrified children when their father had his motor accident in 1917, and rejoicing with him when he was elected Chief Mayor of Cologne. When Professor Zinsser was called into service and Adenauer heard through his children that his neighbor's house was without fuel, he quietly arranged for Frau Zinsser to be supplied adequately by his own coal merchant.

Those who knew Gussi Zinsser at that period remember her as a very pretty and charming girl, of medium height, slim and dark-haired, with a small face and large, romantic eyes. Fond of laughter, equally easily moved to tears, she was kindhearted and ever ready to help where help was needed. She loved flowers and children, and even as a schoolgirl wanted to become a gardener. She admired Adenauer for his knowledge of botany and his chivalrous manner. Proudly she told how she once met him in the street when she was out shopping for birthday presents for her father, and he insisted on carrying her parcels for her and escorting her to her door. "He treated me like a lady," she said.

The Zinssers esteemed Adenauer very highly, and there had been genuine regret when after his wife's death the two families had ceased to meet. They were sincerely glad, therefore, when one day, about two years later, Gussi told them, "I had a long conversation with Chief Mayor Adenauer today." She had been hoeing potatoes on a plot of land leased by the Zinssers and bordering on Adenauer's garden. Adenauer had come up to the garden fence and watched her at work, giving her advice on how to hold the hoe so as to obtain the best effect with the least waste of energy. A few days later she met him again while she was busy in her parents' front garden, and again there was a lengthy conversation about gardening and the cultivation of flowers. Henceforth Gussi Zinsser usually found something urgent to do in the garden around the hour in the morning when the Chief Mayor's car called for him at his house to take him to the office. Frequently he would bid her good morning over the garden fence, linger a little and engage her in conversation before getting into his car and driving away. These chats in the morning, Frau Zinsser did not fail to notice, tended to get longer and longer, and when she asked her daughter what on earth the two had to talk about at such length, Gussi answered, "Gardening—beans and potatoes." But to her sister she confided, "He's the best, the cleverest, the most chivalrous man I know."

One day Gussi Zinsser surprised her parents by announcing that she intended to become a Roman Catholic. "That's Adenauer's influence!" her mother said at once. "I think she must be in love with him." Professor Zinsser and his wife took counsel and considered the new situation thoroughly.

Konrad Adenauer was certainly a man of excellent repute. There could be no doubt of his ability and his success. At forty-three he was Germany's youngest Chief Mayor and head of the fourth largest city in the Reich. Still, the Zinssers felt, there were one or two things to be said against the wisdom of their daughter's choice. There was the difference in age—he was eighteen years older than she. There was the fact that Adenauer was a widower with three children, the eldest of whom, Koko, was closer in age to Gussi Zinsser than she to his father. Adenauer's first marriage had been a happy one. Would not his second wife perforce have to live in the shadow of the first? Would his children accept her as a mother? Finally, there was the question of religion. The Zinssers were Protestants, and although they had never laid much emphasis on their religion and had always been liberal, tolerant, and open-minded on all questions of practical life, they nevertheless felt some genuine reluctance to see their daughter transplanted into Catholic surroundings.

After much heart-searching deliberation it was decided to send Gussi away. She was to stay with relatives at Wiesbaden for six months. It was an old and well-tried method often employed by circumspect parents, relying on time and distance, fresh surroundings and new ideas, perhaps even on the chance of some other man, more suitable in their view as a son-in-law, crossing their daughter's path. Gussi submitted to her parents' wish and went to Wiesbaden. But before very long she returned home, declaring emphatically, "I shall never give up Adenauer." Soon afterward she joined the Catholic faith.

A few weeks later, on September 25, 1919, the marriage of Chief Mayor Adenauer and Fräulein Auguste Zinsser was solemnized in the Chapel of Trinity Hospital, Canon Hans Adenauer, the Mayor's brother, officiating. There were no official receptions or celebrations, no honeymoon trip. Times were complex and difficult, and Adenauer felt he could not absent himself from his duties for any length of time. His young wife understood and willingly adapted herself to his strenuous way of life. Only once, in later years, she confided to her mother, "There are moments when I wish Konrad had become a gardener. We would have a little house out in the country, surrounded by nature, and he wouldn't have to bother about the world."

But Adenauer, much as he himself often longed for a quiet and secluded life in the country, was destined to "bother about the world," and his young wife at once devoted herself enthusiastically to the new tasks and duties which had fallen to her. It was not easy. Soon there was resistance. The servants, used for so long to running the widower's household after their own fashion, refused to accept the authority of the young woman, and one of the maids declared defiantly, "I wouldn't dream of having this girl in her twenties telling me what to do." It was difficult enough to be a housewife in these circumstances; it was even more difficult to replace for the three children the mother they had lost. The two smaller ones, nine-year-old Max and seven-year-old Ria, soon grew used to the new ways in their home, although they found it a little odd that the two Zinsser girls known to them as "Lotte" and "Gussi" should all of a sudden have to be called "Auntie" and "Mummy." A real problem was the eldest boy. He had been ten years old when his mother died, and it had been a very conscious experience for him. He could not bring himself to concede to his father's wife the place in the family which had belonged to his mother. Once he burst out in heartfelt indignation, "How can I call her 'Mother' when I've seen her going to school with her satchel!"

Young Frau Adenauer fought all these obstacles and vexations with the only two weapons she possessed—and they were the only ones that could and did win in the end—inexhaustible patience and endless kindliness. In this she had her husband's unfailing support; whatever she was up against, he stood by her and took her side. When the obstreperous servants failed to respond to his earnest remonstrances, he did not hesitate but simply dismissed them and engaged a new staff. Much of what her mother had feared had in fact come true. And yet things turned out totally different. There was one thing Frau Zinsser's motherly shrewdness had failed to include in her anxious calculation—the strength and power of love. It never changed and never faltered throughout the thirty years of their married life.

In the spring of 1920 Gussi Adenauer fell ill. She was expecting her first child, and the discomforts of her condition went rather beyond what had to be considered normal and natural. The doctor diagnosed an irritation of the kidneys and thought her condition gave cause for anxiety, since eclampsy was to be feared.

This diagnosis struck terror into the hearts of the family. No one spoke about it but everyone in the house remembered only too vividly that Emma Adenauer's illness had begun in a very similar manner.

The child, a boy, was born on June 4, 1920, but he was so weak that he had to be baptized privately. He was christened Ferdinand. Mother and child required constant attention and observation, and Frau Adenauer's sister Lotte, who was a trained nurse, moved in. Adenauer himself was unable to stay away from his duties. The steadily rising inflation had thrown the city's finances into complete chaos, and every day, almost every hour, decisions had to be made which his subordinates feared to take alone and which required the authority and sanction of the Chief Mayor himself. Adenauer spent every free minute in the sickroom, sleeping half dressed in an easy chair so as to be available at a moment's notice.

When he returned to his home late in the evening of June 7, he was told that the doctor who had called in the afternoon had declared that there was no hope for the child. Adenauer at once went into the sickroom. The child was in his cot, breathing heavily. The nurse had fallen asleep in her chair. He roused the exhausted woman, sent her to bed, and took over in her place. Toward midnight the child's breathing began to rattle. Adenauer telephoned the doctor, who was willing to come at once but said his visit would be to no purpose since he could not save the child. Adenauer returned to the sickroom. He took the baby from his cot and held him in his arms until, as dawn broke, it was all over. Then, with the telephone ringing incessantly and clamoring for his presence at the Town Hall, he hurried back to his office.

It is often said that Cologne is ruled by an "Adenauer Dynasty," the implied reproach being that Konrad Adenauer used his authority as Chief Mayor to favor his kin by moving them into various influential key positions. Appearances seem to confirm the truth of this allegation. Both Adenauer's brothers, August and Hans, at one time occupied leading posts in the public life of the city. Hans Adenauer, as Dean of Cologne Cathedral, was one of the high church dignitaries of the community. August Adenauer was a professor of law at the university and represented the interests of the municipality in many court actions. Dr. Willi Suth, husband of Adenauer's only sister Lilli, was for many years City Treasurer, and after 1945, *Oberstadtdirektor*, or permanent nonpolitical head of the city administration, a position which, since his retirement in 1953, has been occupied by the Federal Chancellor's second son, Dr. Max Adenauer.

On the surface all this looks indeed like nepotism. But appearances are deceptive. August Adenauer had been conducting legal actions on behalf of the municipality long before Konrad Adenauer entered the municipal administration. Dr. Suth was already well known in local government and regarded as a very promising official before he married Lilli Adenauer. And as for Max Adenauer, the Chancellor's son, even a political opponent like Socialist Mayor Robert Görlinger conceded frankly, "We elected him in spite of his father."

No one, in Adenauer's own view, is better or more fully informed on the work and achievements of the Cologne city administration under Chief Mayor Adenauer during the years following World War I than Dr. Willi Suth. "He happens to be my brother-in-law," the Chancellor remarked, "but I think he is objective enough to give you a correct picture." Dr. Suth has known Adenauer for more than forty years, and for more than twenty of them worked under him in the city administration.

"I have often asked myself," Dr. Suth says, "what were the reasons for his success. His uncommon, penetrating intelligence alone does not explain it. There is some other quality besides, an unusual power which eludes definition—his power of suggestion, his ability to compel others to work to the utmost of their capacity. Working under such a man was not always easy. His justification in the eyes of others was that he treated himself quite as ruthlessly as he did his colleagues. That silenced his critics. He is a psychologist by intuition. He loathes talkers and chatterers, and in general anyone unable to concentrate on essentials. He is very quick in seeing through such people even though they may be trying to cloak their inadequate performance with an outward show of zealous officiousness. I remember how once he told a municipal chief inspector who used to blow into his office like a whirlwind, 'You're walking too fast, Herr Meier, you'll never reach your goal!' Another official, notoriously lazy, pleaded his insomnia. 'I don't know what more I can do, *Herr Oberbürgermeister,*' he complained. 'I've tried every conceivable drug, and nothing helps.' Adenauer answered sarcastically, 'How about trying to work until you're really tired?'

"On the other hand," Dr. Suth continues, "he would be of truly overwhelming generosity toward people whose achievements convinced and impressed him, and inevitably this earned him the reproach, on the part of the city fathers, of waste and extravagance. One of his favorites was Professor Fritz Schumacher, a well-known architect and city planner. Adenauer had 'borrowed' him from the city of Hamburg to help in the Cologne development planning, and he made every effort to retain this unrivaled expert permanently in Cologne. Despite the acute postwar housing shortage, he obtained a house for him, and Schumacher's financial requirements were met even before he had mentioned them. But even Schumacher, who truly worked like a horse, I once heard sigh, 'I don't think the Chief Mayor has any conception of the limits set to human capacity and stamina.' "

With extraordinary single-mindedness the effort of this team which Adenauer, in this way, gathered around him in the course of the years were directed toward one goal: Cologne. To make his home town the largest, the most beautiful, the most powerful city of the Rhineland was the task on which Adenauer concentrated all his energies and the energies of those working with him. At the back of this activity, however, there was more than just local patriotism; there was a dominant political conception: Cologne was to become the bridge connecting Germany with democratic Western Europe. Hence the enlargement and improvement of the great inland river port, hence the construction of the huge trade fair exhibition halls, hence the deliberate and planned boosting of the university and its institutes. All this was meant to combine in making Cologne an economic and cultural shop window for all Germany, looking out toward her Western neighbors.

These plans must have struck anybody who knew Cologne in those days as thoroughly fantastic. At the time Adenauer became Chief Mayor the city of Cologne seemed definitely set on the path of steady decline. Its great period seemed irretrievably a thing of the past; grandeur and splendor had steadily diminished in the course of the centuries, political independence had been lost, cultural life had been laid waste by the closing of the university, and the transformation of Cologne into a military fortress city seemed to have set the seal of finality on this sad and depressing development. The belt of fortifications which had been laid out around the city proper had the effect of a suffocating embrace and slowly but surely had strangled the city's natural organic growth.

Then came the defeat of 1918. Adenauer had been in office for barely eighteen months when the national disaster occurred. In those black days, Dr. Suth thinks, no one in Cologne dared to make plans for the future, and people counted themselves fortunate indeed if they were allowed to "keep what they had." Not so Adenauer. "It seemed almost presumptuously arrogant," Dr. Suth recalls, "when one day he declared, 'Times of political catastrophe are especially suitable for new creative ventures!' And what was even more remarkable, he put this bold assertion to the proof. Almost all his great projects were conceived and initiated during the years of catastrophe, 1919 and 1920—parks and open spaces, new harbor installations, the university, sports and playing fields. In the initial stage of every one of these projects Adenauer came up against the resistance of the city parliament. The councilors were terrified of the enormous expenditure to which these far-reaching plans were bound to commit the city. They saw Cologne dragged into a bottomless pit of utter bankruptcy. They called Adenauer a 'Utopian,' a 'reckless gambler and wild speculator,' and finally 'Germany's most expensive mayor,' a nickname which clung to him for years to come."

Still, he persevered and eventually prevailed in almost every case. The way he contrived to get his views accepted, using perfectly constitutional means in gradually reducing a reluctant or hostile majority and winning it over to his side, was in many respects an object lesson in the democratic conduct of politics. Indeed, it foreshadowed the methods and technique which, after World War II, he was to employ so successfully on a much higher level and in a much wider field.

How did Adenauer do it?

"His first principle," Dr. Suth recalls, "was to make himself complete master of the subject under discussion. This enabled him to counter every objection raised by the opposition immediately and effectively. At every meeting he would appear accompanied by his experts and armed with a brief case full of figures and statistics. His second rule was: do not interrupt your opponent but let him speak until he has truly finished. Wait with your own views until he has advanced the whole store of his arguments and has none left in reserve. Almost cynically he once told me, 'The most successful man in politics is he who can outsit the rest.' For this reason he often saw to it that council and committee meetings dragged on far into the night. When everyone was dog tired from the endless pro and contra of the debate, he would finally come out with his own motion or proposal which to the hazy and sleepy minds would then appear like a summary of their own views, and they would adopt it without further ado.

"He treated the city parliament with a mixture of seriousness and a superior sense of humor. During noisy scenes he would remain quietly seated and, arms folded, watch the spectacle. When a Communist councilor once grabbed a glass tumbler standing on his desk and angrily threw it at his opponent, Adenauer did not interfere. But at the next meeting the drinking glasses had been quietly replaced by paper cups—by order of the Chief Mayor.

"It was sometimes a little depressing," Dr. Suth continues, "to watch the initiative of a creative personality being balked at almost every turn by the resistance of a short-sighted or narrow-minded parliament. But Adenauer never despaired of parliamentary processes. He believed in democracy, he was convinced that it was the only political system allowing the individual a maximum of freedom and initiative, and therefore he never shirked the Herculean labors of converting his obstreperous parliament to his own views with reason and argument. Occasionally, of course, his patience snapped, and then he would simply confront the city parliament with accomplished facts. The best known example of this is the story of the Cologne 'Green Belt.' From that time onward Cologne spoke of its Chief Mayor as 'Adenauer the autocrat.' "

A city map of Cologne shows the core of the old town girdled by a broad green ribbon. This used to be the so-called "Fortress Rayon" or fortification belt, some twenty-five miles in length and averaging a width of two thirds of a mile. For military reasons all building was prohibited in this ring-shaped area, and the private owners of this land had been paid compensation for their loss from state funds. After the defeat of 1918 things changed. The Fortress of Cologne was razed and demolished, and the fortification belt, all of a sudden, was once more available for building. What was to happen to the land?

The occupying power intended to leave the entire area untouched as wasteland. This would have been possible at best for a few years, but certainly not over any length of time. Before long speculators would have gotten hold of the land in one way or another, and wild and uncontrolled building would have begun. Adenauer perceived the danger and intervened. Secretly, with only his closest assistants knowing about it, he got in touch with the British occupation authorities. He suggested to them the transformation of the entire fortification belt into one large, open park. Plans for this had been prepared some time ago, they were lying ready in his desk drawer, and he had brought them along. He succeeded in convincing the British of the soundness of his idea, and they agreed to his proposal.

This first step was immediately followed by a second, and once again Adenauer acted alone. He took a train to Berlin, mobilized his political contacts, and succeeded in obtaining a Prussian Government Order authorizing the city of Cologne to expropriate the entire fortifications area. Still he was not satisfied. It seemed more than likely that negotiations over compensations with the large number of individual owners would take years, and Adenauer wanted to act swiftly. Again he traveled to Berlin. This time he brought back a law issued by the National Assembly enabling the city of Cologne to carry out its expropriation measures without lengthy negotiations. This law had been especially drafted and adopted to answer Cologne's particular requirements, and those who knew of its origins referred to it openly and spitefully as "Lex Adenauer."

"Now, of course," Dr. Suth recalls, "there could be no more question of secrecy. A week after the adoption of the law Adenauer summoned the city parliament. It was only now that he submitted his plans to the public. The dimensions of the project caused general surprise but there were hardly any factual objections. It was clear to everyone: green open spaces of such size were a true gift to every single one of Cologne's citizens. But this is not to say that Adenauer was thanked for what he had done. Not at all—he was reproached with having acted on his own authority; he was told that he should have consulted the city parliament beforehand; and it wasn't long before he heard himself called an 'autocrat.' Adenauer smiled quietly and remained silent.

"The real opponents of his scheme, however, did not pipe up until some time later. They were the 1,500 private owners of the expropriated land who considered themselves damaged by the new law. They got together, formed an association to protect their interests, and with meetings and an extensive press campaign set about mobilizing public opinion for their cause. Branding the expropriation law as a 'revolutionary assault on the sanctity of property,' they called Adenauer nothing less than a 'lackey of Socialism.' With the help of arguments like these, the association managed to win the support of the peasant population of the surrounding countryside and to turn them into their allies. The agitation reached a stage where the peasants and dairy farmers of the county did in fact pass a resolution to discontinue the delivery of milk to the city of Cologne as soon as the first act of expropriation was carried out. This was a threat which had to be taken seriously; if such a decision were carried out it was, in those early postwar years of scarcity and starvation, tantamount to a sentence of death on thousands of small babies.

"It was an unbelievable and unexampled case of selfishness," Dr. Suth remembers, "and I was just as infuriated by it as most Cologne citizens. Not so my brother-in-law. His reaction was quite different. 'Now we've got them,' he said. 'With these methods they've put themselves morally in the wrong.' He arranged for posters and advertisements in the press denouncing the moral attitude of the 'Belt Owners' in the strongest terms, and, taking a personal hand in the campaign, wrote a pamphlet in which he not only told the 'Belt Owners' what he thought of them, but also fully explained his own scheme and submitted his projects to public discussion." The little pamphlet, widely distributed, had a powerful effect. Enthusiasm for the bold schemes of the new Chief Mayor combined with furious contempt for the attitude of the "Belt Owners" carried the counteroffensive to victory. Finding themselves in moral isolation, the "Belt Owners" capitulated. Adenauer refrained from all vindictiveness and showed himself a wise and moderate peacemaker by assuring the expropriated owners of generous compensation.

"In later years," Dr. Suth says, "Adenauer did much more and much greater things for Cologne, but of all his achievements the Green Belt has always been his favorite. I remember a day in 1945 when we walked together through the streets of the ruined city and he said to me sadly and yet full of pride, 'The churches have gone but my Green Belt has remained.' "

As Federal Chancellor, Adenauer has made it his practice to leave economic affairs in the Federal Republic entirely to the experts and to intervene only in critical situations. However, his struggle with one of the large and powerful industrial combines in the Ruhr shows that when necessary he is perfectly capable of taking on the most formidable opponent even in the economic field.

The conflict began when the *Rheinische Braunkohlenwerke,* the Rhenish soft coal mining concern which supplied the city of Cologne with electricity, gave notice that in view of rising production costs it had to cancel the current tariff and charge increased rates. Negotiations for a settlement continued over a long period, and Adenauer, bearing in mind the needs of a large working population under his care, fought stubbornly and grimly for the retention of the old rates. The coal syndicate, however, was in a much stronger position, and no one in Cologne doubted that the quarrel would end with their victory.

Suddenly, one morning, people read an astonishing news item in their papers. It said blandly that the cities of Cologne and Frankfurt had jointly purchased the hard coal fields of Rossenray on the Lower Rhine, where they intended to build a large new power station which would supply both cities with electricity.

The Ruhr magnates burst with wrath and indignation. But the soft coal syndicate suddenly found itself willing and able to supply Cologne with electricity at the rates stipulated by Adenauer. And the Chief Mayor was able, as soon as a settlement was reached, to dispose of the city's holdings in the Rossenray coal field with not inconsiderable profit.

The year 1926 not only marked his fiftieth birthday. In several other respects, too, it was a crucial year in Adenauer's life. It was the year which brought to his home town the end of foreign occupation. It was the year which saw him at the height of his popularity as Chief Mayor and which marked the beginning of his decline. It was also the year in which he was within an inch of becoming Reich Chancellor and head of the German Government.

In January, 1926, the last British occupation troops left the city of

Cologne. Adenauer's bearing on this occasion was characteristic of the man who in his public speeches never abandoned his restraint to give way to emotional mass appeals. Cologne was in a delirium of rejoicing. The British, it was generally conceded, had carried out their occupation duties correctly and with due regard for the feelings of the population, but the fact remained nevertheless that they had been a foreign occupying power and their departure was felt as a release from heavy pressure. A howling, hissing, and booing mob escorted the British regiments as they marched through the streets to the railway station.

This, understandable though it may have been, was not to Adenauer's liking. He made it plain in the great speech he delivered during the "liberation celebrations" in the cathedral square at midnight on January 31, 1926. He spoke from the steps of the cathedral, to a crowd of tens of thousands, in the white glare of searchlights floodlighting the façade of the great church and its noble spires. A recording was made of his speech which Dr. Suth, his brother-in-law, has preserved. Adenauer said:

"The hour has come for which we have longed so fervently, the day of freedom is here! Our hearts go out in gratitude to Almighty God for having lent us strength in our days of trial and leading us safely through danger and distress. Once more we are reunited with our state, our people, our fatherland, reunited and free after seven years of separation and bondage. . . . In these seven years we have had to endure much and suffer heavy burdens. But let us not speak of this in this solemn hour! Indeed, let us be just! Let us recognize, despite the many troubles we've had to bear, that in the political field our departed adversary has played a fair and just game. Let us hope that our period of suffering has not been in vain, that the peoples of Europe will henceforth be animated by a truly new spirit. The laws and rules of justice and morality which are valid for the relationship between individuals and which declare all human beings free and endowed with equal rights must henceforth be valid for the society of nations not only in words but in spirit, in fact, and in truth!"

Nine years had passed since Konrad Adenauer had been unanimously elected Chief Mayor of Cologne in 1917. When, after twelve years of office, he came up for re-election, on December 17, 1929, he won with the smallest possible majority—one vote. Yet these twelve years had seen an unbroken chain of successful achievements in local government.

What was the explanation for this astonishing decline in his fortunes? Whence this reverse?

The man to answer this question was Robert Görlinger. "If you want dark colors for my portrait," Adenauer had said with a smile, "go and see Görlinger. He can supply you with all the somber hues you require." Robert Görlinger had been a life-long political opponent of Adenauer's. At the time this was written, he was Mayor of Cologne, a small, almost dwarfish man with sharply cut features, a working-class Socialist who had worked and fought his way up from humble beginnings through the trade-union movement and the Social Democratic party. For many years he had been the leader of the Socialist opposition in the Cologne city parliament and one of Chief Mayor Adenauer's severest critics, until after World War II he finally became Mayor of Cologne himself and ended up in the chair of his old adversary.

"One can almost pinpoint the day when the reversal of Adenauer's fortunes set in," Görlinger said. "It began with the story of the bridge across the Rhine at Mülheim, a most instructive story because it shows Adenauer the autocrat in the most striking fashion. This is the story."

When the neighboring town of Mülheim was incorporated in the city of Cologne, it was promised a bridge of its own across the Rhine, and this promise was to be honored in 1926. A committee of experts was set up which included five well-known architects and technicians of international standing and four representatives of the city of Cologne. The committee decided on an open competition for the best and most suitable design, and finally chose the project submitted by the firm of Krupp's, a beautifully curved arch bridge. Seven of the nine judges in the competition were in favor of this design, two were against. One of these was Chief Mayor Adenauer, who pleaded in favor of a suspension bridge.

"He talked like a book," Görlinger recalled, "trying to persuade the rest of the committee of the advantages of 'his' suspension bridge, mostly on aesthetic grounds. The arch bridge, he argued, would block the wonderful view toward the mountains in the north, whereas the delicate filigree work of the suspension bridge would leave it unobstructed. It was truly wonderful to see what poetical images this dry-as-dust lawyer's brain was able to conjure up when it suited his purpose! However, the vote went against him and the municipal council endorsed the vote of the judges with a large majority.

"Now, a genuine democrat would have submitted to this majority decision. But that was not Adenauer's way of doing business. This man knew only one authority which he respected, and that was his own will. The manner in which he got his way was a masterpiece of parliamentary artistry. He got hold of every single one of the municipal councilors and over a glass of wine to which he invited them belabored them individually for hours on end with his unceasing flow of arguments. He even harnessed the Communists, whom he professed to hate so implacably, and made them pull his cart! With real warmth and glowing conviction he talked to them of the architectural wonders of Leningrad, and, lo and behold! it was the suspension bridges to which Leningrad owed its beautiful modern appearance! And would you believe it, the Communists, these idiots, actually fell for this twaddle!

"But his best trick this smart stage manager saved up for the final and decisive meeting. Suddenly, to the great surprise of everyone, the spokesman of the city administration—I think it was Adjunct Billstein—advanced a totally new argument which until that moment had never been mentioned in the debate. It had become doubtful, he said, whether the foundation of the river bed was in fact capable of supporting an arch bridge. There was a likelihood of its shifting, and this made it almost a public duty to raise grave doubts regarding the safety and durability of the Krupp bridge. For almost an hour this representative of the city administration poured a cataract of figures over the city parliament, figures which he read from a piece of paper and which, in all probability, he understood just as little as nine tenths of the assembly. All the time this was going on Adenauer sat enthroned in his mayor's chair, watching quietly the confusion he himself had engineered.

"For the whole story of the alleged shifting of the ground and its sudden appearance at this stage was his own work. What had happened was that some municipal official had told him that Max Woltmann, the city architect, in a casual conversation had expressed some doubt whether the river bed of the Rhine would support the weight of an arch bridge. Adenauer picked this up immediately. Although it was a Sunday, he sent for the architect, who was eventually tracked down enjoying some carnival festivity, and overwhelmed the baffled and perplexed man with angry reproaches for not having announced his doubts long ago. Having suitably crushed poor Woltmann, he locked him up in his office until he had sweated out a lengthy expert opinion complete with all the relevant supporting figures—which Billstein then paraded before the assembly!"

It may be added here that Görlinger's version of the incident does not agree in all respects with the records of the municipal assembly, and Woltmann's expert opinion, which was later thoroughly scrutinized by a special committee of professionals, was found to be correct and well grounded.

"Be that as it may," Görlinger said, "at any rate, what matters is that Adenauer got his way. At its meeting of April 28, 1927, the city parliament with forty-three votes against thirty-six decided in favor of Adenauer's suspension bridge—the very same assembly which only a few weeks earlier had approved the committee's choice of the Krupp arch bridge with a large majority! And, here is my point, the point of the whole story. Adenauer had emerged victorious, but it turned out to be a Pyrrhic victory. The press, and not only the opposition papers, were infuriated by this spineless lack of character on the part of the municipal councilors, and inside the city parliament there were a good many who felt rather ashamed of their own irresolution and fickleness. Many of the Chief Mayor's former supporters and political friends drew away from him. Adenauer had overdone it, and he had done it once too often."

Adenauer was intelligent enough not to underrate this change of feeling. As the end of his period of office approached, Görlinger recalled, he left no means untried to ensure his re-election. A month before the election date he organized a large public meeting in the Hansa-Saal, the main ceremonial hall of the Town Hall, at which he gave a full account of his work, justifying everything he had done, and outlining at the same time the future plans and aims of his administration.

"I was among the audience at this meeting," Görlinger said, "and I admit I found it hard not to be impressed by what he said. His dry and sober, occasionally even sarcastic, method of expounding the most fantastic schemes created an impression on his hearers that, given a little honest good will, all these Utopian projects were really child's play. What did he not conjure up! The old city was to be replanned, new streets, full of light and air, were to take the place of the old, narrow, crooked, and unsanitary passages, skyscrapers were to be erected, a girdle of modern cottages and flower gardens laid out encircling the town, workers' settlements—at election time Adenauer invariably discovered his social conscience—fast nonstop buses to take the workers to their places of employment, and so on and so forth!

"Who was to pay for all this? The fact that he had, with his previous schemes, already burdened the city with a loan debt of 301,000,000 marks Adenauer brushed aside with the remark that the city treasurer, after all, had 926,000,000 in the bank! And an astonishing thing happened: our burghers, those niggardly cheeseparers who would bite through a farthing before contributing it to the social services, jubilantly cheered this pyrotechnist who under their own eyes blew the remnants of the city funds sky high in a dazzling display of projects for the future!

"It was not only through platform oratory that Adenauer tried to win the support of public opinion for his re-election. His real strength lay in his ability to influence individuals. Thus, he would make a special point of inviting opposition members to his house; I, too, once went to Max-Bruch-Strasse. It was on that occasion that I understood, for the first time, the secret of Adenauer's personal success. The man is generally considered cold, reserved, unfeeling. This notion is quite wrong. Rather, he possesses the remarkable gift of generating warmth and friendliness in precisely the direction where he senses his own advantage. This is, I think, his real secret. He feels genuinely sympathetic toward people whom he can use, and as soon as they have fulfilled their function this sympathy dies away and is extinguished.

"Before that stage is reached, however, Adenauer develops a kind of personal charm which is very hard to resist. He has a 'politeness of the heart' which never fails to touch naive souls. He never forgets a birthday or a promotion, on happy occasions he unfailingly sends his congratulations, on sad ones equally unfailingly his condolences. He always answers all his letters promptly and reliably, fulfills the wishes of his 'friends' as far as possible, and continually nurses their gratitude and sympathy with the help of small presents and courteous attentions. . . ."

Still, when election day came, he barely scraped through with a majority of one vote, and this, it was said, was the vote reserved for the municipality and thus, in a sense, Adenauer's own casting vote. Almost exactly twenty years later, on September 17, 1949, the same thing happened again, a few miles away from Cologne, at Bonn, when Konrad Adenauer was elected first Chancellor of the new Federal Republic, again with a majority of one, and again, it was said, with his own casting vote.

Adenauer continued in office as Chief Mayor of Cologne for another three years. He was well paid and comfortably off, yet continuing in local government meant considerable material sacrifice for him. Shortly before his re-election there was a fierce and somewhat unedifying quarrel in the city parliament about his financial position. The opposition, wishing to clip his wings, argued that he was overpaid: a salary of 41,500 marks per annum plus 37,000 marks toward his residence and another 6,000 marks towards light and fuel, making a total of 84,500 marks, or the approximate equivalent of $20,000 a year. It was true that the allowance for his private residence was extraordinarily high, but what his critics did not point out was that the city had failed in its obligation to put an official residence at the Chief Mayor's disposal free of charge, and that it was now merely paying interest toward the mortgages with which Adenauer, with the city's consent, had built his own house. However, as a result of this investigation of his finances, he was compelled by the opposition to hand over to the city treasurer his director's fees which he received as a member of the board of the Rhenish-Westphalian Electricity Works, and of the German Bank, and one radical opposition group even demanded that his total emoluments for his next period of office should be reduced to 35,000 marks. This motion was rejected by the city parliament, and one reason for its rejection was that the Social Democrats and their leader, Robert Görlinger, refused to support it. Why?

Görlinger, Adenauer's life-long opponent, was quite frank about it. "We knew," he said, "that Adenauer could earn a great deal more in private industry. At that time he had been offered a position carrying a salary of 200,000 marks. Don't misunderstand me, though! I'm the last person to charge Adenauer with money-grubbing and financial exploitation of his position. As long as we have a capitalist society, everyone is fully entitled to sell his labor at the highest price he can get."

A few weeks after he had given this account, on February 10, 1954,

Robert Görlinger, the combative old Socialist, died. When the Federal Chancellor saw the portrait his one-time adversary had painted of him, with plenty of "dark and somber shades," he refused to have it altered or toned down. "Leave it the way it is," he said. "Much of it is seen through the spectacles of political antagonism and distorted by hatred, but I hope and trust that Görlinger is now in a place where he has a better and juster view of things."

## CHAPTER V

THE STORY of the decline and fall of the Weimar Republic has been told many times, and this is not the place to retell it. But in order to appreciate the part which Konrad Adenauer played in it, at a critical juncture and in one short but illuminating episode, it is necessary briefly to recall some of the circumstances which led to the extraordinary situation in which he found himself, at the age of fifty, in May, 1926.

German political and parliamentary life had split up into a multitude of different parties, groups of parties, and factions. No single party was strong enough to form a government. Coalition succeeded coalition in a growing variety of combinations, and it became increasingly difficult to find a stable majority on which to base a cabinet. In the short span of thirteen years, between 1920 and 1933, there were no fewer than eight general elections, and twenty-one different governments took office. The life of any government depended on the confidence of the Reichstag, or Parliament, and Parliament, composed as it was of a multitude of mutually antagonistic and warring factions and splinter parties, was able to dismiss any Reich Chancellor and his cabinet with a vote of "no confidence" whenever they failed to unite a majority of the splinter groups in support of any given measure. This inevitably led to rapid succession of governments whose average span of life was about nine months.

Since such short periods of office obviously did not permit the planning or execution of long-term political and social programs, successive governments were compelled to improvise. An ever-growing number of important issues on which the people expected and demanded decisions—such as the burning question of the revaluation of small savings deposits devoured by the inflation, or the compensation payable to the former ruling princes for their expropriated estates—were shelved or delayed year after year because they carried within them the seeds of yet another government crisis and threatened the life of yet another cabinet.

This was the broad political situation when in the middle of May, 1926, the Chief Mayor of Cologne, Konrad Adenauer, was asked to become Reich Chancellor and head of the German Government. A few days earlier Chancellor Dr. Hans Luther and his cabinet had been brought down after less than five months in office. The incident which brought about Luther's downfall seemed trifling but it was significant. The Weimar Constitution stated that all measures and decrees issued from the office of the Reich President (or Head of State) required the countersignature of the Reich Chancellor, who, if necessary, had to obtain parliamentary sanction for it. Chancellor Luther, in this particular case, had countersigned Reich President von Hindenburg's so-called "Flag Decree," which provided that the flag of the German merchant navy should in the future show the old Imperial German colors, black, white, and red, with the colors of the Republic, black, red, and gold, in the form of a small "jack" inset in the top left-hand corner. This contrivance aroused a great deal of violent feeling in parliament. The Old Imperial colors were felt to be discredited and their reintroduction in this way was regarded by the Socialist and Democratic parties as a concession to the right-wing and "reactionary" groups which undermined the prestige of the Republic. Chancellor Luther's plea that he had introduced the black, white, and red merchant navy flag only in deference to the feelings of Germans abroad was found unacceptable by the majority of parliament, and a motion of "no confidence," tabled by the Democratic party, resulted in his dismissal. War Minister Otto Gessler, a democrat, was entrusted with the interim conduct of affairs until a new government could be formed.

In this confusing situation leading parliamentarians in Berlin, casting about for a man of sufficient standing and authority to break the deadlock and lead them out of the political cul-de-sac, thought of the Chief Mayor of Cologne. Many things seemed to count in his favor. He was known as a highly intelligent, resourceful, and energetic man. His successful career in local government had made him a well-known figure far beyond his immediate Rhineland province. Politically, he had risen rapidly in his own party, the Catholic Center party, and was next to men such as Adam Stegerwald and Theodor Von Guérard, the party's General Secretary, one of the most prominent members of its National Executive Committee. He was not a deputy to the Reichstag but was known as an experienced and skillful parliamentarian, and, finally, as President of the Prussian State Council—an assembly of appointed representatives of the provinces of Prussia with over-all legislative and administrative functions—he had, ever since his appointment in 1920, won general respect and confidence and accumulated a considerable store of political credit.

Thus, summoned by Stegerwald and Von Guérard, Adenauer took the road to Berlin. He remained in the capital for three days. Soon after his return he drafted, for his own records, a detailed *aide-mémoire* of the conversations he had during these three days, and the various negotiations in which he took part or was involved. This memorandum, which reflects the tragic confusion then reigning in German politics with sober and dispassionate clarity, has never been published before and is here printed for the first time, verbatim and unedited, as the Federal Chancellor's own personal contribution to his biography. It reads as follows:

On Thursday, May 13, 1926, at 9:45 P.M. I received an urgent telegram forwarded via Aachen which ran thus: "Request your presence urgently Berlin tomorrow—signed Von Guérard, Stegerwald."

Having a shrewd idea why these gentlemen desired my presence in Berlin and feeling no inclination to take over the post of Reich Chancellor, I put matters off a little by wiring back that their telegram had arrived too late to enable me to reach Berlin the following day; if however they still wanted me on the day after tomorrow, I could arrange to be in Berlin by Friday night or Saturday morning. Next I had a telephone conversation with Stegerwald on Friday, May 14, at 10 A.M., when he urged me emphatically to come. I undertook to leave Cologne by the two-eighteen train, arriving in Berlin at ten-forty in the evening.

I was met at the station by Messrs. Von Guérard and Stegerwald. They accompanied me to the Kaiserhof Hotel where we had a lengthy discussion lasting until 12:30 A.M.

In essence the two gentlemen told me the following:

The time had now come for the formation of a majority government. Only a "Great Coalition" embracing all parties, from the Social Democrats on the left to the German People's Party on the right, could now meet the situation, and all the parties in question were agreed that such a coalition was desirable. They had, they said, gotten in touch with the Social Democrat leaders in parliament immediately after Dr. Luther's resignation, on Wednesday, and the Social Democrats had declared themselves ready to join a Great Coalition. As things stood, however, there still were three issues on which at present the Social Democrats and the German People's Party did not see eye to eye. As soon as these were resolved and out of the way, the formation of a Great Coalition would become possible without further difficulty. These three issues were the following:

1. The revaluation question. Their discussions with the Social Democrats had shown, however, that regarding this problem it would be easy to obtain agreement between all parties included in the Great Coalition.

2. The question of the Flag Decree. On this the Social Democrats had declared they quite understood that in view of the actual position and taking into account the character of the Reich President, the decree, once it had been promulgated, would have to be brought into effect, and they would tolerate its going through.

3. The question of expropriation of the former ruling houses. On this Stegerwald and Von Guérard stated the position was that the matter was taking its prescribed course, and it was generally assumed that a plebiscite would fail to muster the necessary number of votes. Such a result would automatically remove the entire issue from the parliamentary sphere, the Reichstag would no longer have to deal with it, and the matter would be referred back to the three states which so far had not reached an agreement with their former ruling princes.

Stegerwald and Von Guérard went on to say that the day before (which was Ascension Day) they had had talks with the leaders of the German People's Party, in the course of which they had been told by them that, as soon as the three above-mentioned issues had been cleared up, their parliamentary group would be prepared to set aside any other doubts they might entertain and be very glad indeed to join a Great Coalition.

Stegerwald and Von Guérard finally told me that they, in the parliamentary Center Party, had until now always deliberately refrained from proposing me for the post of Reich Chancellor, because they felt I was too good and valuable a man to be wasted on a purely temporary or interim term of office. Now, however, following the conclusion of the plebiscite, the road was clear for a Great Coalition and a stable and durable majority government. They would insist on the plebiscite, scheduled for June 20, taking place at an earlier date. Meantime, it was their plan to form a transition cabinet, with myself at its head and retaining the present ministers, with the ultimate object of forming, after the plebiscite, a majority government broadly based on a Great Coalition, with myself as Reich Chancellor, which would have a longer life. They would ask me most urgently and earnestly, they said, to cooperate in this and put myself at their disposal. I owed it to the fatherland.

What I was told by these two gentlemen regarding the creation of a stable and durable majority government, and, resulting from it, the possibility of contributing something of lasting value to the general good of the country remained not without its effect upon me. I had to ask myself seriously whether in such circumstances it was not my duty to make a great personal sacrifice and take over the post of Reich Chancellor. I told them I would think things over during the night and let them have my answer in the morning.

They now stated they had already arranged a meeting between myself and Herr Gessler, the acting Reich Chancellor, for nine o'clock the following morning. Provided my answer was in the affirmative, they suggested we should together go and see Gessler, who would then suggest to the Reich President that he entrust me with the formation of a government. I should then immediately appoint my ministers in time for the news of the formation of the new government to be published that same Saturday night. They would call on me at eight-thirty in the morning to hear my final answer. I asked them not to rush matters unduly and to give me until nine o'clock.

I thought things over during the night and the next morning at nine o'clock told Stegerwald and Von Guérard the following:

From my point of view the whole proposition raised a number of doubts and difficulties. Assuming the Reich Chancellorship was, for me, a very grave decision which I would take only reluctantly since it meant relinquishing my present sphere of work to which I was deeply attached and which extended far beyond the confines of Cologne, in order to use myself up in Berlin within a relatively short period. The example of Dr. Luther, I said, was not encouraging. However, I would feel under an obligation to put my personal interests aside provided there really was a chance of my doing something for the good of the whole country. My doubts and scruples concerned the following points:

1. The Dawes Reparations Payment Plan. It was clear to all concerned—in particular, the then Reich Chancellor Dr. Marx had told me so on his return from London—that by 1927 it would already no longer be possible to fulfill its terms. In my own personal view, we should never even have signed the Dawes agreement. I must admit, however, that I was not fully conversant with all the facts of the situation and that one had to accept things as they stood; still, the impossibility of fulfilling the Dawes plan from 1927 onward represented in itself a serious difficulty for the new government.

2. My views on Locarno were known to them. Although I was prepared to accept the situation as it resulted from the conclusion of the

Locarno Pact, without material or mental reservations, in order to secure from it the greatest possible advantages for Germany, I was profoundly unhappy about the unsteady, seesaw character of German foreign policy, and could not approve of the manner in which this policy was conducted. In my view, Germany, being a totally disarmed nation, should endeavor, as far as possible, to keep out of all conflicts of the other nations until she was needed. Furthermore, as far as I knew and was able to judge, negotiations at Locarno had been conducted rather less than skillfully on our side. Further developments in Geneva might easily lead to a defeat for Germany, and that again would inevitably be charged against the new government. As far as I was able to form my own judgment without inside knowledge of events, I could not feel that our foreign policy, as conducted up to the present, had been very happy. On the other hand, it was imperative that Herr Stresemann remain in the cabinet—quite apart from the fact that he was the leader of one of the future coalition parties—and I could foresee running into difficulties with him if we could not reach agreement.

3. Regarding current parliamentary issues, in the light of what I had been told by them, I could see no substantial difficulties, neither concerning devaluation and the Flag Decree nor in respect of the indemnification of the former ruling houses. Especially since the last issue, according to what I had been told, would no longer be the concern of the Reichstag.

Therefore, in order to clarify all this, I suggested the following course. I should first of all see Gessler alone and talk the situation over with him. Next, I would ask Dr. Ernst Scholz of the German People's Party, and Dr. Rudolf Hilferding of the Social Democratic party, to discuss matters with me. I was anxious to see these particular two gentlemen (who were not the official leaders of their parties) to avoid lending my soundings an official character. Scholz, I said, was known to me as a former colleague, and I had a high opinion of him as a man of integrity. Dr. Hilferding I knew from the time when we were both members of the State Council, and I had met him occasionally and discussed political questions with him even after he had ceased to be a member. As soon as I had talked things over with these three gentlemen, I told Stegerwald and Von Guérard, I hoped to be able to give them my final answer.

Stegerwald and Von Guérard agreed. As a result I had an interview, at ten o'clock that Saturday, with the acting Reich Chancellor, Herr Otto Gessler, whom I had known for some time. I informed him of my negotiations with Messrs. Stegerwald and Von Guérard, and of my intention to clarify the position regarding a majority government straight away.

Gessler told me that a minority government of the type they had had up to now had become impossible. Such a cabinet would be able, at best, to administer but could not govern. I was quite right, therefore—especially in view of Germany's internal difficulties (unemployment, equalization of finances as between the central government and state budgets), and the difficulties in the foreign situation—to demand a firm and solid majority government, particularly as the Reichstag intended to go into a four months' recess. It was also necessary, he said, before committing myself definitely, that I should discuss present policy with Stresemann, who was a little worried by my appearance in the capital. They would then place before me all confidental matters with regard to foreign affairs, so that I should be able to form my own opinion. He asked me to let him know my decision as soon as possible, perhaps in the early afternoon, to enable the Reich President to charge me immediately with the formation of a cabinet.

At eleven o'clock on the same day, I had an interview with Herr Scholz. Our conversation lasted one hour. I began by telling Scholz that I had asked him to see me because I was anxious, in view of our long-standing acquaintance, to have a man-to-man talk with him. I asked him to be as completely frank with me as I intended to be with him. At the conclusion of our talk I suggested we should agree between ourselves on how much of the substance of this interview was to be made public, and in particular how much of it I should be free to impart to Von Guérard, Stegerwald, and Hilferding, who would see me immediately afterward. Herr Scholz agreed to this procedure.

I told Scholz the same things I had previously told Stegerwald and Von Guérard, with the exception of my doubts and reservations regarding foreign policy. These I did not mention because I had no wish to hurt Stresemann's feelings through lack of consideration, and because I meant to discuss them with Stresemann himself, providing matters progressed far enough. I emphasized that I felt it necessary for me to be quite clear regarding the prospects of a majority government, and furthermore that I must make it a condition, after full consultation with the parties, that I should be free to select my own ministers and would not be bound to accept the nominees of the coalition partners. I then asked Scholz for permission to make notes of what he was going to tell me, and I made these notes under his eyes, at the conference table.

Scholz said that, from my point of view, my attitude and the position I took were correct and wholly justified. He fully appreciated that I could relinquish my position as Chief Mayor only if I was assured a safe and stable majority in the Reichstag. If he were in my place he would proceed in exactly the same manner. However, the difficulties resided in the proposition itself. On principle his party would be prepared, if this was the wish of the Reich President, to take part in negotiations for the immediate formation of a Great Coalition. But such negotiations had no prospect of succeeding, for several reasons.

The principal stumbling block, Scholz said, was the question of compensation for the former ruling princes. Stegerwald and Von Guérard were quite wrong in believing that this matter had ceased to be the concern of parliament. There were people in all parliamentary parties who insisted on seeing this matter settled by the Reichstag, even in the event of a negative result of the plebiscite. This was a question where the Social Democrats were attacking the basic foundations of the state itself, and his party—and, he hoped, also the Center Party—would resist them with all their might. As a result, a very serious conflict was unavoidable.

Another matter which was bound to cause negotiations to fail was the question of the Flag Decree. Even if the Social Democrats declared themselves willing to tolerate the decree, the situation remained impossible, with the Social Democrat leaders being in the government while the party itself carried on their black-red-gold nuisance in the country at large. This would cause the Great Coalition to break apart within a few weeks.

But even apart from the present situation, Scholz said, a Great Coalition was an impossibility. The swing to the right had to come. His party agreed that, owing to the attitude taken by the German National party in foreign affairs and the annoyance felt by the Center party toward the German National party, it was not yet possible, at the moment, to bring about this swing. For this very reason they desired a neutral Cabinet, even if it were a minority government.

He admitted, Scholz said, that a minority government was in itself an absurdity, but at present it was the lesser evil. Nor was it admissible to regard the cabinet now to be formed as a kind of transition cabinet leading to a Great Coalition. It was true that his party was not yet in a position to form a coalition with the German National party, but there was increasing recognition among the German Nationalists that Stresemann's present foreign policy was the right one, despite some grumblers among them who continued to object; but such grumblers could be found in every parliamentary party. His party also agreed that the Center Party, who at present were very angry with the German National party, must be allowed time to come around before it was ready to join the German National party in a coalition.

Following a meeting their parliamentary party had held a day or two ago, Scholz said, feeling in his party was now such that it had become very doubtful whether they could remain in the same government with the Democratic party. For this to be possible it would be necessary for Dr. Erich Koch, their leader, explicitly to withdraw the notice he had given to the present coalition, and furthermore the Democrats would have to declare unequivocally that they would cease their resistance to the Flag Decree and withdraw their mental reservations against it. His party, Scholz said, did not wish to force the Democrats into a Caudine yoke, but in respect of these two points they had to insist on the Democrats giving them adequate assurances, and they, the German People's party, must be free to make use of them in public. What was totally out of the question for them was to join the Social Democrats in a government. Not even a government based on Social Democrat support in parliament was acceptable to them. As for the Reich President, his political attitude was precisely the same as that which he had just outlined to me.

For the rest, regarding myself personally, he had only one thing to say: he himself and his parliamentary party, despite some objections which were bound to be voiced, would be very glad indeed to welcome me at the head of a neutral cabinet.

In reply I told Scholz the following: that what he had just said sounded very pleasant in one of my ears, and very sad in the other. I was very glad indeed, and thanked him for it, that his frank and open statement had allowed me to come to a clear-cut decision: in these circumstances it was, of course, quite impossible for me to accept the office of Reich Chancellor, and this corresponded to a large extent with my own personal wishes. On the other hand, what he had said could really make one weep with sorrow, since it made one realize the terrible, self-destroying length to which internecine party quarrels had gone in Germany. I could well understand, I said, that there were many elements among the German Nationalists, especially among their supporters in the country, who were of value to the state, but surely it was the foremost duty of everyone having the well-being of the fatherland at heart to educate the many millions of Social Democratic supporters everywhere in the country toward loyalty to the state and to make them responsible citizens. This was manifestly impossible, I said, if the Social Democrats were simply barred and excluded from all share in the government.

Scholz answered that he shared my views in principle, and our opinions differed only with regard to the method to be employed. In view of the experience his party had had with the Social Democrats there was only one way for the future, and that was the formation of a purely bourgeois middle-of-the-road government. It would be up to such a government to govern so efficiently and well that the masses would become gradually estranged from the Socialists and won over to its side.

I told Scholz that possibly such an idea was a feasible proposition in times of sound and stable economic conditions. We were faced, however, with a big economic depression and enormous unemployment. In my view this unemployment and this economic depression were not of a temporary, transient nature but would be with us for years. For this reason alone I thought his whole conception impracticable.

After Herr Scholz had left, Dr. Hilferding called on me. I informed him of my conversations with Stegerwald, Von Guérard, and Scholz. I told him I wished him to acquaint me with the views and feelings of the parliamentary Social Democratic party, just as I had acquainted myself, through Scholz, with those of the German People's party, since I was not prepared to assume office unless my two basic conditions were fulfilled: I must be assured of a stable majority in parliament, and I must be allowed to select my own ministers, after due consultation with the parties.

Dr. Hilferding told me the following: With regard to major issues pending between the parties, only three had so far been mentioned in the talks between the parties, namely, those to which I had referred—indemnification for the ruling princes, revaluation, and the Flag Decree. There was, however, a fourth issue which he had not raised so far in order not to add to the difficulties of negotiation. This was the future of the decree on corn tariffs, which was due to expire on August 1 of the current year, and which his friends wished to see extended. With reference to the three other points mentioned by me he had this to say:

1. He supposed that, even after a negative result of the plebiscite, the matter of compensation for the former ruling princes would have to be settled in parliament, after all, but he thought in that event a compromise solution would be necessary and also possible.

2. Regarding the Flag Decree, Herr Külz was of the opinion that the Reich President would agree to a postponement of its coming into effect as long as the question of creating a new flag was left in abeyance. Meanwhile the entire problem could be conveniently referred to a commission which should include not only members of parliament but also others.

3. With regard to the problem of revaluation, he no longer anticipated any difficulties.

Coming to the fundamental problem, Hilferding said his party felt a Great Coalition was in itself desirable, but only if it were given an assured and fairly long lease of life, and on condition that a binding undertaking in this respect was given by the German People's Party. There must be no repetition of the situation where the German People's Party simply walked out of the Great Coalition and left it in the lurch. It seemed doubtful whether the formation of a Great Coalition was possible while the question of the expropriation of the former ruling princes was still pending. However, his party would support me as Reich Chancellor even before a Great Coalition had come into being, and this support in parliament would be considerably stronger and more extended than in the case of the Luther government, because they felt convinced that under my Chancellorship the present constitution of the state would be maintained and safeguarded. Therefore, my government would only in theory be a minority government; in actual fact and in practice it would be a majority administration.

I realized that he knew as well as I did that a minority cabinet which owed its life to Socialist support from day to day would sooner or later be presented with a bill and would have to pay the price of this support, and this was an expensive pleasure to indulge in. It was much better and more businesslike, in every respect, to have a lump sum paid down once and for all; therefore, I should much prefer it if firm and definite agreements were concluded between the parties concerning a Great Coalition.

Following this conversation with Dr. Hilferding, I asked Messrs. Von Guérard and Stegerwald to see me. I reported to them the results of my soundings and told them that in view of these results it was out of the question for me to engage in further activity in this direction. The two gentlemen told me that the statements made by Herr Scholz had changed the situation, which now appeared very different from what they had understood it to be following the declarations of the German People's Party on Ascension Day.

In the early afternoon I called on Herr Gessler and repeated to him what I had told Stegerwald and Von Guérard. Gessler was highly surprised, having been told previously that Scholz, at a private party the previous evening, had expressed himself as very satisfied when it was mentioned that the Center party would propose me as Reich Chancellor. Gessler suspected all this might be due to Stresemann, who feared that I was too strong a man for him to deal with. Stresemann, Gessler said, had some rather violent encounters even with Dr. Luther, and he feared I might turn out to be an even stronger man than Luther. I asked Gessler to report the entire matter to the Reich President in as much detail as possible, and left it to his discretion to inform the Reich President that I had gained the impression from my conversation with Scholz that the Reich President could perhaps bring about a Great Coalition if he were prepared to tell the German People's Party that a majority government was a necessity and that for patriotic reasons it was their duty to join a Great Coalition.

A short while afterward I received a telephone call from Herr Thomas Esser, one of the Center party deputies in the Reichstag, asking me, if at all possible, to come immediately to a meeting of the executive committee of the parliamentary party. I went, and there was told the following:

Dr. Marx, who had been kept informed of my conversations with Scholz, Von Guérard, and Stegerwald, had mentioned the matter at the cabinet meeting which took place at four-thirty that afternoon, stating in particular that, in view of the statements made to me by Scholz, it seemed that the German People's Party obviously did not wish to join a Great Coalition. Thereupon Stresemann had declared that this must certainly be incorrect. He had called Scholz on the telephone, and on his return to the meeting had said Scholz had told him it must be a misunderstanding on my part.

Following this, I gave the executive committee of the parliamentary party a full and detailed account of my conversation with Scholz based on my notes taken during the interview, and assured them there could be no question of a misunderstanding having arisen in the course of an interview lasting one hour. The position was then discussed by a meeting of the parliamentary Center party which followed.

While this meeting was still in progress, Scholz personally, and Stresemann by telephone, asked for Herr Von Guérard and told him they were quite sure there must be a misunderstanding. It was later stated at the meeting of the parliamentary party that the news agency of the German newspaper owners' association, which I knew to be in very close touch with Stresemann, had subsequently toned down a news item reporting my negotiations with the German People's Party to the effect that Herr Scholz had told me they could not consider entering a Great Coalition—at the present time.

The general view was that Stresemann had used Scholz to make it impossible for me to take over the Chancellorship. This view received support from the Reichstag Deputy Ulitzka, who told me the following:

On the Saturday morning, at half-past seven, Frau Antonina Vallentin, a friend of Frau Streseman's, had telephoned Herr Rudolf Breitschied, a prominent Social Democratic Reichstag deputy, and told him that she had just heard that Adenauer was to be appointed Reich Chancellor. This was impossible and quite out of the question. Adenauer was politically on the extreme right and was associated with Wallraf and other people of his kind.

This concludes Konrad Adenauer's personal account of this historic episode.

Adenauer returned to Cologne, and on May 17, 1926, Dr. Wilhelm Marx was appointed Reich Chancellor. His government was the thirteenth to be formed since the foundation of the Weimar Republic, and six more cabinets were to follow, until, in January, 1933, the

Hitler dictatorship struck the final and mortal blow at this sick parliamentary democracy.

Subjectively and from his own point of view, Adenauer was undoubtedly right in keeping out of this senseless and irresponsible party squabble. All the same, there remains the intriguing question whether he would not have been the man to put an end to this undignified spectacle and thus forestall and prevent the disaster which subsequently engulfed the German nation.

When, a quarter of a century later, the Parliamentary Council at Bonn drafted the constitution for the new German Federal Republic under the chairmanship of Konrad Adenauer, it took care to apply the lesson learned in the Weimar days and deliberately strengthened the position of the Federal Chancellor against the fickleness of an irresponsible parliament. Article 67 of the new constitution says:

"The Federal Parliament can express its lack of confidence in the Federal Chancellor only by electing, by simple majority, a successor to his office, and requesting the Federal President to dismiss the Federal Chancellor."

This article makes it impossible for any government to be dismissed without the majority of parliament having previously agreed by vote on a successor assured of the necessary support. More than any other single article in the constitution, this stipulation, based on costly and dire past experience, has made a decisive contribution toward political stability in Western Germany and toward renewed confidence among the German people in the validity and efficiency of parliamentary democracy.

# CHAPTER VI

AFTER the failure of the attempt to unite Germany's major political parties under his leadership and place him at the head of a broadly based and stable Reich Government, Konrad Adenauer continued in his office of Chief Mayor of Cologne for another seven years. But, three years after his re-election in 1929, his work came abruptly to an end. The man whom Adenauer might have frustrated for all time, had things gone differently in Berlin in May, 1926, had arrived. On January 30, 1933, Hitler and National Socialism took power. Adenauer was fifty-seven years old. The second of his three lives came to an end.

"The man to tell you about the circumstances which led to my dismissal by the National Socialists is Dr. Billstein," the Federal Chancellor had said. "In 1933 he was in charge of the administrative department responsible for the Cologne municipal police force, and he witnessed most of what happened at close quarters."

This was an understatement. Dr. Heinrich Billstein, who nowadays lives quietly in retirement in Cologne, had witnessed a great deal more at close quarters than the fateful events of 1933. Except for a short interval during World War I, he worked for a full twenty-one years, from 1912 until 1933, in various departments of the city administration, always under Adenauer's direction, and no man living can have a more intimate knowledge of this period than he.

The repercussions of the world economic crisis, Dr. Billstein recalls, hit Cologne especially hard from 1929 onward. Over one fifth of the city's total population, some 160,000, were unemployed and had to be supported from public funds. In Adenauer's view this steady increase of want and misery was the real danger, and it may be said without exaggeration that his struggle against National Socialism began even then, when he strained every nerve and every resource within his sphere of activity and influence to combat this demoralizing pauperization. "We've got to free people from the misery of having nothing to do," he said to Billstein. He set up the Cologne *Nothilfe* or Emergency Organization, which ran courses in adult education and training centers for various crafts, and organized a system of economic self-help among those hit by the crisis.

"Of course, we all knew perfectly well," Dr. Billstein recalls, "that the problems thrown up by a world economic crisis could not be solved by the municipal administration of Cologne. Therefore, Adenauer tried hard to bring his influence to bear on things at the highest level. Only a few people know of the interview he and Heinrich Hirtsiefer, the Prussian Minister of Economics, had with the then Reich Chancellor, Dr. Heinrich Brüning. Adenauer and Hirtsiefer implored Brüning to make an attempt to overcome unemployment by organizing a large-scale and comprehensive program of public works. Plans for a nationwide network of modern motor highways, *Autobahnen*, were lying ready for execution in the desk drawers of the various ministries. But they remained waiting there until Hitler came and carried them out.

"Adenauer returned from this interview with Brüning in a mood of profound depression. 'Brüning remained deaf to all our suggestions,' he told me. 'He told us a public works program of such dimensions was bound to endanger the stability of the currency, and that in no circumstances could he contemplate it.' Adenauer added with biting bitterness, 'Brüning will hold onto the currency and drop the political reigns of government from his hands. There is nothing left to stem the onrush of disaster.' "

When disaster came, Adenauer was not prepared to make even the slightest concession to the new rulers. The National Socialists demanded that the swastika flag should be hoisted on the Town Hall. Adenauer refused. His municipal administration, he declared, occupied a neutral position in party politics, and this did not permit him to show the flag of a particular party.

Thus his trouble with Adolf Hitler began.

Hitler had been appointed Reich Chancellor on January 30, 1933. One of his first acts was to dissolve parliament and hold new elections, which he hoped would result in a majority for his party. These elections were scheduled for March 5, 1933, and the interval was filled with a whirlwind election campaign of hitherto unheard-of clamor and violence.

In the course of this campaign Hitler reached Cologne on February 17, 1933.

"I remember the date very well," Dr. Billstein recalls. "It was toward evening and I was still busy at my office when I was telephoned from the airport. I was told that Hitler was holding an election meeting at the nearby city of Essen, and would immediately afterward proceed to Cologne. His private aircraft was expected to land at Cologne airport at 11 P.M. I informed the Chief Mayor and asked for his instructions regarding official reception formalities. 'Let me think this over for a bit,' was Adenauer's reply. 'Remain at your office, I'll let you know.' Half an hour later he called me back. 'Since Hitler is coming to Cologne not in his capacity as Chancellor but as a speaker at a party election meeting,' he said, 'I see no reason why I as Chief Mayor should officially receive him. Your department, on the other hand, is responsible for police protection and the safety of the airport area. I would ask you, therefore, to represent the city authorities at the reception.'

"I feared immediately that this attitude was likely to get the Chief Mayor into very serious trouble. But I knew Adenauer's feeling about National Socialism well enough to realize that it was hopeless to try to make him change his mind. So, full of forebodings, I drove out to the airport. Everything was ready to receive the *Führer*. In the glare of the searchlights I recognized the representatives of the Nazi party and of the armed forces, all of them in uniform. I was the only civilian. Shortly after eleven o'clock the aircraft touched down. Hitler alighted and briefly greeted the assembled party members and officers. Then for a moment his eyes went around, searching for someone. A member of his entourage whispered something in his ear. He gave me a cold, critical stare, and, without addressing a word to me, walked past me to his waiting car. He got in and drove straight to the Hotel Dreesen at Godesberg, where he could be sure of a more hospitable welcome than at Cologne.

"Two days later, on Sunday, February 19, a National Socialist election meeting was scheduled to take place in Cologne, at which Hitler was to be the main speaker. The ideology of the Third Reich having not so far fallen on very fruitful ground in Cologne, it was planned to build up the meeting with a large-scale propaganda show as a prelude. Storm troopers and SS were to march through the streets, and the population was asked to put out flags. This was done, although not as thoroughly as had been desired. There were no flags on any of the municipal buildings. But in the early morning of Sunday a message came through to me: 'Swastika flags are flying from the two pylons of the Rhine bridge at Cologne-Deutz.' Obviously storm troopers had secretly put them up during the night. The bridge across the Rhine, however, was municipal property. I telephoned the Chief Mayor at his home. As always in tricky situations, he considered the matter calmly and thoroughly before giving his instructions.

"In this case his instructions—and I admit I was at first thoroughly frightened by his boldness—were as follows: 'Dispatch a group of municipal workmen to the bridge and have the swastika flags removed. Call out a detachment of police and with them assure the safety of the enterprise. In case you are challenged by storm troopers, tell them that you are acting upon my orders. These orders were given by me because the flags have been hoisted without permission from the municipal authorities. If the situation threatens to become serious, you may tell them that I am prepared to have the flags put up in front of the large trade fair hall. That is where Herr Hitler is making his speech this afternoon. Therefore, without suffering in our authority or dignity, we can temporarily regard the trade fair hall as National Socialist party premises.'

"Accompanied by some workmen and a small detachment of police, I went to the Rhine bridge. What I feared happened soon enough. While the workmen were still busy taking the flags down, a group of storm troopers appeared on the scene. Their leader demanded categorically that work should be stopped forthwith. I referred him to my orders given to me by the Chief Mayor but declared myself ready, in accordance with Adenauer's instructions, to have the flags put up again at the trade fair hall. There was a lengthy and rather agitated discussion, watched by a rapidly growing crowd of spectators. Eventually the leader of the storm troopers walked across to a nearby restaurant, where he telephoned to his superiors. Upon his return he said with an angrily twisted face, 'Carry on! But let me tell you, I have orders to see that the flags are put up in front of the trade fair hall.'

"This turned the dramatic incident into a farce. Before the flags could be rehoisted, the flagpoles had to be sunk into the ground in front of the hall, and this took considerable time to accomplish. Since my small labor force proved insufficient for the job, the fire brigade had to be summoned from the suburb of Deutz to help. While all this went on, the storm troopers, shivering miserably in the winter cold, stood by and grimly watched the proceedings."

It was generally assumed that in view of these occurrences Adenauer would be immediately dismissed from office, and there was much surprise when at first nothing happened at all. The tactics of the National Socialists in getting rid of their opponents were not yet generally known or appreciated. They consisted, in the first place, in mobilizing the mob in the street against anyone not acceptable to them, and then, by seemingly yielding to the pressure of public opinion, sacrificing him to the outraged populace. Thus, during the next few weeks National Socialist party organizations in Cologne and the local press seemed to regard it as their most important task to prepare the way for a swing of popular feeling. There was nothing too crude or far-fetched to serve in discrediting Adenauer and undermining his reputation. He was charged with squander mania, with wasting the taxpayer's money, even his personal integrity was called into doubt, and in the end storm troopers, rattling their boxes during street collections, would call out, "Every penny a bullet for Adenauer!"

"In those days," Dr. Billstein recalls, "Adenauer came to know the fickleness and inconstancy of the human character. It was barely a fortnight since the masses had jubilantly cheered him during the carnival, and now these same masses hurled abuse at him wherever he showed himself in public. Many of his so-called friends withdrew from him, and soon there was around him that well-known vacuum which quickly forms about anyone whom it may be damaging or dangerous to know. Adenauer endured all this with admirable fortitude. I cannot recall his uttering a single embittered word about the deep personal disappointment he must have felt. What hurt him profoundly, however, was that people did not hesitate to inflict the same indignities and humiliations upon his wife, old friends of the family turning away brusquely upon meeting Frau Adenauer in the street. That he found hard to forgive. Once, having told me of such an experience, he added, 'It is really very hard to know the human race and not to despise it.' "

The Reichstag elections of March 5, 1933, resulted in a very large increase in the National Socialist vote in Cologne, and immediately party measures against the Chief Mayor stiffened. A permanent detachment of storm troopers was quartered in his private house in Max-Bruch-Strasse, ostensibly, as in the days of the "Soldiers and Workers Council" fifteen years earlier, to insure his safety, but in fact to keep him under surveillance. With the arrival of this prison guard, Adenauer's fate as Chief Mayor was sealed.

Still he remained at his post. On March 12, a week after the Reichstag elections, local government elections were due to be held. It was generally expected that serious trouble would break out on that day. It was intimated to Adenauer from National Socialist quarters that he would be wise to ask for his retirement on a pension forthwith, and the *Regierungspräsident,* or Provincial Governor, implored him to take at least a fortnight's leave of absence for a vacation trip away from the city. But Adenauer refused to budge or yield. His only concern was the safety of his children. Fearing that on election day the Hitlerites might storm and ransack his house, he took the children to the Catholic Caritas Hospital at Hohenlind and placed them in the care of the director, who was a friend of the family. "I don't want them to see what happens in their parents' house when the storm troopers arrive," he explained. His wife alone remained with him.

"I believe most of us secretly dreaded this twelfth of March," Dr. Billstein admits frankly. "But there was no sign of fear in Adenauer. On the morning of election day a memorial meeting for the dead of World War I was held at the Gürzenich, one of Cologne's most famous historic buildings. Although he had been warned that it might not be safe for him to attend. Adenauer duly appeared. I accompanied him and with my own eyes saw the complete isolation in which he found himself. People avoided him like a leper. But it was a good thing, nevertheless, that he went. For here, at the Gürzenich meeting, he received a warning without which his fate, in all probability, would have taken a very different turn. A man who had joined the National Socialist party for purely opportunist reasons took Adenauer aside and told him in great haste that the storm troopers were preparing a plot against his life. It was planned to 'liquidate' him by an assault squad in the Town Hall, on Monday morning, as soon as he arrived at his office. They were going to throw him through the window into the street.

"After the meeting Adenauer went straight to his office at the Town Hall to take leave, as he told me later, of the rooms of which he had grown so fond. He never saw them again. They were destroyed in World War II. When the warning he had received in the morning was repeated in the evening, he telephoned the Chief of Police of Cologne, Lingens, and asked for protection. The day before, at a conference concerned with safety measures for the municipality, Lingens had declared emphatically, '*Herr Oberbürgermeister*, I know that at the moment you are the man in the greatest personal danger in all Cologne. In spite of this, I would ask you to come to us at Police Headquarters, if you feel threatened. My officers and I have pledged ourselves to defend you to the last man.' Now, scarcely twenty-four hours later, the same Lingens, when asked for police protection, answered, 'I'm sorry; without orders from Berlin I'm unable to do anything.' Adenauer asked for no further explanations. He replaced the receiver."

His decision was made. He was going to Berlin to lodge a personal complaint with Hermann Göring, in charge of the Ministry of the Interior, about conditions in Cologne. It was a bold and risky move, but Adenauer felt it was the only way still open to him. As always, he had ordered his official car to call for him at his house at nine o'clock in the morning on Monday. He was certain that the storm trooper detachment quartered in his house would try to prevent his journey. Therefore, he did not cancel his official car, but instead asked a friend, Dr. Robert Pferdmenges, a well-known Cologne banker, to lend him his own car for a trip to Dortmund, at seven o'clock in the morning. At Dortmund he intended to catch the train to Berlin.

Early on Monday morning he informed his wife. He would be back within a few days, he told her; meanwhile she should join the children at the Hohenlind hospital. She should also inform his secretariat at the Town Hall that he had gone to Berlin. Walking past the sleeping storm-trooper guard, he left the house which he had built himself and which he loved dearly. The car took him to Dortmund, as planned, where he took the train for Berlin. He had hoped to return within a few days, but it took twelve years before he again set eyes on the places where he had lived and worked, and then the Town Hall lay in ruins, and a lone goat was nibbling the grass which grew among the heap of shattered masonry that had once been his house.

"The following day, March 13, 1933," Dr. Billstein tells, "the

Cologne newspapers announced with banner headlines the news of the flight of the Chief Mayor and of his dismissal from office. Slander and abuse reached a new climax. 'Cowardly deserter' was one of the milder expressions used. In fact, Adenauer proved anything but a coward or a deserter. He had merely shifted his struggle onto new ground. Immediately after his arrival in Berlin, he requested an interview with Göring, who kept him waiting three days before receiving him.

"In later years Adenauer once gave me a description of this interview. Göring received Adenauer in his office in the Prussian Ministry of the Interior. Wearing civilian clothes, he sat on a sofa between two large windows, which had the effect that Adenauer, blinded by the light which fell across his face, at first did not see Göring at all. Proceedings, at least outwardly, resembled a police interrogation. The face of the accused man is exposed in glaring light, while the investigating magistrate remains in the shadow.

"At first Göring refrained from assuming the role of a magistrate. He offered Adenauer a chair and asked him calmly, almost courteously, to submit his case. He even listened to Adenauer's complaints without interrupting him. Then he suddenly asked, in the same quiet, almost polite tone of voice, 'And what about those millions which you took from the City Treasury before you fled?' Adenauer answered equally calmly, 'I cannot assume, Herr Minister, that you should believe nonsense of that sort.'

"Göring dropped the subject at once. But his next question was a new accusation: 'Why was it, Herr Adenauer, that you ordered the flags to be removed from the Rhine bridge on the occasion of the *Führer's* visit to Cologne? You appreciate that your attitude caused very bitter feelings among the Cologne party comrades.' Adenauer risked a great deal when he answered, 'Because I had the impression that the majority of the citizens of Cologne did not approve of the hoisting of the flags. It was done at night and without permission from the municipal authorities.'

"Next Göring referred to Adenauer's complaint about his unlawful dismissal. 'This dismissal was ordered without my knowledge,' he said. 'I have given orders to former Undersecretary of State Schmidt to conduct an investigation of your affairs and to go closely into the charges leveled against you in Cologne. My further decisions will depend on the results of this investigation.'"

That ended the interview. Adenauer heard or saw no more of Göring. Many years later he learned by accident that as early as February, 1933, Göring had issued instructions to Nazi party organizations in Cologne to proceed energetically against the Chief Mayor and render life as difficult for him as possible.

Meantime, however, a systematic drive had begun in Cologne against all members of the former municipal administration. Not only Adenauer himself but many of his former staff were now openly abused by the press and at public meetings, and denounced for alleged grave offenses. Immediately after Adenauer's departure, a new man, one Günther Riesen, had been installed as acting Chief Mayor, and to this man Adenauer now addressed a letter from Berlin. Appealing to his successor's sense of loyalty, he asked him for protection for the officials who had worked under him, and in particular requested Riesen to give them at least an opportunity to defend themselves before dragging their names publicly in the gutter.

Riesen's answer has been preserved. A copy was made at the time by Dr. Billstein, who rightly felt that this was a "document of the times." "You are the accused," Riesen wrote, "I am your Counsel for the Prosecution, and the people are your Judge. That is the position between us."

There was something unreal about the life Adenauer led in Berlin after his departure from Cologne. He was still President of the Prussian State Council, and he lived in his official apartment in the Prussian Ministry of State which had been placed at his disposal some years before. It consisted of several rooms equipped with furniture from the former royal Prussian palaces. In these stately surroundings, which reminded him at every step of better days gone by, he lived the life of a man who had no idea how to support himself and his family in the immediate future. Apart from the small cash he had taken with him on his escape, he possessed no money whatsoever. The city of Cologne had suspended his salary from the day of his unlawful dismissal, and his bank refused the political suspect permission to draw on his account.

Politically, his elimination was complete. There was only one instance when his cooperation was requested. This was the dissolution of the former Prussian Diet, or State Parliament. It still continued in existence, and in order to remove this obstacle in the path of complete unification along National Socialist lines, the then Reich Commissar for Prussia, Franz von Papen, summoned the body of men entitled, in accordance with the Prussian constitution, to authorize the Diet's dissolution. Among them were the Prime Minister of Prussia, and the Presidents of the Prussian State Council and of the Diet itself. The Prime Minister of Prussia, however, Dr. Otto Braun, a Social Democrat, had removed himself to Switzerland, and Adenauer denied Von Papen's claim that he was entitled to take Braun's place and exercise his vote. At the same time he refused to lend his own hand to the dissolution of the Prussian Diet. In the position in which he then found himself, early in 1933, this was a challenge of unheard-of boldness, entailing incalculable risk, and many of his old friends of the Center party trembled for his life.

Whenever, in later years, Adenauer told of this time, he emphasized the great importance the Church had for him in those perilous days. It was not only, physically, a peaceful and protected enclosure where he knew himself safe, at least for some hours, from arrest by the Secret State Police, the Gestapo, but it also gave him strength to overcome his fear of the threats the future held for him. Often he visited the Hedwigskirche, the principal Roman Catholic church of Berlin, and the inner calm and renewed faith in God he brought back from these hours of prayer and contemplation are reflected in the letters which he wrote daily to his family at Cologne, comforting them and asking them not to lose their courage.

Help came from an unexpected quarter. One day a visitor called. He was Mr. D. N. Heinemann, a wealthy American industrialist who lived in Brussels and was a personal friend of Adenauer's. Walking up to Adenauer with outstretched hands, and greeting him in his new surroundings with the same respectful cordiality as of old, he declared without further preliminaries, "I imagine, Herr Adenauer, that you must now be in need of money. I have brought you 10,000 marks in cash because you may have difficulties in trying to cash a check."

It was one of the rare moments in Adenauer's life which found him utterly nonplused. "But this is impossible," he protested. "You can't do that. I have no idea whether I shall ever be able to repay you this sum. My salary has been cut off, and my bank account—" Heinemann cut him short with a reassuring gesture. "I know that my money will be well invested," he said, pulling out his wallet and placing an envelope containing the notes on the table before him. He refused to accept a receipt or an I.O.U., and when Adenauer tried to thank him he rose hastily, shook the dumfounded friend's hand and left, as swiftly and busily as he had arrived.

When Adenauer, as Federal Chancellor, made his first official visit to the United States, in 1953, one of his first calls immediately after his arrival was not on the Mayor of New York or on some American politician, but on D. N. Heinemann at his house in Greenwich, Connecticut.

Heinemann's surprise intervention had banished acute material distress for some time to come. There remained the danger of arrest, and this grew steadily as the days went by. There was little or nothing in the newspapers from which to guess the relentless and ceaseless activity of the Gestapo. But among those who refused to come to terms with the state of Adolf Hitler it was an open secret that almost daily well-known people were whisked away and disappeared —into the cellars and torture chambers of Columbia House, into Gestapo Headquarters in Prinz-Albrecht-Strasse, into some prison or other, without charge, without questioning or interrogation, without legal aid or any other means of defense.

In this perilous situation Adenauer turned to an old friend and former schoolmate at the Apostel-Gymnasium, Ildefons Herwegen, Abbot of the world-famous monastery of Maria Laach. He asked him for sanctuary at the Abbey.

It was a hard decision to take. Although the Abbey promised greater safety, it meant further, prolonged separation from his family. Adenauer asked his wife to come to Berlin, to consult with her. Frau Adenauer had greatly missed her husband during the weeks she had spent alone with the four children at the Hohenlind hospital, but realizing in what acute danger he was, she put all her personal wishes aside and urged her husband to place himself under the protection of the monastery. Ildefons Herwegen's answer, when it arrived, was positive. The Abbot of Maria Laach asked Adenauer to come at once. "I shall be glad to have you with me," he wrote, "and you're welcome to stay as long as you like."

The Adenauers left Berlin the very next evening, taking the overnight express so as to disappear from the capital, if possible, unseen. At the railway station of Neuss, near Cologne, they were met by the car their trusted friend, banker Pferdmenges, had sent. It was to take them up into the remote Eifel mountains and to the beautiful, eleventh-century Benedictine Abbey situated picturesquely at the edge of a deep crater lake and surrounded by endless forests. The car had to make a wide detour around the city of Cologne. Adenauer had been formally and officially expelled from his home town and was forbidden to enter the city's confines.

Once more Adenauer gave his wife the necessary instructions, telling her to whom to turn in case she needed help or advice, and agreeing with her on methods by which they could keep in touch without arousing suspicion or betraying his whereabouts. "I hope you will be able to visit me from time to time," he said. Then he pulled the bell rope of the Abbey and was let in.

Adenauer remained at Maria Laach for almost a year.

Behind the protective walls of the ancient monastery an altogether new and unaccustomed life began for him. After years of tireless activity which had seldom left him time to think about himself, he now found himself surrounded by the timeless contemplative calm of monastic life. But it was impossible to forget that he was only a guest in this quiet seclusion. Abbot Ildefons urged him to be cautious and keep his presence in the monastery as secret as possible. His wife visited him from time to time, and the Abbot suggested it would be safer to see her outside the monastery walls. So they went for long walks together through the woods until they parted again at the gates.

Adenauer read a great deal in these months of seclusion and inactivity, mainly historical works, including ancient Roman history. Art history was another field which interested him deeply, and he made a special study of the life of Rembrandt and his works. But more important than all this were the two great papal encyclicals on social questions, *Rerum Novarum* and *Quadragesimo Anno*, which Adenauer encountered for the first time at Maria Laach and which made a decisive impression upon him. In these two fundamental papal pronouncements the practitioner of the day-to-day political struggle discovered a comprehensive and coherent program inspired by belief in an order willed by God which was perfectly practicable in terms of modern society. They represented, it seemed to him, an impressive attempt to overcome and defeat the idea of the class struggle in the spirit of Christian charity, and to release the working masses, under the watchword of "Deproletarianization of the Proletariat," from the spiritual and material pressure of their seemingly hopeless situation.

These views impressed him deeply, and the conception of the role of the state which he encountered in this social teaching of the Church henceforth greatly influenced his thinking. It was this fundamental notion which guarded him more securely than all written democratic constitutions against the temptation to extend the powers of the state at the expense of the personal liberties of the individual. It is probably accurate to say that Adenauer's political work in later years has its roots in these months at Maria Laach and could not be explained without reference to them.

Adenauer himself does not seem to have been conscious, at that time, of any such distant possibilities. He was safe at Maria Laach, but obviously he was far from happy. He suffered from his inactivity and above all, as is clear from his letters, from the separation from his family. During the summer holidays he arranged for the eldest son of his second marriage to stay with him. Paul, then a boy of ten, accompanied his father to daily divine service in the Abbey church and kept him company on his long solitary walks. For the sensitive youth these were important impressions which gave his later life its decisive turn; from school he went on to study theology and become a priest, and only consideration for his invalid mother prevented him from following his true inclination and entering Maria Laach as a Benedictine friar. Even today, as a grown man, Chaplain Paul Adenauer remembers with some emotion the weeks he spent with his father at Maria Laach. "Once toward evening," he recalls, "I walked with my father through the woods above the Abbey. Suddenly my father stopped and pointed northward, where we saw the quarries of Oberkassel standing like fiery walls in the sunset. 'In that direction lies Cologne,' my father said, in a voice I shall not forget."

As Christmas approached it was decided that, despite all the risks and difficulties, the family should spend it together, reunited, if only for a day or two. Since Adenauer was prohibited from visiting Cologne, it was arranged that the family should visit him at Maria Laach. There was a hotel by the lakeside, not far from the Abbey, and here Adenauer took a couple of modest rooms for his numerous family. After a somewhat adventurous journey up into the snow-bound Eifel mountains, they arrived unmolested and unrecognized, all eight of them—Frau Adenauer; the three grown-up children of the first marriage, Konrad, Max, and Ria; and the four "little ones," Paul, Lotte, Libet, and Georg, known as "Schorsch." It was a happy reunion under the Christmas tree, but it had an unhappy result.

Despite all precautions, the family visit had not gone unnoticed. News of it reached the authorities, and presently the Abbot received a peremptory request from Freiherr von Leuninck, the Governor of the Rhineland Province, not to tolerate Adenauer's presence in the monastery any longer. Ildefons Herwegen indignantly rejected this interference and refused to comply. But Adenauer feared that sooner or later the Abbey would get into serious trouble on his account, and he looked around for a refuge elsewhere which would allow him, at the same time, to be reunited with his family.

Through a fortunate coincidence he heard of a family living at Neubabelsberg, just outside Berlin, who were preparing to emigrate from Germany. They were looking for a trustworthy tenant for their house, and the common bond of silent understanding and solidarity which then united all those opposed to the Hitler regime made their choice fall on Adenauer. It was true that the nearness to Berlin represented a certain danger for Adenauer, but, on the other hand, the prospect of being able to live again with his family, after a separation of nearly a year, outweighed all his doubts, The arrangement was made, and soon Adenauer took leave of Abbot Ildefons and his monks and moved with his family to Neubabelsberg.

It was a handsome and well-appointed house to which they came, surrounded by a large garden and with a small private swimming pool, and it seemed that here at last was peace and rest for the hunted fugitive. Above all, for the first time in many years, Adenauer found time and leisure to devote himself to his family, and he did so with the same zest and energy he gave to everything he undertook. He looked after the housekeeping, worked in the garden, did the shopping, and made the children, too, render their small daily services to the household. Paul had to clean the shoes for the whole family, Lotte was detailed to do the washing up, and Libet to do the dusting.

The remuneration was weekly pocket money carefully graded and ranging from fifty pfennigs to one mark, according to age and services. "You must learn," Adenauer told the children, "that one never gets anything for nothing in life, and one has to earn the fulfillment of one's wishes by hard work."

He devoted much more time and attention to his children than he had ever done before. He helped them with their homework, went for walks with them, and taught them all to swim, including three-year-old Schorsch, who was as yet free from domestic duties. For the children this was a happy and carefree time when they had their father all to themselves. They could not guess how uncertain the foundations of this family idyll were. The danger of sudden arrest was by no means banished, and the material situation, too, remained disquieting. The city of Cologne was still not paying Adenauer his salary, and his bank account continued to be blocked. On the other hand, he was determined not to use up the Heinemann loan but to save as much of it as possible. He found another way out of his straits. During the good years of success and prosperity Adenauer had collected a fair number of paintings, and in his purchases had been guided more by his personal taste than by the prominence or reputation of individual artists. He now found that his artistic judgment had been sure and good. He was able to sell part of his collection with considerable advantage.

Things seemed indeed to be taking a turn for the better when suddenly a new and threatening cloud gathered above Adenauer's head. This was the case of Anton Brüning. It happened in March, 1934, when Adenauer was living in Neubabelsberg, and all but ruined his fortunes forever.

Among the few permanent officials of the Cologne city administration who remained loyal to the fallen Chief Mayor, Josef Giesen occupies a special position. In contrast to most others he kept in touch with his former chief after his own dismissal by the National Socialists, and during the twelve years of persecution which he shared with Adenauer remained an untiringly helpful and loyal friend. Giesen, an expert gardener and fruit grower, had been in charge of the city's horticultural department. After his dismissal from municipal service he retired to a village halfway between Cologne and Bonn, where he bought a small fruit farm. This he developed within a few years into a remunerative model enterprise which not only kept him going but enabled him generously to help others during the lean years of food rationing, among them the family of his former chief.

"I felt Adenauer's fall in the Third Reich much more severely than my own dismissal," Josef Giesen says. "Complete elimination from public affairs was a much harder blow for a man of his dynamic energy than it was for the rest of us. What was for us a fact with which we managed somehow or other to reconcile ourselves was to him real tragedy, a complete paralysis of all his creative political strength. Besides, his actual fate rather differed from that of most other dismissed officials. With us they were content with firing us, and thereafter we were more or less left alone. But he was kept under continuous, unceasing observation by the powers above. Through all those years they watched him with implacable hatred and secret fear, and again and again tried to destroy him, not only politically but also morally. Toward this end every means, however despicable, served, including outright defamation and attacks on his personal integrity. The most characteristic example of this relentless persecution was the way in which they attempted to involve him in the Brüning case."

This is Josef Giesen's account of this remarkable affair.

At the beginning of 1934, Anton Brüning (not to be confused with Dr. Heinrich Brüning, the former Reich Chancellor), a former director of the Deutsche Bank at Cologne, was arrested on a charge of fraudulent conversion and embezzlement. Early in March, 1934, Adenauer received a summons to appear as a witness at the trial of Brüning. The form of the summons struck Adenauer as unusual. No date was mentioned when the trial would take place. Adenauer was merely requested to keep himself available, from a certain time onward, for his testimony as a witness.

Adenauer immediately got in touch with his brother, August Adenauer, a prominent lawyer in Cologne, who telephoned the presiding judge of the court. To his amazement he learned that it was not intended to hear Adenauer as a witness during the public trial but that he was to be interrogated by a special examining magistrate. "But why all this?" Dr. August Adenauer asked. "Dr. Adenauer is a sick man," the judge answered, with special emphasis. Adenauer, of course, was not sick at all, and it took his brother some time before he saw through the perfidy of this procedure. The alleged illness was merely an excuse to prevent Adenauer's public appearance in court. It was rightly feared that he might easily be able to demolish the charge which was but an unscrupulous tissue of falsehoods, and score a public triumph over Hitlerite justice.

It was finally arranged between the President of the Court and Dr. August Adenauer that the examination of the witness was to take place in private at the house of Hans Adenauer, the second brother, who was a member of the cathedral chapter. The Court seemed to feel that nothing unforeseen or compromising was likely to happen at the private residence of so high a dignitary of the Church.

The meeting took place on a gray morning in March, 1934. Adenauer arrived early at his brother's house in Cathedral Square. He felt certain that the unusual circumstances of this examination presaged an unusual course of proceedings. At length the others arrived. They were a judge, a public prosecutor, a junior assistant judge functioning as a clerk to the court, and between two police constables, the defendant Brüning, and his counsel.

Proceedings began with an interrogation of the accused. Pale-faced but outwardly calm and composed, Anton Brüning made his statement. It was truly sensational. Brüning accused the former Chief Mayor of Cologne of nothing less than "passive bribery." According to him, Adenauer had received from the bank of which Brüning was a former director the sum of 35,000 marks (approximately $8,800) for the purpose of repaying a mortgage debt. In the books of the bank this payment had been camouflaged as profits from Stock Exchange speculations, whereas in fact, Brüning said, all concerned had been well aware that it was a complimentary payment in recognition of certain financial transactions of the city of Cologne in which the bank had received preferential treatment.

This was a surprise indeed! Adenauer perceived at once the deadly danger hidden in this charge. He knew that, unless he succeeded in proving the utter falseness of this monstrous accusation, he was finished, a heavy sentence of hard labor awaited him, and there was no hope, however distant, of any political activity whatsoever, even after the downfall of the Hitler Reich. There was nothing to do but to take the bull by the horns there and then. Turning to the public prosecutor, Adenauer said:

"Brüning has been prompted to tell this lie in order to secure a lighter sentence for himself."

The Public Prosecutor protested indignantly against "this insinuation," but the Judge remarked ironically that some allowance should be made for the excitement felt by the witness. "Herr Brüning himself is probably best qualified to clear up this point," he said. Brüning had visibly winced under Adenauer's words. Now, with all eyes upon him, he stammered, "My statement was made voluntarily." The Public Prosecutor asked him to repeat it.

Brüning repeated, "Chief Mayor Adenauer received through my intervention and good offices bribery money to the amount of 35,000 marks."

"When and where?" Adenauer asked like a shot.

His question gave the cue for a game of questions and answers lasting hour after hour. Adenauer, of course, knew the Deutsche Bank well. He had worked with its Cologne branch for many years, first during his term as City Treasurer, and later as Chief Mayor, and his private and personal funds, too, had been very largely administered by it. Now every single one of these transactions was closely scrutinized in every detail. As the scrutiny proceeded, Brüning's composure and self-assurance gradually weakened. He entangled himself in contradictions, hesitated, remained silent. Adenauer was able to disprove every single one of his allegations, but, each time Brüning found himself cornered and had to admit the falseness of his claims, he invariably took refuge behind his original statement, repeating with the monotony of an automaton:

"Chief Mayor Adenauer received from us 35,000 marks bribery money."

The meeting had begun in the early morning, and in the late afternoon the struggle still continued. There was not a point left that had not been raised, discussed, disproved. But still Brüning insisted on his allegation. At last Adenauer turned to him direct. Pointing at the crucifix in the corner of the room and looking his accuser firmly in the face, he said slowly and solemnly:

"In the name of all that is sacred to you I ask you: tell the truth at last!"

The words hit Brüning like a hammer blow. He lowered his head and remained silent. After a time he looked up and glancing helplessly at Judge and Prosecutor, murmured almost inaudibly:

"It is possible that the Chief Mayor is right. Yes, he is right."

The Public Prosecutor jumped up, yelling, "Have you gone mad?

Do you realize what you've just said? This is the most important point in the whole indictment. Just think of the damage you're doing yourself!"

But somehow Brüning had become a changed man. He repeated, this time in a firm and clear voice, "My original statement was untrue. I withdraw my accusation against Chief Mayor Adenauer." Once more there was a struggle. The Prosecutor refused to be beaten. He left nothing untried, threatening, imploring, begging, abusing the accused. But Brüning stuck to his guns: "I withdraw my accusations." The Prosecutor had lost his battle.

"Take the defendant away," ordered the Judge. The two police constables took Brüning away between them. Adenauer went up to the prisoner and shook his hand, as a sign that he bore him no grudge. Then he slipped one of the constables a few marks. "For a taxi," he said. He wished to spare Brüning the ignominy of having to walk through the streets of Cologne as a prisoner.

"That was the Brüning affair," Josef Giesen said. "Unfortunately most people have already forgotten these things, but it is as well to remind oneself from time to time of the methods used in the Third Reich to bring down and destroy perfectly blameless and honorable men. You just fired off your slanderous allegations, and if you happened to miss the target, you just kept silent and said no more. There was never a word of apology or exculpation.

"No one ever thought of withdrawing the charge of bribery or any of the other infamous lies which were spread among the public about the Chief Mayor of Cologne and his municipal administration. The file of the Göring Investigation Committee against Adenauer contained over a thousand pages. What remained of all these charges? The separatist charge collapsed like a house of cards, and not a shred of proof was left of all the countless cases of alleged corruption. But has anyone ever heard of Adenauer having been rehabilitated? On the contrary, the spying, the surveillance, the slander continued, and there was no pretext too flimsy to get him into new trouble. They thought they'd get him yet."

Indeed they did. On June 30, 1934, Adenauer was arrested by the Gestapo.

# CHAPTER VII

June 30, 1934, was the day of the so-called "Röhm Revolt," when Hitler, with unexampled violence and brutality, made short shrift of all his enemies, rivals, and suspected opponents within his own party, and of a great many others as well. The reckoning was a massacre, and Adenauer's arrest was as sudden and arbitrary as everything else the regime perpetrated on this memorable day.

Paul Adenauer, then a boy of eleven, was a witness of events and remembers them well.

Already on the morning of June 30, he recalls, the family had heard rumors that something unusual was afoot in Berlin. Motorized SS detachments, it was said, were tearing at top speed through the city, and storm troopers were marching through the streets in long columns, silent, without singing. A little later it became known that General Kurt von Schleicher and his wife, who lived near the Adenauers at Neubabelsberg, had been shot by an SS detachment. Then came news of a whole wave of arrests and shootings in Berlin, one worse than the other. To Adenauer the most terrible blow was the murder of Erich Klausner, the leader of the "Catholic Action" group, who was shot down by SS men in his office in the Prussian Ministry of the Interior.

"Meanwhile," Paul Adenauer tells, "details about the alleged Röhm Revolt became known, and I remember my father saying, pale with anger, 'Hitler is simply using the opportunity to get rid of all his opponents.' Anxiously my mother asked, 'Do you think they will come to us, too?' My father shook his head. 'I'm already finished and done with,' he said, to comfort her. He tried hard to conceal his agitation from her and the children, and carried on with his work in the garden as usual, but we all sensed his inner restlessness, and the whole family was caught in this nervous tension.

"Toward seven o'clock in the evening a small car drove up in front of the house. A man got out and rang the bell at the garden gate. When it wasn't opened at once, he simply climbed over the low gate and walked across the lawn, straight up to my father, who was busy, as every evening, watering his flowers. 'Secret State Police,' the man said, without introduction, showing his tin badge. 'You're under arrest. Pack your bag and follow me at once!' My father put down his watering can and they walked up to the house together.

"My mother had watched the scene from the terrace. 'What do you want of my husband?' she asked anxiously. 'Temporary arrest,' the official answered laconically. 'No need to get worried,' my father intervened at once. 'I've done nothing wrong. I'm sure the mistake will be cleared up very quickly, and I shall soon be back with you.' While my mother was hastily packing a small suitcase, she asked the official, 'Do you think my husband will be back soon?' The man answered, 'I'm afraid it will take some time.' My father said good-by to us. He was calm and composed as he left and waved to us from the garden gate."

For the family there began the agony of waiting. The town was full of the wildest rumors. Thousands were believed to have been arrested. At Spandau, it was said, an uninterrupted series of executions was taking place, and in the cellars of Police Headquarters at Potsdam ceaseless interrogations, accompanied by cruel torture, were proceeding day and night.

"On Monday morning," Paul Adenauer recalls, "my mother could bear the uncertainty no longer. She went to see the Gestapo at Police Headquarters in Potsdam, where we understood my father had been taken along with many others arrested. She returned in despair, having met with a brusque rebuff. They had refused to tell her anything—where my father was, and what was the charge against him. 'Now there's nothing left to us but to pray,' she said.

"On Monday evening my father was back. He looked pale and worn with lack of sleep, but was unhurt. However, what he told us sounded bad enough."

Things had been uncomfortable even during the car journey. When they reached a certain crossroads where a narrow path through the woods forked off from the main road to Potsdam, the Gestapo man asked suddenly, "Are you carrying any arms?" The question was a well-calculated piece of mental cruelty. Like everyone else in Neubabelsberg, Adenauer knew only too well that previously many arrested prisoners had been "shot while attempting to escape" along this particular path through the woods. "At that moment," he told his family later, "I felt sure that my last moments had come." But the Gestapo car continued along the main road to Potsdam.

Since all Potsdam prisons were filled to capacity with suspects alleged to have been involved in the Röhm Revolt, Adenauer was taken to a country house requisitioned by the Gestapo as a supplementary detention center. Here he found twenty-nine fellow prisoners waiting, men of all walks of life, including several bankers and army generals. They were kept under strict surveillance, their every move closely watched, but otherwise nothing happened and no one seemed to bother about them. They were simply left to their own torturing uncertainty, apart from being made to listen to a broadcast harangue by Goebbels, a gruesome and bloodthirsty account in which the Propaganda Minister tried to justify the massacre of June 30. On Sunday all but three of the arrested were released. One of the three who were kept back was Adenauer.

Finally, on Monday, Adenauer was taken to Police Headquarters at Potsdam. For several hours he was left alone in a small room with no furniture except a table and a couple of chairs. Eventually a Gestapo official, a tall, heavy, brutal-looking man, appeared. He went straight at Adenauer:

"We've had you under observation for several weeks. We know all about you. The only way you can ease your situation is by making a full and frank confession. So you'd better tell me—who else was involved with you in the conspiracy?"

Adenauer answered calmly and firmly, "I know nothing of a conspiracy."

The Gestapo man stepped close to him.

"Very well," he said, "if you prefer to be obstinate we shall continue the interrogation in the cellar. Do you know what that means?"

Adenauer repeated, "I have nothing to confess."

At this the man turned and left the room, slamming the door furiously behind him. Again Adenauer was left alone for several hours. And in the evening he was released—without warning, without reasons being given, in the same abrupt and arbitrary manner in which he had been arrested. He learned later that Hitler had issued orders, that very Monday evening, to release all those arrested and discontinue further persecutions.

"We were hoping then," Paul Adenauer recalls, "that these orders would also mean the end of further police measures against my father, and that henceforth he would be left in peace. But my father did not share this view. 'Hitler will never lose a single one of his former opponents from sight,' he said to an old political friend who visited him at Neubabelsberg, 'and if the regime blunders into mistakes we shall have to pay for them.' "

Events were to prove Adenauer right. Soon after his release he received a confidential warning from Ildefons Herwegen at Maria Laach.

"Danger approaching. Recommend urgently to travel."

Thus began the harassed life of a hunted fugitive which for many weeks took Adenauer from place to place, throughout the length and breadth of the country. He never stopped anywhere for more than twenty-four hours, and no one knew where he was.

Josef Giesen, his loyal friend and colleague, was one of the few men with whom Adenauer remained in touch during these weeks of restless wanderings. It was Giesen who eventually advised him to retire to some quiet and inconspicuous spot, some out-of-the-way small village where he could go underground with his family and shake off the tribulations of his persecutors. He agreed that this was sound advice and asked Giesen to look for suitable quarters for his family and himself somewhere, if possible, in the wooded hills of the Siebengebirge, not far from his native Cologne.

Giesen found an empty house in the village of Rhöndorf, in the little-known Löwenburg valley, which seemed suitable. It was not a beautiful house. It was old, neglected, and damp. But to someone in Adenauer's circumstances it offered many advantages. The rent was low, the location lonely and isolated, and, although the rooms were small, there were a great many of them—a distinct help in installing so numerous a family.

"In 1935 the Adenauers moved into this house," Giesen recalls. "I had hoped that now at last they would be left alone. But I had underrated the hostility of the Hitler regime against Adenauer. Today one is inclined to laugh about the ridiculous excuses which were used to get a man into trouble, but in those days there was nothing laughable about them. The traps and pinpricks designed to trip him up continued even at Rhöndorf, and they were very serious and very dangerous for Adenauer. At one time the local Gestapo post designed a regular plot to get rid of Adenauer. They suggested to some 'reliable' toughs in the village that they should drag Adenauer from his house at night and do to him what was known as 'People's Justice.' The plan miscarried because no one could be found at Rhöndorf willing to lend his hand to it."

When this "spontaneous action" failed to materialize, intervention came "from above." Suddenly an official order was issued expelling Adenauer for an indefinite period from the *Regierungsbezirk*, or administrative county area of Cologne. Rhöndorf was situated within this area, and within twenty-four hours Adenauer had to leave his house and his family. In vain he protested against the unwarranted harshness of the order. From Freudenstadt, in the Black Forest, where he had gone with his wife, he addressed a long and detailed application to the Provincial Governor, asking for the order to be rescinded. His appeal was refused, the expulsion order confirmed.

This time Adenauer found ways and means of mitigating the rigors of his banishment and maintaining contact with his family. He established himself at the village of Unkel, immediately on the border of Cologne county and less than four miles from Rhöndorf. Here he found a refuge in the Pax Home, a leave and convalescent home for Roman Catholic priests. But the large house which stood empty during the autumn and winter months was a comfortless and cheerless abode for the lonely man.

"Many years later," Josef Giesen tells, "Adenauer once told me how on the Day of Prayer and Repentance, in November, 1935, he very nearly felt his spirit broken by an overwhelming sense of frustration. There seemed to be neither meaning nor purpose left in his life. He was sixty years old, without office, without work, without a task to perform, and his future seemed hopelessly dark. He felt, he said, like a tree torn up by the roots and drifting aimlessly down the river of life. In those hours, he confessed, he all but despaired of the wisdom and mercy of God. Only his unshakable faith gave him certainty that somehow these sufferings, too, must be part of the trials of life.

At the beginning of December, 1935, his ten-year-old daughter Lotte fell seriously ill with an inflammation of the throat glands. Once more Adenauer appealed to the authorities at Cologne to permit him to return to his family. Permission was granted but only for the three Christmas holidays. Thereafter he had to return to

Unkel. He continued to bear these iniquities, not cheerfully, but with seemingly inexhaustible patience, and once again his patience was rewarded. Unexpectedly, in 1936, the expulsion order was rescinded, and he was allowed to return to his family at Rhöndorf. At about the same time, and equally unexpectedly, his straitened finances took a more hopeful turn.

In Cologne, his original successor in office, rabid Günther Riesen, had made way for a new Chief Mayor with a somewhat more pronounced sense of justice. In the course of a private conversation with Adenauer's brother, lawyer Dr. August Adenauer, this man remarked casually and in confidence, "I know your brother has been treated unjustly. But, of course, officially I could never admit this." This casual remark caused Adenauer to raise once more, and very cautiously, the question of compensation or a pension. He got in touch with the new Chief Mayor, and in the spring of 1936 a compromise settlement was reached. Adenauer was to receive part of his pension—approximately 1,000 marks a month (or the equivalent of $245)—and he was awarded payment in compensation for his two houses in Cologne which had been expropriated. This compensation, however, was far below the real value of the two properties, and when at first he refused to agree to such a settlement he was clearly given to understand that, unless he signed the agreement, the Gestapo would soon be after him again.

With the money he received from the enforced sales of his two Cologne houses, Adenauer purchased a plot of land and building site at Rhöndorf—No. 8a, in Zennigsweg, his private address to this day. It is magnificently situated, a fairly steep hill slope giving a wide and unrestricted view across the Rhine Valley as far as the distant chain of the Eifel mountains. There is a local legend according to which this is the spot which Byron praised in "Childe Harold" in such glowing terms:

> The river nobly foams and flows,
> The charm of this enchanted ground,
> And all its thousand turns disclose
> Some fresher beauty varying round:
> The haughtiest breast its wish might bound
> Through life to dwell delighted here;
> Nor could on earth a spot be found
> To nature and to me so dear. . . .

Whether or not this was, in fact, the place Byron had in mind, this was where Adenauer built his new home. Considering the uncertainty of his circumstances at this time, this building enterprise was a rather bold move, and the large house with its wide terrace and its many rooms something of a luxury. But, after many doubts and misgivings, Adenauer decided to face the heavy expenditure and not to stint himself. One thought was uppermost in his mind: after all these years of homeless wanderings and insecurity, he was determined to create at last a truly beautiful and comfortable home for his family.

Building this house and laying out its garden now became his passion and sole preoccupation. He visited the building site every day, supervising the work, suggesting alterations and modifications, giving practical advice to the building workers which at first was not altogether welcome, but was freely accepted later on when it was recognized how well thought out his hints were. Even more intensively he devoted himself to the garden. This was a difficult and complex job in which Giesen, Adenauer's faithful gardener friend, helped with experienced advice. As the steeply sloping ground of the mountain shoulder did not permit the laying out of the usual flower beds, a plan was designed which followed the pattern of the terraced vineyards on the sloping banks of the Rhine, each terrace being supported by a low wall built of locally found field stones. Most of these stones Adenauer, then a man past sixty, carted up the steep hill himself, and most of the low terrace walls he built with his own hands. From early spring until late into the autumn he spent practically his whole time working in his garden, setting out the rows of "pedigree" roses which even today are his joy and pride, and in later years, when food began to grow short, planting his terraces with vegetables.

Beside his passion for gardening, his former hobby of "inventing things," for which there had been little or no time during his years in office, now took on a new lease of life. In this, too, he was as punctilious and systematic as in everything he undertook. He arranged his day according to a carefully worked-out schedule, certain hours being reserved for gardening, for reading, for helping the children with their homework, and others again strictly set aside for "inventing" and not to be interfered with. A visitor who called, unannounced, at the house in Zennigsweg in 1937, believing he would find an elderly retired official with ample time on his hands, was most astonished when the maid refused to admit him. "I'm sorry, between five and six the Chief Mayor works on his inventions and must not be disturbed."

For his family and his friends, Adenauer's inventions were an unceasing source of amusement. There was the luminous darning egg, the electric insect killer (a device to protect trees against the larvae of destructive bugs), and, above all, Adenauer's "Dazzle Protection Spectacles," a pair of special glasses designed to shield motorists and pedestrians against the dazzle of unlowered headlights of oncoming cars. None of these achieved much recognition—except the luminous darning egg, which, unbeknown to Adenauer, had been invented a few weeks earlier by somebody else and had been duly patented—and Adenauer bore the mocking banter of his family and friends with unvarying, serene imperturbability.

"Indeed," his friend Josef Giesen recalls, "his visitors at Rhöndorf always marveled at his calm, his composure, his placid temper. It seemed to them that he had finally resigned himself to the prospect of spending the rest of his days in the quiet seclusion of his house and garden. But they deceived themselves. Deep inside him things looked very differently. I noticed this to my great astonishment one day, in the last year of the war, when we drove together to Cologne.

"I was driving, and he sat beside me. I observed him closely as the car bumped along the bomb-scarred streets. Adenauer had not been to Cologne for many weeks, and the sight of the destroyed city moved him deeply. He sat beside me, pale, silent, lips pressed together. Suddenly he put his hand on my arm and murmured, in an almost toneless voice, 'Please, turn back, I can bear no more of this.' But, a little later when we had left the city behind us and were driving along the open road, he turned to me and said emphatically, 'Giesen, we've got to start thinking right away how we shall rebuild all this after the war.' "

The three years which followed until the outbreak of war Adenauer spent living quietly with his family at Rhöndorf. They were uneventful and undisturbed years. The children were growing up. The eldest daughter Ria was married to Walter Reiners, an engineer; the second son Max completed his law studies and like his brother

Konrad obtained a position in industry; and the four "little ones" developed well and promisingly, chiefly Paul, who did exceptionally well at school.

There was little contact with the outside world, few visitors, and little visiting. Occasionally the Adenauers would see some of their old and trusted friends in Cologne, banker Pferdmenges and his family, or Professor Benedikt Schmittmann, whose wife, Ella Wahlen, was a cousin of Adenauer's first wife.

Benedikt Schmittmann, professor of social sciences at Cologne University since 1919, was an unusual and remarkable man, a noble and fearless character and a gifted teacher whose views, inspired by Christian idealism and a somewhat Utopian belief in the future of human society, exercised considerable influence on Adenauer's thinking. The two men did not always agree in their long discussions of political, social, and moral issues, and often Schmittmann's enthusiasm came up against Adenauer's skepticism and reserve. "You have much too high an opinion of the human race, Benedikt," Adenauer would tell him. But he considered him "one of the finest men I've ever known," and Schmittmann's maxim, "Work as though you were to live forever. Pray as though you had to die today," was very much Adenauer's too.

The fateful year of 1933 had dealt the two men identical blows; they were summarily dismissed from their posts. Having lost his chair at the university, Professor Schmittmann and his wife retired to their country house near Düsseldorf.

One day, in the summer of 1939, Frau Schmittmann recalls, the Adenauers invited the Schmittmanns to their house at Rhöndorf, and after coffee Adenauer asked them to his study. "How soon do you plan to go on your vacation?" he asked them. Schmittmann answered that he had planned to go away toward the middle or end of August. "I would advise you," Adenauer said, "to leave earlier, and to go abroad. Your best plan would be not to return at all." He went on to explain that he was certain war would break out very soon. "The moment war breaks out," he said, "Hitler will arrest all political suspects and send them to concentration camps, you, Benedikt, and me too."

"I've known for a long time," Schmittmann replied calmly, "that in the event of war they're planning to carry out mass arrests, and I know also that you and I are on the Gestapo proscription list. But what is the use of fleeing the country? What could I, a man of sixty-seven, hope to do out there? No, we shall stay in Germany."

Adenauer explained that he himself had no thought of emigrating, either. That was not the issue. "The point is," he said emphatically, "that one mustn't be 'available' at the crucial moment. That is what matters. After a period of waiting for things to settle down, one would probably be able to return without much risk."

"I shared Adenauer's view," Frau Schmittmann recalls. "We discussed the pros and cons for a long time that night, but reached no decision."

In August Frau Schmittmann succeeeded in persuading her husband to take a vacation trip to Austria. When they reached the Italian frontier, she made a last attempt to induce him to cross over into safety. Schmittmann refused. "I'd rather die of politics in Germany than of homesickness abroad," he said. They returned to Cologne, and here Schmittmann met his fate. On September 1, the day war broke out, he was arrested, and a fortnight later, on September 13, his wife was officially notified by the Oranienburg concentration camp authorities that he had died suddenly of a heart attack during parade. Later statements by fellow prisoners proved this to be untrue. During a "penalty exercise," an SS detachment leader had crushed Schmittmann's chest with the heel of his jackboot.

Adenauer followed his own advice. Shortly before the outbreak of war he took his wife on a trip to Switzerland and did not return for several weeks. His calculation had proved correct. The initial wave of arrests had rushed past, and no one seemed to be interested any longer in the fate of the retired Chief Mayor of Cologne. Adenauer learned later that at the last moment his name had been crossed off the Gestapo list. He was never able to find out who was responsible for this. When Frau Schmittmann telephoned him after his return to tell him of her husband's death, he received the news in deep silence. There were no words left, it seemed, to say what he felt.

The first years of the war, apart from many difficulties, also brought some peaceful and pleasant changes to the house in Zennigsweg. The family continued to grow. Both of Adenauer's elder sons were married, Max to Dr. Gisela Klein, and Konrad to Lola Hunold, a young lady from neighboring Aachen, and both were warmly and cordially welcomed into the family by their parents-in-law. New friends were made, too, forming a close little community which meant rather more to the Adenauers than just ordinary social intercourse. Among them was a next-door neighbor, Frau Schlüter-Hermkes, widow of a high-ranking civil servant and herself a writer much interested in social, religious, and political questions. She and Adenauer had much in common, and their joint thinking and debating in the small literary and musical circle which met once a fortnight for lectures and discussions was to produce very practical results in later years.

One after another the three eldest sons were called up into the army, first Max, then Paul, and finally Konrad. Their father helped them by looking after the families they left behind. First he took Lola, Konrad's wife, into his house; she was working in Berlin as a secretary and expecting her first child. Next he took in Gisela, and toward the end of the war his daughter Ria and her two children joined the rest of the family.

"The house in Zennigsweg was not really equipped to receive such an invasion," Lola Adenauer tells, thinking back to those days, "but there couldn't have been anything more natural than the way in which my parents-in-law received us. There was no sacrifice they would not make, no discomfort they would not gladly put up with. Everyone just moved a little closer together, and soon every room in the house, except my father-in-law's study, was filled to capacity."

Not counting his youngest son, twelve-year-old Schorsch, Adenauer, now approaching sixty-eight, found himself the only man in the house among eight women. All agree that he exercised a benevolent and mild rule, but his authority remained undisputed and, on occasion, extended as far as the kitchen. Whenever some small tension arose between the women, a word from "Father Konrad" sufficed to calm the waves.

There is no doubt that Adenauer, in those days, strictly refused to have anything to do with politics, and deliberately and studiously refrained from trying to interfere with the course of events in Germany. Sometime in 1943, he was, in fact, approached by an intermediary on behalf of Carl Gördeler, who was anxious to get in touch with Adenauer and sought an interview with him, and this intermediary gave Adenauer some cautiously veiled hints indicating the existence of a widespread conspiracy against the Hitler regime. Adenauer flatly declined to have anything to do with it and told the emissary emphatically that he would in no circumstances be a party to such a move. His reasons were very simple: he had no faith in the success of an undertaking led by Gördeler.

The events of July 20, 1944, justified his doubts. On this critical day the entire family sat around the radio set until far into the night, following with mounting anxiety the dramatic course of events.

Bad news arrived the next day. Returning from a visit to friends in the neighborhood, Frau Adenauer reported in great agitation, "Giesen was arrested this morning by the Gestapo!" The reason for it was a letter Giesen had written to his son who was serving as a soldier at the front. In it he had described, among other things, a British bombing attack which had succeeded in destroying an armaments works near the village of Urfield where he lived. "This time the English have tailored the job to measure," he had written to his son, expressing the hope that this horrible war would soon be over. The letter had been opened by the censor. Giesen's offense was "undermining the armed forces' strength to resist." The Gestapo had arrived early in the morning, searched the house for several hours, confiscated all food stores, and subjected Giesen to lengthy interrogation. In the course of this day they had again and again inquired after his contacts with Adenauer. Giesen had said nothing to compromise Adenauer, but all the same, before being taken away, he had whispered to his wife, "Warn the Adenauers!"

"We were all terrified beyond words by this news," Lola Adenauer tells. "The first thing we did was to hide all our food and provisions, which came mostly from Giesen's farm. Apart from this, we did everything we could think of to prepare the house against the dreaded visit, burning letters and papers and hiding undesirable books. My father-in-law did not take part in this, but did not interfere, probably because he felt this frantic activity would divert women and children from the dreadful tension of waiting.

"They did not come until three days later. We were at lunch when a car drove up down below. Then we saw six men come up the steps toward the house. The leader of the group was a man who had only one arm. Without anyone having said a word we all knew at once: the Gestapo were here! They didn't ring the front doorbell, but walked around the house to the terrace where we were all sitting. 'We have orders to search your house, Herr Adenauer,' the one-armed leader said, showing my father-in-law a paper bearing some official rubber stamps.

"My father-in-law gave the paper a quick glance and nodded silently. 'Besides, we require some information from you,' the one-armed man continued. Looking at the women and children sitting terrified around the table, he said, 'I think it would be better to have this conversation privately.' Again my father-in-law nodded. He rose. The one-armed man and another official in a dark leather coat took him between them, and they disappeared into the house. We heard them walk up the stairs to the second floor, and little Schorsch said, 'Now they're going into Father's study.'

"During this entire scene my mother-in-law had not spoken a single word. She sat petrified. Now she suddenly roused herself, and, with a calmness the rest of us could only admire, said to the four remaining men who were standing about irresolutely, 'Gentlemen, carry out your search. We have nothing to hide.' The search of the house lasted a full five hours. They went through every single room, from the attic down to the cellar, opening every cupboard, wardrobe, chest or box, investigating even the radio set to see if the dial was not by chance set on a foreign station. At seven o'clock in the evening interrogation and search were broken off. The two officials emerged from the study, carrying a pile of books and papers, and the room was sealed. I can still see my father-in-law watching them with mingled pride and contempt as they fixed their lead seals to the door.

"After they had gone," Lola Adenauer's account concludes, "he told us about his interrogation. They had inquired after Giesen and many other friends and acquaintances of former days. Strangely enough, the revolt of July 20 had not been mentioned by a single word. Following this they had got to work on his files, papers, letters and books. Although the library had previously been carefully cleared of anything remotely suspicious, they had nevertheless found a number of books to confiscate, among them the works of the great Norwegian novelist Sigrid Undset.

"Before they left, the one-armed leader had declared threateningly, 'We shall be back tomorrow,' and in fact they did come back the following day, going once more through the whole house, from early morning till midday. Then they disappeared without a further word, and we never heard of them again."

* * *

Ever since the events of 1933 Adenauer suffers from insomnia. As a rule he rises early while the rest of the house is still fast asleep, drinks a cup of strong coffee, and then sits all by himself on the terrace of his house, or on a wooden bench he has had installed at the highest point of the garden, looking out over the misty Rhine Valley towards the Eifel mountains and watching their summits glow in the light of the rising sun.

One morning, in August, 1944, he was roused by a loud, impatient ringing of the bell. He rose, walked through the sleeping house, and opened the front door. Facing him in the doorway stood two men, the local Rhöndorf policeman and another man in plain clothes easily recognizable, even without his tin badge, as a police detective. The policeman spoke first. He had known Adenauer for a long time, and was visibly embarrassed.

"I'm very sorry, *Herr Oberbürgermeister*," he stammered, "but I'm afraid we shall have to take you with us . . . it's orders from above . . . nothing against you personally . . . a general measure, it seems . . . there's six of them we have to collect in Rhöndorf and Honnef. . . ."

"Most comforting," answered Adenauer.

The loud ringing of the bell had awakened the house. Even while the policeman spoke, the women appeared.

"Arrested again?" Frau Adenauer inquired anxiously.

"Only a protective measure," the policeman answered reassuringly. "You'll have your husband back with you before long, I'm sure."

The detective, however, gave him a sternly discouraging look, and the policeman said no more. "Get ready quickly," the detective turned to Adenauer gruffly: "we haven't got much time!"

While his daughter-in-law Lola helped Adenauer pack a small suitcase with his toilet things and other necessaries, Frau Adenauer lured the village policeman into the drawing room, where she tried, cautiously, to draw him out. The good-natured man, feeling sorry for the terrified woman, told her what he knew. It wasn't much, but it sounded menacing enough: a comprehensive police swoop throughout the whole Reich had been scheduled for this day, August 23, 1944. The code word was "Operation Thunderstorm." All remaining prominent politicians of the Weimar Republic who were still at liberty were to be arrested at one fell swoop.

"But why?" Frau Adenauer asked.

"Perhaps," the policeman suggested, not quite sure of himself, "those up above are afraid these gentlemen might do something if the war goes wrong. . . ."

"And where are they going to take my husband?"

"I'm afraid I couldn't tell you. Our orders are to hand in all those arrested in Rhöndorf and Honnef at the Security Service in Bonn. But I don't think they'll stay there. . . ."

The detective returned with Adenauer from the bedroom, and the frightened village policeman said no more.

More than once the Adenauers had taken leave of each other in similar circumstances, but never had the separation been so painful. The grandchildren crowded around their grandfather, crying and screaming, and none of the women was able to hold back her tears. They implored him to let them at least accompany him as far as the streetcar stop, but Adenauer refused sternly. He took leave of them in his own house.

The two officials took Adenauer to Bonn, where they handed him over to the State Security Service of the Gestapo at their headquarters in Kreuzbergweg. Here quarters were filled to capacity. Those arrested in Bonn had been brought in several hours earlier, and there were more new arrivals all the time. The victims of "Operation Thunderstorm" were mostly elderly gentlemen whom the police had literally fetched from their beds. They had just as little idea of the reason for their arrest as Adenauer, and consequently the place was full of the wildest rumors.

At Rhöndorf the women were left behind in a mood of helpless despair. At length Frau Adenauer could no longer bear the waiting and the suspense. After lunch she and her daughter-in-law Lola went down to Bonn, to the Security Services headquarters. By that time Adenauer was no longer there, and their desperate inquiries after his whereabouts were answered by the officials with a silent shrug.

They ran through the streets, asking shopkeepers, passers-by, anyone they met, whether they had seen or heard anything. A bookseller was able to tell them that he had seen a column of men marching to the Rhine Railway, and he had recognized Mayor Adenauer as one in the column. They hurried to the railway station. The stationmaster confirmed the bookseller's story. He thought most probably the prisoners had been taken to Cologne, where the Trade Fair grounds with their large halls were being used as a detention camp.

The two women took the train to Cologne and went out to the Trade Fair ground. It was late when they arrived. Standing at the barbed wire enclosure, they gazed across to the wide empty lawn. "I shall stand here until I have seen my husband," Frau Adenauer said. She remained standing there until darkness fell and the guard chased her away.

## CHAPTER VIII

IN HIS youth Eugen Zander had been a Communist, and his early idealistic extremism had earned him long spells of imprisonment. When he first met Adenauer, in August, 1944, in the Trade Fair concentration camp, he had already served nine years of hard labor in Siegburg prison and was one of the "old-timers" of the Cologne camp. Somehow, through luck and fortitude, Zander survived all these vicissitudes. Today he is an inspector of parks and gardens employed by the Cologne municipality, a mellowed, middle-aged man comfortably established in his little suburban house, and his youthful radicalism is very much a thing of the past. But the days when Konrad Adenauer was his fellow prisoner are still fresh and vivid in his memory.

"I was then what used to be called a 'Kapo'," he tells, "meaning a cadre policeman, one of the privileged convicts who were entrusted with certain administrative responsibilities in the camp. Each Kapo had his specific duties of supervising the rest of the prisoners, in the kitchen, in the clothing depot, and during the work outside the camp area. It was my duty to receive all new arrivals, fit them out, and detail them to their barracks and bunks. One day a large new batch arrived, and there were many prominent and well-known faces among them. I recognized Thomas Esser, a former Vice-President of the Reichstag, Undersecretary of State Schmidt, Reichstag Deputies Theodor Babilon and Hermann Gerig, and of course, Konrad Adenauer, the former Chief Mayor of my home town, Cologne.

"I took my new charges to the clothing depot, where they had to hand over their money, watches, pocket knives, collars, ties, and suspenders, and received a filthy blanket in return. As they were lining up in front of the depot, one of the old-timers walked up to Adenauer. 'How do you do, *Herr Oberbürgermeister*,' he said. 'I'm sorry I have to greet you in this way, but we're both no longer considered worthy of saying "Heil Hitler,"' Adenauer replied in a friendly tone, 'How do you do,' and I liked the way in which he simply ignored the other man's cheap irony. 'May I offer you a welcoming drink?' the old-timer went on, handing him a tin mug which was disgustingly dirty, with blobs of toothpaste sticking to it. Adenauer took it and had a drink of water from it without turning a hair. I liked that, too, and decided to take the Chief Mayor under my protection."

Quarters were narrow and gloomy. The prisoners' bunks were in three tiers, the air was stale and stifling, and the place was infested with millions of bugs. When Zander met Adenauer again a few days later, he seemed in very bad shape, looking pale and worn, with reddened eyelids, and complaining about lack of sleep and the plaguing vermin. Feeling sorry for him, Zander decided, on a sudden impulse, to quarter him in the clothing depot, which until then he had inhabited alone. Permission for this preferential treatment was not easy to obtain, but Zander persisted and finally wangled it.

"So Adenauer became my roommate," Zander tells, "and he remained with me for the rest of the time he spent in the camp. In the beginning he seemed very quiet and depressed. He had not been detailed for work outside, and after the roll call at six o'clock, when the 'politicals,' Social Democrats and Communists, had been marched off to work, he would return to our room and just sit there quietly, for hours. I made him lie down and spend the morning resting on his mattress, and tried to make life generally a little easier for him as far as I could. When the weather was fine the prisoners who didn't have to work spent most of the day in the open air, sitting in the sun in front of their barracks, delousing themselves, talking to each other, or else going for 'walks,' that is, pacing up and down restlessly along the barbed-wire enclosure like caged animals. Sometimes relatives would appear on the other side of the fence, and they would try, behind the backs of the guards, to communicate with them in sign language.

"One day Adenauer returned from such a 'walk' in a particularly dejected mood. He paced the room restlessly, then sat down on his mattress, brooding silently. Eventually I asked him, 'What's the matter with you, *Herr Oberbürgermeister*?' Everyone in the camp, even the guards, used to call him by his former title, as a matter of course. He told me he had seen his wife and daughter. They had been standing at the barbed wire fence, crying. When they had waved to him, the guard had come up and chased them away. They had not been able to exchange a single word. I looked at Adenauer as he sat there in front of me, on the edge of his bunk. He was as thin as a skeleton, his clothes were flapping loosely about him, and with his collarless shirt and his soup spoon stuck in his breast pocket, he must have been a heartbreaking sight for his wife."

The sad encounter, however, had a most welcome result. Frau Adenauer obviously had wished to make sure where her husband was. As soon as she had seen him with her own eyes, parcels arrived for him almost daily, at first only from his family, and later from friends and acquaintances and all sorts of people who had heard of his fate and whereabouts—food, cigarettes, tobacco, occasionally even a little genuine coffee. He shared everything with Zander; between roommates that was understood practice. But the way he allowed anyone who came to the room to partake of what he had went far beyond the customary comradeship of the camp. His liberal attitude became well known, and visitors to the clothing depot became frequent.

Gradually his mood became less gloomy. There was no scarcity of intelligent and highly educated men among the prisoners; there were doctors, lawyers, politicians, civil servants, and university teachers, and after a while a small debating circle formed in the clothing depot around Adenauer, discussing for hours problems of religion and politics, art and science.

"I can still remember some of those conversations," Zander tells. "Especially one occasion when Adenauer explained his views on what the political situation would be after the war. The unnatural alliance between America and Russia, he said, would break up again. The world would be divided up into two giant power blocks, one communist, the other democratic, and vanquished Germany would have to choose once and for all for either East or West, unless she wished to be ground to dust between the millstones of the world powers.

Outwardly and superficially, then, life seemed not too bad once he had settled down and accustomed himself to it. But everyone in the camp knew, and so did Adenauer, that below the tranquil surface horrible and terrifying things went on all the time. Almost daily batches of prisoners were taken out and deported to the various extermination camps from where no man could hope to return, and at night special squads would suddenly burst into the barracks, tear this man or that from his sleep, and drag him away. Next morning he had disappeared and was never heard of again. His papers were endorsed, "shot while attempting to escape," and filed away.

"None could know whether he wasn't going to be the next victim," Zander says. "As it happened, in my position as Kapo I had free access to the camp administrative office, and one morning, glancing quickly through the files in an unobserved moment, I came across Adenauer's name. I was terrified. Adenauer was listed among those scheduled to be taken out the coming night. None of us had expected that it would come to that. I hurried back to our room. Adenauer was resting on his mattress. I told him, 'I've just been to the office. Tomorrow another batch is going to Buchenwald. Your name is on the list, *Herr Oberbürgermeister*!' I just couldn't bring myself to tell him the full and horrible truth. Buchenwald, I felt, was bad enough. He raised himself, and although he said nothing I could sense his alarm. 'You've got to get out of here, *Herr Oberbürgermeister*!' I said. 'The best plan would be for you to report sick.' He thought for a moment. Then he said, 'Get Dr. Richarz.'"

Like all interned doctors, Dr. Richarz, to whom Adenauer had often talked, enjoyed a special position, because as a rule the official camp physician left all preliminary treatment of prisoners to their medically qualified fellow inmates. Zander immediately went to find Richarz. Having been told of the imminent danger in which Adenauer was, he did not hesitate to help. He came at once. On their way to the clothing depot they passed the camp dispensary, where Dr. Richarz picked up a small bottle of Sympathol, a commonly used restorative. Outside, he poured half its contents into the sand and, handing Zander the half-filled bottle, said:

"Now just understand this, Eugen. I've been treating the Chief Mayor for some time for his heart condition. According to my prescription, you've been giving him thirty drops of Sympathol daily. Is that quite clear?"

It was. Eugen Zander nodded.

When they reached the clothing chamber, Adenauer was no longer alone. Another prisoner had come in to get some blankets. Zander knew him only too well. He was working as an informer for the camp commandant and reported everything he heard and saw to his superiors. Zander was terrified lest Adenauer and Richarz should venture to speak openly to one another in the presence of this man.

"But I had underrated the two," he recalls. "They were much too smart for this fellow. Adenauer sat up in his bed and in a weak voice said, 'I'm ill, Dr. Richarz. I feel sick unto death.' Richarz bent over him, and, examining him carefully, murmured so audibly that everyone in the room could clearly hear, 'Grave . . . very, very serious indeed. . . .' As soon as the informer had left, they dropped the comedy. Richarz turned to me. 'Go at once to the Camp Commandant and report that Dr. Adenauer had a serious heart attack this morning. Tell him he collapsed as he got up. Tell him I ordered his immediate transfer to the hospital. Meantime, I shall inform the camp doctor.'

"I doubted very much that Dr. Richarz would get away with it. After all, Adenauer was scheduled to be shot and it seemed highly unlikely, therefore, that the Camp Commandant would intervene to save his life. But Dr. Richarz knew his 'customers' better than I did. The Camp Commandant, for some reason, was terrified when he heard that Adenauer was seriously ill. He telephoned the camp doctor at once, and, having spoken to him, sent for an ambulance and ordered Adenauer's immediate transfer to the hospital. The camp doctor apparently had been very willing to authorize the move. A medical colleague of his at Honnef (the neighboring village to Rhöndorf) who knew Adenauer well had previously been in touch with him, in an effort to ease Adenauer's situation, and it seemed that he was glad to have this opportunity, or excuse, to oblige.

"At all events, the ambulance arrived within the hour. I accompanied Adenauer to it. As he got in, he shook me by the hand and said, 'I shan't forget this, Eugen, not ever.' Frankly, I didn't believe he meant it seriously. I thought to myself, if we two manage to see this through and survive the Third Reich, you will return to your world and I will go back to mine, and there's a gulf between these two worlds which nothing will ever bridge.

"But," concludes Eugen Zander, "my opinion of the Chief Mayor was wrong. Some time after Adenauer's departure I, too, was deported to Buchenwald concentration camp. We were liberated by the Americans in the spring of 1945, and one morning a large bus drove up to the main entrance to the camp. It had been sent by the Cologne city council to get all prisoners whose homes were in Cologne. The driver of the coach came up to me and said, 'I have a message for you. Kindest regards from Chief Mayor Dr. Adenauer.'"

A spell in the hospital is a blessing for any prisoner, after the filth and brutality of the concentration camp. For Adenauer his transfer to Hohenlind hospital had particular advantages. Professor Paul Uhlenbruck, the head physician, was an old and close acquaintance of his, and he saw to it that Adenauer was treated almost like a patient in a private ward. He was allowed visits from his family at all hours, and, since Frau Adenauer and the children made full use of this permission, he was seldom alone.

But even so he remained depressed and racked with anxiety, and lived in perpetual dread of things to come. What was going to happen to him once he was pronounced fit again—as eventually he would be—and had to return to the camp in the Trade Fair grounds? The advancing American armies had reached the German frontier at Aachen, and it was more than possible that the retreating National Socialists, faced with the Allied advance into Germany proper, would rid themselves of all their more prominent opponents. At Aachen something like this had already happened. Why should things take a different course at Cologne?

Yet it would have been easy for him to escape. The nursing staff knew him well, they were aware that he was a personal friend of the head physician, and most probably he could have left the hospital under some plausible excuse and disappeared. But this would have endangered Professor Uhlenbruck, who bore responsibility for the prisoner, and getting him into trouble seemed to Adenauer too high a price to pay for his own freedom.

For a long time he kept his worry to himself, but one day revealed himself to his wife. Frau Adenauer was aghast. She had not visualized her husband to be in so perilous a position, and immediately urged him to escape and await the arrival of the Allied armies in some well-concealed hideout. From this grew a plan, so astonishingly naive and simple that no one would credit Adenauer with having thought it out.

One afternoon a car drew up in front of Hohenlind hospital. From it emerged a major of the *Luftwaffe*, wearing dark goggles, who walked straight up to the reception desk and in a peremptory voice demanded that the prisoner Adenauer be handed over to him immediately. His authority was an official-looking document stating that former Chief Mayor Adenauer was required at once in Berlin

Adenauer's first wife, née Emma Weyer, with their son Konrad, Jr.

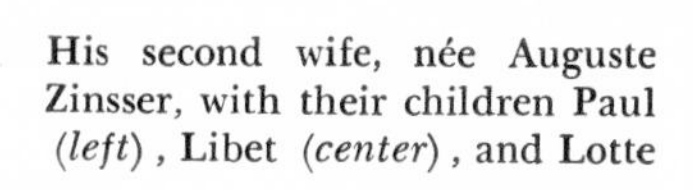

His second wife, née Auguste Zinsser, with their children Paul (*left*), Libet (*center*), and Lotte

*Rheinisches Museum*

The Rathaus, Cologne, where Konrad Adenauer had his offices as Chief Mayor from 1917 to 1933

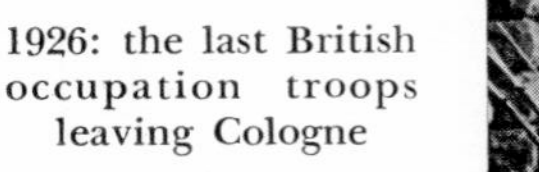

1926: the last British occupation troops leaving Cologne

*Wündshammer*

An official visit to Cologne in 1926. President von Hindenburg (*left*) and Chief Mayor Adenauer before the Rathaus

*Rheinisches Museum*

for interrogation. No one felt the slightest suspicion. Adenauer was brought down. Because of an alleged inflammation of the eyes he, too, had been wearing dark glasses for some time. The officer took him to the waiting car and drove off.

Huddled in the corner of the car and waiting for him sat Frau Adenauer. There wasn't time for more than the briefest of welcomes. The car leaped forward with one bound and at breakneck speed tore through the quiet suburban streets toward the open country. It did not stop until the city was left well behind at a safe distance. Now Adenauer was able to thank his liberator. He was Major Hans Schliebusch, whom Adenauer had known in earlier days. Frau Adenauer had gone to see him and asked for his help in organizing the escape. Schliebusch was delighted to cooperate. "If it's a question of cocking a snook at the Nazis," he had said, "You can count on me."

The first part of the plan had succeeded. Now the three conspirators had to decide what to do next. It was a lovely, sunny day in September. From the west came the steady thundering of the battle front. "The drums of freedom," Schliebusch said. The approaching liberation was to be the basis for their further plans. They would call on an acquaintance at Bonn in whose house Adenauer should remain concealed for a few days until a suitable hideout had been found where he could safely "sit out" what could only be a brief interval until the arrival of the Allied armies. For this hideout Frau Adenauer suggested a place called Nister Mühle, a quaint old mill in an isolated and secluded part of the wooded hills of the Westerwald, to the southeast of Cologne, which her daughter Lotte had discovered.

Next they jointly drafted a letter to Gestapo headquarters in Cologne in which Adenauer informed them that for "reasons of health" he had gone to stay at the Nister Mühle, where he was at their disposal any time, if required. This letter was to be left behind with their friend in Bonn, who should appear to have forgotten to mail it. In this way Adenauer hoped to avoid punishment for his escape, and to protect his family from reprisals. In case he should be caught again, the letter could be produced as proof that his abscondence from the hospital was not meant as flight or escape.

In the light of this sunny autumn afternoon this seemed a brilliantly contrived way out, and in a lighthearted mood the three conspirators jokingly anticipated the baffled face Gestapo commissar

Bethge was bound to make if this letter were suddenly to turn up, and Schliebusch thought optimistically, it'll never come to that; the Americans will be here long before the Gestapo.

It was evening when they reached Bonn. Darkness fell, and the optimistic mood of the afternoon suddenly seemed all too lighthearted. Frau Adenauer was suddenly filled with gloomy forebodings. Her doubts were justified. They reached their friend's house at Bonn, and he opened the door himself. Seeing three figures with dark spectacles in the dim light of the landing, he was taken aback. It was Schliebusch who now took the initiative. Pushing the two Adenauers inside, he closed the door behind him and asked quickly:

"Can you have Dr. Adenauer and his wife stay with you for a few days?"

Without answering the question, the man turned directly to Adenauer. "I thought you were under arrest?"

"I've granted myself a spell of leave of absence," Adenauer answered, trying to lend the embarrassing situation a jocular turn.

But their friend failed to see the humor of it.

"And you come to me?" he said. "Haven't you thought of the danger to which you're exposing me?"

No, frankly, they had not thought of that. The spontaneous way in which Schliebusch had come to their assistance had led them to assume, mistakenly, that anyone would feel it his natural duty to help a fugitive in such a situation.

"I'm sorry to have troubled you," Adenauer said. He turned away and was about to leave.

But now Schliebusch intervened again.

"Have you really got the heart to turn a man like Adenauer away in this situation?" he asked. "Couldn't you let him stay at least for one night? Where else could he go now? Rhöndorf is out of the question, and a hotel would be much too dangerous. . . ."

For a moment the man hesitated, and thought. Then he said, "All right, then, you can stay the night. But tomorrow you've got to leave. . . ."

Adenauer thanked him, and Schliebusch promised to pick up the fugitives first thing in the morning.

That night Adenauer and his wife had little sleep. Sitting up most of the night in the strange room, they considered what to do next. The plan with the letter to the Gestapo had obviously failed.

There was no hope of their host being willing to run such a risk, and a very considerable risk it was, as they had to admit to themselves.

"There is no other way," Adenauer said in the end. "Tomorrow morning we shall separate. This is what you'll do. You'll go back to Rhöndorf and keep quiet for a few days. Then you'll go to Cologne, and, as harmlessly and ingenuously as possible, ask for me at the hospital. They will tell you that I've been taken to Berlin for interrogation. After that, wait for a few more days . . . and then go to the police station in Rhöndorf and report me as missing."

Frau Adenauer did not like this plan. She hesitated to agree, and felt all sorts of scruples. But he insisted. "You've got to do it," he said emphatically. "Whatever happens, you've got to see that you're covered."

She pleaded with him to allow her to go with him. But he shook his head. "No," he said. "Believe me, it is better like this, for you and for the children."

He found it hard to convince her. In this mood they separated the following morning.

In the beginning everything seemed to be going according to plan. At the Nister Mühle Adenauer was well received. The miller and his wife, a good-natured and warmhearted old couple, knew perfectly well who the belated summer guest who called himself Dr. Weber was, but they kept their mouths shut, and if they felt any anxiety they managed to conceal it, even from Adenauer himself. "Let him enjoy his vacation," the old miller said, and that apparently was what Adenauer did. He went for long walks through the autumnal woods, venturing even as far as the neighboring little market town of Hachenburg, where he terrified his friends by walking quite unconcernedly, in his conspicuous light raincoat and wearing his blue sunglasses, among the crowds in the streets.

Probably this lack of concern was in itself the best and most effective form of camouflage, for nothing happened to him. On the contrary, he even succeeded in re-establishing postal contact with his family by way of Hachenburg. People he scarcely knew willingly allowed him to use their addresses as a cover for his mail, and at Rhöndorf, too, friends were found who were prepared to do the same at the other end.

Once again, everything seemed to be taking a turn for the better.

Even the five terrified women at Rhöndorf—Frau Adenauer, her two daughters, and the daughters-in-law, Gisela and Lola—began to hope confidently that the escape would work out as planned and without further hitches. It was true, the advance of the American armies was held up and their arrival delayed, but on the other hand there was comfort in the thought that the visible breakup of the Third Reich was bound to act as a brake on the terror measures of the Gestapo. The Allied air forces were giving the cities of Western Germany a terrific pounding, and it was reasonable to hope that in the resulting chaos the disappearance of a single prisoner would not be noticed.

But all this proved to be an illusion which was rudely shattered on the morning of September 24, 1944, when two strangers suddenly called at the house in Zennigsweg. They happened to find Frau Adenauer alone with her daughter Libet. The two daughters-in-law had gone to the village shopping, and Lotte, who had enlisted as a Red Cross nurse, was away working at a nearby army hospital. It was Libet who opened the door to the two strangers. They did not trouble to say who they were, but one of them, a fat man, simply asked, "Where is your mother?" and Libet Adenauer knew all there was to know. She went to find her mother in the kitchen, whispering, "Gestapo!"

"Where is your husband?" the fat man asked without introduction as soon as Frau Adenauer appeared.

"I don't know," she said. "I have myself reported him as missing——"

The fat man cut her short with a gesture of dismissal.

"Come along with us," he ordered.

"Where?" she asked, frightened.

"Interrogation."

Frau Adenauer mustered all the courage she had. She knew it would be fatal to show any weakness at this moment. It would only be interpreted as a sign of a bad conscience. "I'm ready," she said firmly.

The official smiled. "I would advise you to take some toilet things along. I don't think you'll get back home for a little while yet." While the other man, a youngish, pimply-faced fellow, accompanied her to the bedroom to supervise the hasty packing of a bag, Libet Adenauer approached the fat man. "Please leave my mother here," she begged. "Surely you can interrogate her here just as well. How can we get along, all alone, with the small children?"

For a moment the man seemed to consider the proposition. In a friendly voice he asked:

"Do you know where your father is?"

"No," she answered, looking him firmly in the face.

"There, you see!" he said gruffly, all benevolence gone again.

A few minutes later Libet Adenauer tearfully saw her mother, escorted by the two men, walk down the stone steps of the garden path and disappear below, beyond the gate.

At lunchtime a family council was held. It was a desperate and utterly helpless gathering of four young and forlorn women struggling vainly against their tears and torturing anxieties. Libet Adenauer was barely sixteen, her sister Lotte nineteen, and the two sisters-in-law were not much older than they. They were at a complete loss to know what to do. In the end it was Libet, the youngest, who proved the most energetic and circumspect.

"We must send a telegram to Max, first of all," she declared. "Max is an officer, and that always makes an impression on the Nazis. He's got to intervene with the authorities on Father's and Mother's behalf. And then I'll go and see Uncle Toni. He must help us to find out where Mother is."

This was done. "Uncle Toni" was Anton von Weiss, the Swiss Consul General at Cologne, an old friend of the Adenauer family who had removed himself temporarily to Rhöndorf to escape the ceaseless air bombardment of the city. He was aghast at the news Libet Adenauer brought him, and, without waiting for her to say anything further, telephoned the Rhöndorf police station. Within a few minutes he had extracted the information that Frau Adenauer had been taken to Cologne for interrogation at Gestapo Headquarters in Elisenstrasse.

"I'll go there myself tomorrow," he declared emphatically, "and move heaven and earth to get your mother out of that place!" Sixteen-year-old Libet Adenauer, however, was skeptical. She did not believe that representations from the Swiss Consul General, at this stage of the war, would make much impression on the Secret State Police. She meant to go there herself and see her mother. If she was unsuccessful, there was still time for Herr von Weiss to intervene. All she asked him to do for her was to drive her to Cologne in his car the next morning. Allied air attacks had completely disrupted the railway system, and there were no more trains.

The following day Consul General von Weiss took Libet Adenauer to Cologne. Adenauer's youngest daughter, who, since her marriage in 1950, is Frau Werham, wife of an enterprising industrialist in the neighboring city of Neuss, and mother of two children, has herself told of her memorable adventure on that day, September 25, 1944.

The following is her own account:

"Uncle Toni" took me to Elisenstrasse and let me out on the doorstep of the Gestapo headquarters building. As on the previous day, he offered to accompany me, but I felt it was better for me to go alone. I had discussed my plan carefully with Lotte, Gisela, and Lola, and we thought that, since not all Gestapo officials were necessarily subhuman, a girl of sixteen might with luck achieve more with an appeal to their human instincts than would a man with legal arguments.

An SS man in black uniform was guarding the entrance door. I went up to him and said, "I am Libet Adenauer from Rhöndorf. My mother was arrested yesterday and I understand she is here now. Would it be possible for me to speak to her?" The man gave me a superior and rather pitying look. Then he said good-naturedly, "Well, in that case you'd better see Commissar Bethge, second floor, room 116." And he let me pass.

Upstairs in Commissar Bethge's anteroom I was told to wait outside on the landing. It was a long and gloomy corridor with innumerable doors, and, after I had waited for two hours on a wooden bench, my hope and courage had very nearly gone. It was too late by then; I was not admitted and had to leave without having achieved anything. It was only several days later that I finally succeeded in penetrating into Commissar Bethge's inner office. He was a short, stocky man, with black hair, fanatical eyes, and a skin like tanned leather. He remained seated behind his desk as I entered and for a long time scrutinized me in silence. Then he asked gruffly:

"What do you want?"

"Please, I should like to see my mother, Frau Gussi Adenauer," I said.

He shrugged his shoulders and didn't seem to think it necessary even to answer.

I repeated my request: "Please, allow me to see my mother, only for a brief moment." Although I had been firmly resolved to control myself at all costs, I could hold on no longer, and began to cry.

Bethge said, "You'd better go back home! Your mother will be back sometime, never fear."

I made no move. Suddenly he narrowed his eyes and gave me a crafty look. "Do you happen to know, by any chance, where your father is hiding out?"

I shook my head and said nothing.

Impatiently Bethge repeated, "Come on, now, get out of here!" He took a file from his desk and began to leaf through it. I don't know even today where and how, at that moment, I found the courage, but I simply sat down and said, "I won't leave this place until you've told me where my mother is."

Now Bethge got furious and yelled at me, "You impertinent little beast! Get out of here at once! Or I'll have you arrested on the spot! And then you'll see what happens to you!" I said nothing. I remained sitting where I was and went on crying. After a while I asked again:

"Couldn't you, please, tell me where my mother is?"

At this Bethge furiously brought his fist down on his desk. "This is really the limit!" he shouted. "This is the biggest piece of insolence I've ever come across! Who do you think you are?" He stared at me, quite beside himself with anger. But gradually, as he went on staring, the expression on his face changed. It seemed almost as though my stubbornness had begun to amuse him.

"All right, then," he growled at last. "Just to get rid of you. Your mother has been taken to the Brauweiler prison."

I rose, and wiped my tears with my handkerchief. Then I said:

"Please, Herr Commissar, you couldn't perhaps give me a note of introduction to the prison administration at Brauweiler, could you?"

Bethge gasped for breath several times. I was afraid he might burst out again, but suddenly, without speaking a word, he reached for his pen and began making out a form. When he had finished he handed me the paper across his desk; it was a visitor's pass for the prison at Brauweiler.

"Thank you," I said.

"Get the hell out of here, and double quick!" he barked.

There I was then, standing in the street, holding my precious piece of paper. The visit at Gestapo headquarters had lasted for more than three hours. The question was now how to get to Brauweiler. The streetcars had long ceased to run in bombed-out Cologne. So I started out on foot. It was a day of sweltering heat, and the way along the dusty streets of the ruined city seemed endless. But I was determined to get to Brauweiler and see my mother that day, and stubbornly walked on. After about two hours' walk, an army truck gave me a lift as far as Weiden. There I knew my parents had a friend, a linen manufacturer named Sinn. I went to his office, and he lent me his bicycle for the rest of the way. The country road to the village of Brauweiler was almost impassable. The last air attack had turned it into one big bomb crater. Most of the time I had to push the bike and climb over trees which had fallen across the road. Once two low-flying British aircraft came over and machine-gunned the road, and seeking cover I fell into a water-filled ditch. It was growing dark, the moon rose in the east, and I was so exhausted and desperate that I began to cry.

I finally reached Brauweiler at eight in the evening. The large prison gates were already closed. I rang the bell at the side entrance. After a long time of waiting the door was opened by a grumpy old official who asked me what I wanted at this late hour. "I should like to speak to my mother, Frau Adenauer," I said. He took me across a courtyard to a large, dark building with endless long corridors dimly lit by blue blackout lamps. He unlocked a door somewhere and showed me in. "The visitors' room," he said. "Wait here." He left, and locked me in from outside. I was alone. The small room with its naked walls and its bright, unshaded bulb dangling from the ceiling was empty except for a plain wooden table and two uncomfortable chairs.

After a while I heard the sound of two people approaching outside. Then the key was turned in the lock and the door abruptly flung open. In the doorway stood my mother. Behind her, and much taller than she, was a wardress, a lean and hard-mouthed woman.

I had jumped up from my chair. I stared at my mother. She had changed terribly during these few days. She looked pale and worn from lack of sleep, her eyes were reddened and swollen from crying. Her hair, always so carefully done up, hung loosely and unkempt about her face and was tied at the nape of her neck with a shoelace. For a few moments we just gazed at one another, unable to speak. I felt like rushing up to her and embracing her, but the wardress seemed to guess my impulse and kept me back with her outstretched hand.

I remained standing where I was and just stammered, "What have they done to you?" She did not answer my question but shook her head as if in mild reproach and said, "But my poor child, what a mad thing to do, to come out here! I shall soon be with you again!" Her voice sounded toneless, almost dead. Again I asked myself anxiously what could have happened to change my mother so utterly during these few days.

"How are Lotte and Schorsch?" she asked. "And Lola and Irene?" And again she spoke in this tired and apathetic voice which cut like a knife into my heart. "They're well, Mother," I answered hastily, "they're quite all right. We've sent a telegram to Max asking him to come as soon as possible. I'm sure it'll all be cleared up soon, this mistake about you and Father. . . ."

"Father has been arrested again," she murmured.

At this, the wardress intervened. "It is forbidden to speak about other prisoners! Besides, your three minutes are nearly up!"

My mother and I said no more. In the glaring, merciless light her face seemed suddenly aged and unspeakably tired. There were deep shadows around her eyes, which began quietly to fill with tears.

"Time is up!" said the wardress.

At that moment the door opened, and a prison inspector appeared. He looked at my mother. Then he looked at me.

"You can take your mother with you straightaway," he said to me. Then to my mother, "Frau Adenauer, you are released." And after a moment, "You have permission to speak briefly to your husband. He is here, in the men's wing."

We were led across the courtyard, to the visitors' room of the men's prison. After a short while the door opened, and a warder showed my father in.

I was the witness of a heartbreaking meeting. . . .

This concludes Libet Adenauer's account. But it is not the whole story. Libet Adenauer did not know, then, what this story was.

After they had reached their home at Rhöndorf that night, Frau Adenauer refused to tell of her experiences in prison and gave but monosyllabic answers to her daughters' questions. Some deep, convulsive horror seemed to shake her whenever her imprisonment was mentioned, and she was terribly, frantically worried about her husband. Again and again she insisted that "something must be done at once" to get him out of Brauweiler prison before the Americans arrived. During the last air attack one of the wardresses had said to her, "You'd better not rejoice too soon, you political ones. As soon as the Americans arrive, you'll all be shot."

It was clear that in those days Gussi Adenauer had gone through some agonizing experience which weighed heavily on her heart and mind.

## CHAPTER IX

THE TWO Gestapo agents who had arrested Frau Adenauer had handed her over to the police station at the neighboring village of Honnef. There she had been interrogated for several hours, without result. She maintained firmly that she had no knowledge of her husband's whereabouts.

In the late afternoon of the same day she was taken to Gestapo headquarters in Elisenstrasse, in Cologne, where she was sent to the cellar of the building. There she found herself in unexpected and unaccustomed company. The young SS man who escorted her told her with a smirk, "I'm sorry I can't give you a private room, *Frau Oberbürgermeister.* You'll have to move in with the criminal cases. But there's no need to be afraid. They're not dangerous people. Just some prostitutes who have evaded police control. Once you've got used to it, you'll feel quite at home with them. . . ."

The cellar was a noisy place. Shrieks of laughter, high-pitched giggling, blaring dance music which seemed to come from some unseen loudspeaker, filled the dimly lit corridor, and when the SS man finally opened a door and pushed the terrified woman inside, a suffocating cloud of mingled smells, perspiration, human excrement, and cheap scent, enveloped her. The SS man announced, "A guest of honor–*Frau Oberbürgermeister* Adenauer!" and shut the door behind her. The music came apparently from the SS prison guardroom just overhead, and the girls took the opportunity of having a dance among themselves, reinforcing the hit tunes with their own shrill singing. The room was lit by a single dim bulb, and after her eyes had grown used to the poor light, Frau Adenauer, picking her way painfully through the throng of dancing street girls, discovered many others lying stretched out on the stone floor or sitting huddled against the walls, their knees drawn up. In one corner stood two white enameled bins. There was no other furniture.

Gussi Adenauer was not in a mood to join the prostitutes' amusement, and, when she failed to respond to their advances, the girls at first grew rather hostile and threatening, but after a while decided simply to ignore her. She sat huddled against the wall, gazing desperately into the teeming, shrieking, smelling semidarkness, waiting. This was a world she had never known before. It terrified and revolted her beyond words.

After what seemed an endless time of waiting, the door was opened and someone called, "Adenauer—for interrogation!" She stumbled outside where she was received by an elderly, hard-faced SS man who told her, "I'm taking you up to see Commissar Bethge. I'd better warn you right away. Don't try to tell him any fibs. He's softened up people much tougher than you." The warning, uttered in a toneless, casual voice, sounded terrifying.

She was pushed into a room on the second floor, and at first had to shut her eyes against the blinding electric light which came from a desk lamp and hit her in the face.

"Where is your husband?" a voice rasped at once from the semidarkness behind the powerful lamp.

Haltingly Frau Adenauer once again told the agreed story: "He was taken from the hospital for interrogation. . . . I don't know where he has been taken. . . . I have myself reported him as missing. . . ."

"Stop telling me these fairy tales!" Bethge interrupted her. "Where is your husband?"

"I don't know," she answered.

"But I know that you do. And that is why you won't get out of here until you've told me where your husband is."

Frau Adenauer remained silent. Bethge began, very slowly, to tap his pencil against the edge of the desk, and waited. Tap, tap, tap went the pencil. It was like Chinese torture. "Very well, then," he said after a while. "You can think it over if you like. We're in no hurry." He ordered the SS guard to conduct her back. When she reached the cellar the dance was over and the girls had stretched out on the floor to sleep. There was no room left for her. She had to stand. Two hours later she was taken out again, for another interrogation.

"Well, have you thought it over? Where's your husband?"

"I don't know."

"All right, then," said Bethge. "In that case let me help your memory a little. If by three o'clock you still haven't remembered where your husband is, your house at Rhöndorf will be cleared out by tonight and confiscated as property belonging to an enemy of the state. And your two daughters . . ." Bethge paused for a moment, then asked in a changed voice, "By the way, how old are the two young ladies?"

Frau Adenauer felt her whole body begin to tremble.

"Nineteen and sixteen," she answered in a faltering voice.

"As young as that?" Bethge had become quite jovial. Lighting his pipe, he said casually, "And how do you feel with us, in here, Frau Adenauer? I mean, down there, in the cellar?"

"It's horrible!" she gasped.

"Of course, of course, I quite understand," Bethge said. "Considering who you are . . . and naturally for young girls like your daughters the shock would be even greater."

The Commissar rose behind his desk. His voice had an almost fatherly tone.

"Now, let's be reasonable, Frau Adenauer. If you will tell me now where your husband is, I shall let you go home right away, even today. Nothing will happen to your children, and your husband, too, will be treated leniently. But if you continue to deny everything—you've got to be clear about this—we shall get your husband in any case. It's ridiculous to think that anyone can hide forever from the Gestapo. And in that case . . ."

Bethge stepped forward from behind his desk and stood close to the prisoner.

"In that case," he continued, "your husband must expect a very severe penalty; you will remain under arrest yourself, and I shall have your two daughters arrested today. And one thing I can promise you—they'll stay down there in the cellar until we've got your husband, even if it takes months!"

Gussi Adenauer felt completely stunned. Deliver Lotte and Libet into this hell! It was unthinkable. But what about her husband? Could she even think of revealing his hideout? How could she ever face him again if she betrayed him now? And if she remained silent? What was to happen if Commissar Bethge did as he had threatened? What would her husband say, the best and gentlest of fathers, if that came to pass?

"I'm waiting, Frau Adenauer," Bethge urged. He had returned behind his desk. "I'm still waiting, but I shan't wait very much longer.

If I have to send you back to the cellar now, all the things I have just mentioned to you . . . will happen."

At that moment Gussi Adenauer made her decision. She was absolutely certain in her own mind that her husband would never have consented to her sacrificing the children for his sake. About that she felt no doubt. In a toneless voice she said:

"He is in the Westerwald—at the Nister Mühle . . ."

"There now," Bethge said, satisfied. "Couldn't you have told us that right away?" Suddenly his eyes narrowed in suspicion. "Are you telling the truth?"

She nodded.

"All right, we shall check your statement very carefully."

The interrogation was over. The SS guard took Frau Adenauer back to the cellar.

The following morning Frau Adenauer was transferred to the Gestapo prison at Brauweiler, where she was placed in solitary confinement. There were no more interrogations, and no one troubled her any further. The wardress who brought her food, told her casually that her husband had been arrested again and was also held at Brauweiler.

No one seemed to remember that they had promised to release her. As far as she herself was concerned the Commissar had lied, after all. What guarantee was there that he would not break his other promises as well? Perhaps Lotte and Libet had been arrested all the same and were even now in the cellar at Elisenstrasse. And what was happening to her husband? Who could know what horrible punishment he might have to suffer at this very moment for his escape?

She tried to query her wardress, but the woman had all of a sudden become very taciturn, pretending grumpily that she knew nothing. Her mental depression deepened, her gloom overpowered her, she began to have hallucinations and to doubt her own sanity. For hours she would sit on her prisoner's mattress, staring in front of her, asking herself the same questions over and over again: what is happening to my husband, what is happening to my children?

Meanwhile the prison doctor had told Adenauer, who felt very ill himself, that his wife was in the same prison as he and was suffering from severe depression. But it would pass off again, the doctor thought, and there was no reason for Adenauer to worry unduly. September 25, 1944, their Silver Wedding day, they both spent in prison, together, and yet separated. It was not until several days later that Frau Adenauer was released.

For a long time afterward Gussi Adenauer suffered deeply from the mental strain of her days of imprisonment. The greatest psychological shock of all had been her unexpected meeting with her husband. What her daughter Libet had only been able to hint at was later told in some detail by the prison inspector who was present.

As Adenauer entered the visitors' room in the men's wing of Brauweiler prison and suddenly found himself facing his wife, neither of them was at first able to move or speak. They just stood facing each other, speechless. Then he went slowly up to her.

"Gussi," he said tenderly. She remained silent, unable to stir, unable to utter a single word. At last she began to stammer. "I have . . . you know, they threatened . . . the children . . . I could think of no other way out . . ."

"I know it all," he interrupted her. She flung herself into his arms and burst into a flood of helpless tears. Gently he stroked her hair. "Don't, Gussi," he said. "Don't torture yourself. We're all in the hands of God."

Adenauer himself had passed through a harassing time when he met his wife in Brauweiler prison, and for him the end was not yet.

September 25, 1944, was to him a day of special significance to which he had been looking forward with joyous anticipation. It was the twenty-fifth anniversary of his marriage to Gussi Zinsser, in 1919. Often in the past they had made plans about how they were going to celebrate the day together, but when it finally came it turned out very different. He was alone, separated from his family, a hunted fugitive hiding under a false name in the forest of the Westerwald. Through their secret postal connection his wife had inquired whether she might come and pay him a clandestine visit, but he had refused her wish, with a heavy heart. It was too dangerous a thing to do. Instead she had sent him a cake and a letter, through the good offices of the kindly man at Hachenburg who functioned as their illegal post office, and the children had included their letters of congratulation and good wishes.

He had collected the parcels and letters toward evening and had walked back through the dark forest to his hideout in the old mill. Before going to bed he had read the letters once more, and then had lain awake for hours, considering his situation. The iron self-control and discipline with which, during the day, he played his part of an inconspicuous and friendly holiday guest was apt to give way at night, and he would be a prey to moods of profound gloom.

Thus passed the long, sleepless night. Outside it was still dark and there was only the rustling noise of the wind in the trees outside his window, when suddenly he thought he heard the throbbing noise of an engine slowly coming nearer. When it was quite close it ceased abruptly, and with a sudden flash a dazzling searchlight played on the house and fell straight through his window.

He knew at once: it was the Gestapo; he had been given away; they had come to get him.

All those who know Adenauer well and have watched him in critical situations are unanimous in testifying that complete fearlessness is among his most outstanding characteristics. During the war air attacks left him wholly unruffled and, except when, in the last days of the fighting, his house and garden were actually in the front line, he never deigned to seek safety in an air-raid shelter. The overzealous measures of protection devised by his police escort arouse in the Federal Chancellor an ironical smile, and on occasion he succeeds in dodging them. Even the threats of the separatists, who for years swore they would carry out the death sentence passed on him at Koblenz and murder him in an ambush, left him completely unmoved.

But this time, for once, it was different. At that moment, in the dark autumn night of 1944 when the Gestapo car stopped in front of the mill, Adenauer admits that he was suddenly seized by nameless terror.

"At that moment," the Federal Chancellor confesses frankly, "I completely lost my nerve. I grabbed my clothes lying on a stool by my bed, and on my bare feet rushed frantically up the wooden stairs leading to the attic, where I hid behind the chimney stack. My hope was, of course, that when they did not find me in my room they would drive away again, thinking I had escaped through the back door into the woods."

But the Secret Police thought no such thing. It was no use for the old miller to protest that he knew nothing of any Dr. Adenauer, the gentleman staying at the mill was Dr. Weber—they searched the house, from bottom to top, and eventually the terrified man who had trapped himself behind the chimney stack in the attic, paralyzed with fear and unable to move a limb as he listened to their approaching steps, heard them come up the stairs. There were three of them. The flashlight beam played across the attic. And a slightly ironical voice said reproachfully:

"But *Herr Oberbürgermeister*, really!"

The humorous mockery of the address immediately restored Adenauer's composure and self-control. One of the three Gestapo men said later:

"It was wonderful to watch the instant change which came over the man at that moment. He straightened himself up and, with a dignified voice which betrayed no fear whatsoever, said 'With your permission, I shall get dressed first.' He did so, calmly and leisurely, while we waited in the doorway to the attic. Then he emerged from his hideout behind the chimney stack, and from that moment onward was in complete control of the situation. 'With your permission, I shall have my breakfast first,' he said. It was much more an order than a request, and after a moment's hesitation he added, 'Gentlemen, I'm sure you feel as much in need of breakfast as I do. May I invite you to have a cup of coffee with me?' When the three of us looked somewhat uncertain, he added, 'I can even offer you something special. I've got some real coffee, and a cake of almost peacetime quality. You should know that it is my Silver Wedding anniversary today.' "

The invitation was accepted. It became a strange banquet. The miller had roused his wife, who had made the coffee, and with trembling hands served the four men at table. At first a slight air of shyness and embarrassment seemed to hang over the company, but Adenauer's courtesy and amiability soon dispelled all inhibitions. When they rose, an hour later, and bade good-by to the miller and his wife, Adenauer had learned everything these minor officials knew about his case. He knew that his wife was under arrest. And he had picked up a veiled hint to the effect that in all probability Frau Adenauer had betrayed her husband's whereabouts during her interrogation.

"I observed Adenauer very closely," one of the Gestapo men said later. "Not a muscle in his face twitched when he heard that his wife had put the Gestapo on his track. Only, from that moment, he grew very silent."

It was a dull, gray morning when Adenauer arrived in a police car at Brauweiler prison. The place looked unspeakably desolate and depressing, and Adenauer was given a particularly bad cell. It was narrow, had no heating facilities, and even in the daytime was plunged in semidarkness, its only source of light being a tiny barred window high up in the wall. The Gestapo commissar in charge knew Adenauer from earlier times. He insisted on accompanying him personally to the clothing depot where he was relieved of his suspenders, tie, shoelaces, and pocket knife, and on the way there said to him, "Now, please do not commit suicide. You would only cause me no end of trouble. You're sixty-eight years old, and your life is over anyway."

On the fifth day after his arrival at Brauweiler Adenauer was summoned for his first interrogation by the redoubtable Commissar Bethge. When this man told him with unconcealed spitefulness that Frau Adenauer had betrayed the hideout in the Nister Mühle, he answered calmly, "She has done right." Possibly it was just this attitude of Adenauer's which caused Bethge's surprise move of arranging the meeting between husband and wife immediately before Frau Adenauer's release.

Shortly after this meeting Adenauer fell ill, and Dr. Temmer, the prison doctor, ordered his transfer to a heated room, special invalid's diet, and daily walks in the fresh air. The change of surroundings brought other welcome improvements. In his new quarters Adenauer came under the jurisdiction of another supervisor, and this man, Chief Constable Dahmen, was an official of the traditional old-fashioned type, fair, just, and humane, who was outraged by the chaotic conditions the Hitler regime had introduced into what he had been brought up to consider proper prison routine. Dahmen expressed his angry dissatisfaction with these new and irregular ways by allowing the political prisoners in his charge a degree of latitude which went far beyond official regulations. He saw to it that Adenauer received books and writing materials, and did everything he could to make life a little easier for the sick old man. And when one day Lieutenant Max Adenauer called at the prison and wished to see his father, Dahmen, contrary to all regulations, left the visitor alone with the prisoner, to talk freely without supervision.

Libet Adenauer's telegram which she despatched immediately after her mother's arrest had taken ten days to reach her brother. Not knowing precisely where her brother was, she had sent it to his last garrison, at Rastatt, in the Black Forest, from where it had been forwarded. It read:

> PLEASE INFORM ME URGENTLY OF PRESENT ADDRESS LIEUTENANT MAX ADENAUER AND TELL HIM HIS RETURN TO RHÖNDORF URGENTLY NECESSARY SINCE BOTH PARENTS NOW ABSENT–LIBET ADENAUER

When Lieutenant Adenauer received this telegram on October 4, 1944, he had not a moment's doubt as to what was behind the cryptic wording: both his parents had been arrested. He applied at once for compassionate leave, but toward the end of 1944 this was not easy to obtain in the German Army. His first application was refused. He then sent his wife Gisela to see his commanding officer, Lieutenant Colonel Reile, on his behalf, and when she told him of the circumstances of her father-in-law's case, she found immediate sympathy and willingness to help. This was mainly due to the general deep resentment felt among the fighting services about the way the Gestapo ruled Germany behind their backs. Whenever it was a case of resisting these arbitrary excesses, the soldiers as a rule formed a common front of solidarity.

"Thus, on October 24, I was granted four weeks' leave," Lieutenant Adenauer tells. "The reason given was 'To attend to private matters in Berlin.' Two days later I was at Brauweiler, with my father. I had not expected to be allowed to see him for more than a few minutes in the visitors' room, and was surprised by the goodwill I encountered. A chief constable took me to my father's cell and left us alone there for a full three hours. My father received me sitting on his bed. He looked pale and in poor shape, and, wearing a shirt without a collar and shoes without laces, presented a somewhat neglected outward appearance. But he did not complain. On the contrary, he gratefully acknowledged the many favors granted to him by his supervisor. Only two things troubled him seriously: his sleeplessness, and the fact that his cell was immediately above the room in which interrogations took place. 'It is horrible,' he said, 'to have to listen to the screams and the slashing noise of the beatings, sometimes for hours on end. These Gestapo people have no human feelings left at all. The other day one of these torturers came to see me. He seemed to think he must tell me all about it in every detail. "Some of them," this fellow said, "scream with fear before I've touched them, and they always get a double dose!" '

"My father, too, had been interrogated several times, but had not been maltreated physically. Commissar Bethge had summoned him to his office and asked him about his participation in the July 20 revolt. Apparently my father was suspected of having been in touch with Gördeler. He was able to reply truthfully and with a clear conscience that he had nothing whatever to do with the conspiracy. Bethge apparently believed him, for my father's statements were taken down into the protocol without queries or objection, and he was thereafter left in peace. I told my father that I planned to go straight to Berlin to intervene there on his behalf, and he agreed with my plan. We discussed details of how it would be best for me to proceed, and I was much reassured when he told me emphatically, again and again, that he still did not know why in fact he had been arrested on August 23. The only offense he was conscious of having committed, he said, was his escape from the hospital at Hohenlind."

After the conversation with his father, Lieutenant Adenauer looked forward with some confidence to his negotiations in Berlin. But his private contacts proved ineffective. He approached a number of men in influential key positions in banking and industry well known to the Adenauer family, as well as several high-ranking officers, but none of them felt able to intervene on his father's behalf. By late autumn of 1944 the Gestapo had become all-powerful in Germany, and there was apparently no way of influencing their decisions.

So Lieutenant Adenauer went to see the Gestapo himself. On November 3, 1944, he called at their headquarters in Prinz-Albrecht-Strasse and was referred to a branch office in Meineckestrasse, where an official named Kunze was believed to be dealing with his father's case. Kunze was reserved but correct. The "Adenauer File" had been forwarded to him from Cologne, he said, but he had not yet found time to study it. He promised to do so immediately, and asked the son to come back the next day.

"When I called again on the following day," Lieutenant Adenauer tells, "a second Gestapo man named Hahnenbruck was also present. The two men had meanwhile studied my father's file and gained the impression that the charge of complicity in the Gördeler conspiracy could not be maintained. Still, Hahnenbruck, whose bearing was much more aggressive than Kunze's, kept referring to my father's flight from Hohenlind hospital, a fact, he said, which weighed heavily against him. For why should a man escape, Hahnenbruck argued, unless he knew he was guilty?"

"There was, of course, an obvious answer to this: all too many perfectly innocent people had fallen victims to the Gestapo. But this being no suitable answer, I suppressed it. Instead I referred to my father's advanced age, his illness, and the mental depression which unjustified and indefinite imprisonment were bound to cause in a sick old man. These considerations, however, failed altogether to make an impression upon the Gestapo officials. Therefore I changed my tactics. I told them two of my brothers and myself were soldiers at the front, and asked them, 'How do you think, gentlemen, a soldier fighting the enemy feels when he hears that one of his family at home has been arrested for no reason at all and thrown into prison?'

"This argument made an impression. Kunze declared obligingly that he would forward the 'Adenauer File' at once to the Reich Security Office, for the personal attention of Kaltenbrunner, and with his own recommendation that Dr. Adenauer should be released. During the following days I called several times more at the office in Meineckestrasse to make sure things were really moving. But the Reich Security Office took their time over it. My leave was up, and when I departed from Berlin I was still uncertain about my father's fate. I asked my brother Paul, who was serving with the Army Medical Corps at Jüterbog, and my father's old friend, banker Pferdmenges, to pursue the matter further.

"On the return journey to my unit I visited my father once more at Brauweiler and told him of the results of my efforts. He thanked me and said, 'I only hope I shall no longer be in prison when the Americans arrive. . . .' "

The American advance into the Rhineland was delayed much longer than Adenauer had expected; but there was no news from Berlin either, for several weeks. Outwardly at least Adenauer remained unperturbed. "I've rarely had so patient a prisoner as Dr. Adenauer," Chief Inspector Dahmen recalls. "He never complained and always seemed content with everything. With him I never noticed any of the violent changes of mood to which people in prison are normally prone. He seemed like a sage who is no longer affected by the ups and downs of life."

Suddenly, however, something happened which shook Adenauer deeply.

One day, walking in the courtyard, he recognized among the other prisoners Major Hans Schliebusch. He asked Dahmen, if possible, to arrange for him to see the major and speak to him privately. The inspector thought it prudent to make inquiries first. He arranged for the transfer of Schliebusch to his own section of the prison, and on this occasion learned that Schliebusch had been arrested on a charge of having helped Adenauer to escape the Hohenlind hospital. Fearing that the major might not care, in the circumstances, to see Adenauer again, he had a private talk with him. To his surprise, the major was neither afraid nor embittered. He spoke of Adenauer with great respect and sympathy and declared roundly he would not hesitate, in similar circumstances, to do exactly the same thing again. As for the consequences to himself of his action, he shrugged them off lightheartedly. "There's nothing much they can do to me," he said. "There was no legally valid warrant of arrest against Adenauer. The man was sick, and it was my human duty to get him to a healthier place. That's what I've done, and nothing else."

After this Dahmen had no hesitation in letting the two men meet. He quartered Schliebusch in a cell opposite Adenauer's, and whenever opportunity offered left their doors unlocked so they could slip in and out and visit one another. "Sometimes their whispered conversations would go on for hours while I watched outside to warn them, if necessary," Dahmen recalls.

Schliebusch's arrest weighed heavily enough on Adenauer's conscience, but there was worse to follow.

One day, Schliebusch's son, a young soldier serving at the Western front, joined his father as a prisoner at Brauweiler. During a recent leave period he had visited his father in prison, and although their talk had lasted only three minutes, it had deeply upset the son. While waiting at the streetcar stop outside the prison, a girl had spoken to him, they had become friendly and made the return journey together, and by the time they left the train at Bonn, the unwary and deeply troubled young soldier had opened his heart to her. Now that they had put his father in prison, he had said, he had no intention of going back to the front. He would try to escape to Switzerland, and his father was in agreement with this. The next day young Schliebusch was arrested. The pretty young girl who had won his confidence with a tale of woe of her own was an informer employed by the Gestapo with the special duty of spying on the relatives of the Brauweiler prisoners.

Major Schliebusch was in despair. As an officer he knew the penalty for desertion, and the man who had never given a thought to his own situation was now tormented by fears for the life of his son. Adenauer did his best to calm and reassure the desperate man, but it was of little avail. Uncertainty grew as the weeks went by and neither Schliebusch nor his son were even summoned for interrogation.

"His own situation Adenauer never mentioned with a word," Inspector Dahmen says. "Only occasionally he would ask me whether there was still no reply from the Reich Security Office in Berlin. Unfortunately there was none, and personally I had little confidence that he ever would get one. I knew of too many cases who had been waiting for months for a decision which never arrived."

On November 26, 1944, however, there was a heavy air raid, and all prisoners were taken to the shelter in the basement where, for safety's sake, the Gestapo officials joined them. Spotting Commissar Bethge among them, Adenauer went up to him and asked:

"Has the order for my release still not come from Berlin?"

"Yes, it's here," answered Bethge. "Arrived this morning."

"In that case I wish to be released this day," Adenauer declared.

Bethge objected. "Today is Sunday, and the depot is closed. You can't have your belongings back until tomorrow when the officials are back on duty."

"I can do without the stuff," Adenauer answered. "I'll go as I am."

Commissar Bethge gave a shrug. "All right," he growled, "if you must, please yourself."

As soon as the air raid was over and the all clear had sounded,

Adenauer went back to his cell and packed his little bag. He asked Dahmen, his friendly jailer, to telephone Herr Sinn, the linen manufacturer at Weiden. Would his friend be willing to drive him in his car to Rhöndorf, tonight? Sinn was delighted to help. There was one last difficulty. "I'm still a little weak after my arrest," Adenauer confessed. Was there anyone available who could help him carry his suitcase as far as Weiden?

"As it was my duty-free Sunday," Dahmen says, "I offered to go with him. It was just after two o'clock in the afternoon when we left the prison together. I was pushing my bicycle with the suitcase on it, and Adenauer walked beside me, without collar or tie, without shoelaces or braces. And as we walked, we talked about the two Schliebuschs. 'If the war goes on much longer,' Adenauer said sadly, 'they'll probably be tried before a People's Court and sentenced to death. . . .' "

It never came to that. Major Schliebusch and his son were transferred to a prison in Cologne, and when all of a sudden the American troops arrived at the beginning of March, father and son profited from the ensuing chaos at the prison and made good their escape. But possessing no papers and fearing to be picked up, either as deserters by the Germans or as spies by the Americans, they spent days wandering between the fronts, hiding in barns at night, and occasionally calling on a trusted friend for something to eat. The last man who sheltered them was Adenauer's loyal friend Giesen. They were then both gravely ill, having contracted spotted typhus while in prison. Giesen did what he could for them, but urged them to report to a hospital. The two men could not make up their minds whether it was safe to do so. A few days later they were picked up by the Americans, who transferred them to a hospital at Bergheim. There they died. They were buried together at a nearby military cemetery.

# CHAPTER X

THE WAR was nearing its end, but it was by no means over when Adenauer returned from prison to his home and family at Rhöndorf. He was pale, emaciated, and worn from lack of sleep, but as always calm, unperturbed, and uncomplaining, finding it a little difficult at first to adjust himself, but soon resuming his old patriarchal routine. The house was full, and soon it became fuller still. The day after his return from Brauweiler his eldest daughter, Ria Reiners, appeared unexpectedly with her two children. Their home town, München-Gladbach, on the western outskirts of the Ruhr, was too close to the approaching front for safety or comfort.

The house was overcrowded and nervous tension rose all around when at last the great American spring offensive opened. Gunfire in the west grew louder every day, and at night the sky was bright with flashes. Many National Socialists packed their bags and withdrew into the interior. Wherever people met, only one question was discussed: "Shall we stay or pull out?" Adenauer refused to consider the alternative. He was firmly determined to remain where he was, awaiting events with complete calm. The war, he was sure, would by-pass his house.

But the war had its own mind and refused to conform. When news arrived that the Americans had crossed the Rhine at Remagen, Adenauer, utterly unprepared for this development, saw his theory confounded. Now there was a new situation indeed. Now it had to be assumed as certain that the American forces would follow up their advantage at this point and cross the Rhine in strength almost directly opposite Adenauer's house. There was no denying it. Rhöndorf was right inside the fighting zone.

Despite the approaching danger, the Adenauer family remained calm. On the evening of March 8, Adenauer ordered the small storage cellar which, as far back as 1938, he had had converted into an air-raid shelter, to be made ready with chairs, mattresses, blankets, and pillows. The entire family, except himself, his wife, and their youngest son Schorsch, who remained in the house, were to spend the night there. At first this precaution seemed unnecessary. There was only sporadic firing from either front. Toward midnight, however, the gunfire increased rapidly in intensity, and at about three-thirty in the morning it grew into a terrific artillery bombardment. Crashing shell bursts came closer and closer, in more and more rapid succession, shaking the house to its foundations. At four o'clock Adenauer, his wife, and young Schorsch decided to join the others in the shelter. There were now fourteen people, including a small baby, crowded into a tiny space. It was anything but comfortable, and it became increasingly doubtful whether it was even safe.

Toward daybreak the artillery fire eased up, but instead the air was now filled with the roar of airplanes ceaselessly bombing and machine-gunning the Rhine Valley, with particular attention to the thick woods just above Rhöndorf where the retreating German troops had hastily taken up defense positions. On the whole, however, this first day of siege passed off without incident. It was a fine and sunny day, and toward noon everyone ventured outside to take a breath of fresh air.

In the afternoon there was a sharp knock at the front door and someone loudly called out Adenauer's name. Although his wife warned him to be cautious, Adenauer went himself to see who it was. In the doorway stood a man who seemed almost out of his mind with fear. He was Louis, one of a group of French prisoners-of-war who, a few weeks before, had been helping in the garden.

"Can you give me shelter, please?" he stammered. "I've escaped from the prison camp . . . they were going to deport us to Central Germany . . . I wanted to hide in the woods but the woods are full of German soldiers . . . if they find me I shall be shot!"

It seemed a modest request to make in the circumstances. But Adenauer immediately saw all its possible consequences. It was scarcely three months since he himself had been released from the Gestapo prison at Brauweiler. If now an escaped prisoner were found in his house, if it became known that he had given shelter to a fugitive Frenchman, he would pay for it with his life, and his entire family would be in mortal danger. SS men were ceaselessly combing through the neighborhood looking for deserters, and often came into the houses. In this closing stage of the war they held power over life and death and were authorized by Hitler personally to shoot anyone by summary justice without trial, on the spot.

Frau Adenauer had followed her husband to the door. "Please help him," she pleaded, and the terrified Frenchman repeated, "Please, help!" Adenauer helped. "Yes, you may come," he said. Louis came toward evening, but not alone. He brought four other French who, like himself, had escaped from the prison camp. "They're comrades," he pleaded, "Christians like you and me——" Adenauer cut him short with a gesture. Instead he beckoned the five Frenchmen to follow him through the darkness up the hillside. Halfway up stood a small wooden shed used for gardening tools. Adenauer unlocked the door and said, "You can stay in here. If you're hungry you may come down to the house and get yourselves something to eat." Before Louis was able to thank him, he had disappeared in the dark.

In the evening the artillery fire regained the force of a full bombardment. This time the whole family at once repaired to the shelter and spent the night there. Their hope that it would slacken the next day was disappointed. On the contrary, it increased in intensity, for by now the Germans, too, had brought their artillery into position, and a Tiger tank was posted down below in Rhöndorf next to the village church, and vigorously shelled the opposite bank of the Rhine. Now the house in Zennigsweg was right in the middle of things, and the first shells fell into its grounds. Nevertheless Adenauer and his wife ventured across to the house to prepare breakfast for the shelter inhabitants and boil a supply of potatoes for lunch, for the fugitive Frenchmen, after all, had to be fed too.

At midday, as they were eating, a shell exploded in the immediate vicinity, rocking the shelter with the force of an earthquake. Cautious investigation revealed that the house had received a direct hit. The first floor corner had been ripped away, demolishing a bedroom. In the afternoon things grew worse. The house received a second hit, and in the garden shell hits felled several trees. At dusk Louis appeared at the shelter entrance. The tool shed was becoming rather unsafe, he reported. Could they possibly join the family in the shelter? The five Frenchmen were admitted without argument, and the population of the tiny dugout rose to nineteen.

Adenauer had expected the battle to pass over them like a fierce but swift thunderstorm, and every reasonable argument seemed in favor of this view. The Allied armies possessed undisputed air supremacy, and all resistance was but a senseless prolongation of a war by now well and truly lost. But the thunderstorm lasted for a full week before it abated and the family were finally able to leave their underground dungeon. During this time Adenauer insisted on himself going regularly "on patrol." Entirely heedless of the danger, he would climb to the top of his garden and its solitary wooden bench, and from this vantage point would calmly survey and appraise the military situation. Most times he would return to the shelter with reassuring news. "The Americans have now crossed the Rhine to the north as well," he would report, and this would be followed by a detailed appreciation of the strategic position. One day, however, he returned from patrol pale and mud-bespattered. The American gunners on the far side of the river, it seemed, had discovered his observation post and had taken direct aim. He had recognized the first shell from the "swish" it made in the air before it actually hit the ground. He had thrown himself flat on the ground, and this and the two shells that followed had passed over his head and exploded against the hillside above him, less than fifteen feet away. Apart from his hearing, which had suffered temporarily, he was none the worse for his experience, but henceforth he was more careful. But even then he allowed no one else to go scouting.

On the morning of the seventh day the guns fell silent. There were only a few thunderclaps in the far distance; the storm had drawn away. Adenauer climbed up to his observation post and returned within a few minutes, reporting excitedly, "The Americans are here!"

So they were. Down below an endless chain of American tanks and armored vehicles was rattling and clanking down the road which runs alongside the river embankment, followed by column after column of jeeps, the steel helmets of the soldiers glistening in the sun. The inhabitants of the dugout watched the spectacle with breathless fascination. Little Schorsch was the first to find his voice again.

"The war is over!" he cried

The following morning an American jeep drew up below at the gate in Zennigsweg, and two officers came up the garden path. One of them, a tall, dark man speaking faultless German, asked to see "*Herr Oberbürgermeister* Dr. Adenauer." They were asked inside, and someone went to bring Adenauer from the garden. He appeared, still wearing his gardening apron and his old straw hat, carrying a pair of garden shears.

"Gentlemen, what do you wish to see me about?" he asked coolly.

"We are calling at the request of the American commander in chief," one of the officers explained. "We have orders to ask you, Dr. Adenauer, whether you would be prepared to resume the direction of the city administration of Cologne. In that case, you would be reinstated at once as Chief Mayor, and our Supreme Command would invest you with all required authority."

Adenauer did not agree at once. He was in a difficult position, and the proposal had to be considered carefully.

On the one hand there was Cologne, his home town, bleeding from a thousand wounds. He had seen it with his own eyes only a few weeks earlier, in the company of Giesen, and the impression had been a nightmare weighing on his mind ever since. What he had said to Giesen on that occasion had been more than a fleeting impulse. He knew it would be a great task to rebuild this city to which he had devoted the best years of his life, and lead it out of its misery and desolation. He knew that Cologne needed him. He was in his seventieth year, but he felt strong enough to shoulder the task.

But on the other hand there were his three sons, Konrad, Max, and Paul. They were still soldiers on active service, and the war was not over yet. What would happen to them if it became known that their father was collaborating with the Americans? Just now, in the last phase of this death struggle which spelled their doom, the masters of the Third Reich knew no inhibitions and no mercy. The sons of a collaborator faced certain death.

Adenauer stood irresolutely, facing the two officers.

"If you agree," one of them urged, "our orders are to take you to Cologne immediately in our car."

"I should have to stipulate certain conditions," Adenauer declared. "For the present my cooperation would have to remain secret. Until an armistice is concluded I could work only unofficially as an adviser to the American commander in chief." Seeing that the officer, in mingled astonishment and suspicion, raised his eyebrows, he explained, "Three of my sons are still serving with the German Army."

"I understand," said the American. "Your condition is accepted. May we drive you over to Cologne straight away?"

"You may," said Adenauer.

A quarter of an hour later he was on his way. His wife accompanied him. There was still fighting on the right bank of the Rhine as they drove into the city.

Cologne was in ruins. The gay and beautiful ancient city where before the war 780,000 people had lived, worked, and enjoyed themselves had lost all semblance of its former self. More than half of its 59,000 houses and public buildings were totally destroyed, and only 300 had escaped undamaged. There was no water, no gas, no electricity; there were no streetcars or automobiles. Streets and pavements were filled with mountains of shapeless rubble through which army bulldozers, here and there, had cut rough thoroughfares to replace the original configuration of streets and passages which had entirely disappeared under a vast mass of debris defying all topography.

Yet there were people living in this desert of ruins. A census taken by the Food Office on the left bank of the city, while German units still fought their last rearguard actions on the far side of the river, revealed a population of 32,000. They were alive, but how they lived was almost impossible to say—like cave dwellers in the cellars and basements of their destroyed houses, cooking their food by day out in the open on primitive fireplaces built from a few bricks on the tops of the rubble mountains, and bringing their water in buckets and tin cans from the few hydrants still functioning.

Such was the situation when in March, 1945, Konrad Adenauer once more took over the administration of his native city, succeeding, incidentally, his own brother-in-law, Dr. Willi Suth, who at the request of the American authorities had been temporarily in charge, as an emergency appointment. The Chief Mayor's working conditions reflected the general misery and destitution of the population. The magnificent historic Town Hall lay in ruins. Emergency office quarters were found in the building of the Allianz Insurance Company. Adenauer's own former town house was totally bombed out and uninhabitable. With his wife he lived in two rooms in a hospital in the suburb of Lindenthal. Every morning he drove the long way through the rubble lanes to his office, every evening and often late at night he drove the long way back, tired to death. Every day was now a desperate struggle with men, things, and conditions, against an unending stream of difficulties which instead of lessening, seemed ever to increase in magnitude.

The difficulties began with trifles. There was no writing paper, there were no pencils to be had, there was no telephone. And above all, and this was anything but a trifle, there were no suitable people available to help. Most of the few officials and municipal employees who had remained in the city had formerly belonged to the Nazi Party, and in accordance with the directives issued by the occupation authorities were therefore excluded from employment. Adenauer's most pressing problem was thus to find a suitable staff with a clean and acceptable political record.

One municipal official who had been a member of the Social Democratic Party before 1933 has told how Adenauer endeavored to secure his cooperation.

"He promised nothing. And, indeed, what could he have promised? In view of the galloping inflation and the rapid decline of the purchasing power of the currency, there was little inducement even in a very high salary, and promises of steady employment and a secure position in the future sounded almost like mockery in the conditions which then obtained. All Adenauer had to offer was work, mountains of work which would tax the strength and capacity of every single man to exhaustion. The astonishing thing was that Adenauer did not even attempt to pretend that things were otherwise. He never thought of glossing over the stark realities.

"His tactics were different. He appealed to my local patriotism, to my sense of duty toward our common native city. 'Cologne needs you,' he would say. 'We need every single available man, and above all men capable of thinking and acting independently.' "

In this way Adenauer succeeded, step by step, in bringing together a staff of devoted and loyal helpers, and the first stage in the battle against overwhelming chaos was won.

The most urgent and pressing task was to feed the population. Food was the topic uppermost in everyone's mind. People no longer reckoned in terms of money or money's worth, but calculated in calories, and there was nothing in their daily lives that was not subordinated to the paramount necessity of obtaining something to eat. But no food stores of any significance had survived the fighting in the city, and private trade, paralyzed by the disruption of all means of transport, was unable to bring up supplies. In this situation Adenauer turned to the American military commander for help. He met with understanding and active support, and the food depots of the occupation army were opened to the starving citizens.

Adenauer did not leave it at that but simultaneously, as he had done after World War I, developed a German self-help organization. Although it could be argued that under the Hague Convention the conquerors were fully responsible for the support and sustenance of the inhabitants of occupied territories, Adenauer declared publicly what was then by no means a popular view—namely, that it was essentially immoral to rely upon foreign assistance beyond the most urgent necessities. As a consequence, he had all available means of transport requisitioned forthwith and sent them out into the surrounding countryside to purchase from the peasants whatever could be obtained—potatoes, grain, vegetables, and cattle.

Next to food the most pressing problem was housing the homeless, and this was complicated by an unforeseen new factor. As soon as actual fighting ended anywhere, a great stream of "returnees" began to flow back into the cities, and after the armistice this flood took on truly frightening proportions. Between six and seven thousand people formerly resident in Cologne who had been evacuated during the war flocked back every day, and almost without exception they faced destroyed homes, factories, offices, and shops, unemployment, and starvation.

There was only one effective remedy for all this. Building had to be started as quickly and as extensively as possible, the ruins had to be made habitable, and new houses must be constructed. One would have thought that Adenauer, the passionate builder and fanatic of town planning, would have been the first to agree to this priority. But to everyone's surprise Adenauer reacted differently. He had succeeded in obtaining from the American Military Governor a supply of so-called "Iron Coupons" which had enabled him to purchase, on behalf of the city, very substantial quantities of steel, temporarily stored in a large industrial works on the Lower Rhine. As soon as this "deal" became known, house and property owners besieged the city administration, demanding allocations of steel for the rebuilding of their properties. But Adenauer refused point-blank. "First the Rhine bridges!" he declared. Without the bridges the city remained cut in half and could never be restored to normal life. The functioning of these vital arteries had first priority. Once communications and transport were again in running order, building materials could be brought up all the faster and more efficiently. Adenauer's attitude met with little understanding from the would-be builders, and there was much disappointed criticism. It took many of his fellow citizens years to see how right he was at that moment.

In 1933, Konrad Adenauer took refuge from Nazi persecution at the Monastery of Maria Laach

A general view of the Monastery

*Verlag Ars Liturgica*

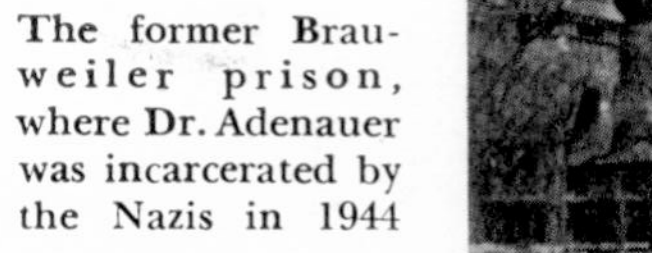

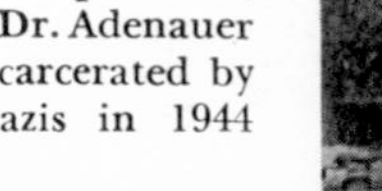

The former Brauweiler prison, where Dr. Adenauer was incarcerated by the Nazis in 1944

*Wündshammer*

General Lucius D. Clay (*right*), U. S. Military Governor, and General Sir Brian Robertson, British Military Governor, talking with miners at Bochum in the Ruhr (*Wide World Photo*)

Konrad Adenauer receives the congratulations of his family after his election as Federal Chancellor. *Left to right:* Paul Adenauer, Libet Adenauer, the Federal Chancellor, Lotte Adenauer, and Konrad Adenauer, Jr. (*Wide World Photo*)

One of the men who worked closely with Adenauer in the reconstruction of Cologne immediately after the war was Johannes Albers, who began as a typesetter, worked his way up through the Christian trade unions, became a cofounder of the Christian-Democratic Party (CDU) in 1945, and is today one of its deputies in the Federal Parliament.

"There was one thing," he recalls, "which was most characteristic of Adenauer's activity in this immediate postwar period. Despite the flood of urgent day-to-day decisions which pressed around him, he was never satisfied with mere improvisation. There was always a great and overriding conception in the background which dominated all his planning: the new Cologne. He surrounded himself with a staff of architects who, fired by his own enthusiasm, set about working out schemes there and then for the future replanning of the city. At a time when no one thought of anything but expedients to get a roof of some sort over his head, he devoted himself with great seriousness and absorbing interest to planning for the rebuilding of the old, slum-ridden medieval inner city on new and healthier foundations.

"This simultaneous devotion to present-day tasks and planning for the future which was so striking a feature in Adenauer was made possible only by a strict and methodical planning of his own working day. Even in those early and stormiest days when our city administration was submerged by a flood of applicants, when every departing visitor literally passed the door handle to the next caller, Adenauer was always available, and always had time. There was never in his office any of the hectic busybodiness which all too often makes the atmosphere in government buildings so unbearable. Adenauer has a remarkable capacity for concentrating on any single task in hand and grasping its essentials after the briefest of study. This enabled him, and enables him still, to get through an incredible amount of work every day.

"We were often surprised, in 1945, by the variety of things to which he attended personally. One day he telephoned to the municipal transport company and ordered them to send a fleet of large buses to the concentration camps of Buchenwald, Dachau, and Theresienstadt and bring home all prisoners formerly resident in Cologne. The reason he gave was as characteristic of his attitude as the order itself. 'We owe this to these poor people,' he said. He always rejected the thesis of collective guilt and responsibility of all Germans, but with equal emphasis he took the view that it was the collective duty of us all to repair the injustices of the past.

"The relationship of mutual trust and loyalty which Adenauer succeeded in establishing between the American occupation authorities and himself took some time to develop," Albers recalls. "In the beginning the atmosphere was often difficult and far from friendly. But gradually Adenauer managed to convince the Americans that at least some Germans were honest, fair, reliable, and trustworthy. As for himself, he adhered strictly to his orders—as long as they were not utterly unreasonable or conflicted with his conscience. If that were the case, he objected frankly and openly. It will be remembered, for instance, that in the summer of 1945 he flatly refused to join the then newly founded Christian-Democratic Party in Cologne, on the ground that the formation of new political parties was still prohibited by Military Government. As soon as the Allies lifted this ban, he became a member."

It is probably true to say that in essence Adenauer's attitude toward the occupying power was in precise conformity with the principles laid down by the Allies themselves for what was then called the "re-education" of the German people. They explicitly discouraged a spirit of uncritical subordination and preferred to place in positions of responsibility men whose record showed them not to have been blind and willing tools of their former masters. However, when actually faced with a man who had the courage to refuse to carry out the orders of the occupying authorities, for good and valid reasons, their reaction was very different from what might have been expected. Instead of appreciating and respecting an attitude they themselves had fostered and encouraged, their answer was instant and humiliating dismissal.

This did not happen, however, until the American Army, with whom Adenauer had worked fairly well, withdrew from Cologne, and British Military Government took over from them. The question as to why the British authorities, in October, 1945, dismissed Konrad Adenauer from his post of Chief Mayor has often been discussed and no genuinely valid reason has so far come to light. The view generally accepted in Germany at the time was that Adenauer had to make room for someone less obstinate and strong-willed and more compliant with British wishes. This is certainly only part of the truth, and there may well have been other, deeper reasons which caused the British Labor Government, which came to power in July, 1945, to feel that Adenauer's political outlook was out of harmony with the development they envisaged and favored in their zone of occupation.

Whatever these reasons and motives may have been, the actual incident which led to his dismissal was trifling, if not downright ridiculous, and the form used undignified and grossly offensive. In the long run it did Adenauer no permanent harm but it certainly poisoned British-German relations for years to come, and exposed the pompous shortsightedness of the British authorities to well-deserved ridicule.

What actually happened was this. In order to supply the population with a minimum of domestic fuel during the approaching winter months, the British Military Governor had given orders to cut down wholesale the trees in the parks and public highways of Cologne. Adenauer refused to carry out these orders. He pointed out that such a measure would merely cause irreparable damage to the city without sensibly alleviating the fuel shortage. Instead he asked that the coal reserves requisitioned by Military Government should be released and that steps should be taken to increase the supply of coal from the Ruhr and an adequate allocation made available for domestic consumption.

So as to underline his request and lend his argument additional strength, Adenauer made use of a means of publicity which in later years he formed into one of his most effective political instruments—he gave an interview to important representatives of the foreign press. At that time this was an unusual and somewhat spectacular thing to do, but seeing that Germany did not even exist then as a state, and possessed no representation of any kind in foreign countries, it was the only way open to a German politician to make his views known abroad and attempt to influence world opinion. In later years Adenauer made frequent full and effective use of it.

On October 5, 1945, the correspondents of the London *News Chronicle* and the American Associated Press called on him at his office. The obvious topic was, of course, the supply of coal and domestic fuel for the population of Cologne during the coming winter. Adenauer did not hold back his views, pointing out the calamitous consequences which the Allied decision to leave the civil population without any fuel whatsoever was bound to have. "The inevitable result of this," he declared passionately, "will be the death of untold thousands by epidemics and a permanent undermining of the health of the entire population."

The two newspapermen, obviously impressed by this remarkably courageous and forthright German, seized the opportunity to obtain his views on the political situation in general. At that time a French suggestion was being widely discussed which advocated the establishment of an independent or self-governing Rhine-Ruhr state which was to be carved out of the bankrupt former Reich and set up as an autonomous political unit. The two journalists, recalling vaguely that after World War I the Chief Mayor of Cologne had sponsored some sort of Rhineland state, and believing him therefore in sympathy with the French suggestion, asked his views on it. To their surprise Adenauer flatly rejected the plan.

"If you set up a Rhine-Ruhr state, detached from the remaining parts of Germany," he said, "you're immediately faced with the question: what is to become of the territories to the north and south of this new state? Russia, following her traditional imperialist tendencies, will probably immediately proclaim her zone of occupation to be the true German Reich, and the carved-up parts of the three western zones will naturally work for their reunification with the Russian-occupied German Reich. The result must be that you've turned the face of Germany as a whole toward the East, instead of toward the West. In my view the Western powers would be wise not to disrupt the political cohesion of the three zones occupied by them. If Russia is unwilling to cooperate in the unification of the whole of Germany, the best thing by far would be to unite at least the three western zones in a federal state, and the sooner the better. In order to satisfy French security wishes with regard to such a West German Federal State, the economy of this West German territory should be integrated with that of France and Belgium as intimately and closely as possible. Common economic interests are the best foundations for a rapprochement between the nations and the safeguarding of peace."

To appreciate the significance of this statement, it must be remembered that it was made in the autumn of 1945, at a time, that is, when scarcely anyone in Germany dared look beyond his immediate problems into the more distant future, and that however improbable they sounded in October, 1945, these ideas had become solid reality four years later, in almost precisely the shape which Adenauer had suggested. The two newspapermen were obviously impressed with what they had heard, and, in order to end the interview on a pleasant note, they mentioned that General de Gaulle had declared in a speech at Saarbrücken that Frenchmen and Germans should cease all recriminations about the past and henceforth work together, remembering that they were all Western Europeans. Adenauer responded, not without bitterness, "I wish that for a change some British statesman would speak of us as Western Europeans."

The very next day Adenauer was summoned by the Military Governor. The reception was icy. None of the British officers rose from their seats when he entered the office, and no one offered him a chair. While standing, a letter was read to him which amounted to little less than a political death sentence:

Headquarters Military Government
Cologne Regierungsbezirk (808 Det.)

Herrn Oberbürgermeister
Dr. h.c. K. Adenauer
Allianz Building
Cologne

6th October, 1945

1. I am not satisfied with the progress made in Cologne with regard to reconditioning of buildings, street cleaning, and the general task of preparing for the coming winter.
2. About two months ago I reminded you personally of your responsibility in this respect. You have not discharged your duties to my satisfaction. I am fully conscious of the difficulties with which you have had to contend. I know that many of your colleagues have been eliminated for political reasons. I am aware of the difficulties with regard to the supply of labor in Cologne. I am fully cognizant of the situation with regard to transport, fuel shortage, etc.
3. I am nevertheless convinced that, given proper supervision and energy on your part, more could have been done to solve these problems than has actually been achieved.

4. In my view you have failed in your duty toward the population.
5. You are therefore relieved, as of today, of your office of Chief Mayor of Cologne.
6. You will leave Cologne as soon as possible and in no case later than 14th October.
7. You will immediately hand over your tasks and duties to the Deputy Mayor of Cologne, Herr Suth.
8. Until the appointment of a Chief Mayor, Herr Suth will temporarily assume the duties of Chief Mayor.
9. After handing over to Herr Suth you will cease to take any further part in the administration or public affairs of Cologne or any part of the North Rhine Province.
10. You will not pursue any political activity whatsoever, either directly or indirectly.
11. In the event of your not complying in any way with the orders contained in this letter, you will have to stand trial before a Military Court.
12. You will acknowledge receipt of this letter below.

Barraclough
Brigadier Comd. Mil. Gov.
North Rhine Province.

BAOR/Jb/FPH

Adenauer was handed the original of the letter for signature. He was asked whether he had any observations to make.

"No," he answered, signed, and left.

It is probably idle to ask whether the newspaper interview of the previous day contributed to Adenauer's dismissal. What is certain is that a form was chosen which was bound to wound him deeply. He was charged with political incompetence and dereliction of duty toward his fellow citizens, and the British Military Governor even went so far as to underline this particular charge in a letter addressed to Adenauer's brother-in-law, Dr. Suth, who was temporarily appointed his successor.

"Herr Dr. Adenauer," this letter says, "has been dismissed because in my view he has not implemented Military Government policy with sufficient energy and farsightedness."

One can only guess what Adenauer felt when he returned to Rhöndorf that day. But we know what he did. He went to his study, opened the drawer of his desk, and took out a folder marked "Dismissal by the Nazis." He took a second folder, and with his stiff Gothic handwriting marked it "Dismissal by the Liberators."

# CHAPTER XI

No one could have blamed Adenauer if after his dismissal he had finally retired to Rhöndorf and, surrounded by his growing family, devoted himself to his private passions—flowers, pictures, music. Regarded superficially, his situation in 1945 seemed but a repetition of what had happened to him in 1933, after Hitler came to power. He was dismissed from office, banished from Cologne, and forbidden all political activity. Yet there was a vital difference. In 1933 the blow had been struck against him by people whom he had always regarded as his opponents and enemies. This time the representatives of Great Britain, a nation whose democratic way of life he had always greatly admired, had pronounced sentence upon him. In the days of Hitler his dismissal had been part of a general measure affecting many others besides himself. This time he alone was singled out for humiliation. And what hurt him most and more profoundly than the dismissal itself was the reason given for it; he was supposed to have been a failure. They had given it to him in black and white: incompetence. This wounded his pride more than anything else. Besides, time, too, had not stood still. In 1933 he had been fifty-seven years old. Now he was in his seventieth year and had reached an age when a man is inclined to accept a gradual diminishing of his physical and mental strength as an inevitability of fate, and resigns himself to quiet and leisurely contemplation during his remaining years.

All this might have been discouraging enough. Added to it, however, there was domestic misfortune. Frau Adenauer was ill. For months, during his term of office as Chief Mayor, she had been tirelessly traveling back and forth between Cologne and Rhöndorf, dividing her heart and her time between husband and children, and spending alternate weeks with each. But now she was in the hospital, in the care of Professor Uhlenbruck at Hohenlind. And Adenauer was prevented from seeing her because the British authorities, simultaneously with his dismissal, had expelled him from the city of Cologne. He sent an application to the occupation authorities asking for permission to visit his sick wife. From this short letter one gathers, not without a pang of emotion, that Adenauer was under no illusion regarding his wife's condition. He did not know for certain then, but in his heart could not doubt that it was an ailment which could only end in death.

He wrote, "As a result of a poisonous infection which she contracted in September, 1944, in the Gestapo prison at Brauweiler, my wife has fallen seriously ill. She requires treatment by a specialist, as hers is a rare and unusual case of osteomyelitis." His request was granted, although with qualifications. He was allowed to visit his wife twice every week and must not stay with her for more than an hour. The route he had to take through Cologne to reach the hospital was prescribed to him in detail.

These were his circumstances when, in the late autumn of 1945, Adenauer began to build up the Christian Democratic Union in Germany, a new political party since known as the CDU.

There was a great deal of movement among the politically interested groups of Christians in Germany immediately after the final defeat, and their general outlook and aims were familiar to Adenauer. His own political allegiance since the beginning of his career had belonged to the Roman Catholic Center party, and he was well acquainted with the two important papal pronouncements on social questions, *Rerum Novarum* and *Quadragesimo Anno*, in which a bold attempt was made to overcome the idea of the class struggle by a "Deproletarianization of the Proletariat."

But Adenauer had never considered this problem on strictly and exclusively confessional lines. His own conception was more broadly based, and it was for him not a new departure. As far back as August, 1922, when he was President of the *Deutscher Katholikentag* (German Catholic Assembly), he had asked in a widely noted speech for a political alliance between Catholic and Protestant Christians who should make it their task to "struggle jointly for the practical realization of Christian principles in public life." This early call had met with little response. It was not until the cataclysm of 1945, which left behind it not only a ruined land but also, among large masses of the people, a deep despair of the validity of party programs, that the time seemed ripe for a political program broadly based on the Christian spirit.

In all parts of Germany people were coming together, simultaneously, independently, and often unbeknown to each other, who felt that the principles of Christianity offered a last possibility of creating order in a world desperately out of joint. In the Rhineland, in Lower Saxony, in Bavaria, and Schleswig-Holstein, in Berlin and the Soviet Zone, everywhere groups and associations were forming which felt themselves to be germ cells of a new political party. Their names varied, and their aims differed in many ways, but one thing they all had in common: the rigid and exclusive framework of confessionalism had been broken and abandoned. The traditional old Center Party itself had stepped forth from its ivory tower and called upon devout Christians, irrespective of confession, to unite in battle against the materialism of the *Zeitgeist* and for a new order of life in the spirit of the gospel.

Cologne was one of the chief centers of this new movement. Here a Christian-Democratic party had formed itself under the leadership of Dr. Leo Schwering, and as early as June, 1945, had approached Adenauer with a request to join and support it. At that time Adenauer had been obliged to decline. There was still a ban on the formation of political parties, imposed by the occupying power, and the new party was, strictly speaking, illegal. Adenauer declared that he was ready to join it as soon as its formation had been authorized by the occupation authorities. When permission was granted a few weeks later, he became a member of the Christian-Democratic party, and the weight of his personality as well as his position as Chief Mayor of Cologne soon advanced him to a leading position in the party's regional executive committee.

His duties as Mayor of Cologne, however, had left him with little time to devote to political party work, and with his dismissal this political work came to an end, too. In a letter to the executive committee he pointed out that the "Military Government had debarred him from all political activity," and he resigned his party offices. But there was nothing to prevent him, in his exile at Rhöndorf, from continuing to think out and develop the ideas which he regarded as a basis for the salvation of ruined Germany. In those quiet weeks of his second banishment he became more firmly convinced than ever that henceforth Germany must be governed on Christian principles or perish.

Adenauer had always been a "man of lonely decisions," and it was particularly fortunate therefore that during this period of theoretical groundwork he had a partner in discussion against whom to test his views and clarify his conclusions. This partner was Frau Maria Schlüter-Hermkes, the well-known author and next-door neighbor of his, who had formed part of the small circle of close friends during the Hitler years and who shared many of his beliefs and hopes for the future. With her Adenauer discussed the program of the new party at length and in great detail, and eventually she recorded a summary of their discussions by his Rhöndorf fireside in a memorandum to which Adenauer later added numerous marginal notes and observations in his own hand.

This was, of course, no more than a prelude to Adenauer's later work on the final party platform of what became the Christian Democratic Union, but most of the basic principles of the definitive version are already contained in this draft, and the continuous exchange between the text of the draft and Adenauer's marginal notes lends this memorandum, retrospectively, the attraction of a vividly conducted dialogue.

Thus, to give an example, Frau Schlüter-Hermkes had propounded a basic concept of Christian ethics as one of the fundamental tenets of the new program: "The human person is endowed with unique and inalienable dignity, and the value of each individual human being is irreplaceable." This principle, which is the fountainhead of all detailed postulates of the program, inevitably leads to "a conception of state, economy, and culture in which the state, its economy, and its culture can never be a purpose in themselves but must fulfill the function of a servant of the individual person."

Adenauer elaborates this when he observes, with reference to this point, on the back of the memorandum: "For a Christian statesman the individual person and the community must fundamentally be of equal weight. Only a proper balance of these two fundamental factors of human existence will insure a healthy life for a people. The individual, valuable in himself and responsible for the whole, must develop fully within the framework of the state. It follows that a state based on, and governed by, Christian principles must conceive it as its duty to create space and opportunity for such development. This in turn imposes upon every member of a democratic state an obligation to form himself, and allow himself to be formed, into an independent and responsible personality. Democracy, then, is not to be understood as a process of leveling down toward a mediocre average. On the contrary, true democracy is the soil in which a fully developed individual personality is rooted. . . ."

The ban imposed upon him by the British authorities made it necessary for Adenauer to conduct his preliminary conversations with political friends in places outside the British zone of occupation. During the next few weeks they would meet on an estate near Koblenz, just beyond the zonal boundary, in French-controlled territory. In December, 1945, however, an officer from British headquarters visited Adenauer at his home in Rhöndorf. When he indicated his wish to discuss certain political questions with him, Adenauer declined, referring the officer to the exhibition prohibition, but suggesting that he might wish to accompany him to the nearby French zone, where he was prepared to talk to him. The result of this was that the officer caused the ban on Adenauer's political activity to be rescinded forthwith.

This was the signal for the beginning of a life of ceaseless and untiring activity, which Adenauer has led ever since. He still had no private motorcar of his own, but his brother-in-law, Dr. Suth, now lent him a car, and in this Adenauer began to travel systematically up and down the country, from place to place, reviving old political contacts, seeking out new people who had been recommended to him, speaking at meetings, establishing new local branches, and endeavoring everywhere to smooth out differing opinions and to unite disparate views in the common goal of the new party.

This was not always easy. In most cases the new popular Christian movement—and that is what the Christian-Democratic Union was in its beginnings—had its origin with men and women who had formerly belonged to the Catholic Center party, and, looking back as they did on the experience gathered in almost a century-old tradition of political Catholicism in Germany, they naturally claimed for themselves the leadership in local branches and district and county organizations. The claim was not altogether unreasonable since the Protestants, owing to the regional establishment of their churches, manifestly lacked political training and tradition.

However, German Protestantism had now belatedly embarked on a political road and was catching up with the Catholics, and Adenauer, himself a Catholic and former member of the old Center party, considered it politically unwise to place the Protestant groups at a disadvantage in what was intended to be a united and unifying Christian movement. His main anxiety at this stage was to prevent confessional splits and schisms from developing and endangering the life of the new party, and he insisted in every instance, and often in most acrimonious debate, on absolute parity at all levels. In his notes which he made as he drove from meeting to meeting, from conference to conference, we often find such remarks as "good cooperation between the confessions, *Una-sancta* atmosphere," or else "tension must be eliminated, X too autocratic."

These notes, hastily scribbled in pencil during the journey, are instructive in many ways. Above all they dispel all doubt in regard to Adenauer's capacity for psychological insight and his ability to understand the minds of others and to size them up. These notes are full of brief and often razor-sharp remarks about individuals, their potential political value, and their usefulness to the new organization. It never took Adenauer long to make up his mind where and how the individual abilities and services of newly encountered men or women could be most profitably employed.

Apart from these extensive journeys up and down the country, he frequently met with those politicians who already occupied leading positions in the new party. The first meeting of this kind in which Adenauer took part was at Bad Godesberg. Others followed later at Herford and Neheim-Hüsten. At all these conferences Adenauer was in the chair, as if by natural right and title, and on occasion he did not shrink from somewhat robust methods to assert his claim to leadership. One of the participants in the Herford meeting remembers a significant little incident: "We all stood about talking in the conference room of the Town Hall. Dr. Holzapfel, who had called the meeting, was already present but the meeting itself had not yet begun and the chairman's seat was still empty. Suddenly Dr. Adenauer appeared on the platform, seated himself in the chair, and declared, 'Having been born in 1876 I presume I am the oldest among those present. If no one objects, I may therefore consider myself president by seniority.' Everyone was flabbergasted and no one said a word. At the end of the conference Adenauer was duly elected its president and permanent chairman."

The description may or may not be a trifle exaggerated but it certainly indicates an important and highly characteristic element—the single-minded purposefulness with which Adenauer pursued his way. He had now reached the age of seventy, and before him, as he saw it, lay an enormous task: the reconstruction of Germany from a Christian spirit. He may have sincerely felt that there simply wasn't time for him to get held up by details of procedure, and one may well find moral justification for his method in the unsparing recklessness with which he treated himself. The demands he made upon himself in this life of tireless, exhausting activity are well illustrated in an account given by Heinrich Schumacher, a robust young native from Cologne who was Adenauer's chauffeur from 1946 until 1949.

"No one can imagine what we went through and had to put up with in those days," Schumacher says. "We traveled in any sort of weather, and despite the shocking state of the roads always drove at an average of seventy-five miles an hour. Dr. Adenauer had his prearranged timetable, and there was nothing to do but stick to it, come hell or high water. In that, he was absolutely merciless. Sometimes, coming out of a meeting at ten o'clock at night, he would say to me, 'You know what, Schumacher, we could save a whole day if we drove through the night.' So we would drive through the night and arrive at Rhöndorf at five in the morning. Then he would calmly say to me, 'Now you go and have a good long sleep. I shan't need you until nine'—which was in four hours' time!

"While traveling he would mostly work on his papers or draft his speeches. In the winter we were often terribly cold in the car, despite blankets, furs, and rugs, and more often than not the food situation was pretty grim, too. Frau Adenauer would always give us sandwiches and a thermos flask of coffee to take on the journey, and we would have short breaks for food by the roadside. But in the restaurants and inns they'd either give you nothing at all or cheat you out of your miserable few coupons. Places in which to spend the night were equally hard to find, unless we were lucky and found a monastery or hospital or some party friend to put us up. There was no fuel, the rooms everywhere were unheated and ice-cold, and often we didn't undress but slept in our clothes.

"Still, even so Dr. Adenauer always insisted on wearing the right clothes for the right occasion. Once when we were in Hamburg he said to me at three o'clock in the afternoon, 'Schumacher, we've got to be in Cologne by tonight. General Robertson is expecting me at Schloss Roettgen at eight o'clock.' Well, Hamburg-Cologne is, after all, a run of 270 miles, and I just stepped on it, doing an average of eighty miles an hour. Just before reaching Cologne, Dr. Adenauer asked me to stop. He took his suitcase and disappeared into the woods. Five minutes later he was back, immaculately dressed in his dinner jacket, black tie, and patent leather shoes. I quickly gave his shoes a once-over with my handkerchief, and we got to General Robertson's on the dot.

"I've kept my old logbook for 1948, and it shows that we did just under 100,000 miles that year. And I'm sure we didn't do much less than that in the two previous years. There were moments, to be sure, when I asked myself why on earth I had to go in for this race. But then, looking at this man of seventy indefatigably at work, I felt ashamed at the mere thought of conking out."

Adenauer was aware from the outset that the far-reaching aims of the new party required long-term planning and could not be realized within a short space of time. He was particularly anxious, therefore, to find, wherever possible, assistants and friends among the younger generation, and, as soon as he had discovered a man whose abilities promised to be of advantage to the party, he spared no effort to win him over to the cause.

A typical example is the case of Dr. Josef Löns, who became the first secretary general of the CDU and who is today director of the Personnel Branch of the new Federal Ministry of Foreign Affairs at Bonn. Dr. Löns had been a prisoner of war and after his repatriation had taken up an appointment in the legal branch of the Cologne municipal administration, where he followed the development of the new Christian party in Germany with intense interest. The story of his "conversion" by Adenauer is vividly told by Dr. Löns himself.

"I was acquainted with the so-called 'Cologne Principles'," Dr. Löns says, "as well as with the various other draft programs, and I had attentively watched the growth of the new organization—the foundation meeting at Bad Godesberg, the unification of the various groups under the name of Christian Democratic Union, and finally the election of Konrad Adenauer as first chairman of the new party in the Rhineland. I must admit that I watched the development of this new movement and the direction it took with some doubt and anxiety. My own origins were in the Youth Movement, and my beliefs were those of a Christian Socialist. I was convinced that the gospels contained political postulates of a social radicalism which left the

Marxist class-struggle slogans far behind. Seen in this light, the weakening and watering down of the social postulates in the CDU platform seemed to me ominous and dangerous. Also I considered it a fatal mistake to have placed the leadership of the new party in Adenauer's hands. In my view Adenauer was the prototype of the Christian conservative of the old and obsolete stamp. Therefore I armed myself with every conceivable objection and reservation when one day Frau Christine Teusch, a former Center Party deputy, called on me and on behalf of Adenauer invited me to a conference in the office of Dr. Pferdmenges, the banker.

"The interview took place the following day, and Adenauer went straight for his goal. He invited me to join the CDU and offered me the post of first secretary general of the party. At first I felt rather baffled. Then I decided to put my objections before him without hesitation or reserve. I said, 'To my mind the new party in its present form is merely yet another attempt to misuse Christian beliefs for political ends. I am a Christian Socialist!' It was meant as a challenge, and that was how Adenauer understood it. He repeated, 'Christian Socialist? What in fact do you mean by that?' I endeavored to explain the essential points of my beliefs as clearly and concisely as I could, and although it took me the best part of half an hour to do so Adenauer listened to me calmly and patiently.

"When I had finished he said, 'I see that you want to transfer all means of production to common ownership. Have you ever considered what the results of this would be, in the first instance, for you personally? Take the railways, the *Reichsbahn*. They are a nationalized industry under state management. Now, when you make a railway journey, have you ever felt conscious of being a coproprietor of this railway system? And as far as the workers and employees are concerned, wouldn't you agree that a fair and just social order which enables the working man, too, to acquire property for himself and his family does far more for the personal happiness of the individual than the idea that he is the co-owner of all nationalized means of production?'

"I argued that Socialism as I understood it by no means prevented or excluded anyone from owning private property, say a small house or a garden. 'My point is,' I said, 'that the socialization of the means of production prevents the capitalist exploitation of labor.'

"Adenauer smiled ironically. 'Do you really believe,' he went on to ask, 'that a worker or employee enjoys more rights, privileges, and liberties in a state-owned industry than under private management? Is it not a fact, rather, that concentration of political and economic power in one single hand subjects the working man to a form of dependence which goes far beyond his dependence on the private, individual employer? Look at Russia, and you will see how many rights and privileges a worker enjoys in the state-owned industries! Would you not agree that it is better and wiser to separate political power from economic power and have the state function as an arbiter between capital and labor?'

"For the first time," Dr. Löns says, "I felt the effect of his personality upon me. His manner of speech was dry, matter-of-fact, almost doctrinaire, and occasionally seasoned with biting irony, but his arguments invariably struck home. I fought hard to break out of his encirclement, but again and again he blocked my escape route. Finally I advanced some personal motives. 'I cannot accept the post of party secretary,' I said. 'I have lost six years through the war and must be thankful for having at least firm ground under my feet again. . . .'

"At this Adenauer flew into a bit of a temper. 'And what are we old ones to say,' he asked, 'if the young, for purely selfish reasons, keep aloof from political work?' We struggled for a full two hours. At the end of the interview I was no longer a Christian Socialist but secretary general of the CDU."

The first conference of the Christian Democrats which the new party secretary attended took place at the end of February, 1946, at Neheim-Hüsten near Soest in Westphalia. It was convened by Adenauer who, in this grimmest of postwar winters, had chosen as a meeting place a Catholic convent where the hospitable nuns had placed their cells and the large refectory at the disposal of the five-day conference.

"I shall never forget my first impression of this meeting," says Dr. Löns. "The participants had come from all over the British Zone, and for most of them it had been anything but easy to get there. They came on bicycles and on foot, some had traveled for days in open coal trains, others had managed to thumb lifts from passing British military vehicles. Most of them were men belonging to the older generation, and as they arrived, dirty from the rough journey, exhausted, frozen to the bone, and half starved, they were indeed a true image of Germany's misery.

"Men and women from all walks of life had come together at the oasis of this hospitable nunnery, differing widely in their social origins, their professions and trades, and their political beliefs. There were former members of the Center party among them, old democrats of the Liberal school, Christian trade unionists, and people like myself who, until a short time ago, had believed in the advent of of Christian Socialism in Germany. The only thing they all had truly in common was a passionate determination to lead their country out of its chaotic state.

"It was on this occasion that I learned to appreciate and admire Adenauer's extraordinary skill in handling and guiding people. There were twenty-seven delegates to the conference, and nearly every single one of them had brought his own ideas and his own definite program. Adenauer found himself faced with an avalanche of suggestions, recommendations, and individual wishes. To thrash these out in open discussion and get them under a common denominator would have been utterly impossible in the five days allotted, and the conference would have ended in failure.

"Adenauer, as chairman, proceeded differently. Sitting calmly, arms folded, at the head of the long table, he allowed every one of the delegates first of all to develop his plans and ideas, letting the torrent of speeches rush past him without interfering or engaging in detailed discussion. In the evening, after the debate, he retired to his cell and there wrote down his own thoughts. In this way the constitution of the new party, its 'basic law,' took shape. Although it incorporates many of the suggestions put forward by the conference, it is in all essential points Adenauer's own work.

The introductory paragraphs of the Neheim-Hüsten party program laid down with all possible emphasis and unequivocal firmness the Christian basis and foundation on which the Democratic Union was to rest. This is where Adenauer took his uncompromising stand against all those who had doubted the wisdom and propriety of calling a political party "Christian," thereby mixing up politics and religion. Adenauer was certain that these conscientious doubters were wrong, and in his own hand inserted these words: "A Christian view of life must once more take the place of materialist beliefs.

Materialist principles must make way for the fundamentals of Christian ethics. These must become the determining factors in the reconstruction of the state and in the delimitation of its powers and authority; they must be the guiding principles for the definition of the rights and duties of the individual, for economic and social life, and for the relations of the nations among each other."

Having laid down this principle, the party program centers—as does the Rhöndorf draft—on the essential freedoms of the Christian person and individual. As a safeguard and protection against interference from the state, basic democratic rights are explicitly listed in detail, and their number even enlarged, for, apart from political and religious freedom for the individual, the program expressly calls upon the state for recognition and protection of the family as one of its inherent duties.

Equally, in the economic sphere, individual freedom is stipulated as the overriding principle. It is in this section of the party program that Adenauer develops a number of ideas peculiarly his own. He fears what he calls "the overpowering concentration of economic forces in the hands of single individuals." He recognizes the "demonism of power which tempts those who wield it into arbitrariness and carries, for those who are subjected to it, the risk of losing their freedom and human dignity." Perceiving this danger, "especially in the inborn tendency of Germans toward recklessness and lack of moderation," he never tires of warning against the fatal consequences of this national failing.

As a safeguard against the development of such dangerous tendencies, Adenauer propounds what he terms "the principle of distributed power," a conception which henceforth dominates all his economic thinking and which recurs, in many variants, in all his speeches, conversations, and interviews. What is meant by it is briefly this: Power must never be allowed to concentrate in undue measure in any one place lest it imperil the freedom of the individual, and wherever it appears that such a concentration is in the process of formation, it must be broken up. The practical application of this principle, inevitably, has far-reaching consequences. It implies, first and foremost, a definite rejection of all socialist economic experiments, since they lead to an accumulation of political and economic power in the hands of the state, enabling it eventually to "overpower" the individual. In the same way it implies rejection of the formation of mammoth trusts, concerns, and combines, and the creation of monopolies over entire branches of the economy. Apart from splitting up and decartelizing such organizations and subdividing them into enterprises of normal size, the Neheim-Hüsten program recommends two further safeguards: "equal partnership between employers and employees in management and responsibility," and "the establishment of enterprises based on a mixed economy."

This last idea was a particular favorite of Adenauer's and he advocated it with special urgency in long private conversations with industrial and economic experts in the party.

"Take, for example, the city of Bochum," he would say. "Now Bochum depends for its entire life on the existence and prosperity of its great steel works, the Bochumer Stahlverein. Not only are the workers and salaried staff employed in the steel works entirely dependent upon the prosperity of this one, single enterprise, but also the vast majority of the middle class in the city, tradesmen, craftsmen, and others. What could be more natural than that the municipal administration of the city should be enabled, in one form or another, to exercise a measure of influence upon the fate of this enterprise? And what is true of Bochum is true of any other city harboring within its walls a large industrial enterprise upon which the great majority of the inhabitants, directly or indirectly, depend for their livelihood."

While the "principle of distributed power" is thus essentially a negative measure, intended to ward off the dangers with which the economy threatens the liberty of the individual, the positive side of Adenauer's social concepts finds expression in other parts of the Neheim-Hüsten program. Characteristic of this is Article X of the party platform, which says: "Moderate property is an essential safeguard of the democratic state. The acquisition of moderate property by all those who genuinely and sincerely create wealth and value is to be encouraged."

This term "moderate property" is, for Adenauer, not just a vague phrase but denotes a perfectly concrete proposition. Creative man, Adenauer feels, should have a house and a plot of land which he can call his own. This was one of the aims for which the Chief Mayor of Cologne always strove, and it recurs emphatically in the program of the new political party. This "Immediate Program," as it was called, demands: "The rebuilding of destroyed cities and villages is to be carried out in such a way as to avoid the damage caused by the concentration of too many people in too narrow a space. Wherever necessary the land required for these purposes should be obtained through expropriation."

The conference at Neheim-Hüsten closed with a vote of confidence for Adenauer. He was elected chairman of the CDU in the British Zone and was granted extensive powers to conduct the policy of the new party until the next meeting of the zonal executive committee.

"Couldn't you get us an invitation to the next conference of the NEI at Luxembourg?"

Adenauer had sprung the question one day without warning on his party secretary. The initials NEI stood for *Nouvelle Equipe Internationale*, an unofficial association of parliamentarians from almost all European countries whose aim it was to arrive in open discussion at a common point of view regarding the most important topical problems of European policy.

"There was good and urgent reason for Adenauer's question," Dr. Löns recalls. "The principal subject on the agenda of the forthcoming Luxembourg conference was, 'What is to become of Germany?' Frankly, we thought it a little hard on us that this gathering of Christian politicians should be debating our future without any one of us being present. But the real reason we wished to receive an invitation from the NEI lay deeper. It was this: as time went on, the total lack of international contacts had begun to be a considerable and serious handicap to the activity of our party, and we found ourselves at a particular disadvantage in our controversy with the Social Democrats who were able to rely on their connections with the British Labor Party, and in many respects got the better of us. I did my best, therefore, to obtain this invitation and was very glad when eventually a letter was received from the President of the NEI inviting Dr. Adenauer and myself to attend the Luxembourg conference as guests.

"The trip to Luxembourg," Dr. Löns recalls with a wry smile, "was Adenauer's first journey abroad after the war, and it took place in somewhat grotesque conditions. We were careful to take enough gasoline for the journey there and back, but, of course, we had no money at all. This was before the West German currency reform, and the old inflated German Reichsmark was not accepted outside Germany. I had foreseen this, and a friend of mine in Brussels had promised to meet us at the Hotel Continental in Luxembourg and bring us some foreign currency. But when we arrived he wasn't there.

"After waiting for him for some time in the lobby of the hotel, Adenauer decided to take independent action. He remembered having made, years ago, in his Cologne days, the acquaintance of a Luxembourg politician. 'I shall pay him a courtesy call,' he said. He left, and was back within the hour. 'The reception was very polite.' he reported, 'but I've got no money. My delicate hints at our precarious situation were obviously not understood.' Suppertime approached, and we were still waiting, surrounded by attentive waiters whom we contrived to ignore with as much superior nonchalance as we could muster. Suddenly Adenauer declared, 'Hang it, I'm going to eat now!' He ordered for both us, and ate with a hearty appetite, while I could hardly swallow anything. He watched my embarrassment with sidelong glances, but said nothing. Only when he had finished he remarked, 'I've always made this a rule of my life—do your work as well as you can, and someone will, in the end, take care of the payment.' His optimism was proved justified. My Brussels friend arrived after midnight, having been delayed by the breakdown of his car, and released us from our vexation.

"The conference opened the following day in the great hall of the Luxembourg town hall. Delegates from eighteen nations took part. We Germans were admitted only as observers. An account published in the newspaper *La Libre Belgique* describes our position very aptly. It says: 'The Germans were sitting in the very last row, in a dark corner of the hall. Calm and immobile, with the face of a Tibetan monk, Adenauer listened to the speeches. There were Frenchmen, Dutchmen, Luxembourgers, even some Basque refugees voicing their opinions, all of them dealing most elegantly with the German problem, solving the intricate question of the German economy and settling the issues of German trade unionism—on paper!'

"Toward the end of the congress Dr. Adenauer was invited to speak; but according to the Belgian newspaper he was merely asked to testify 'as a witness on behalf of Germany.' The way he discharged this difficult task was masterly. He made no bones about anything. He frankly admitted what could not be denied—the guilt and responsibility of National Socialism for the Second World War, the misdeeds and atrocities of the Third Reich. He said: 'During the years of National Socialism the German people behaved in such a manner that I despised them. But since 1945 I have learned to feel some renewed respect for my people. . . .' That was the heart of his plea, the refrain to which his argument kept returning: 'Despite all the misdeeds of National Socialism, the German people have a right to claim that they should not be judged solely by this one epoch in their history.'

"On this occasion, as on others, Adenauer's skill consisted in knowing precisely where and when it was advisable not to insist. He deliberately refrained from entering into polemics with previous speakers and pulling their German programs to pieces. But he won the meeting over by an unqualified pledge to a united Christian Europe. He ended with the words: 'Today I regard myself primarily as a European, and only in the second place as a German,' and a wave of applause thanked him. As he walked back to his seat, stiffly erect and with an unmoved face, a Swiss journalist said to me: *'C'est un homme!'*"

Adenauer's success was more than a momentary flash in the pan, for already on the following day the question of admitting the CDU as a member of this "International of Christian Parties" was discussed by the conference. But this was not without its difficulties. The French delegates insisted that in the event of the Germans being admitted the conference should once more plainly and unequivocally reiterate the crimes of which National Socialism was guilty. This pronouncement, however, was couched in terms which discriminated clearly not only against National Socialists but against all Germans generally. Adenauer protested and, when this had no effect, threatened to depart if the conference proved unwilling to delete the offending sentences. There were protracted negotiations, messengers and couriers hurried back and forth between the various hotels through half the night, the French eventually agreed to tone down the wording of the text, but Adenauer insisted on the radical elimination of the controversial passage.

"He got his way in the end," Dr. Löns concludes his account, "and at the next session Germany was admitted into the community of the NEI as a full member."

# CHAPTER XII

It is not easy today, even though hardly more than a decade has passed, to visualize the complex conditions in which a German politician had to work in 1946. A brief summary of the main factors may help in appreciating Adenauer's hopes, doubts, and decisions during these immediate postwar years.

Germany had emerged from her defeat as a constitutional, political, and economic maze of bewildering intricacy which, moreover, continually changed its pattern. The former Reich had been divided up into four zones of occupation, and new political life stirred in all four almost as soon as the fighting had ceased. Supreme governmental authority was vested in the Allied Control Council in Berlin. This should have insured a unified and coherent development throughout the occupied territory, but it found itself incapable of doing so. One of the very few things of practical consequence the Control Council achieved was the "Plan for Reparations and the Level of Postwar German Economy," which was an implementation of the so-called "Potsdam Protocol" and formed the basis for the dismantling of German industry during the following years. The Control Council failed almost immediately in its task of organizing the four zones of occupation as a unified economic area, and it never even attempted to create a unified political structure.

As a result individual occupying powers took such political and economic measures in their respective zones as seemed right and desirable to them, and these were seldom synchronized and often divergent and contradictory. The Soviet Zone very soon went its own way, being deliberately transformed by its occupying power into a Communist satellite state, and in the three Western zones there was, at least in the earlier stages, no uniform development either.

Political reconstruction progressed fastest in the American Zone. As early as the end of August, 1945, General Eisenhower, the then Military Governor, authorized the formation of political parties on a district level, and on September 19, 1945, he subdivided the American Zone, by decree, into three component states, or *länder*—Hesse,

Bavaria, and Württemberg-Baden—each with its own government. At the end of December, 1945, his successor, Lucius D. Clay, authorized the formation of political parties on state level, and on February 28, 1946, the political parties in the American Zone received permission to constitute and organize themselves on a zonal basis. At the end of June, 1946, one year after the end of the war, the states of the American Zone went to the polls and elected their first parliaments, whose primary task it was to draft their own constitutions or "basic laws."

In the British Zone where Adenauer was domiciled and to which his political activity was restricted for the time being, matters progressed much more slowly. The then British Labor Government took the view that the formation of political parties should not be rushed and that it was sounder policy, in the first instance, to promote the reconstruction of the trade unions, and to develop political life and activity from their midst. Thus, political party newspapers were not permitted publication in the British Zone until March, 1946, the same month which witnessed the first trade union congress of the British Zone, at Hanover.

At about the same time a first and cautious attempt was made by the British authorities to enlist the cooperation of representative Germans in the actual administration of their zone. This was the "Zonal Advisory Council," whose members were appointed delegates of the various branches of the civil administration, the political parties, and the trade unions. It was against the background of this assembly that Adenauer played his next part.

There are not many men in Adenauer's immediate sphere of activity who have not succumbed more or less willingly to the somewhat intimidating spell of his forceful personality, and who have kept an open mind and their independent judgment. But there are some, and one of these critical supporters is Dr. Paul Otto, an energetic and progressive industrialist from Osnabrück, who worked closely with Adenauer during the formative period of the CDU. Despite genuine respect and admiration, he is not blind to Adenauer's human weaknesses, and looks upon the Federal Chancellor with surprising, often sardonic, objectivity.

"I first met Dr. Adenauer at the CDU Conference at Herford," Dr. Otto tells. "That was when he made his *coup d'état* and usurped the leadership of the party by appointing himself 'President by seniority' and gripping the reins before the convener of the meeting, Dr. Holzapfel, had recovered from his astonishment. I confess I was rather shocked by Adenauer's tactics, and during the lunch interval, when we were all standing about on the wide staircase of the town hall, I remarked to an acquaintance, 'This Dr. Adenauer is a talented man but too impertinent for my liking.' When I turned round, I found myself looking Adenauer straight in the face. He was standing one step above me and must have heard every word. But he said nothing and merely gave me a friendly smile.

"That was our first encounter. I met him next at the CDU party conference at Neheim-Hüsten, at the end of February, 1946. It was during this conference that the newly constituted CDU received an invitation from the British Military Government to send a delegate to the Zonal Advisory Council which was to be inaugurated at Hamburg early the following month. Now, this Zonal Advisory Council was a body appointed by the British, with the sole task of advising Military Government on its measures, and it possessed no actual powers of any sort. Our meeting considered who should go to Hamburg and represent the party. When someone mentioned Adenauer, he rose immediately and declared roundly, 'No, I shan't go. There's nothing doing there. Politically, the Zonal Advisory Council is a dead end. I suggest we send Dr. Otto.' And again he gave me a friendly smile.

"As a result I was unanimously elected chief delegate, with Adenauer as my deputy. Naturally I felt rather uncomfortable about this. Adenauer was not only much older than I, but also, politically, incomparably more experienced. Therefore, when we drove up to Hamburg together, I asked him to change places with me. He refused flatly. When I argued my lack of political experience, he remarked with a touch of irony, 'Oh, but we can soon put that right,' and there and then, in the car, gave me the necessary instructions. His advice was brief and pointed, and some of his guiding maxims I have remembered to this day. 'Never tell a lie,' he said, 'not even in politics, because you will never be able to remember all the things you've said. Never attack anyone who is not present and cannot defend himself. But if he's there, don't be mealy-mouthed and let him have it. If there are unpleasant things, put them squarely on the table for everyone to see!'

"His eyes sparkled with mischief as he gave me this lesson," Dr. Otto continues, "and I had great trouble getting him back onto the subject which was worrying me: I still wanted him to take my place as leader of the CDU delegation to the Zonal Advisory Council. Obviously, my embarrassment amused him greatly, and he kept me on tenterhooks until we arrived in Hamburg. That was his revenge for my remark at Herford. It was not until eleven o'clock at night, as we drove up to his *pension,* that he suddenly said, 'All right, then, if I can do you a favor, let's swap places!' "

The inaugural meeting of the Zonal Advisory Council took place on the morning of March 6, 1946, in the building of the former Hamburg Military District Command, and the British had dressed it up in military fashion.

"I was standing beside Adenauer by the window," Dr. Otto recalls, "when there was a sudden roll of drums and a fanfare of trumpets and Marshal of the Royal Air Force Sir Sholto Douglas, the British Commander in Chief and Military Governor, appeared on the scene. Dr. Robert Lehr, Administrative President of the Rhine Province as he then was, introduced us. First to be presented to the Military Governor was Dr. Kurt Schumacher who, as leader of the Social Democratic party, enjoyed the particular sympathies of the British Labor Government. Sir Sholto gripped Schumacher's left hand with both of his own—Schumacher had lost his right arm in the First World War—shaking it with marked cordiality. Adenauer glanced at his watch. Douglas and Schumacher talked for a long time. What was said we couldn't hear, but Douglas laughed loudly several times, and Schumacher, too, smiled. After a considerable time Douglas passed on. Again Adenauer looked at his watch. 'Fifteen minutes,' he whispered to me. 'You'll see, it won't take that long with us.'

"Next the Military Governor stood facing Adenauer. Adenauer was introduced. Sir Sholto asked genially, 'Well, *Herr Oberbürgermeister*, and what was your political career?' Adenauer answered, 'Oh, in 1917 I became Chief Mayor of Cologne. In 1933 I was dismissed by the National Socialists because of political unreliability. In March, 1945, I was reinstated by the Americans, and in October of the same year I was dismissed once more, by the English, because of incompetence. That's why I am now in the Zonal Advisory Council.' For a moment

Douglas stared at Adenauer, speechless. Then he walked on, without a word. 'You see,' Adenauer said to me. 'With us it has taken exactly one minute and forty-five seconds!'

"After the official reception," Dr. Otto continues, "I was taken aside by Hinrich W. Kopf, who was then the Administrative President of Hanover Province. I knew him from Hanover. He was a member of the Socialist Party and very much in Schumacher's confidence. 'You know,' Kopf said to me, 'we ought to make a real effort to get our two party chiefs together for a round-table talk. It must be possible for us to agree on a common German standpoint with which to face the occupying powers. You get to work on Adenauer. I'll deal with Schumacher.' In the evening there was a dinner for the members of the Zonal Advisory Council in the great hall of the Hamburg Town Hall. After the official part was over, Kopf again turned to me. 'Well, how are things going?' he asked. 'Adenauer is willing,' I answered. 'So is Schumacher,' said he. An hour later the two men were sitting together around the same table in a corner of the hall."

Kurt Schumacher was then at the height of his influence. His party was the acknowledged favorite of the British occupying power. The then British Government party, anxious to maintain good and close relations with the German Social Democrats, had invited Schumacher on a visit to London as early as November, 1946. The leader of the Social Democratic party was generally regarded as the head of the future German state. Dr. Otto recalls an incident when delegates of various parties were standing together talking and Schumacher's tall, emaciated frame passed the group. "Here comes the future German Reich Chancellor," one of them said. And no one contradicted him.

Abroad Schumacher was generally regarded as the acknowledged representative of the new Germany. His incisive speeches and sharp, cutting remarks, peppered with biting irony, were widely quoted and extensively commented upon. Schumacher possessed an unusual gift for the apt phrase and hard-hitting, off-the-cuff metaphors. Sayings of his, such as "The modern democracies seem to regard the Horsemen of the Apocalypse as their cavalry," stuck in people's minds and became well-known quotations.

Adenauer could rarely be heard to make brilliant remarks of this kind. He drew his effect from dry, closely argued speeches in which he led even his reluctant hearers, step by step, along an unbroken chain of logical argument toward the conclusion to which he wanted to commit them. These demonstrations of sound common sense were seldom interrupted by sarcastic hits at his opponents or samples of the specific Cologne humor which can be of an almost Gallic acidity. Adenauer mastered it as well as anyone, but in his public utterances rarely made use of it.

"I have always believed more in men than in programs," Dr. Otto says, "and I have often wondered what would have become of Germany if Schumacher had gained the leadership. Of course, such speculations after the event are on the whole idle, but still, I believe one can safely say this: the leader of the Social Democratic party would never have been able to restore foreign confidence in the trustworthiness and reliability of the Germans to the extent achieved by Dr. Adenauer—this fund of trust and confidence which today is Germany's greatest foreign asset. It is true enough that Schumacher's nerves had suffered terribly from years spent in concentration camps. But, even had this not been so, I feel his temperament most probably would not have been able to resist the temptation, in a critical situation, of trumping with the possibility of a political alternative and thus forfeiting his partner's trust. There was only one thing these two men, who now sat facing me, had in common: both their faces bore the stamp of a hard and cruel fate."

Schumacher opened the conversation. Without beating about the bush he went straight to the two central problems which, at that time, dominated the thinking of every German: the food situation and industrial dismantling. "We've got to hammer it into the Allies' heads," he said, "that their endeavors to win the German people to the idea of democracy are doomed to failure unless the occupying powers honor the obligations placed upon them by our unconditional surrender. Their total victory entails, for them, a total obligation, and we Germans must refuse to be shouldered with the responsibility for conditions which are beyond our control and upon which we have no influence."

Regarding industrial dismantling, Schumacher said, "It is clear that a reduction to an exclusively agrarian economy as envisaged by the Morgenthau Plan would be tantamount to an economic atom bomb for Germany. Here, too, we've got to make it clear to the Allies that the dismantling of our industries is the worst and most unsuitable form of obtaining reparations. You don't kill the goose if you're after its golden eggs!" It was a phrase which recurred frequently, in different variants, in Schumacher's later speeches.

"Although we were talking only in a small group," Dr. Otto recalls, "Schumacher spoke with a loud and animated voice, his face twitching with nervous tension and his left hand underlining his words with emphatic gestures. When he had ended, Adenauer said drily, 'It will not have escaped your attention, Herr Schumacher, that the CDU at their party conference at Neheim-Hüsten adopted two resolutions which say exactly the same thing, in different words!' Schumacher nodded briefly. For a moment we all hoped that agreement on the two questions which Schumacher himself had described as the central problems would lead to a joint effort by the two men. It could have meant the beginning of a common foreign policy.

"But then Schumacher said, 'In these circumstances I should be ready for some form of cooperation between us. But there is one condition: yourself and your young party, Herr Adenauer, will have to recognize the SPD's claim for leadership. I don't think this is an unwarranted demand. Every objective observer must admit, after all, that the SPD is, and will remain, the largest party with the best prospects for the future.'

"Adenauer replied icily, 'Personally, I'm of a different opinion. I don't believe the SPD will in the future be the largest party. And I feel the decision about this should be left to the coming elections.'

"For a moment," Dr. Otto concludes, "silence reigned around our table. Everyone felt conscious of one thing: something irrevocable had happened. The struggle between the SPD and the CDU had begun."

The skepticism Adenauer had felt from the very beginning regarding the work of the Zonal Advisory Council was soon justified by actual procedure. The Council met once a month at Hamburg for a session lasting two or three days. Its agenda was drawn up jointly by a German secretariat and a British liaison staff, which meant in practice that the British informed the Germans which subjects should come up for debate. German suggestions had to be submitted to the British liaison staff, who were free to decide whether they should be included in the agenda, or rejected. There was no appeal against these decisions, and the public was excluded from the debates.

The general tone and attitude, too, was anything but friendly and cooperative, at any rate in the beginning. There was a characteristic and much quoted instance when Sir Cecil Weir, chief of the Economics Division of Military Government, rejected a German complaint about the reduction of the fat ration to eight grams daily with the classic remark: "Fats serve no other purpose than to improve the taste of food and render it more easily digestible. The nutritive value of fat is being much exaggerated. Fats do not become necessary until total daily food consumption exceeds 3,500 calories." When the German representatives showed their unwillingness to accept these strange views and on their part mobilized German scientific experts who protested emphatically against Sir Cecil's idea of "fat as a lubricant," a member of Military Government, Mr. Lennox, officially called the Zonal Advisory Council to order: "Gentlemen, I would warn you not to overrate the importance of your own affairs. This always makes a bad impression with us."

Incidents of this kind did not help to create a cooperative atmosphere, and it took some time before these initial acerbities disappeared from the debates. Even greater were the difficulties encountered in the beginning with regard to the second major problem—industrial dismantling. Discussion of this subject in the Zonal Advisory Council was at first prohibited altogether. It was argued that dismantling was closely related to the question of reparations, and this had been settled, on a four-power basis, with the Soviet Union in the Allied Control Council. It is to Adenauer's credit that he refused to accept this proposition and endeavored to obtain a change in the ruling. He went to Berlin and sought an interview with the Deputy Military Governor, General Sir Brian Robertson, informing him in clear terms that the Zonal Advisory Council would inevitably forfeit its entire prestige and authority with the German people if it were debarred from discussing what were, after all, the most important political questions of the day. General Robertson was not slow to see the point of this argument, and henceforth the problem of dismantling was admitted to the agenda, at least as far as the discussion of exceptionally harsh individual cases was concerned.

Adenauer's procedure in this particular instance was characteristic of his realistic approach in any given situation. He had, admittedly, at first regarded the Zonal Advisory Council as a kind of shadow parliament where "politically, nothing was likely to happen," and for this reason he had originally been unwilling to join it. But, once he had joined it, he did everything he could to lead the Council out of its shadow existence and help it to gain genuine influence and authority. He never tired of complaining, frequently in public, of the restrictions imposed upon the German representatives. "We are permitted to discuss the tax on bicycles," he said, "but we are allowed no influence on taxation policy as a whole. Social insurance and land reform, two things which are of decisive importance for the future of Germany, are removed from our competence and are being dealt with by some other bodies appointed by the British without reference to us."

In these circumstances any German politician must have felt considerable temptation to turn his back on this institution and let the occupying powers carry on alone as best they could, trusting that before long they would make thoroughgoing fools of themselves. It seemed inevitable that cooperation in these unfavorable and often almost humiliating conditions must in the long run severely damage the reputation of a politician with his own people and potential electorate. Undoubtedly, there were moments when Adenauer, like the rest of his German colleagues in the Zonal Advisory Council, gave serious thought to this aspect of the matter. But it is characteristic of him that he should not have yielded to this perfectly understandable inclination. For who was likely to profit if the occupying powers made a mess of things, and fools of themselves? The answer was—no one, certainly not the German people. Of course it would not have been difficult to make demagogic capital out of such a mess. Indeed, it would have been easy, temporarily, for such an "upright German" to gain applause from the hungry and despairing masses. But in the last resort this would have been a nationalist, not a national, attitude, and Adenauer was always careful, then as later, to make this fundamental distinction.

Adenauer had no illusions about the Zonal Advisory Council. It was a highly imperfect instrument to wield on behalf of the German cause. But it was not wholly useless or unsuitable, and above all, it was better than no instrument at all. This, to Adenauer's mind, was the decisive point, and he did everything he could to improve the instrument and make it more efficient. There were many ways, he found, in which this could be done.

"For instance, there were the minutes of the meetings of the

Zonal Advisory Council," Dr. Otto recalls. "They were censored by the British liaison staff before being released to the press, and contained only the measures adopted by the Council. Adenauer insisted that they should also contain the motions submitted by the German representatives which had been rejected or defeated. The German public, he felt, were entitled to know what its delegates were trying to achieve and whether and why they had failed to achieve it. In another instance, some German tax office appealed to the Zonal Advisory Council for help and guidance, and Adenauer seized the opportunity to demand the setting up of a Finance Committee. His request was granted, and the Finance Committee was able, in due course, to exercise considerable influence upon the development of the German economy. Among other things it prepared a huge experts' report of more than a thousand pages which two years later served as a basis for the introduction of currency reform.

"Looking back and speaking quite generally," Dr. Otto thinks, "it would be wrong to underrate the influence which the Zonal Advisory Council gradually acquired for itself. It is true that its decisions had no legislative force or authority—it had never been intended to have more than an advisory capacity—but even so the way was prepared, here in Hamburg, for many of Germany's future political decisions, primarily for the 'Basic Law' or Constitution of the Federal Republic. But more important still than this practical work was the gradual change in the psychological climate between the occupiers and occupied to which the Zonal Advisory Council contributed to a considerable degree."

However, the friendly atmosphere in the Zonal Advisory Council which had gradually established itself could not conceal from the German politicians the sad fact that they were, in truth, working in a vacuum and without solid ground beneath their feet. Men like Adenauer and Schumacher had been called upon by the occupying power to cooperate in an advisory capacity because, as leaders of large political parties with clearly formulated political, economic, and cultural programs, they stood in the public limelight. But neither the occupying power, nor, indeed, the party leaders themselves knew as yet with any certainty how large these parties were and how much support they enjoyed among the German people. Very properly

Adenauer had drawn Schumacher's attention to the fact that neither of them as yet possessed a popular mandate. The reconstruction and reorganization of political life on a broad basis was hampered at every turn by restrictive ordinances, and for the present there was no question of a general election which alone could have revealed the true proportions of strength and given the leaders a genuine mandate, if not to take decisions, at least to speak their minds in the name of the people.

All important decisions were taken without the participation of the German representatives, and in all cases where they were asked by the occupying power for their views or even for their approval, they were compelled to act on their own personal authority without being certain of popular support. It was a perpetual dilemma which required men of sure instinct, firm self-assurance, and an uncommon readiness to assume responsibility to overcome it.

A characteristic example of Adenauer's attitude in a dilemma of this kind was the establishment of the "land" or state of North Rhine-Westphalia, in the British Zone.

In July, 1946, Adenauer and Schumacher received an invitation to go to Berlin for a conference with General Sir Brian Robertson, the then Deputy British Military Governor. A British aircraft took them to Berlin, and together with two Berlin representatives they were received at Military Government Headquarters, in Fehrbelliner Platz. The day was July 18, 1946. One of the participants in the meeting later described it as follows:

"Lieutenant General Robertson, then a man of fifty, almost of the same age as Schumacher but nearly twenty years younger than Adenauer, welcomed the German representatives in his own courteously correct but always somewhat reserved way, talking at first separately with each of the German representatives. It was noted then that Schumacher would invariably address the Military Governor as 'Herr General,' while Adenauer, deliberately emphasizing the civilian nature of their relationship, spoke to him as 'Sir Brian.'

"After this brief personal conversation, the General turned to the purpose of the meeting. He informed his visitors that British Military Government had decided to create in their zone of occupation a completely new constitutional entity—the 'land' North Rhineland-Westphalia. An A.D.C. outlined on a map the borders of the new territory, and General Robertson himself gave a brief explanation of the reasons which had prompted this surprising measure. The refusal of the Soviet Union to agree to a unification of the four zones of occupation, he indicated, had caused the British and the United States government to plan for consolidation of political and economic conditions in the parts of Germany under their control and the placing of things on more durable foundations with the least possible delay. The establishment of the state North Rhine-Westphalia was a first and important step in this direction.

"Having given this explanation, the General inquired of the representatives of the two great German political parties whether they were in agreement with this measure.

"Schumacher answered, 'No, Herr General.'

"Adenauer replied, 'Yes, Sir Brian.'

"That ended the interview. As they left the room Adenauer, with a slight movement of his head toward Schumacher, murmured to his companion, 'He's a Prussian, after all.'"

What prompted Adenauer to take this attitude?

This was, it seemed, a particularly glaring instance of the occupying power interfering unilaterally and drastically with the constitutional structure of Germany without taking the prior advice of those German politicians they had expressly appointed to advise them. The measure as such was an accomplished fact. Adenauer knew as well as Schumacher that a "No" from the German party leaders, however determined, could not possibly undo it. But he knew also that the British Government had its reasons for trying to obtain the subsequent agreement of the German party leaders, and that in so agreeing, despite his present lack of authority and influence, he committed himself to a measure of joint responsibility for the future. He was prepared to assume this responsibility, although he foresaw that his "Yes" was likely to be misunderstood and would be interpreted by his opponents as an excessive willingness to yield to Allied wishes, a reproach which later on was, in fact, leveled against him more than once by the Social Democrats. Of course, there was neither point nor purpose in saying no. But was it necessary, for that reason, to give an unreserved "Yes" for an answer? Many people might ask themselves that.

But Adenauer knew very well why he had said, "Yes." All these doubts and reservations could not, in the last resort, prevent him from considering the issue coolly and on its merits. And the fact was that the establishment of the state of North Rhine-Westphalia was a measure which he, as a politician, in the situation as it then was, was bound to welcome.

What was this situation?

General Robertson had told his visitors no more than what any German with an interest in politics already knew perfectly well in the summer of 1946, namely, that the attempt of the four occupying powers to coordinate their German policies under a common denominator had practically ended in failure, and that this failure was due mainly to the attitude taken by the Soviet Union and France.

Not only the Russians had acted unilaterally in their zone. The French were pursuing their own schemes as well. As early as August, 1945, a French Government commission had taken over the administration of the Saar Territory, which henceforth was treated separately from the rest of the French zone of occupation. In February, 1946, the French Government, as a next step, had demanded that the establishment of a central administration for all four zones be preceded by either an internationalization of the Ruhr area, or, as an alternative, a total destruction of the Ruhr's industrial potential, coupled with a permanent military occupation of the Rhineland. These demands had been supported by the Soviet Government.

Then came a surprise development. At the conference of the four Foreign Ministers which met in Paris on April 25, 1946, the Soviet Union suddenly changed its ground. Foreign Minister Molotov dropped his support for the French demand for internationalization of the Ruhr and declared himself emphatically in favor of a unified treatment of Germany. At the same time, however, he rejected all suggestions put forward by the Western powers aiming in this direction, including a "draft plan for the preparation of a peace treaty with Germany" and a proposal made by the United States Secretary of State, James F. Byrnes, for the disarmament and occupation of Germany over a period of twenty-five years.

What was the purpose underlying the Russian attitude?

Adenauer had his own views about this, and at the next meeting of the zonal executive committee of the CDU he explained them in detail to his party friends, giving at the same time a full exposition of the reasons which had prompted him to agree to the establishment of the North Rhine-Westphalia state. He said:

"Apparently Russia has come to recognize that she cannot hope to obtain control over the whole of Germany with the help of the German Communist party and sections of the Socialist party alone. That is why, it seems to me, she is now trying to hoist the national flag on behalf of Germany. The aim of this is clear enough. Russia is trying to win the support of the whole of the German people by proclaiming herself a champion of unified Germany—under Soviet leadership and domination, as we may be entitled to add in parentheses. I believe the danger threatening from this direction is so great that for the first time it has compelled England to take swift and decisive action by creating this new state of North Rhine-Westphalia."

Next Adenauer dealt with the policy of France, and here he was on ground thoroughly familiar to him. A wit once remarked that Adenauer's vocabulary comprised no more than 300 words but the remarkable thing about them was that he always used them in the right way, at the right time, in the right place. There would be more justification in saying that Adenauer's political concept comprises only a few basic ideas which consistently recur and to which he has adhered stubbornly and steadfastly through the decades.

One of them is undoubtedly the idea of creating a large West German state within the constitutional framework of the Reich. He first developed this idea in 1919, in a speech made before prominent representatives of public life in the Rhineland when it was his purpose to frustrate French moves aiming at the seizure of the left bank of the Rhine. Now, twenty-seven years later, the same basic conception recurred as he explained to his political friends in the CDU why it was with an eye on France that he had approved the establishment of North Rhine-Westphalia.

Reminding his listeners of the French demands of February, 1946, he declared that the creation of the state of North Rhine-Westphalia placed an almost insuperable obstacle in the path of French claims for a separation of the left bank of the Rhine or an internationalization of the Ruhr. Indeed, among this circle of close political friends, he went further and confessed frankly that he would have liked to see this new state made even larger, comprising in addition the provinces of Rhenish Hesse, the Rhine Palatinate, Hesse-Nassau, and the Saar Territory.

Was not this particularism, indeed, downright separatism? On the contrary, Adenauer asserted, it was a decisive measure for the retention of the unity of the Reich and the prevention of territorial secessions!

He emphasized again, as he had done twenty-seven years earlier, that it was not from nationalist motives that this solution recommended itself to him. Again, on the contrary! "A West German state of this size," he pointed out, "which in its economic structure and in the general outlook of its people is necessarily orientated toward co-operation with the West is the most reliable safeguard for peace and the best guarantee of French security. France must, and will, understand this, and renounce her plans to split up Germany or annex German territory."

Having thus justified his own point of view, Adenauer went on to explain to his friends why, in his opinion, Schumacher had disapproved of the creation of North Rhine-Westphalia. With a touch of calculated irony, he pointed out that a new state which comprised only the industrial areas of the Ruhr would undoubtedly have been welcomed by the Social Democrats. As the Ruhr was a traditional stronghold of the Socialist parties, such a state would have turned it into a parade ground for Marxist ideology. As it was, however, Adenauer hinted, the CDU also had reason from a purely party political point of view to be satisfied with the new arrangement, since the inclusion of the Rhineland with its predominantly conservative population now offered a chance of breaking the hold of the Socialist parties upon the industrial areas.

The minutes of the meeting record unanimous approval of Adenauer's statement. What was more, his exposition convinced not only his party associates but also a man of whom Adenauer most certainly did not think at that moment, but whose trust and support were, before long, to become a most valuable asset. From his office in the I. G. Farben building at Frankfurt, the United States Deputy Military Governor, General Lucius DuBignon Clay, reported to his government in Washington:

"Of particular interest is the support which the CDU gives to a united Western Europe and to a reconciliation with France."

Adenauer's estimate of the eventual distribution of strength between the various political parties in the new state of North Rhine-Westphalia was proved substantially correct before the year was out. Early in October, 1946, British Military Government summoned the first *Landtag*, or diet, of North Rhine-Westphalia for its inaugural meeting. This body, however, which looked like a parliament but in all essentials wasn't one, could only be regarded as a transitory solution. It possessed neither legislative nor executive powers, and its members were not elected but appointed by the occupying authorities on the basis of proposals submitted to them by the parties. It consisted of a total of 200 deputies, and their seats were distributed among the parties according to a key which had been worked out very roughly from the results of the last free elections in Germany, in 1933. Accordingly there were seventy-one Social Democrat, sixty-six CDU, and thirty-four Communist deputies, while the old Center party was represented by eighteen, the Free Democratic party by nine, and two members were independents.

This distribution soon turned out to be entirely misleading. Communal elections which took place in the British zone on October 2, 1946, for the first time brought to light the true distribution of political forces in the new Germany. Military Government agreed to a request for revision, and appointed a new land parliament whose composition accorded more closely with the new position. The young CDU was the chief beneficiary of this correction. There could no longer be any question of a Socialist claim to leadership such as Schumacher had staked in his fateful conversation with Adenauer only a few months ago. The number of CDU mandates rose from sixty-six to ninety-two, while the SPD were reduced from seventy-one to sixty-six. Even greater were the losses of the Communists, who dropped to fifteen seats, or very nearly half their previous strength. Adenauer's optimism regarding the potential chances of a Christian party proved fully justified, and he could look forward to the "big elections" with calm assurance.

His own personal position within his party was equally secure. His ascendancy was no longer seriously disputed. The first meeting of the CDU deputies at Düsseldorf elected him leader of the parliamentary party in the new Landtag.

This first meeting of the parliamentary party was an unusual and memorable occasion, as Dr. Bruno Six, one of the members, recalls. Since all available meeting halls in Düsseldorf were either damaged by bombs or requisitioned by the occupation forces, the ninety-two CDU members gathered in a small, windowless, badly ventilated, and badly lit movie hall. Here, in a decidedly gloomy and depressing atmosphere, the first discussions took place which were to decide the future strategy and tactics of the new party upon its first entry into parliamentary life. The chief question to be settled was whether on important occasions the party should act as a bloc and whether the institution of the "whip" should be introduced to enforce party discipline. Almost at once Adenauer protested.

"We were all most surprised," Dr. Six tells, "to see Adenauer oppose this idea with passionate determination. He would have absolutely no truck with it. To him the freedom of conscience of every single member in any kind of division was inviolable and inalienable. In great agitation he exclaimed, 'Should there be a majority in favor of introducing a party whip and compulsory voting, I regret I could not be chairman of the parliamentary party, and indeed I should not feel able even to remain a member of it!' "

It was a genuine Adenauer sentence, and most revealing of the man and the part he was henceforth to play in German political and parliamentary life. Naturally, it can be argued that Adenauer at this particular moment somewhat despotically used his personal authority, and his undeniable indispensability, to exert pressure upon his colleagues and impose his will. Charges of this kind were often brought in later years against the Federal Chancellor and leader of a coalition government, and they are not unfounded. But there is little doubt that, if Adenauer coerced his colleagues on this occasion, he did so because he was looking beyond it and was anxious to establish a precedent for the sake of what was to him a higher principle. Individual conscience remained to him the highest authority, in the realm of political decisions as well. It was a principle which in later years was to cause him many an uncomfortable moment, within his own party and in the Federal Parliament, but he firmly adhered to it. His categorical rejection of the party whip deprived him on more than one occasion of the chance of throwing the full weight of his own party in the balance of an important decision. But in view of past German experiences it was probably a wise renunciation, since it did much to banish the danger of a one-party dictatorship riding rough-shod over the new parliamentary democracy.

Among the general mass of the bankrupt's estate which the vanished Hitler Germany had left in the hands of its liquidators, the Ruhr area represented undoubtedly by far the most valuable asset.

Coal and steel were basic commodities most desperately needed, inside and outside Germany, and despite large-scale devastation the industrial area of the Ruhr was still one of their most important producers. Although actual production was still modest, its potential resources were enormous, and, as reconstruction slowly got under way, the question arose on what principles it should proceed.

What was to be the future basic structure of the Ruhr industries? Everyone was aware of the danger of a powerful concentration of economic strength in a comparatively small area and in comparatively few hands. Its evil effects had been experienced before. How was its resurgence to be prevented? By socializing the entire complex of the Ruhr industries, lock, stock, and barrel, as was demanded by Socialists and Communists? Or was it possible to leave these important basic industries in the hands of private enterprise? If this was desirable, as the CDU thought it was, what safeguards could be adopted to guard against a recurrence of the fatal mistakes of the past?

These were the major problems facing the new North Rhine-Westphalia parliament. But it did not seem likely, at any rate, not in the beginning, that this parliament would ever get around to grappling with these issues and to taking decisions of such magnitude. To begin with, the working conditions of the new assembly were as unfavorable as they could be. As no suitable premises could be found in the whole of Düsseldorf, the parliament was reduced to deliberating in the private theater of the Henkel works, with the president and his officers occupying the stage among props and pieces of scenery, and the deputies crowded into the auditorium. Secondly, this parliament barely managed, as it was, to deal with a host of urgent day-to-day matters which crowded in upon it: food and essential consumer goods had to be provided for the starving population, fuel had to be found against the approaching winter, the never-ending stream of "returnees" and refugees had to be looked after.

It was not until March, 1947, in the last month of its existence, that this parliament at last found time to get to grips with the big task of determining the future shape and structure of the key industries of the Ruhr—coal, iron, and chemicals. Each of the four parties, CDU, SPD, Free Democrats, and Communists, had prepared their own motions and draft bills, and each set represented a complete blueprint for the future structure of Germany's economy.

The program of the CDU was contained in six separate and detailed motions signed by Adenauer. Their salient point was expressed in the demand for a "change in the structure of economic ownership and power," and this change or reordering was to be based on the "principle of distributed power" as embodied in the CDU programs adopted at Neheim-Hüsten and Ahlen. It provided for the future participation of land and local governments, communal organizations, workers, employees, and cooperative societies in the ownership and management of all industrial enterprises.

This participation was to be subject to two basic stipulations: first, representatives of nonprivate capital were to participate in the issued share capital of these companies in such a way that they should together command an absolute majority of votes in the shareholders' meeting, but no nonprivate shareholder must alone and singly command such an absolute majority of votes; secondly, no shareholder representing private capital must command more than 10 per cent, no shareholder representing nonprivate capital more than 15 per cent of all votes in the shareholders' meeting, either directly or indirectly.

In contrast to this the Communists demanded total expropriation of all relevant enterprises without compensation and their transfer to state ownership, whereas the Social Democrats asked that besides the state the trade unions should be given a substantial share in ownership and management.

The great debate, for which each party had mobilized its most authoritative and effective speakers, began at 10:15 A. M. on March 4, 1947, and it was followed with tense interest throughout Western Germany. It derived particular significance from the fact that it was the last debate of its kind which would take place before the first free general elections in the Ruhr and Rhineland, and, as these elections were but six weeks away, this great fundamental discussion served as an opening shot in the election campaign and was bound to have an important influence on the result of the poll. The issue itself has meantime long been superseded by events. The interest and fascination of the debate lies in the fact that it gives us a first full-dress view of Adenauer as a debater and parliamentarian.

The overture was disappointing. The Communist speaker, Josef Ledwohn, contented himself with delivering a harangue against "monopoly capitalism" and its sins in the past, ending upon the assertion that the CDU draft bills were no more than a capitalist maneuver to relegate the problem of state ownership once and for all to cold storage. This evoked little response. Of more interest was the spokesman of the Social Democrats, Fritz Henssler, who subjected the CDU motions to a detailed and aggressive analysis, trying to show that they were, in essence, a patchwork quilt of basically contradictory and incompatible views.

"The CDU draft bill," Henssler said, "is undoubtedly a collective piece of work. It bears the stamp of many different and differing minds and tendencies having been at work. They have obviously tried to give a little to everyone, and in attempting to do this they have drifted far away from the basic concept of socialization. . . ."

The main direction of the Socialist attack thus soon became clear. It was to show up the CDU as an agglomeration of conflicting interests and ideas without fundamental unity and without a clear-cut and coherent policy. The opponents of the CDU had apparently come to the conclusion that the dominant personality of Adenauer was the main bracket holding this heterogeneous party together, and their polemical attacks were therefore aimed chiefly at him personally. The debate, on their part, developed into a concentric attempt to undermine and shake Adenauer's hold on his own party, with a good measure of personal defamation of one kind or another thrown in. It culminated in an attack by the Communist deputy, Heinz Renner, with whom Adenauer was to have many a parliamentary brush in later years. Renner declared:

"I don't know, Herr Adenauer, in which concern or combine you are a shareholder. On the day I know it, I shall tell it openly. But one thing we do know even now—that you *are* a shareholder. And we also know that even a wily old fox will one day walk into a trap!"

Adenauer was well aware that his opponents were aiming at the undermining of his authority and the disruption of his party. But he did not allow himself to be provoked into personal polemics, leaving all personal accusations, some of them downright slanderous, unanswered. When he rose to reply, he confined himself deliberately to answering factual criticism leveled against the program of his party. This, however, he did with consummate skill and a dexterity which could surprise only those who had forgotten that the former Chief Mayor of Cologne had once enjoyed the reputation of being a most formidable and redoubtable opponent in debate.

He made straight for the most delicate point which had been raised

—the alleged disunity and differences of opinion in his own party. "We in the CDU," he said, "are in complete and unanimous agreement about the great work we propose to undertake—and indeed, what we are submitting to you here will one day be called a great piece of work in the history of economics—we are all agreed, I say, every one of us, irrespective of his class or station in life, irrespective of whether he happens to be employer or worker, farmer or manufacturer, we've all taken up our position together, jointly, with ranks firmly closed, on this issue.

"Ladies and gentlemen, let me say this to you. If a great party is to come together in common agreement on an issue involving such specific and decisive demands as this, it is no more than natural that there must be a certain amount of give and take, that there must be concessions here and there to the other fellow's point of view. If we in the CDU were all to think uniformly along identical lines, we should soon have another National Socialist party, and that is not really what we want, is it? There is only one thing which matters: that opposing and even contradictory views can be freely voiced, also, inside the party, that people of differing opinions should do their best to persuade and convince each other, and that, when all has been said that needed saying, mutual concessions are made and a sound compromise is found. It is only in this way that genuine progress is achieved, and the gentlemen of the Socialist party will be able to consider themselves fortunate on the day when they have succeeded—as I hope and wish they will succeed—in placing their own so widely divergent views under a common denominator, as we have done!"

No doubt, these words were directed not only at the Social Democrats but equally at Adenauer's own supporters. They showed very clearly what he had had in mind when he rejected the idea of compulsory party discipline. They were not only a reminder to his opponents but also a warning to his own friends not to allow themselves to be deprived again of their invaluable advantage and privilege of freedom of thought, opinion, and speech.

Next, Adenauer explained in detail his party's ideas about the proposed decartelization of large concerns and the future management of the national economy, and with passionate insistence rejected the elimination of the employer's private initiative which had been demanded by both Socialist parties.

"If the German people are ever to rise again from their present state of abject misery," he declared, "if they ever work their way up to prosperity again, they will owe this rise solely to the initiative of the individual, and never to the bureaucracy of the state. Herr Henssler is defeating himself with his own proposals. He wants to turn over ownership of the shares to the state but he is not prepared to grant the state the right of interference in management. Well, then, why isn't he? Apparently because in this respect he has more confidence in the others than he has in the state. Because he believes that the trade unionists to whom he is prepared to grant this right will show some personal initiative. What else do we demand but that full use should be made of the personal initiative of the individual? Are we demanding anything different if we suggest that private capital should be allowed an opportunity to participate, and that individuals should play their full part in the reconstruction of Germany's economy? We shall always stand in need of the initiative of every single individual in Germany, or else our people will become again what they have been during the past twelve years, a blind herd and shapeless mass!"

Up to this point it was Adenauer the party politician and party leader who had spoken, trying to define the aims of his party and marking them out against those of the rest. Now it was the turn of Adenauer the statesman. Moving the entire problem of state ownership of basic industries with one stroke into an entirely new light, he now asked the assembly to give thought and consideration to some aspects of the matter which no one, so far, had mentioned with a single word. And these aspects were of overriding importance. The parties had treated the problem of socialization, Adenauer pointed out, as though this were a matter of purely and exclusively German concern, which they alone had to settle, and in which no one else was able, or had a right, to interfere. This, Adenauer now pointed out, was a thoroughly naive and unrealistic way of looking at it. It required vision and farsightedness to recognize that, in those critical spring months of 1947, every measure taken in internal German affairs must automatically lead to consequences and repercussions in the field of foreign affairs, and it required courage to state openly what these consequences were likely to be.

"Germany will remain politically weak," Adenauer declared, "for long years to come. Once this politically weak German state has become owner of these industries, the slightest political pressure on the part of any other powerful nation will suffice to bring about such economic changes as may be in the interest of these more powerful neighbors. I believe that, precisely for national reasons and in view of Germany's present position, no German should lend his hand to schemes which would transfer these vital industries, on which our entire life depends, to the control of a state which is politically weak and helplessly vulnerable to every kind of foreign pressure. I believe that the day will come when the rules of international law will apply again, and it is one of the rules of international law that the property of private individuals, as well as that of communities and similar associations, is protected against seizure by occupying powers. Such property is protected by international law. It is for these reasons, for eminently national reasons, that I believe an arrangement such as we propose to you to be preferable to the draft bills submitted by the Social Democratic and Communist parties."

Adenauer closed by pointing out the far-reaching importance of the decision about to be taken. "We are about to lay the foundation stone for a new economic structure in Germany," he said emphatically. "May the future call this economic structure by any name it pleases. We on our part have embodied and concentrated in our six draft bills all that is necessary for a new economic era to open in Germany."

The parliamentary record notes "prolonged applause." When the vote was taken on the following day, all six draft bills of the CDU were passed and adopted.

Six weeks after this memorable debate the people themselves gave their verdict. In the first general elections for the state parliament of North Rhine-Westphalia which took place on April 20, 1947, the CDU received 42.6 and the SPD 29.6 per cent of all votes cast. In the new parliament, which now possessed a genuine and direct mandate from the electorate, the two Marxist parties, Socialists and Communists, had been jointly reduced to ninety-two seats and were opposed by ninety-two CDU, twenty Center party, and twelve Free Democratic deputies—a coalition which possessed a clear and undisputed majority.

## CHAPTER XIII

THE FIRST four years of German postwar history, from unconditional surrender to the establishment of the Federal Republic, were a period of twilight in which neither Germans nor Allies could clearly see their way ahead. The specters of wartime propaganda were still abroad, distorting people's views, and one of the worst of these specters took the shape of a disastrous piece of paper which everyone quoted although hardly anyone had ever seen it. This was the so-called Morgenthau Plan. This ill-famed document poisoned the atmosphere between the German people and the Western occupying powers for years, and put endless difficulties in the path of their cooperation. Konrad Adenauer's way across these first four years of German postwar history cannot be properly understood without some reference to this ghost which dogged his every step until in November, 1949, at the Petersberg, he finally succeeded in laying it.

The Morgenthau Plan, or "Program to Prevent Germany from Starting a World War III," as its correct title read, was a paper drawn up by Mr. Henry Morgenthau, United States Secretary of the Treasury, at the suggestion of President Roosevelt, and submitted to the second Quebec Conference, between Roosevelt and Churchill, in September, 1944. It recommended, briefly, the cession of East Prussia and Southern Silesia to Poland, of the Saar and adjacent territories on the Western bank of the Rhine to France, the partitioning of the remainder of Germany into two independent states, North Germany and South Germany, the complete deindustrialization of both states, including the closing of their mines and the dismantling of their heavy industries, the creation of an International Zone in the Ruhr, and the reduction of the whole of Germany to a politically and economically powerless agrarian state.

The Morgenthau Plan never got beyond the stage of a draft paper, but it was nevertheless a gift from heaven to the Goebbels propaganda machine, which exploited it to the full in the closing stages of the war by whipping up nationalist instincts to a last bout of frenzy. This propaganda took deep roots. It purported to show the German people what was awaiting them if they lost the war, and it dominated their thinking for a long time after the war was lost and over. The Morgenthau Plan itself might no longer exist, but the vast majority of Germans were persuaded that the "Morgenthau mentality" dominated all Allied planning.

The facts were somewhat different. The Morgenthau draft paper was never adopted by the Quebec Conference. From the very first, it aroused strong criticism among the Roosevelt administration itself, and it was rejected by Mr. Churchill.

However, the Germans for a long time refused to believe it and suspected the idea of having survived, after all. What did survive, however, was the idea of drastically reducing German industrial capacity, and this found expression in the Potsdam Agreement and in the so-called "First Level of Industries Plan for Germany," promulgated by the Four Power Allied Control Council in March, 1946, as an implementation of the Potsdam decisions. This plan required German industrial production to be reduced to between 50 and 55 per cent of its 1938 level. All industrial capacity exceeding this limit was to be dismantled and handed over to the Allies as reparations for war damage or, where this was not practicable, to be destroyed on the spot.

The area most drastically affected by this industrial dismantling plan was, of course, the Ruhr territory, and this again was part of the new state of North Rhine-Westphalia where Adenauer lived and where his political activity was centered. It is not surprising, therefore, that we should see him in the forefront of those German politicians who at once took up a determined struggle against this mutilation of the German economy. But it is noteworthy that among the wild chorus of passionate protests against the "First Level of Industries Plan" his own voice remained at all times remarkably cool in tone and sober in argument. His was mainly an appeal to reason among the occupying powers, as when he declared:

"The entire industry of the Ruhr, owing to the war, overexploitation, and general wear and tear, is today in such a state of dilapidation that its machinery can only be expected to go on producing for yet a little while longer if it remains where it is and if it is worked by people who know how to handle it. If on the other hand this machinery is now broken up and dismantled and if those parts of it which survive this process get into the hands of people who do not know how to use them, the whole thing would be reduced to a heap of scrap. In that event dismantling would amount to no more than demolition and devastation pure and simple."

Equally soberly and factually he went on to describe the effect which the "First Level of Industries Plan," if carried out, was bound to have on conditions in Germany generally: "If the dismantling plan were carried out, iron and steel would become a commodity of great rarity in Germany. Since every industrial enterprise is inevitably based on iron and steel, the German people would be automatically deprived of all chance to manufacture exportable goods, and this in turn would inevitably, in the course of time, reduce Germany's present population to some thirty or thirty-five million, that is, to a level which would permit it to exist on the produce of its soil alone. This is precisely what the Morgenthau Plan intended to achieve, and, although fortunately this plan was rejected by the Allies, its ultimate aims would nevertheless be realized in this roundabout way."

Just how serious Adenauer considered the situation to be becomes clear, furthermore, from a confidential account which he gave to his party friends at a CDU conference at Lippstadt, in December, 1946. This account, which deserves all the more attention because it was not meant for publication and served no propaganda purpose, shows clearly to what length even a calm and sober politician like Adenauer found himself driven by the attitude of the occupying powers on the dismantling issue. At Lippstadt Adenauer declared:

"We were resolved, unless the British discontinued dismantling, to get together on our part in the Rhenish-Westphalian industrial area and to tell the occupation authorities that henceforth the CDU refused all further cooperation with the British, meaning that we would withdraw, on behalf of the party, all our ministers and representatives in local government on all levels, because we found ourselves unable to cooperate with an occupying power working deliberately toward the planned destruction of 50 per cent of our people."

That things did not come to this pass and the "First Level of Industries Plan" was temporarily halted in the first phase of its implementation was not, however, entirely due to German appeals and protests. A decisive change in the international situation came to the aid of the Germans. The Western Powers were determined to adhere to the Potsdam decisions as long as there seemed a prospect of persuading the Soviet Union to treat Germany as a unified economic area. But in the course of 1946 it became increasingly clear that this was a vain hope. Not only did the Soviet Government strip their own zone of occupation far beyond the limits set in the Potsdam Plan, but in addition they claimed further reparations from the three Western zones to be supplied from current production. This amounted, in practice, to an Anglo-American subsidy to the Soviet Zone and threatened to turn the whole scheme into an exceedingly costly enterprise for the Anglo-Saxon powers. As a result the "First Level of Industries Plan" was gradually abandoned by the Western powers, and, as a first move in a new direction, General Clay received orders from his government to limit all dismantlings to war and armaments industries in the strict sense of the term, to aim at a gradual increase in the German standard of living, and to work toward an eventual independence of the German economy from outside subsidies.

This was a new approach, inspired by a new spirit of understanding for the position of the vanquished, and a first recognition of the overriding need for solidarity on the part of the Western world. "We cannot chain Britain to a corpse," Churchill had said, and President Truman had expressed it even more bluntly: "Hungry people are bad democrats." This sentence, shining like a guiding star above American policy during the following year, soon found its practical application in the project put forward by General George C. Marshall, United States Secretary of State, in an historic speech at Harvard University in June, 1947.

The Marshall Plan envisaged the cooperation of the nations of Europe, ravaged and impoverished by the war, in a joint economic reconstruction program, stimulated and helped by large-scale assistance from American resources, and in this far-reaching planning Germany was to be included. At about the same time a private scheme for the relief of hunger, want, and misery in Germany resulted from a visit paid to occupied Germany by ex-President Herbert Hoover, and owing to his tireless energy and impassioned humanitarian appeal soon grew to proportions, as Adenauer once said, "such as never before in the history of the world have been bestowed upon a vanquished people by the victors." Over sixteen million CARE parcels were sent across the Atlantic to Germany between 1946 and 1949, saving millions from sickness and hundreds of thousands from death by starvation. The Adenauer family, too, were among the recipients of these welcome relief parcels, and on the many occasions when Adenauer, the politician, gratefully acknowledged this great humanitarian enterprise on behalf of the German people, there was always a particularly warm and personal undertone which deeds of genuine charity never fail to arouse in him.

Nor did he fail to respond wholeheartedly—and more readily than many others—to the new political spirit reaching Germany from across the Atlantic. Despite the somewhat embittering experiences he had had in his contacts with the occupation authorities, he welcomed the Marshall Plan without misgivings or suspicion, and even with a certain enthusiasm, and it is characteristic of him that he always regarded Europe as a whole, and never Germany alone, as the true recipient of this message. To a friend he said in those days, "In my mind the ultimate solution must be the creation of one single, enormous internal market in Western Europe, a unified trading area which should comprise England, France, the Low Countries, and Germany . . . ," a sentence he often repeated in public later on.

However, this was a distant goal, and in the reality of political life progress was made but slowly. It was not until the end of August, 1947, that the three Western Powers at their London conference published what became known as the "Second Level of Industries Plan," which applied to the three Western zones of Germany only. It provided for an increase in industrial production to between 90 and 95 per cent of the 1936 level. Steel production, for instance, was raised from 7.5 to 10.7 million tons annually. The most cumbersome and hampering restrictions were lifted. But even under this revised plan 918 industrial enterprises still remained scheduled for dismantling, 338 of them being classified as war industries, and 580 as representing "excess" capacity, and 496, or more than half the total, were located in the British Zone.

The final break with the Soviet Union, who had refused to participate in the Marshall Plan, was now approaching. It became an acknowledged fact at the London conference of the Foreign Ministers in December, 1947, when a last attempt by the Big Four to reach agreement on a peace settlement with Germany ended in failure.

From now on things moved rapidly in Western Germany. The British and American zones of occupation, having been joined together in May, 1947, in a unified economic area commonly known as the "bizone," now witnessed decisive changes. Early in February,

1948, the Bizonal Economic Council in Frankfurt, which had been set up by the two military governments to enable "German organs responsible to the people to help in the reconstruction of German economic life," was reconstituted and transformed, the economic parliament, which was elected by the diets of the eight states constituting the bizone, being supplemented by a *Länderrat* or States Council as a second chamber. It was a first attempt on the part of the Allies to shape an anticipatory model of the future constitutional structure of the whole of Germany—an experiment which, albeit for the present, remained confined to the territory of the two zones, and in its practical application to economic affairs.

The next step came in April, 1948, when the three Western occupying powers at their joint conference with the Benelux countries in London recommended the establishment of a federal system of government in Western Germany and the inclusion of Germany in an International Ruhr Authority, about to be created. A fortnight later, Marshal Vassily Sokolovsky, the Soviet Military Governor, finally disrupted the Allied Control Council in Berlin, ostensibly as a protest against the economic fusion of the three Western zones and the London decisions, and the first blockade measures against Berlin, the former Reich capital, were imposed.

In these weeks and months of rapid and decisive political development which even in normal circumstances would have taxed the energy and resilience of a much younger man, Adenauer lived through a period of deep personal anxiety and profound grief and distress. His wife was gravely ill.

Gussi Adenauer was suffering from a serious hematogenic disorder, a lack of white blood corpuscles, which greatly decreases the general powers of resistance of the whole organism against infections of all kinds. When she was released from Hohenlind hospital in November, 1945, after a successful treatment for dysentery, the doctor had warned Adenauer that in view of her condition she must remain more or less under constant medical observation.

The house in Zennigsweg to which Frau Adenauer returned had greatly changed its way of life since the turbulent days of the capitulation. Ria Reiners with her children and Gisela Adenauer had returned to their husbands, Paul and Lotte had begun their studies at the University of Bonn, and Libet had gone to a boarding school.

Only Georg, the youngest son, and Lola Adenauer, Konrad's wife, had remained behind. With her two children, Irene and little Konradin, Lola was waiting at Rhöndorf until her husband had found a suitable apartment in Cologne.

During this time, when he was devoting all his energies to building up the CDU, Adenauer was often compelled to be absent from home for considerable spells, and he was painfully aware that his wife suffered from these absences, although she never uttered a single word of complaint. "As soon as the new party is firmly on its feet," he would comfort her, "we will go to Switzerland, to Chandolin," a small and isolated place in the mountains which for many years had been their favorite vacation resort. But the much longed-for journey had to be put off again and again. Adenauer had become chairman of the CDU in the British Zone, he was a member of the Zonal Advisory Council in Hamburg, and the summer of 1946 passed with an unending series of meetings and conferences, visits, interviews, and constant urgent journeys from place to place, throughout the British Zone.

In the autumn of 1946 Frau Adenauer fell ill with double pneumonia, and the doctors considered her condition very grave. But the inflammation slowly receded, and she pulled through. The bitterly cold "starvation winter" of 1946-1947, which ravaged Germany with unparalleled fierceness, passed off better than Adenauer had dared to hope, and in the spring of 1947 the condition of the patient took a marked turn for the better. In June Adenauer was at last able to make good his promise. He freed himself of all engagements and took his wife to Switzerland for three weeks. But soon after their return from Chandolin there was again a gradual relapse, and in September, 1947, Gussi Adenauer had to be transferred to the Johannes Hospital at Bonn, where she was placed in the care of Professor von Redwitz, a noted specialist.

Her condition deteriorated steadily. In December, 1947, she was so weak that there seemed little hope for her to see the new year in. Adenauer, despite all his pressing duties, spent many hours every day at her bedside. Often he brought his work along to the hospital, moving a small table up to her sickbed, reading and writing, watching and talking to her at the same time. She rallied once more, but toward the middle of February, 1948, Professor von Redwitz had to tell Adenauer that he had little hope of preserving her life very much longer. But Adenauer refused to give up the struggle. More specialists were summoned and consulted, but none of them was able to hold out more hope. Eventually Adenauer telegraphed Professor Rohr, a world-famous specialist, who hurried over from Switzerland. But even the great Swiss hematologist was powerless. "It is too late," was all he could say.

In the last days of February, 1948, Gussi Adenauer gradually sank into a coma from which she regained consciousness only rarely, for a few minutes at a time. On March 3, 1948, she expired. Her husband and children were with her during her last hours.

Adenauer bore his crushing loss with stoic silence. It was not given to him to show his emotions in an impulsive way. A close friend of the family once said of him, "He is like one of those narrow-necked earthenware jugs in which the Italians store their olives. He's full of olives, but you can only get them out singly and with great trouble." And his youngest son, Georg, said later, "In those days, after my mother's death, we felt how deeply attached he was to us. Without wasting words he quietly rearranged his whole working day so that he could at least spend the lunch hour with his children and we should not feel too lost and lonely. . . ."

He was then seventy-two years old, and he knew that his greatest task still lay before him.

On April 7, 1948, members of the state parliament of North Rhine-Westphalia were specially summoned to hear an important address from the British Military Governor, General Sir Brian Robertson. The Military Governor had not spoken for many minutes when it was clear to all present that a new and momentous step in the development of Germany was about to be taken. Not only was the eagerly awaited currency reform apparently now imminent. General Robertson indicated that the Western Powers had decided to go beyond that and create a provisional separate West German State.

"By genuine and wholehearted cooperation between you and ourselves big things can be achieved," General Robertson said. "If we pull in opposite directions, failure for both of us is inevitable. . . . We have laid a foundation at Frankfurt. Upon that we can build, and build quickly. The primary objective of the Bizonal Administration in Frankfurt is to restore the economy of Western Germany . . . but its ultimate objective is to lay a foundation on which German unity can be restored. By unity I mean real unity with independent, freely elected, and representative government. . . . But for the time being we must accept as a fact that an iron curtain splits Germany. For the time being we must be content with unity so far as it can be achieved, and do not forget that this means the unity of two thirds of Germany. . . . Germany's salvation is in your hands to win or cast away. Only have courage and you will win it. Come forward, determined to make the best of that larger part of your country which is on the right side of the iron curtain. The rest will come in time. We offer you our good will and our cooperation. Don't be frightened by the mischief-makers who scream 'collaborators.' The time has come to realize that the interests of all Europeans are converging. Our needs and your needs cannot be dealt with separately for we all form part of Europe. Nor can you afford to squabble among yourselves. Your divisions are your weakness. . . . It may be very important to be a good party man. It is much more important to be a good German. If you fail to be that, you will wake up one day to find that your party no longer needs your support because it no longer exists. . . ."

The General concluded:

"Is it strange that I should talk to you like this? Yes, it is strange. But these are strange times. They have no parallel in history. . . ."

It was a strange speech indeed in which a general representing a foreign occupying power called upon German parliamentarians to bear themselves as patriots and not be frightened of being called "collaborators." What was the meaning of it all? All those present on that day sensed that a new political leaf was being turned over. The victorious powers had come to recognize that a point had been reached where they needed the help and cooperation of the vanquished if the fruits of victory were not to be lost. That, it seemed, was the heart of the matter. And what was the German answer to be?

Among the listeners to the "strange speech" appealing to them to be "good Germans" was the member of parliament Konrad Adenauer. As he sat there listening, erect, stiff, pale, clad in mourning, nothing in his silent face betrayed the feelings and reactions which the Englishman's appeal aroused in him. It was not until several months later that he gave his considered answer. On September 1, 1948, speaking as the newly elected President of the German Parliamentary Council which had assembled in the Pedagogic Academy at Bonn to draft the new German Constitution, he began his opening address with a personal confession:

"It has been a difficult decision for me, as it has been for every member of this house, whether, in the present condition of Germany, I should lend my cooperation to this enterprise at all. But we must be clear in our minds about the alternative—what would happen if this Council were not to come into being. The present state of lawlessness and absence of rights from which we all suffer would continue and grow steadily more unbearable. Therefore, it is our duty to seize and exploit every opportunity to bring it to an end. What the results of our work will be for Germany depends on factors over which we have no control. Yet we must endeavor to solve the historic problem which has been set us under the protection of the Almighty, with all the seriousness and high sense of duty which the greatness of the task demands of us."

Rarely has a task of such consequence been tackled with fewer illusions, more realistically, and at the same time with a profounder sense of duty. Adenauer was determined to "use every opportunity," yet he did not deceive himself about the limits of his freedom of action. He clearly recognized the "factors over which we have no control" and left no doubt that "the task" of creating the basis for a West German state was not self-chosen but had been "set" from outside.

Who had set the task? What was the basis on which the Parliamentary Council undertook its work? What, in short, had brought these men and women to the Pedagogic Academy at Bonn?

A brief answer to these questions is essential if one is to follow the struggle which Adenauer fought during the nine months that followed, with his German political opponents on the one hand, and with the two men, on the other, who in the Allied Bipartite Control Office at Frankfurt were at once his partners in the new enterprise and his opposing players—the American general, Lucius DuBignon Clay, and the British general, Sir Brian Hubert Robertson.

On July 1, 1948, ten days after the introduction of currency reform, which at one stroke placed the whole of Western Germany's economy on a new, productive footing, the three Western Military Governors summoned the Ministers President of the eleven West German states to Frankfurt where, on behalf on their governments, they handed them three documents. These three papers, generally known as the

"London Documents," had been drafted by the London Six-Power Conference. Their purpose was, as stated in the London Communiqué of June 7, 1948, to authorize the German people in the different states "to establish for themselves the political organization and institutions which will enable them to assume those governmental responsibilities which are compatible with the minimum requirements of occupation and control and which ultimately will enable them to assume full governmental responsibility. . . ."

Document Number One authorized "the Ministers President of the states to convene a constituent assembly to be held not later than 1 September, 1948." This assembly was to "draft a democratic constitution which will establish for the participating states a governmental structure of federal type which is best adapted to the eventual re-establishment of German unity, at present disrupted, and which will protect the rights of the participating states, provide adequate authority, and contain guarantees of individual rights and freedoms." Document Number Two required the Ministers President meanwhile to submit proposals for such modifications of the state boundaries as they thought desirable. Document Number Three defined the rights and duties reserved for the three occupying powers after the constitution had come into force. This "relationship between the constitutional German government and the Allied authorities" was to be formulated in precise detail and laid down in a so-called "Occupation Statute" which was to be made public simultaneously with the approval of the new constitution by the three Military Governors.

This, then, was the "set task." It proved considerably more difficult than had been expected. The eleven Ministers President, after much deliberation, were able to inform the Military Governments at their third joint meeting in Frankfurt, on July 26, 1948, that they suggested the summoning of a Parliamentary Council, composed of deputies from all state parliaments, which was to draft a Constitution. The Military Governors agreed to this procedure, and after the necessary preparatory work had been done by a group of eminent German experts in constitutional and international law, meeting at Herrenchiemsee, the Parliamentary Council was ready, on September 1, 1948, to begin its work.

Meantime the occupying powers, on their part, applied themselves to the drafting of the promised counterpart to the constitution, the Occupation Statute. They found that their own "constitution" presented them with quite as many difficulties as the Germans had to face with theirs. Soon a stage was reached where the Military Governors were keenly and assiduously controlling the work of the Germans but were themselves unable to inform the Germans on the progress of their own work which, after all, had to serve as a basis for what the Parliamentary Council was required to achieve. This contradictory state of affairs caused Adenauer many a sleepless night during the nine months which followed.

Unanimous applause had thanked President Adenauer for his opening address. But soon afterward a Social Democrat member remarked cynically, "We've made old Adenauer President to put this inconvenient nagger and squabbler in a place of honor where he is safely out of the way. The real work will be done in the Main Committee, and there our own Carlo Schmid presides!"

The cynic was not altogether wrong. It was perfectly true that the bulk of the work of the Parliamentary Council was carried by the special subcommittees and the Main Committee under the guidance of genial and massive Carlo Schmid, twenty years younger than Adenauer, a professor of international law at Tübingen University, Minister of Justice and Deputy State President of Württemberg-Hohenzollern, a nimble and widely read intellectual who was generally acknowledged to be among the Parliamentary Council's most persuasive polemical debaters. Professor Carlo Schmid was certainly a great asset for the Socialists, yet the SPD soon found that they had counted their chickens before they were hatched. It was not as easy as all that to put "old Adenauer" in cold storage. Although he did not often take part in the debates of the Main Committee, it soon became clear that he exercised considerable influence on the framing of the Constitution as a whole.

The Bonn assembly was a strange parliament. Most of the delegates of the eleven West German states belonged to an older generation who had been prominent in political life before 1933. Almost without exception they looked back on fearful experiences during the twelve years of the Hitler régime. Condemned to silence and deprived of their political rights, many of them had spent months and years in prisons and concentration camps, and not a few who by rights should have had their place in this assembly were no longer among the living. It was a parliament of those who "had got away by the skin of their teeth," and many met again for the first time here at Bonn, after long years of dispersal and enforced isolation.

Among them was the then chairman of the Free Democratic party, the well-known writer and publicist and former member of the Reichstag, Professor Theodor Heuss. Although they had both for several decades occupied prominent positions in public life, he and Adenauer met personally for the first time in the Parliamentary Council, and the present President of the Federal Republic has some illuminating remarks to make about the Federal Chancellor as he first knew him during the founding of the new state.

"I have admired Adenauer's penetrating mind from the very first," Professor Heuss says. "Of course, I was thoroughly familiar, long before we actually met, with the political part he had played, his bold planning and his outstanding achievements as Chief Mayor of Cologne, and his able leadership of the Prussian State Council. Although there is little of a romantic in him, he had quite early become something of an almost legendary figure. However, after our first few talks, it was clear to me that I was not dealing with the guardian of a successful and, later on, much troubled past, but rather with a most active and elastic man of the present who had a very clear view of the tasks of the future.

"Adenauer presided over the Parliamentary Council. But as the bulk of the Council's work was discharged in committee, his appearance in the public limelight was limited to the rather infrequent plenary meetings. Still, Adenauer showed himself at all times fully informed on all aspects of the committees' work, and he always knew precisely where and why difficulties had arisen. It was then that he intervened, inviting members of all parties to informal discussions of the specific problems involved, and these informal conversations—of which, I believe, no records exist—were as a rule decisive. It was on these occasions that he employed his truly masterly gift for simplifying and unraveling the various knots into which the specialists, for one reason or another, had tied themselves. He had an immense store of practical experience to draw upon, and was able to demonstrate, with the help of striking examples, how this or that paragraph or piece of legal phraseology would or would not work out in actual administrative practice. That brought the theoreticians down to earth, and we were able to carry on."

But even more important than these helpful interventions, the Federal President thinks, was the "background function" which Adenauer fulfilled as President.

"Of course, on account of his position alone, he was the figurehead through whom the Military Governors or their representatives and liaison officers dealt with the Parliamentary Council. Naturally, other members beside him had come into contact with these men, especially the party leaders and chairmen of the various committees. In these conversations people would try to sound each other, exchange arguments, encourage one another, and try to create something like a common atmosphere, but one was often uncertain of the precise rank, weight, influence, and true inner disposition of the partner in conversation. That went for the rest of us. With President Adenauer things were somewhat different. He met the Allies much more on an 'official' level. Although as yet without precise appointment—for who should have appointed him?—he had become in these months, in a perfectly natural way, the obvious and acknowledged spokesman of the nascent Federal Republic with the Western Powers. In this way, these months of early contacts became for him, quite irrespective of his own views and concepts, a kind of apprenticeship during which he thoroughly familiarized himself with the ideas of the 'others' and their ways of thinking.

"As regards our personal relationship in those early days," the Federal President says, "I think the important thing was that we met on common ground in a sober and realistic appreciation of the German situation, the European situation, and the world situation, about which neither of us was given to self-deceptive illusions. Our similar ways of looking at reality created a common bond and helped us, from the very beginning, to establish a relationship of frank and free exchange of views which later on we were able to translate without difficulty onto the 'official' level."

The work of the Parliamentary Council proceeded slowly and thoroughly, altogether too slowly and thoroughly for the taste of the Military Governors. They had allowed three months for the drafting of the Constitution, and toward the end of 1948 they became impatient. It fell to Adenauer to defend the circumspect labors of the German constitution-makers against this pressure, and to draw the Military Governors' attention to the fact that the Western Powers themselves were not altogether without blame for this slow progress.

For how could a "Basic Law" (as the new Constitution came to be called) be formulated as long as the Allied Occupation Statute remained an unknown quantity and the framers of the Constitution were in ignorance of the areas of competence which, until further notice, would be withheld from the jurisdiction of the future Federal parliament and government and remain reserved to the occupying powers?

Whenever it became necessary to discuss these fundamental matters with the Military Governors at Frankfurt, it was Adenauer's thankless task to submit and explain German doubts and objections. The task was made doubly thankless by the fact that in the course of the months that passed very marked differences and tensions developed within the Parliamentary Council itself, notably between the Christian Democratic Union and the Social Democratic party, and that the German conception, as opposed to that of the Allies, was not homogeneous or uniform.

In the course of their joint endeavor the two major German parties, CDU and SPD, had developed sharply diverging conceptions of the structure of the future West German state. The Allies, on their part, stood for a third conception as laid down in the London "Document Number One." This document stipulated "a governmental structure of federal type," and in order to receive the approval of the Western powers, the "Basic Law" had to conform to this specification. But what was meant by "federal type?" The Military Governors themselves could not agree on just how loose this federation would have to be to meet with Allied wishes.

From the very outset Adenauer had devoted his particular attention to the position of the component states within the federation. He was anxious for them to retain a maximum of independence in their relation to the central authority, and for this reason alone, if for no other, it was essential that they should not become financially dependent on the central government. On the other hand, Adenauer had no doubt that state independence as far-reaching as France seemed to think desirable would paralyze the federal government and render it incapable of any decisive action. Beyond this he was primarily anxious to see the basic rights of the individual citizen firmly and explicitly safeguarded in the constitution, and this included the right of parents to secure religious education for their children.

It was on these two basic issues that the CDU collided with the

SPD. The Social Democrats were unwilling to regard the Bonn Constitution as more than a provisional measure of transition which must not anticipate or prejudice a future constitution for the whole of Germany. At the same time, the Socialists wished to knit the federation together as tightly as possible and to transfer a maximum of executive power to the central government, especially in the field of finance legislation. There was good reason for this. The Social Democrats were convinced that they would emerge from the first federal elections as the strongest party, and that as a result they would form the first federal government. To carry out their far-reaching program of socialization and economic planning, especially the transfer of the Ruhr heavy industries to state ownership, they required above all a government with strong central executive powers. There could be no hope of such powers as long as the government was not firmly in control of federal finance legislation but remained largely dependent upon the component federal states. This firm financial control, however, was precisely what Adenauer and the CDU were determined to prevent.

In this situation there arose a conflict which put Adenauer's steadfastness and resilience to a severe test. It was the so-called "Frankfurt Affair."

On December 2, 1948, Adenauer addressed a letter, "in agreement with the Council of Elders of the Parliamentary Council," to the three Military Governors, asking them for an informal and confidential conference in which, besides himself, several other members of the Parliamentary Council were to take part. "I consider it advisable," he wrote, "to suggest a discussion of the results so far reached in the Bonn deliberations, at the present juncture when the Basic Law is not yet cast in its final shape, whereas the Occupation Statute has presumably been determined in its essential points. It would be of great value to the Parliamentary Council if it could be informed at this stage, informally and confidentially, of the main features of the Occupation Statute, before reaching its final conclusions with regard to the Constitution."

The purpose of the required interview was clear enough. Adenauer was above all anxious to avoid a situation where subsequent Allied objections against the Basic Law were likely to discredit the work of the Parliamentary Council with the German public. He hoped to persuade the Allies to raise such objections as might result from the Occupation Statute in good time, before the final adoption of the Basic Law, thus enabling the Parliamentary Council to take them into account.

However, there was one flaw in this calculation, and Adenauer could not possibly have been aware of it. His request for a conference reached the Military Governors at a particularly unfavorable moment. There was no basis for such a meeting because the Occupation Statute, contrary to what Adenauer had imagined, did not yet exist. So far from its essential points being settled, differences of opinion between Generals Clay and Robertson on the one hand, and the French Military Governor, General Pierre Koenig, on the other, had sharpened to an extent where cooperation between the three Military Governors was about to break down.

In his book *Decision in Germany*, General Clay writes that "French representatives were unyielding and were also expressing alarm at what they believed to be a trend to dangerous centralization in the work of the Parliamentary Council." He adds that he felt that "the French Administration in Germany . . . was determined to delay if not to thwart the establishment of West German Government," * and in a long cabled report to his government in Washington, dated November 22, 1948, he complained bitterly about General Koenig's attitude:

"Koenig's stand in the recent meeting is that the French may not accept Western German Government as they dislike the present climate. . . . Although the French Government has officially accepted German recovery as necessary to European recovery, many of the actions taken by its representatives in Germany have been to delay recovery. . . . The French do not really want a united Germany with Berlin as the capital. Our policy calls for a united Germany. Any act on our part which would indicate that we oppose a united Germany would lessen greatly our influence in Western Germany. . . . The French say that there are evidences of a tendency to make Germany the strongest economic power in Europe and the center of the continental economy. . . . I do wish to point out that there is an increasing conflict between American and French policy which leads

* From *Decision in Germany,* by Gen. Lucius D. Clay (Doubleday & Co., Inc.) © 1950.

to almost daily disagreements in our operations in Germany. . . . This conflict of policy is at a critical stage. Each compromise retards our efforts for German recovery. . . . There is no ready solution of this problem. . . ." *

This was the position, largely unknown to Adenauer, when the Military Governors invited him and his colleagues, as requested, to a conference to be held in Frankfurt on December 16 and 17, 1948. It was on this same day, December 16, that the Military Governors finally decided to refer the draft Occupation Statute, on which the German parliamentarians desired to be informed, back to their own governments for a decision, since they were unable to compose their differences.

When the German delegation, led by Adenauer, called at Allied Headquarters in Frankfurt on the afternoon of December 16, they were received by General Koenig, whose turn it was to be in the chair that month. The welcome was polite but markedly reserved. Adenauer gave a brief account of the work of the Parliamentary Council so far achieved, mentioning in conclusion, for the sake of correctness and completeness, that a number of questions still remained open. These unsolved problems included cultural matters such as religious education, the question whether the Basic Law was to be ratified by the state parliaments or by plebiscite, and, of course, the paramount question of the financial powers of the Federal authorities.

Next, General Koenig asked the German representatives to express their wishes in regard to the Occupation Statute, and Adenauer answered by requesting more detailed information which would enable the Germans to put precise and specific questions. General Koenig took silent note of this request—what else could he have done in his situation?—and the interview ended. A further meeting was arranged for the afternoon of the following day.

What followed was the subject of a private and confidential account which Adenauer, later on, gave to a small circle of his closest political friends. According to this account, the members of the German delegation remained together in informal conversation for a short while after the official meeting, talking peacefully and ap-

* From *Decision in Germany*, by Gen. Lucius D. Clay (Doubleday & Co., Inc.) © 1950.

parently in complete harmony about the impression they had gained of their interview with the Military Governors, and even as they walked out into the street Carlo Schmid conversed with Adenauer and no word of reproach was voiced by anyone.

The German delegates had agreed to meet again the following morning for a preliminary discussion before their second interview with the Military Governors. Adenauer was among the first to arrive, and he was soon followed by the Socialist delegates Carlo Schmid and Walter Menzel and Dr. Hermann Höpker-Aschoff of the FDP. They made a surprisingly solemn entry, and in measured tones Höpker-Aschoff made this declaration:

"Herr Dr. Adenauer, I find myself obliged to express to you my pained astonishment. At our meeting yesterday you called upon the Allies to arbitrate between the differences of opinion which have manifested themselves in the Parliamentary Council!"

It was a monstrous accusation, charging Adenauer with an attempt to use the Allied generals to gain an advantage over his German political opponents. Adenauer was utterly baffled and perplexed by this insinuation, and asked for thirty minutes in which to consider the matter. Then he told them:

"If you are genuinely of the opinion that the three Military Governors must have misunderstood my words at yesterday's meeting in this way, I shall be ready this afternoon, before the beginning of the second meeting, to make a personal statement which will correct this alleged error!"

The suggestion was accepted and the statement drafted and agreed upon by all concerned. Despite the statement and an additional declaration to the same effect made by Carlo Schmid, the afternoon meeting with the Military Governors passed off in complete harmony. Tea was served, there was an informal round-table conversation, in the course of which General Robertson underlined once more the importance of adopting the Constitution as soon as possible. The atmosphere was decidedly friendly, infecting even the hostile brethren of the SPD and CDU, there was no further mention of the incident, and after a cordial farewell the German delegates returned to Bonn in the evening.

The next day the Main Committee of the Parliamentary Council met at Bonn, and Carlo Schmid, its chairman, asked Adenauer to report on the Frankfurt meeting. Referring to the "incident,"

Adenauer emphatically rejected the reproach of having appealed to the occupying powers to give their ruling with regard to differences within the Parliamentary Council. In principle, however, he pledged himself to loyal cooperation with the Military Governors, declaring, "It is my considered view that personal contacts and exchanges of opinion with these three men whose voices exercise a decisive influence on our future can only favor and help German interests. I believe that every one of us should take advantage of this possibility."

This plea on his own behalf, however, missed its effect. As soon as he had ended, Adenauer had to defend himself once more against the ferocious onslaught of his opponents. Now Carlo Schmid declared on behalf of the Social Democrats, "By bringing the Military Governors into this, one lath after another is being broken out of the fence we have erected with so much trouble around the autonomy of the Parliamentary Council," and the Communist member Max Riemann tabled a motion requesting the house to "express their disapproval of the attitude displayed by Dr. Adenauer during the talks with the Military Governors and to dismiss him from his post as President of the Parliamentary Council."

This last move, however, seemed somewhat excessive even to most of Adenauer's opponents. When the vote was taken on the admissibility of the Communist censure motion, it appeared that the Socialists apparently did not seriously desire to see Adenauer removed. Carlo Schmid, as chairman, ruled that the Main Committee was not competent to decide this question.

Returning to his office after the meeting of the Main Committee, Adenauer found waiting for him a letter from the Socialist party in the Parliamentary Council, the salient passage of which read: "We regret to have to inform you that . . . you no longer possess, with our party, the confidence which the spokesman of a delegation must enjoy with all concerned." The Socialist party called a press conference that same afternoon, in which this letter was read out. Commenting on it, Carlo Schmid took the view that it was altogether wrong for the German side to enter into any negotiations whatsoever with the Military Governors over the Basic Law. They should, he said, take their decisions in complete autonomy and then face the Military Governors with the clear-cut alternative: "Take it or leave it, accept or reject."

This was not Adenauer's view. It was not only a misjudgment of the actual position, but, moreover, in Adenauer's opinion, not at all in the German interest. Despite all the obstacles and discouraging difficulties he encountered, he was working toward a genuine partnership which he hoped would result not only in a German but in a European consolidation. For that reason, if for no other, he could see nothing dishonorable in giving the Military Governors a clear picture of German difficulties. He was convinced that such trust would be rewarded by trust, and in the long run he was proved right.

During the following weeks the "Frankfurt Affair" became the subject of endless polemics in the German press until it finally petered out. It was a trifle, and Adenauer survived it. He remained President of the Parliamentary Council, and neither his reputation with the German people nor his prestige abroad suffered any damage from these charges. Indeed, it may be said that the stand he took over this incident served to attract additional attention to his personal and political qualities. This is indicated in an account which was written under the fresh impression of the Frankfurt incident:

"Dr. Adenauer is an interesting personality whose activity and energy belie his seventy-three years. Having spent a long life in the political field, during which he achieved the leadership of the Christian Democratic Union, he is a capable politician. His extensive knowledge of government and of parliamentary procedure combine with ability and intelligence to make an effective leader. His shrewdness enables him to create conditions favorable to his party and he is not above using criticism of others to further party interests. . . . When he rises above party politics he has the intelligence and character to act as a statesman. He exhibited this quality of statesmanship at critical periods in the life of the [Parliamentary] Council." *

The writer of these lines was no German. He was the American general, Lucius D. Clay.

* From *Decision in Germany,* by Gen. Lucius D. Clay (Doubleday & Co., Inc.) © 1950.

# CHAPTER XIV

THE OLD YEAR, 1948, had closed on the jarring note of the "Frankfurt Affair." The new year opened at once with fresh difficulties for Adenauer.

He now occupied three important political key positions, every one of which would normally have taxed a man's energy and capacity for work to the full. He was President of the Parliamentary Council. He was leader of the parliamentary party of the CDU in the North Rhine-Westphalia parliament. And as chairman of the zonal executive committee of the CDU in the British Zone he was generally acknowledged as undisputed head of the party in all three Western zones of occupation.

This time, at the beginning of 1949, it was chiefly his own party which caused him anxiety. The attempt at fusion between the CDU and the remnants of the once powerful and influential Center party, to which he had devoted months of patient negotiation, finally came to nothing, and the great hope for a single, large, and all-embracing Christian party which would decisively balance the two Marxist parties, Social Democrats and Communists, had to be abandoned for the time being. For Adenauer this was a distressing disappointment, especially as cooperation between the CDU and its counterpart in Bavaria, the CSU or Christian Social Union, was not standing up too well to the various stresses and strains to which it was exposed, and the common front was not as firmly joined as he would have liked to see it in the interest of the common cause.

A second major anxiety was the difficult progress of the new constitution. Completion of this work was now endangered from two sides. There were the obstructionist tactics of the Social Democrats, whose general attitude toward the CDU had further stiffened after the "Frankfurt Affair," and there were the continuing differences of opinion between the Military Governors, who found themselves unable to agree on the type of federal constitution which would be in accord with their own as yet nonexistent Occupation Statute. "Fortunately," as General Clay notes, "German political leaders in Council recognized the danger of delay, and advised us in late December that it would proceed to complete the Basic Law without waiting for the Occupation Statute." Thus on February 16, 1949, Adenauer transmitted to the Military Governors on behalf of the Parliamentary Council the first complete draft of the Basic Law. The Western Powers found no fault with its basic democratic conception, but objected to "the excessive concentration of power in the hands of the central authority," General Koenig in particular insisting sharply on this point. The draft constitution was referred back to the Parliamentary Council for adjustment and modification. It was clear that final agreement might now take weeks, if not months, to be reached.

Despite this new setback, Adenauer remained unshakably confident that the Constitution would eventually reach port safely. Indeed, looking further ahead, he simply ignored the new difficulties which had arisen, and in the early months of 1949 began actively to prepare his party for the coming electoral contest. Even his closest party friends shook their heads at this display of seemingly incomprehensible and wholly unwarranted optimism. The new German Constitution was, after all, still far from complete; there was as yet no electoral law, and not even an approximate date was envisaged for the first general election to be held in the new Federal Republic. Still, Adenauer acted as though all this were already settled and required no further attention. For him, the time had come for attention to be fastened on the next move.

The next move was to win power in the new state. Unlike many others, Adenauer had a very clear idea of the importance of this first electoral decision. He had no doubt that the victorious party, which would be the first to form a government in the new state, would set the pattern and determine the course of developments for a long time ahead. He appointed Dr. Alois Zimmer, Minister of State in the Rhine-Palatinate government, a tough and energetic man, "Plenipotentiary General" of the CDU in charge of preparations for the election campaign, and Zimmer recalls that Adenauer told him even then, "We must now win power. And we must remain in power for at least eight years. If we can achieve that, we shall have placed Germany firmly on the road along which she can safely proceed."

That was a bold thing to say, especially for the leader of a young and untried party. For, compared with its great rival, the Social Democratic party, which was based on a settled program and whose organization was able everywhere to rely on the foundations and traditions of the old pre-Hitler party, the Christian Democratic Union was at a great disadvantage. It was still organized only within individual states, possessing as yet no over-all central direction, and although in 1947 these CDU associations in the various states had been brought together in a loosely knit joint committee, there were still considerable differences of view with regard to a number of important points in the program. This had enabled Dr. Kurt Schumacher, the Socialist leader, to speak of the CDU as a "haphazardly blown together bunch of bourgeois voters," and when in March, 1949, a South German newspaper conducted a poll among its readers about the electoral prospects of the two great parties, nine tenths of all those asked were convinced of a Socialist victory.

Adenauer was well aware of these weaknesses, and the closer the time for the election approached, the more energetically he worked to tighten up and streamline the organization of the party and to arm it for the impending contest. The work he did in those months, supported by Dr. Zimmer, the plenipotentiary, and the general secretaries Herbert Blankenhorn and Bruno Dörpinghaus, was decisive for the later success of the CDU. The divergent views of the CDU state associations had to be reconciled under an over-all common denominator. Personal differences had to be smoothed away. Suitable candidates had to be found for the various constituencies. And, above all, initial suspicions and reservations among Protestant circles against the new party had to be overcome. This was a point Adenauer never tired of emphasizing. Again and again he hammered it home to his party friends that confessional differences must not be allowed to stand in the way of the common Christian task of resurrecting Germany, and, if he paid any attention at all to questions of confession in selecting and appointing his associates and party workers, it was only to make sure of a fair balance and parity within the organization.

During these months of preparation, Dr. Zimmer recalls, Adenauer devoted himself personally to every aspect and every single detail of the plenipotentiary's work, supervising the nomination of candidates, the adaptation of propaganda and publicity to the varying regional conditions in the states and provinces, and the raising and expenditures of election funds. Of far greater importance, however, than this detailed organizational work was a fundamental step which Adenauer took at that time, a full six months before the election, which determined the future not only of the CDU but of the whole of the West German State.

How was the German economy, disrupted and destroyed as it was by the war, to be reconstructed? That, Adenauer recognized, was bound to be the paramount election issue. Was there to be a planned economy along Socialist lines with supreme power of direction and control vested in the state? Or was there to be a free economy, based on the law of supply and demand and the free competition of private enterprise, with the state intervening as a regulating factor only in the interests of social justice? It was a decisive question, and as yet an open one. The new state was faced at the outset with a clear-cut alternative, and the choice it made would obviously exercise a profound influence on its internal structure and mold its whole social outlook.

In its various draft programs, chiefly in the so-called "Ahlen Program" of February, 1947, the Christian Democratic Union had been wrestling with this problem for some time, and after rejecting a purely capitalist solution as well as the Socialist concept, had finally evolved a set of proposals of its own which attempted, in essence, to banish the dangers of a capitalist system dominating the state by extending the principle of distributed power to the economic field.

The Bizonal Economic Council at Frankfurt had in its majority arrived at similar conclusions. Here, too, the view had eventually prevailed that German economic reconstruction should follow neither purely capitalist nor rigorously socialist principles. Under the influence of an uncommonly brilliant economist, who was, moreover, an unusually forceful and strong-willed character, the Frankfurt Council had, after much trial and error, struggled and worked its its way through to a uniform economic concept which appeared to combine freedom and state control of the national economy in a peculiarly happy synthesis. The new formula was known as "Social Market Economy," and its creator was the fifty-two-year-old former Bavarian Minister of Economics and Professor of Economics in the University of Munich, Dr. Ludwig Erhard.

Erhard had quickly become one of the most fervently admired and furiously hated men in Germany. Liberal economists regarded his Social Market Economy as "an ill-conceived attempt to revive the economic theory of state absolutism," while Dr. Schumacher, the Socialist leader, referred to it derisively as "the fat propaganda balloon of private enterprise filled with putrid gases of decaying liberalism."

Adenauer saw in Ludwig Erhard the man with the requisite theoretical and practical abilities to carry the economic program of the CDU into effect. He invited the controversial professor to address the zonal executive committee of the party and explain his theories. Erhard accepted the invitation, and the meeting, which took place at Königswinter on February 21, 1949, became a milestone in the history of the party.

It cannot be said that the meeting received the guest from the very beginning with unreserved enthusiasm. On the contrary, several delegates immediately and sharply inquired why Dr. Erhard had not yet joined the CDU as a member? The question contained an implied reproach against Adenauer: why was a man allowed to speak in their midst who had deliberately refrained from identifying himself with the economic program evolved by the party? Adenauer replied on behalf of his guest, "I asked Professor Erhard myself," he said, "why he wouldn't join our party. He answered me with a counter-question: 'If you lived in Bavaria, would you join the CSU?'" "And what did you answer him?" a heckler wanted to know. "I decided not to have heard the question," Adenauer said. The remark provoked general hilarity. As everyone in the meeting knew, the Bavarian CSU had been ridden, in its beginnings, with a whole series of internal crises and unedifying quarrels and dissensions, and even now "Bavarian Separatism" kept causing the Parliamentary Council awkward and troublesome moments.

The introduction had broken the ice, and Professor Erhard was able to explain to an assembly which followed him with growing interest his theory of Social Market Economy. Starting from a criticism of planned economy, Erhard explained that its mechanical interference with the structure of the national economy, especially in the shape of maximum prices fixed by the state, tended to destroy the natural order of supply and demand. This, he demonstrated, had the effect of driving the goods from the market and inducing producers and retailers who endeavored to escape this price dictatorship of the state to seek refuge in the black market—at the expense of the consumer, who was made to share the risk and cost of such illegal transactions. Hinting clearly at experiences of the most recent past, Erhard compared a state which ignored the price-regulating function of free competition to an engineer who shuts off the safety valve of a high-pressure steam boiler.

Social Market Economy, Professor Erhard maintained, proceeded very differently. It accepted the interplay of economic forces as a fundamental principle, indeed it explicitly favored and sponsored open competition within free enterprise, recognizing that the effect of such competition must inevitably be to lower prices. "For it is the aim of Social Market Economy," he emphasized, "to invest the nominal income of the large masses with the highest possible purchasing power." It was only when prices began to rise that state intervention was called for. In that event, however—and this was the essential point of the new theory—the modern state had at its disposal means of regulation far more effective than the merely mechanical fixing or pegging of prices. Tariff, finance, and taxation policy, Erhard explained, enabled the state to exercise a controlling influence upon prices to an extent which no enterprise could ignore or evade.

Erhard had spoken for nearly three hours, and when Adenauer amid prolonged applause moved a vote of thanks to the "man from Bavaria" and suggested having the speech printed at once as a pamphlet and distributed to all CDU speakers in the election campaign, he carried the meeting without much difficulty.

Politically, the enlistment of Professor Erhard and the adoption of his economic policy was a master stroke. The phenomenal economic recovery which had set in, in the wake of the currency reform, was the only major event in postwar Germany which had profoundly affected the lives of the great mass of the people, who took little or no interest in politics. By incorporating in its program, upon Adenauer's initiative, the basic principles of the economic policy which, in the eyes of the nonpolitical masses, had brought about this prosperity, the CDU had secured for itself an invaluable asset in the coming election campaign. Adenauer's calculation was soon proved correct. The indisputable fact that the individual citizen could, at long last, feed and clothe himself again and freely buy with his money what he needed or desired carried more conviction than all economic theories. The additional fact that Professor Erhard himself, generally acknowledged as the creator of the "German Economic Miracle," soon afterward overcame his "Bavarian reservations," joined the CDU and became one of its more effective election speakers greatly increased the prospects of the young party.

Meanwhile work on the Bonn Constitution proceeded with agonizing slowness. Negotiations continued with the three Military Governors, who were still not agreed among themselves about the extent of power and authority to be reserved for the central government in the new federation. Compromise solutions were suggested by both sides and rejected, and new proposals made. Final agreement was not yet in sight.

Amid these difficult and wearying negotiations, the President of the Parliamentary Council left Bonn for a few days and on March 25, 1949, traveled to Switzerland. The Interparliamentary Union at Berne had invited the acknowledged leader of the CDU to address them on the subject of conditions in postwar Germany, and Adenauer welcomed the opportunity of giving before a neutral audience an account of the situation as he saw it.

The meeting took place in the auditorium of Berne University. When "the pale, lean German with his hard Tartar face," as a Socialist Swiss newspaper described seventy-four-old Adenauer, mounted the rostrum to speak, no one among his audience expected the explosive effect his words were going to have. They expected a well-tempered, dispassionate speech along soberly academic lines which would send them home somewhat better informed on German problems than they had arrived. They were in for a surprise.

There was nothing "academic" about Adenauer's speech. With his very first sentences he made it clear to his Swiss hearers that any consideration of German problems inevitably involved the whole of Europe, and he intended therefore to speak about things which were the immediate concern of the entire "European Community of Fate," and this included Switzerland.

The dividing line separating the two great power blocs of the United States and the Soviet Union, he declared, ran straight across the middle of Germany, and the western half of Germany, which held the largest industrial potential in all Europe, was in an untenable condition of disarray and disorder. "Even today," he said, "a very considerable part of its forty-three million inhabitants live in housing conditions of such abject misery and in such civic bondage as may have been imaginable in the Balkans a hundred years ago but has not been encountered in Western and Central Europe for centuries!"

The unadorned frankness of his opening immediately secured for Adenauer the close attention of his hearers. But there was also growing astonishment among many of them when he went on to declare that at least part of the responsibility for these conditions must be placed squarely on the shoulders of the Allied Military Government. "The unconditional surrender of the German armed forces in May, 1945," Adenauer said, "has been interpreted by the Allies to mean complete transfer of governmental authority to their hands. This interpretation was of doubtful validity in international law, and in my view it was also a grave mistake. It would have been better and more correct for the Allies to have left it to the Germans to reorder their affairs and rebuild their national structure, and to have confined themselves to control and supervision."

Having made his position clear in principle, Adenauer went on to deal with conditions in detail. There was much with which he had to reproach the victorious Allies, but this did not prevent him from recognizing, justly and fairly, the more recent change in the attitude of the occupying powers, or from appreciating fully the outstanding merits of the Marshall Plan which, he said, "will remain for all time a glorious page in the history of the United States of America." All the more incomprehensible was the wide discrepancy between this readiness to help and the rest of the measures decreed by the Allied military authorities.

There was above all the continued policy of industrial dismantling. With emphatic bluntness Adenauer declared, "The intention seems to be to maintain Germany's economic potential at a level which is incompatible with the aims of the Marshall Plan." And he did not hesitate to assert roundly, "In many instances the underlying motive for these dismantlings is the desire to eliminate German competition from the world's markets."

An assertion of this kind was, at that time, very "strong meat" indeed, bound to shock profoundly, especially a neutral audience. But there was proof of the allegation, and Adenauer furnished it. He mentioned, as an example, the dismantling of the Kolibri comb factory, carried out, he asserted, at the instigation of a British officer who ran a similar, competitive enterprise in England. He quoted, as another example, a statement issued by the Association of British Watch Manufacturers thanking their president for having succeeded, by means of dismantlings, in reducing the production capacity of Western Germany's watch industry below the level of 1936. The British manufacturers, Adenauer said, had "noted with satisfaction that the German watch industry was now working only with obsolete machinery," and at the end of their conference they had transmitted a request to their own government to "reconsider the entire problem of industrial dismantling in the event of Germany succeeding once more in inconveniencing British exports to world markets."

All this was strong, controversial stuff indeed, but there was more to come. Before his hearers had time to digest it, Adenauer turned to the next problem: the question of German industrial patents and their wholesale expropriation and transfer to foreign interests. Here again, facts and figures were furnished as proof. According to a statement made by an expert of the American chemical industries, Adenauer said, the patents formerly belonging to I. G. Farben, the great German chemical trust, had given American industry a lead of at least ten years over their competitors. Basing his statements on a report issued by the American office in charge of exploiting German industrial patents and research processes, Adenauer went on to declare that the Soviet Union alone had bought, in a single month, over 2,000 secret German Wehrmacht documents concerned with armaments research and weapon development at the price of $6,000. The damage caused to the German national economy by this one transaction alone, he said, could not be even approximately estimated in figures.

Completing his survey of German economic conditions, Adenauer turned to most recent developments—the so-called "Ruhr Statute" establishing an "International Authority for the Ruhr" and promulgated by the occupying powers in December, 1948. The Ruhr Authority, he pointed out, being in a position to fix the level of production, as well as the prices, for coal, iron, and steel, had concentrated enormous power in its hands which enabled it to influence decisively the entire German economy. As the establishment of the Ruhr Authority had aroused strong criticism and bitter resentment in Western Germany from the very day of its inception, the majority of Adenauer's hearers obviously expected the German party leader to take the strictly national view and denounce the Authority in emphatic terms. Such a protest would have but voiced existing feelings in Western Germany where the main charge against the occupying powers was that, as in the Marshall Plan Organization in Paris, Germany herself was not represented in the Ruhr Authority by her own delegates but merely by the Military Governors who purported to speak and act on her behalf. The question had even been raised in various quarters whether in these circumstances any useful purpose was served by cooperating with the Western Powers in the joint construction of a new German state.

All these arguments were available. But Adenauer declined to use them. To the great surprise of his audience he declared, "Everything will depend on the spirit in which this Ruhr Statute is applied in practice. If it is applied as an instrument to repress the German national economy and keep it down, the Marshall Plan becomes plainly nonsensical. Nor will any nation be able, in the long run, to tolerate such restrictions upon its economy. If, on the other hand, the Ruhr Statute is used as an instrument to serve German and European interests, if it is the beginning of a new order in the economy of all Western Europe, then it can become a promising starting point for general and comprehensive cooperation among the nations of Europe."

This was indeed the most important point of the entire speech, little though it was grasped at the time, either at home or abroad. It showed the leader of the new Christian party in Germany determined to rise above traditional nationalist thinking, prepared to commit his people to painful sacrifice if at this price supranational unity among the community of nations could be bought. His words were an earnest of the change of heart which the world had demanded of Germany after 1945, but that was not how they were understood. While the outside world furiously denounced "Adenauer the archnationalist," an equally furious opposition at home charged him, in the name of national consciousness, with "lack of resistance against the wishes of the victors."

But Adenauer had not finished yet. There was still more in the Berne speech. Economic distress was by no means the full tale of Germany's misery. There was other severe damage, Adenauer declared, which the postwar years had inflicted upon the body of the German people, and again he quoted as proof facts and figures worked out by the American authorities which made his point much more tellingly than any protest of flaming indignation could have done:

"Thirteen and a third million Germans from the Eastern provinces have arrived in the three Western zones. Six million Germans have disappeared from the face of the earth. They have perished, they are dead."

These expulsions from Eastern Germany, Adenauer declared, were the result of the Potsdam Agreement concluded by the victorious powers on August 2, 1945. His criticism of this agreement was confined to a single sentence: "I am convinced that in time history will pronounce a very severe verdict upon this document."

In the spring of 1949, it must be remembered, Western Germany's refugee problem had assumed the proportions of a major catastrophe, of which the outside world had little or no conception. Adenauer seized the opportunity to demonstrate in plain terms the avalanche of misery and destitution these masses of refugees had carried with them to the West. There were, on an average, two persons per dwelling room in the three Western zones. Tuberculosis had risen, against 1938, by 250 per cent. Because of the lack of beds and hospital space only a small proportion of cases could be isolated from the rest of the community. Infant mortality in the second quarter of 1946 was 135 per thousand. The birth rate, which in 1915 was still 1,500,000, had decreased for the whole of Germany to 600,000. By 1980, Adenauer explained, the population of Germany would have fallen below 40,000,000.

"It is extremely difficult," Adenauer said, "to forecast with any degree of certainty how the German people will react psychologically to this growing destitution." However, one or two fairly reliable observations on this subject he felt able to make: "Owing to the atrocities committed by the Soviet troops during their advance into Germany, and the tales brought back from the East by returning prisoners of war, popular feeling toward the Soviet Union is now so thoroughly negative that numerically speaking communism is of no great importance in Western Germany." All the same, Adenauer warned against underrating the influence of infiltration from the East upon the workers in important branches of industry. As for National-

Socialism of the Hitlerite stamp, Adenauer declared that it had comparatively few supporters in Germany. But what was making itself felt distinctly was a renascent sense of nationhood, a reawakening national consciousness and pride.

"The existence of a genuine and healthy national sentiment," Adenauer declared, "can only be welcomed. For a people without a sense of nationhood will lose confidence in itself and surrender to its fate. Nor is it fair or right to expect the German people to offer resistance to the infiltration from the East if they are not allowed to feel as a nation."

It was in the name of this sound and healthy national sentiment that Adenauer protested as firmly against the frontier adjustments in the West, which he called ill advised, as he denounced the detachment of the Eastern provinces beyond the Oder-Neisse line. "This frontier we shall never recognize!" he declared emphatically, thus pledging himself, even before this neutral audience, unreservedly to the cause of German unity and reunification which, he said, was the most ardent wish of all Germans.

Adenauer's Berne speech closed with a reference to relations between France and Germany. This was indeed a problem on which Adenauer had spent a lifetime of thought and toward whose solution he worked whenever opportunity offered. The French desire for security he recognized as fully justified without reservation, but, with reference to the present situation, added, "I believe that France need no longer have the slightest fear. Germany is disarmed, her armed forces are disbanded, her war industries have been dismantled, she is occupied, she is paralyzed."

But those were merely mechanical safeguards. Far more durable guarantees, Adenauer felt, were provided in the spiritual and mental reorientation of the German people. He said, "The overwhelming majority of Germans is profoundly convinced that Europe can be saved from Asian domination only through union and firm integration of all the nations of Western Europe. If France at this juncture can show herself wise and generous toward Germany, she will render historic service to the cause of Europe."

Could the first steps toward such union and common purpose be recognized even then? Adenauer asked. He pointed to the promising attitude of Robert Schuman, the French Foreign Minister, to the change in the outlook and attitude of the Benelux countries, and noted with deep satisfaction that in Great Britain, too, the idea of an integrated European community was gaining ground.

Adenauer's Berne speech caused a political sensation far beyond the frontiers of Switzerland. Almost everywhere it was received with stormy indignation, and Social-Democrat newspapers in particular took the CDU leader and President of the Parliamentary Council severely to task. The Swiss newspaper *Volksrecht* asked the challenging question: "Do the British and American generals comprehend the damage they have caused, and continue to cause, by sponsoring and supporting the Christian Democratic Union led by Dr. Adenauer?" *The Daily Herald*, the official organ of the British Labor Party and of the then Labor Government of Clement Attlee, declared in a banner headline across its entire front page: "German Accuses Allies." The Liberal *Manchester Guardian*, in a long leading article devoted to the Berne speech, summarized its criticism thus: "We can only assume that Dr. Adenauer deliberately attempted to deceive his hearers." Other smaller papers expressed their views even more drastically. "A Nationalist Shows His True Face," and "The Wolf in Sheep's Clothing" were some of the headlines.

Even the British House of Commons occupied itself with this German account of conditions rendered to a small circle of hearers. The matter was raised in several parliamentary questions calling the British occupation authorities in Germany to account, and Mr. Christopher Mayhew, Under Secretary of State for Foreign Affairs, replied to one questioner, "It is clear that this speech does in fact contain certain expressions of opinion which show a regrettable lack of political responsibility and are bound to cause Germany serious damage in the eyes of the world."

On the whole Adenauer remained silent to these reproaches. It was only in a letter to the Swiss *Neue Zürcher Zeitung* that he briefly commented on his own speech, in order to clear up an obvious misunderstanding. In this letter he made a sharp distinction between nationalism, which he called "a danger to peace and to good-neighborly relations with other countries," and national consciousness and sentiment, which, he said, "are vital and essential to any people, and especially to the German people in its present situation."

Looking back, it may be said that the Berne speech, despite the initial shock it caused, or possibly because of it, by its unreserved sincerity contributed much to the establishment of genuine confidence and trust between Germany and her future partners in the international field, and Adenauer had no reason to regret this appeal to the conscience of the world.

## CHAPTER XV

At the end of March, 1949, when Adenauer returned to Bonn from Switzerland, the German situation seemed as uncertain and contradictory as at any time since the capitulation.

Most plainly visible was the rupture in the Allied camp. The blockade of the three Western-occupied sectors of Berlin, imposed by the Soviet authorities as a reprisal against West German currency reform, had been in force for a full nine months, exposing over two million Germans, cut off and seemingly adrift in the heart of the Soviet Zone, to mortal peril. It was a monstrous act of political blackmail, directed equally at the Berliners and the three Western powers. The Berliners, however, stood fast, and the three Allies stood by them. Vigorous counteraction was taken in the form of the Anglo-American "air lift," a gigantic and successful attempt to feed and supply the isolated city with the help of a vast air transport fleet. This was a momentous and decisive development. It not only saved the blockaded city from starvation and surrender, but beyond this immediate purpose created for the first time a firm bond of genuine solidarity between Germany and the Western World. Until then Germans in general had regarded the Western Powers merely as victors bent upon demanding repentance and exacting reparation for past misdeeds. Now they found them to be allies fighting by their side in the common struggle against the murderous stranglehold from the East. The Berlin Air Lift radically and profoundly changed the mental and political climate in occupied Western Germany. All the harder to understand were the apparent contradictions which persisted in the Allied attitude. For, while they spared no effort and went to unparalleled lengths of exertion and material sacrifice in succoring Berlin, the selfsame Western powers continued to carry out their program of industrial dismantling in their three zones of occupation. Indeed, they pursued it with a new vigor and relentlessness which recalled the most uncompromising periods of the immediate postwar era, even threatening to use troops wherever German workers actively opposed the destruction of their work places. It was, it seemed, truly as Adenauer had said at Berne, "What the right hand builds the left tears asunder."

Nor was this the only glaring inconsistency which troubled Adenauer and greatly added to his difficulties in advocating a policy of cooperation and trust with the Western powers. In his own immediate sphere, in the Parliamentary Council, sharp differences had arisen which at the last moment seemed to threaten the completion of the Constitution. This time the point at issue was the so-called *Finanzausgleich*, or equalization of burdens as provided for in the new Constitution. This article was designed to enable a future federal government to effect an equalizing balance between constituent states of the federation with poor taxation revenue and those enjoying a higher internal revenue, and naturally this entailed a measure of controlling authority for the central government over the financial policies of the various confederate states. The Military Governors, holding fast to the federal principle they had laid down, felt that this was allowing altogether too much power to the central government, and they had therefore rejected this particular section of the draft constitution.

Their rejection aroused the bitter opposition of the German Social Democrats. The SPD had from the very beginning advocated a West German state with a strong central authority, leaving only minor and nonessential powers in the hands of the confederate states, and in the course of months of negotiations they had been compelled to yield on many points and submit to the federalist wishes of their political opponents. Now apparently the limits of their readiness to compromise had been reached. One of their spokesmen in the Parliamentary Council had declared roundly, "Our party will not surrender one iota of their draft proposals for the equalization of finances."

In Adenauer's view this new bone of contention was of secondary importance; among his closer political confidants he declared that he thought it absurd to risk jeopardizing the great over-all objective for the sake of a detailed claim which, if it proved justified, he was sure would in any case eventually and gradually be fulfilled. The great over-all objective, however, was to put an end, at last, to Western Germany's constitutional anarchy and create the nucleus of a democratic state, a germ cell of a new and stable order which in time could serve as a rallying point for the rest of Germany, and offer to the Soviet Zone a model and example, and new hope for the future.

Such, in broad outline, was the situation of the three Western zones of occupation in March, 1949. But now, instead of a hoped-for relaxation of tension, a new sharpening of differences made itself felt. As General Clay noted, the SPD "now insisted that the new proposal be submitted to a plenary session of the Parliamentary Council for approval regardless of our comment. The CDU would not agree and declared that compromise was essential. . . ." In other words, the Socialists were determined to complete the Constitution without further reference to the occupying powers, and subsequent rejection of a Basic Law passed by a majority in the Parliamentary Council would therefore place the entire responsibility for the failure to establish a West German state on the shoulders of the three Military Governors.

This was the stand taken by Carlo Schmid, the Socialist leader, even on the occasion of the "Frankfurt Affair." At that time it had been a threat uttered by an individual representative; but now this threat had hardened into a definite decision backed by the full authority of the Socialist party executive. Dr. Schumacher, the all-powerful party chief, had changed his ground; he was now conducting his struggle against the occupying powers from a national platform, and with national slogans.

In view of the approaching elections, this new strategy offered obvious advantages to the Social Democrats. The party felt it could count on strong support among the broad masses of the German people if it proclaimed, in a "sovereign" manner, its bold defiance of the explicit wishes of the occupying powers. Even if this were to result in the wrecking of the Constitution, the responsibility for such a calamity would lie with the Allies, and the Socialist party could still bask in the glory of heroic resistance stoutly maintained in the interest of the nation as a whole. What was more, by this strategy they were able to maneuver their great opponent at home, the CDU, whom they had come to respect during the preceding state parliamentary elections, into a most awkward dilemma. If the Christian Democrats continued to uphold Adenauer's thesis that the new West German state could be built only in cooperation with the Western democracies—represented as they were in Germany by the three Military Governors—it would be easy enough to accuse them of undignified and spineless compliance with the wishes of the occupying powers, if not of worse things. If, on the other hand, they abandoned their stand, they would inevitably be forced into the wake of the new national policy proclaimed by the SPD, thus acknowledging indirectly Schumacher's claim to leadership.

It was characteristic of Adenauer that he simply refused to recognize this dilemma. He continued unperturbed along the road he considered the right and correct one, and the next aim along this road was the speedy completion of the Constitution in agreement with the three Military Governors. There remained, of course, the question whether the rest of the Parliamentary Council would find it in them to show the same strength of character and steadfastness of purpose. But world events conspired to spare them this test. The decision was made without them, beyond the Atlantic.

On April 2, 1949, the Atlantic Pact was signed in Washington. The Foreign Ministers of twelve nations—Belgium, Canada, Denmark, France, Great Britain, Iceland, Italy, Luxembourg, the Netherlands, Norway, Portugal, and the United States—had come together to conclude an alliance for their joint protection and mutual defense, committing all members of NATO, the North Atlantic Treaty Organization, to come to each other's aid in the event of outside aggression. Germany was not mentioned in the Atlantic Pact. She was apparently not considered a potential aggressor against the West, and this in German eyes was a distinct step forward. For even the Treaty of Dunkirk, from which this great defensive organization of the Western World had grown, by referring explicitly to a "threat from beyond the Rhine," had been clearly pointed against the former wartime adversary. Now Germany as an object of Allied anxieties had evidently receded to the background, and it seemed clear, moreover, that there was now no intention of treating the Western half of the former Reich, for which three NATO members—Great Britain, France, and the United States—bore the responsibility, as a political no man's land, unless they were prepared to run the risk of other than democratic influences obtaining a hold on it.

What was more, the friendly atmosphere created by the alliance just concluded offered an opportunity for swift settlement of outstanding Allied differences over Germany, and the Foreign Ministers of the three occupying powers, Dean Acheson, Ernest Bevin, and Robert Schuman, did not allow their chance to slip. Six days of joint discussion around the Washington conference table sufficed to hammer out a common pattern for their future German policy. The draft Occupation Statute, evolved by their representatives in Germany—the three Military Governors—and by now swollen to a monstrously complicated and tangled document, was quickly consigned to the wastepaper basket. In its place, a brief document of less than three typescript pages was drafted, which confined itself to the stipulation of a few basic essentials. Henceforth the future federal government would know where it stood and what limitations were placed, for the time being, upon the sovereignty of the new state. These so-called "reserved fields" included, chiefly, disarmament and demilitarization, foreign affairs and currency control, the Ruhr Authority and other international organs of control. These remained in the hands of the occupying powers. Within eighteen months after coming into effect, however, the Occupation Statute was to be revised, and as many of these restrictions as possible rescinded.

Two days later, on April 10, 1949, the American Military Governor, at the request of the three Foreign Ministers, handed Konrad Adenauer as President of the Parliamentary Council this document outlining the essential points of the Occupation Statute. In a covering letter, transmitted by General Clay at the same time, the Parliamentary Council was informed that as soon as a West German government had been formed, Military Government in Western Germany would be dissolved and replaced by a civilian High Commission. In conclusion, the Foreign Ministers urged the Parliamentary Council, once more, to complete its work on the Constitution as speedily as possible.

There was, however, a second letter from the Foreign Ministers which General Clay did not pass on to Adenauer but kept locked in his desk, and this letter was subsequently to play an important part in German politics. It contained alternative proposals by the three Foreign Ministers which went a long way toward meeting German, and particularly German Socialist, wishes regarding the controversial issue of equalization of finances and the general position of the central authority within the federal state. It was left to the discretion of General Clay to decide at which moment this letter should be communicated to the Parliamentary Council.

There could be no doubt about the purpose of this move. The three Foreign Ministers continued to feel that the new German state should be as decentralized a federation as was possible and practicable, but they were willing to make further concessions in the event of the entire conception threatening to be wrecked on the rock of Socialist obstruction. Seen from the heights of the Atlantic Community and its overriding requirements, the question of German finance equalization, indeed the entire problem of the structure of the future German federal state which so exercised the minds of German politicians, no doubt reduced themselves to comparatively unimportant trifles. The only really important thing was that Western Germany should receive, as soon as possible, a democratic constitution and acquire stability. This was essentially the view taken by Adenauer all along.

But, even so, without knowledge of the existence of the second letter from the Foreign Ministers, Adenauer had reason to be satisfied with what had been achieved. By far the most important point was the Allied undertaking for a revision of the Occupation Statute within eighteen months. This insured continuity of development and left the door open for further negotiations. Adenauer had always placed his faith in the inherent logic of events and the ultimate victory of sound common sense, and consequently regarded the prospect of early revision held out by the Allies themselves as a direct encouragement to continue on the path of a gradual whittling away of Allied prerogatives and privileges, until eventually full sovereignty was attained.

The Social Democratic party reacted very differently. Suddenly and without warning, it rejected the entire draft constitution so far completed and announced that within a few days it would submit to the Parliamentary Council a completely new draft of its own, considerably shorter and following more closely its own ideas. The next day, April 14, the three Military Governors met a delegation from the Parliamentary Council, led by Adenauer, for a conference at Frankfurt. Every attempt was made to persuade Carlo Schmid, the Socialist spokesman, with reasoned argument to reconsider his party's attitude, and to desist from the uncompromising stand they had taken. One by one the three Military Governors spoke to him at some length. There was no precedent, General Clay said finally, "for three Military Governors trying so hard to divest themselves of authority and with so little success."

In vain they pleaded. Carlo Schmid merely declared that all further steps would have to be deferred until after April 20. On this day the Socialist Party Conference, called by Schumacher, was to meet at Hanover.

This meeting of the Social Democratic party executive committee at Hanover on April 19 and 20, 1949, was deliberately dressed up as a major political demonstration, designed to focus the attention of all Germany, indeed of the entire world, upon the historic decision about to be taken. There was but one question in everybody's mind: would Dr. Kurt Schumacher, the all-powerful leader of the party, have the courage openly to challenge the three Western Allies, Great Britain, France, and the United States, reject their proposals, and insist on his own uncompromising "No" to the present draft of the Basic Law?

The meeting of the party executive lasted for two whole days, from early morning until late at night. Schumacher opened it by giving a lengthy and detailed account of the situation, referring to the Allied recommendations for the Basic Law as "an attempt to permit the resurrection of Germany only in the form of a very loose federation of states." This was a dramatically pointed description of the actual state of affairs, sounding very effective but in fact doing less than justice to the true position. Even more summarily Schumacher dealt with the CDU, declaring, "You can only be a German patriot, and not a patriot of eleven German states. That is the whole difference between the Social Democratic party and the Christian Social Union!"

The debate which followed showed that, at first, by no means all members of the executive committee shared Schumacher's views. A number of voices were raised questioning the wisdom of challenging the Western Powers in this way, and warning against the fatal consequences which were bound to ensue if the work done at Bonn was brought to naught at the last moment. But Schumacher brushed all these objections aside with an impatient gesture. With supreme optimism he declared, "Nothing will be brought to naught! Germany will receive her Basic Law!" A correspondent of a British news agency reported, "In the face of this great decision Schumacher seemed possessed of unshakable calm, indeed of almost Olympian serenity. Despite his grave physical disability he remained in his place from morning till night; he even had his lunch brought to him in the conference room and again and again intervened in the debate, encouraging the waverers and compelling the undecided to make up their minds."

These tireless labors bore their fruit. On the evening of the second day, the party executive committee, with fifty-one votes out of a total of sixty-three, adopted a resolution prepared by Schumacher which, in form and content, was nothing less than an ultimatum. The party proclaimed a whole catalogue of conditions and requirements to be incorporated in the Basic Law, and declared it would reject the Constitution in its entirety in the event of any single one of these demands not being met. The die was cast. When later in the evening Schumacher called the press, he told them:

"We have spoken our last word. We answer NO to the Allied memorandum. We answer NO to the compromise demanded of us. We demand a new Basic Law."

On the following day, April 21, the Socialist party submitted their own draft constitution which they had promised earlier. What would the Military Governors say now? How would they react to this open disregard of their authority? The answer came swiftly, and it was a surprise. On April 22, General Clay announced on behalf of the Foreign Ministers that the Allies would not insist on their objections but were prepared to make a number of important concessions. These concessions, it turned out, coincided so closely with the demands made by Schumacher that they amounted to little less than acceptance of his ultimatum. The "Man of Hanover" had prevailed.

Or so it seemed. The Socialist press announced triumphantly, "Although three victorious nations, England, France, and America, are keeping Germany occupied, it is in fact Dr. Schumacher who determines the destiny of Western Germany. . . ." And even solidly conservative papers such as *Die Zeit* of Hamburg acknowledged, "The SPD has won the game. Its trump card was the executive committee's 'No' to all further compromise over the draft constitution, and it settled the issue. . . . With the outlines of a federal republic becoming discernible and German politicians, too, having henceforth to be measured by standards of statesmanship, the question now arises whether Kurt Schumacher will succeed in effecting the transition from being a people's tribune to becoming a genuine statesman. The 'No' of Hanover was a debut of much promise."

In the light of such resounding success, which even the opponents had to acknowledge, it seemed of small consequence that General Clay now took the second letter of the Foreign Ministers from his desk and handed it to the Parliamentary Council. True, it enabled the three Military Governors to re-establish their authority by showing that they had not, in fact, yielded to Schumacher's ultimatum but had acted in accordance with instructions previously received from their governments. But in the eyes of the public this did nothing to lessen the magnitude of Schumacher's success.

Nevertheless, the delayed transmission of so vitally important a document caused some political minds to wonder what had really happened behind the scenes. During a press conference of April 25, at Frankfurt, a London journalist asked General Robertson, the British Military Governor, point-blank:

"May one ask why General Clay did not transmit the second letter from the Foreign Ministers to the Parliamentary Council until April 22, although it had been in his possession ever since April 10?"

The British General answered with his well-known poker face: "One may ask but one may not get an answer."

For the moment Adenauer remained silent in the face of his opponent's great triumph. A deputy of the CDU who was also a member of the Parliamentary Council at that time later said:

"Never have I admired Konrad Adenauer as much as during those days. He had every reason to feel annoyed at the attitude of the Military Governors. They had withheld from him, the President of the Parliamentary Council, a letter which had been meant for him, and by doing so had helped his opponent to a political advantage the repercussions of which upon the coming elections were impossible to estimate. What would have been more natural than that he who had always been a loyal partner to them should now reproach the Military Governors? Nothing of the sort happened. Rather the contrary. His political friends were bitterly resentful, and Adenauer did his best to calm them. In lengthy conversation he explained to them that the reason for the attitude of the Allies must presumably be sought in the fact that on account of its long-established tradition the Social Democratic party seemed to offer them a better guarantee for democratic development in the new Germany. "We must never forget," he said, "that the CDU/CSU is a very young party. We cannot blame the Allies if they feel that they have no very clear view of our future development."

Adenauer did not confine his loyal attitude to the three Military Governors. It would have been open to him now, for his part, to move the CDU into opposition and to defeat Schumacher's proposals in the Parliamentary Council. "I believe," the CDU deputy's account continues, "that few party politicians would have resisted this temptation. Again Adenauer refrained from taking the obvious step, but instead tried his best to coordinate and harmonize the new Socialist proposals as quickly as possible with the bulk of the work already achieved. Again and again he impressed upon us at the meetings of the parliamentary party the urgent necessity of 'bringing in' the Constitution as early as possible, and that for the sake of this great objective we had to put up with adjustments and sacrifices of some of our own wishes. Even now, in this situation when it was clear that his opponents would claim the entire credit for the completion of the Constitution and enter it as a major success in their books, Adenauer remained stoutly faithful to his principle."

Three days after the announcement of the Allied concessions, the Parliamentary Council had reached agreement on all outstanding controversial issues, and on the evening of April 25, Adenauer, in his capacity as President of the Council, was able to inform the Military Governors of the good news.

Speed was now the essence of the contract. For on April 27, 1949, the Soviet Government announced its willingness to lift the blockade of Berlin provided the Western Powers agreed to hold a Four Power Conference to discuss the reunification of Germany. The object of this diplomatic move was clear. The Soviets were endeavoring through prolonged negotiations around the conference table to delay the creation of the Federal Republic, if not in fact to prevent it altogether.

The Western Powers were not deceived. They agreed with the Russians on the lifting of the Berlin blockade and the summoning of a conference which was to begin on May 23, in Paris, but at the same time the American Government informed General Clay through Ambassador Robert D. Murphy that they "desired the prompt formation of a West German government." In other words, the Western Powers were not prepared to have the creation of the West German state made an object of barter at the forthcoming conference. Therefore the Federal Republic must be an accomplished fact by May 23, 1949.

Adenauer appreciated the position and acted accordingly. Having so far always defended the deliberate and thorough pace of the work at Bonn against undue haste and pressure, he now pressed urgently for its speedy completion. But the Communists, too, appreciated what was at stake. They transferred their struggle to the Parliamentary Council and made Adenauer the chief target of their attacks. Their spokesman, Max Reimann, declared:

"General Clay is, of course, fully aware that the creation of a separate West German state can be accomplished only with the help of the leading political parties. . . . He is conducting a policy of realism, and this realistic policy compels him to take note of the fact that, with England outmaneuvered by U.S. capital and, consequently, the German Social Democrats pushed aside, the decisive party here in this Council is now the CDU. This cool political calculation has prompted him to put his money on the CDU. But Herr Adenauer, on his part, was sufficiently clever as long as eighteen months ago to put the money of the CDU/CSU on the dollar horse. He woke up to the true facts of the situation a little earlier than you, gentlemen of the Social Democratic party. In your block-headed conceit you so misjudged the position that you failed to notice that you had ceased to play a decisive part in this game and had meantime been reduced to the status of U.S. reserve troops."

The Communists did not confine themselves to political accusations but once again resorted to personal incrimination. The old charge of separatism was revived, and Reimann declared, "I shall prove to you, Herr Adenauer, that in 1919 you took a leading part in the establishment of the Rhenish Republic." This time Reimann asserted that material from the archives of the former Reich Chancellery had come into his possession which proved Adenauer's separatist past beyond any doubt.

Adenauer challenged him to make this material public. Reimann did so, at the next plenary meeting, which was also the last the Parliamentary Council was to hold, but to all those reasonably familiar with the history of the separatist movement, his "revelations" brought no surprise whatever. All Reimann had to offer was a string of quotations from Adenauer's well-known speech of February 1, 1919, at Cologne City Hall, suitably distorted and falsified to support his allegation that the former Chief Mayor of Cologne had demanded the detachment of the Rhineland from the German Reich.

Adenauer protested vehemently, "If Herr Reimann makes an assertion to this effect he is simply telling an untruth and is speaking against his own better knowledge." So as to lend greater emphasis to his own countercharge, Adenauer proceeded to give an account of the proceedings taken against him during the Hitler regime, which had been initiated for the express purpose of clarifying his participation in the separatist movement. "This commission of inquiry," he declared with raised voice, "came to the conclusion that all charges leveled against me were wholly untrue."

Having said this, he dealt his accuser a smashing counterblow. He revealed the motives which had prompted Reimann to make his slanderous attack.

"Last Thursday," Adenauer now told the assembly, "Herr Reimann asked me for a personal interview. In the course of this conversation he invited me to arrange for the Basic Law to be defeated, or else he would come up with his revelations. Ladies and gentlemen, I will leave it to your judgment to decide which paragraph of the criminal law applies to an action of this kind. Personally I wouldn't even trouble to consult the criminal law. I feel that a politician, and Herr Reimann aspires to be a politician, who resorts to such means passes judgment upon himself."

When Reimann protested angrily, Adenauer gave precise chapter and verse for his charge. Reimann, he said, had taken him aside and told him at least three times, "I warn you! I've got the entire material of 1919 to hand. You had better see to it that this Basic Law is thrown out!"

Adenauer's statement caused an uproar among the assembly, and a storm of indignation against the Communists. Such was the turmoil that the session had to be suspended for over an hour. When it was resumed, Adenauer returned to the chair which, during this personal argument, he had vacated to Adolph Schönfelder, the Vice-President, and presided over the final stages of the last reading of the Constitution. There was not a trace in him of the violent emotion which had agitated him during the preceding personal episode. Indeed, his calm and superior chairmanship was particularly noticeable during this last session.

Standing on his feet continuously from midday onward, he supervised the voting on article after article, paragraph after paragraph, and, when on one occasion renewed objections were raised, he warned good-humoredly against further delay. "May I remind the assembly that we are not here to vote on the Ten Commandments but on a law valid only for a period of transition." His urgency and dispatch carried the rest of the assembly with him. The whole enormous bulk of the Constitution was "whipped" through its third reading in a matter of ten hours.

At midnight on May 8, 1949, the fourth anniversary of the end of the war, the Basic Law was finally adopted by fifty-three votes against twelve. Immediately afterward Adenauer made his concluding speech which ended on this note:

"We have completed the greater part of the task the Parliamentary Council was called upon to perform. Even though there has been some disharmony here and there, our work was nevertheless inspired throughout by a feeling of love and devotion toward the German people. Ladies and gentlemen! Let us wish that God may bless this people and this work, for the benefit of all Europe and for the sake of peace in the world!"

Four days later, on May 12, 1949, at the head of a delegation from the Parliamentary Council, Adenauer received from the hands of the Military Governors at Frankfurt a formal letter confirming the official approval of the new Constitution by the occupying powers.

In his account General Clay remarks, "The structure of West German Government was thus established prior to the May 23 conference of the Four Foreign Ministers in Paris. It served notice that the three Western Powers would no longer be thwarted in their efforts to reconstruct a democratic Germany, and that this was the end of Communist expansion." *

But the Bonn Constitution marked not only the end of Communist expansion. It marked at the same time the beginning of a new development which started in the West. Article 24 of the Constitution laid it down that "the Federal Republic shall be empowered to transfer, through appropriate legislation, such of its sovereign rights to international institutions and to agree to such limitations of its sovereignty

* From *Decision in Germany*, by Gen. Lucius D. Clay (Doubleday & Co., Inc.) © 1950.

as may be required to integrate it in a collective system of security for the preservation of peace."

It was not without good reason that Adenauer in his first speech as Federal Chancellor placed particular emphasis on this specific article of the Constitution. It was this article, embodying a voluntary renunciation of unrestricted national sovereignty, which enabled him during the years to come to achieve his most notable successes in the field of foreign affairs—the Schuman Plan, Western European Union, and the acceptance of Germany into the Atlantic Community.

With the foundations for the new German state well and truly laid, only two questions remained to be solved, both of which fell within the competence of the Parliamentary Council. An electoral law had to be drafted and adopted, and the provisional capital of the Federal Republic chosen.

Over the electoral law a last tussle arose with the Military Governors. Always anxious to emphasize the federal character of the new state, the Military Governors had insisted that the framing of the regulations governing the election to the Federal Parliament should be left to the individual constituent states. This seemed an impossible condition. It was absurd to authorize eleven different confederate states to issue eleven different electoral laws for one and the same joint Parliament. Truly grotesque results were inevitable if each political party which happened to command a majority in any given constituent state shaped the electoral law according to its own preferences.

This time it was not only the Social Democrats Carlo Schmid and Walter Menzel who protested against the Military Governors' ruling. Adenauer, too, rejected such a solution but advised against a precipitate and intemperate answer. "With a little patience," he said, "anything can be explained to the Military Governors, and their agreement obtained." He was proved right. The electoral law, as finally approved by the Military Governors on June 2, 1949, corresponded on all essential points to German wishes and requirements.

Two West German cities were competing for the privilege of harboring the future federal government within their walls—Frankfurt and Bonn. It was an alternative typical of the birth pangs of the new German state and the contradictory forces at work in the renascent German body politic. No agreement could be reached between the two contenders. Both cities were already busily at work erecting future parliament buildings and ministries and planning for additional housing when, on May 10, 1949, the controversial issue came before the Parliamentary Council to be finally settled by a vote. The debate had lasted all day in sultry summer heat and everyone was exhausted when at last, at midnight, the vote was taken.

For Adenauer this was an important moment. Bonn was almost a sister city to his native Cologne, and hardly a stone's throw away from his own home across the river. He had spent his entire life in its immediate neighborhood and was attached to it by a thousand bonds. Was it, or was it not, going to be the center of the new national life which in his old age he had labored so strenuously to kindle?

Nothing betrayed his feelings. Blank ballots were distributed on which each deputy in the great hall, overcrowded by excited spectators, had to write the name of the city of his choice. One by one the folded papers were collected and taken up to the President's desk on the elevated dais. There, tall, erect, clothed in black, pale, and visibly tired, stood Konrad Adenauer, unfolding paper after paper and announcing its contents in a clear voice above the general hubbub of growing excitement, while a clerk entered it on a list:

"Frankfurt . . . Bonn . . . Bonn . . . Frankfurt . . . Frankfurt . . . Bonn . . . Bonn . . ."

With an unmoved face Adenauer announced result after result. Excitement rose from minute to minute as it became clear that the race between the two rival would-be capitals was extremely close. At one moment Frankfurt had gained a clear lead, and the Frankfurters were already certain of their victory. Then the last few papers were brought up.

"Bonn . . . " Adenauer announced, "Bonn . . . Bonn . . . Bonn . . . "

The lead was lost. Bonn won by the narrowest of margins.

The new German state had its provisional capital.

Forty-eight hours later the Soviet sentries at the zonal frontier post of Helmstedt opened the barrier and the first convoy of trucks carrying fresh food and vegetables from Western Germany thundered along the autobahn toward hungry Berlin. The capital of the old German state was freed of the deadly stranglehold of the blockade.

## CHAPTER XVI

SUNDAY, AUGUST 14, 1949, had been fixed as the day on which the new Federal Republic of Germany was to hold its first general election.

The Christian Democratic Union opened the election campaign three weeks before polling day, on July 22, with a mass meeting at Heidelberg intended by the party leadership as a solemn demonstration. Against the historic background of Heidelberg Castle trumpeters were sounding fanfares, heralds clad in red velvet were receiving the guests, and an orchestra played the march from Wagner's *Tannhäuser*. Three prominent speakers, among them Adenauer, had been chosen to announce to the nation in broad, inspiring outline the fundamental principles and objectives of Christian Democratic policy.

Such had been the intention of the organizers. But Adenauer all but wrecked their plans. Deliberately ignoring all pomp and circumstance and casting high-flown solemnity to the winds, he descended at once into the political arena, firing point-blank at his opponents.

Now it was suddenly seen that Adenauer had only given the appearance of surrendering the "national field" without a struggle to his great opponent, Kurt Schumacher. He had remained silent when the defiant "No" was uttered from Hanover. To the astonishment of many of his political friends he had not contested with a single word the triumphant claim of the Socialists to have forced their will upon the occupying powers. Indeed, well-meaning friends in the Parliamentary Council had found a perfectly plausible explanation of his attitude. In those critical April days, they were sure, Adenauer had been above all anxious not to endanger the completion of the Constitution by indulging in a German party quarrel.

But since then three months had passed, during which time the Socialist party had made much valuable capital of their "act of liberation," and still Adenauer had said nothing. Why? Now the puzzle was solved, and its solution gave to many an unexpected insight into Adenauer's ways of thought and action. He had bided his time, bearing the resentment of his friends with the same patient equanimity which made him put up with the victorious exultation of his opponents, waiting for the right time and the right occasion to open his counteroffensive under the most favorable conditions and with the greatest possible effect. It was a genuine example of the characteristic Adenauer strategy.

The opportunity had now arrived. The first large election meeting of the CDU would insure the strongest possible resonance for what Adenauer had to reveal. An audience numbering several thousands was present, as was the press, not yet weary from innumerable election speeches and awaiting the first appearance of the young party on a nationwide stage with tense excitement. The moment, too, was advantageous. Even if it must be assumed that people would quickly forget what they heard during these three weeks, the period was still short enough for Adenauer's revelations to stick in the memory of most and to make their impact on polling day.

The Heidelberg meeting began with what looked like a serious hitch. Adenauer failed to turn up. Party secretary Blankenhorn, who had left Bonn two hours after his chief, had long reached Heidelberg, and still there was no sign of Adenauer. Frantic telephone calls were made in all directions, and a rumor went round that Dr. Adenauer had had a motor accident. When eventually he arrived, literally at the very last moment, he showed himself most surprised by the general unrest he had caused. As it turned out, he had stopped his car somewhere on the way and taken a short walk into the nearby woods. There, seated peacefully on a tree trunk, he had drafted the speech he was now going to make.

Mounting the rostrum he was greeted by an enthusiastic ovation, and at first it seemed as though he meant to confine himself, like the rest of the speakers, to a sober and dispassionate exposition of the party's aims and tasks. Very soon, however, he left the well-trodden path and went straight over to the attack. With passionate indignation he protested against the claim of the Social Democrats to have shown greater courage and energy than the CDU in standing up for, and defending, the national interest. In the light of the undeniable success which Schumacher's "No" had achieved, this seemed a very risky protest indeed. But Adenauer was ready to back it with proof, and in doing so provided not only the Heidelberg meeting with a major surprise. It had its effect far beyond the meeting and was everywhere felt to be the severest and most damaging blow Schumacher's party had suffered for a long time.

Calmly and soberly Adenauer told the meeting that "about a week before the Hanover conference the executive committee of the Social Democratic party had been confidentially informed to the effect that the Allies would not insist on their recommendations, and that the Foreign Ministers' Conference in Washington was prepared to meet German wishes with regard to a strengthened position of the central governmental authority in the future Federal Republic."

"This information," Adenauer declared with a raised voice, "was imparted to the representatives of the Social Democratic party by a high-ranking officer of the British Military Government at headquarters in Frankfurt as early as April 14, while I, as President of the Parliamentary Council, did not receive the same news until April 20."

That was a sensation indeed! It was now clear that the second letter from the three Foreign Ministers which General Clay had kept in his desk had been known to the Socialist party executive, at least in its essentials, before they sat down to take their "far-reaching decisions." Now the Hanover "act of liberation" appeared in a new and highly dubious light.

The outcry of indignation which arose the very next day from the Socialist camp proved that Adenauer had hit a bull's-eye. Schumacher was outraged and called Adenauer a liar. A Social Democrat newspaper correspondent described him as "a master of rhetorical body blows." As was to be expected, the British authorities denied having given any prior information to the Socialist party executive.

Adenauer answered this denial by revealing his sources. He called a press conference at which party secretary Blankenhorn disclosed the fact that a British officer, indignant over the way in which members of the Labor Party passed the German Socialists useful trumps for the election campaign, had fully informed him on what had been happening. Shortly afterward the British Foreign office took official note of the incident. Its spokesman admitted that "on April 14, at Frankfurt, certain indications had been given to representatives of the Social Democratic party regarding the version of the Basic Law which, in the British view, could still, in an extreme case, count on approval by the Allies."

"If ridicule could kill," an American newspaperman wrote, "there should now be a great many dead among the Socialist executive committee at Hanover."

Several important developments had taken place before polling day, inside as well as outside Germany, which were not without their effect upon the course of the election.

Most important of all, the dark cloud of the Paris conference had passed. After nearly four weeks of fruitless negotiation the Allies had terminated their discussions on German reunification on June 20, without result. This negative outcome was frankly welcomed by many Germans, since it relieved them of their fear that the three Western Powers might after all, at the last minute, reach an understanding with their one-time Soviet ally behind the back, and at the expense of, Germany. To Adenauer the Paris result was definite confirmation of the view he himself had held all along. During the closing days of the Parliamentary Council he had remarked, "As soon as the Federal Republic stands firmly established on its feet, the Allies will have created an accomplished fact which they can no longer ignore or by-pass." The correctness of this view was now plain for all to see. It seemed clear that henceforth the Western Allies could not and would not pursue a "German policy" of their own over the heads of the men at Bonn, and without reference to them.

Internally, too, several shadows had passed. The Allied Military Government had been abolished; with it the arbitrary division of Western Germany into three zones of occupation had disappeared. Military Government had been replaced by a civilian Allied High Commission composed of three High Commissioners and their staffs, whose official headquarters was at the Petersberg, just south of Bonn. Their duty was to administer the special rights and prerogatives reserved to the occupying powers and specifically defined in the Occupation Statute.

With them new men had appeared on the political scene. General Clay, the American "Pro-Consul," had left Germany, and his place had been taken by John J. McCloy, a prominent banker and former Assistant Secretary of War. As it happened, he and Adenauer were distantly related by marriage, Mrs. McCloy having been born, as was Adenauer's second wife, a Zinsser. On the French side, General Pierre Koenig had been replaced by a career diplomat, André François-

Poncet, who had been Ambassador to Germany once before, knew the country intimately, and spoke its language fluently. Of the Old Guard of the immediate postwar period, only Sir Brian Robertson was left. But, having retired from the Army and divested himself of his military rank, he too was now performing his duties as a civilian.

It had been generally assumed by observers inside and outside Germany that the last major thorn in the German flesh, industrial dismantling, would inevitably become the principal issue on which the election would turn. "Whoever denounces dismantling loudest and most vehemently will win the German elections," a well-known French publicist had predicted, and it remained to be seen whether this skeptical view of the Germans as "a nation of incorrigible industrialists" would be confirmed by events. Looking back on the election, it can be said that on the whole the skeptic was proved wrong. True, the subject of dismantling figured to some extent in the election speeches of all parties, but it remained in the background. Three major problems which primarily occupied the minds of the electorate took precedence over it. They were unemployment, housing, and the destitution of the refugees from the East. And these three major problems affecting the existence of the nation could in turn be summed up in one cardinal question:

Was Professor Erhard's Social Market Economy in a position so to boost the German economy that these three vital problems could be effectively solved?

Adenauer, who had boldly placed the Social Market Economy at the head of his party's election program, had full confidence in Erhard and the soundness of his conception, and Erhard himself had equal self-confidence, asserting in unequivocal terms that the economic policy sponsored by the CDU could and would create the conditions necessary for the solution of these problems.

Against this, the Social Democratic party adhered steadfastly to the economic views they had already propounded in the Frankfurt Bizonal Economic Council. "The continuation of the social market economy," their leaders declared, "will only make the rich even richer and the poor yet poorer. It is bound to lead to catastrophe." In their election manifestoes and addresses they demanded state ownership of heavy industry, socialization, and a planned economy, and their economic experts declared roundly that Erhard must go before his ideas could cause even greater damage.

With fundamental views thus clashing sharply, the election campaign was not an easy one to conduct, and its drama was heightened by the shortness of time in which the issues had to be fought out. Little more than three weeks were available before polling day, and the electorate consisted to a large extent of young people who had never voted in their lives before and were only vaguely familiar, if at all, with democratic processes. Three weeks was not a great deal of time in which to "educate" a largely ignorant electorate. For it was necessary to explain to them thoroughly not only the issues on which they had to decide, but, moreover, the extent and weight of the responsibility they assumed in making these decisions, of which many who had never experienced any but authoritarian rule were but dimly aware.

During this period Adenauer was on the road from morning till night, traveling and speaking day after day. There were days when he addressed as many as three or four separate meetings, drafting his speeches in the car while traveling from place to place, mostly using no more than briefly sketched pencil notes, but never making the same speech twice and carefully basing each one on detailed knowledge of local conditions judiciously obtained beforehand. Frequently, too, after a meeting he would briefly jot down his impressions for future reference. Thus, at Cologne, he noted, his "pledge to work for a united Europe met with a very strong reaction," and to a traveling companion he remarked, "Now I know for certain that I'm on the right road."

The election campaign made tremendous demands, physical and mental, on all German politicians without exception, and for many of them it was, in addition, a severe test of character and nerves. Deep personal animosities between the leading protagonists lent an extra edge to their political differences. Thus, after the Heidelberg speech, Kurt Schumacher nursed a profound personal antipathy to Adenauer bordering on unmitigated hatred and seeking release in utterances which went considerably beyond the customary and accepted polemics of an election campaign. "Herr Adenauer," Schumacher said on one occasion, "maintains a very reserved relationship with truth and honesty."

In general, Adenauer preferred to ignore such purely personal attacks. Only once, during a meeting of the executive committee of the CDU, he took actual notice of them, saying, "Personal feelings always create a higher temperature than factual differences of opinion." In their ultimate effect Schumacher's exaggerated polemics probably were to Adenauer's advantage. Even more than his achievements in building up the party to its present status, the violent and acrimonious attacks of his opponents now made him stand out visibly from the rest of the CDU leaders and made him appear in the minds of the people as the central figure of the election campaign and Schumacher's only opponent of true consequence. For it must not be forgotten that, although the CDU had undoubtedly gained ground during the campaign, most neutral observers remained convinced until the very last of a Socialist victory. As late as the eve of polling day the odds among foreign newspaper correspondents in Frankfurt were seventy to thirty for Schumacher.

Then came the surprise.

Sunday, August 14, 1949, was a hot and sultry day. Before midday Adenauer went to his local polling station at the village of Rhöndorf to cast his vote. Returning home, he devoted himself to his private correspondence, catching up on it, and in the afternoon there was the customary Sunday family gathering with his children and grandchildren who had come up from Cologne and München-Gladbach, devoted mainly to the discussion of domestic topics such as cooking, baking cakes, and educating the children. Although himself a candidate for the neighboring constituency of Bonn, the father of the family firmly declined to speculate on the probable outcome of the election. "Children," he said, "I'm tired. What could be done, we have done. And the outcome is not in our hands. Tomorrow we shall know anyway, and therefore it is idle to think about it now."

Toward nine in the evening there was a telephone call from Bonn. A party friend announced the local result: 28,000 votes for the CDU, Adenauer elected member of the Federal Parliament with a clear majority. The family rushed up with its congratulations. Adenauer warded them off. "Let's wait and see how it goes on," he remarked laconically. At ten o'clock he went to bed.

In Hanover, too, at the Socialist party headquarters men were waiting to see how it would "go on." But they were not retiring to bed. Result after result came in over the teletype. At the hour when Adenauer withdrew for the night there were congratulations for Kurt Schumacher who, in his constituency of Hanover South, had been elected with an absolute majority. But as the night drew on the position gradually deteriorated, and when the anxious party officials finally dispersed at dawn, they knew: the CDU had won.

Before noon on August 15, the whole of Germany knew the final result.

Of a total electorate of approximately 32,000,000 in the German Federal Republic, 78.8 per cent had exercised their right to vote—a high proportion, it was felt, and testifying to anything but political indifference and lack of interest in the future of Germany. A count of 7,360,000 votes had gone to the CDU, 6,930,000 to the Social Democrats. The lead was by no means overwhelming but it was sufficient to decide the principal issue at this election—who was henceforth to lead in Germany, the SPD or the CDU. The FDP (Free Democratic Party) had emerged as the third strongest party, with 2,790,000 votes, while the remaining parties, including the Communists, had been left far behind.

What would the *Bundestag*, the first Parliament, look like?

In all it comprised 402 deputies representing ten different parties. Of these 402 members, 139 belonged to the combined CDU/CSU, and 131 to the Socialist party. The FDP had obtained fifty-two seats; two smaller parties, the German Party and the Bavarian Party, seventeen seats each. The Communists, with their fifteen members, had been relegated to the place of an insignificant and uninfluential splinter group.

Seven days after the election, on August 21, 1949, Adenauer invited the leading men of the CDU/CSU to a confidential discussion at his house in Zennigsweg, at Rhöndorf.

The moment had come to decide on the future strategy of the party. In accordance with established parliamentary tradition, it would fall to the CDU/CSU as the strongest party in Parliament to form the first federal government. But this was easier said than done. They must first of all agree among themselves on who was to assume the important offices of Federal President, or Head of State, and Federal Chancellor, or Head of Government, and they had to decide on what sort of a majority they intended to base themselves in Parliament. The combined CDU/CSU could not govern alone. They fell short of the required absolute majority of 202 by 63 seats. In order to form a government commanding a secure and stable majority they had to enter a coalition partnership with one or several other parties. Who were these political allies to be?

Two solutions seemed to offer themselves: a coalition between the two major parties, CDU and SPD, which would result in a form of national government, or cooperation with the smaller, non-Socialist parties, which would place the SPD in opposition.

Should there be a coalition with the Social Democrats or not? That was the basic question to which the Rhöndorf meeting had to address itself. There were many who thought such a coalition by far the best solution, if not indeed the only natural and obvious answer to the problem. The three occupying powers, too, although studiously refraining from all semblance of interference, shared this view. There was much to be said for starting the new republic off with a joint effort by the major parties. The Social Democratic party had already let it be known that in principle they were in sympathy with the idea of entering a coalition with the Christian Democrats. However, they had made one condition: they must be given the Ministry of Economics in the new government. Acceptance of this condition, on the other hand, would mean for the CDU an abandonment of the economic principles they stood for and which had very largely contributed to their success at the polls.

So far Adenauer had voiced no opinion on this crucial question, and there was therefore much tense expectation among those he had invited to his house. It was, in a sense, the General Staff of the party which had foregathered. Nearly all prominent CDU/CSU politicians, including the Ministers President of several confederate states, were present. One of those taking part unofficially in the discussion was Dr. Robert Pferdmenges, the Cologne banker and personal friend of Adenauer's, who since 1945 had been a member of the CDU executive of the Rhineland province.

"After their victory," Dr. Pferdmenges tells, "I had expected to find the CDU leaders in high spirits. The opposite was the case. Arriving rather late at the meeting, I found a gathering of men standing about in groups, serious and rather depressed, while others were walking up and down the garden engrossed in agitated discussion. It was a blisteringly hot summer afternoon, as more and more cars drove up down below in Zennigsweg and politician after politician panted and sweated his way up to the house. This path from Zennigsweg up to Adenauer's house is fairly steep and long—thirty-five steps, to be exact. Adenauer himself has a high opinion of them. 'Climbing stairs,' he says, 'keeps a man young.' Not all his visitors share this view.

"As soon as all the guests had arrived, Adenauer invited us into the house, where a large table was laid for afternoon coffee. In any other place than this, doubts might conceivably have arisen as to who should preside over so prominent a gathering. But here, in Adenauer's house, the question could not even arise. With complete naturalness Adenauer, as host, claimed the chairmanship for himself. He rose, welcomed his guests, thanked all those who had contributed to the success in the elections, and immediately attacked the central problem."

Coalition with the Socialists or not?

"I am aware," Adenauer said, "that many of those here present take the view that a coalition with the Social Democratic party would be the best solution. I consider this wrong. Our party has fought this election with the Social Market Economy as the chief point on our program, and the majority of the electorate have decided in favor of this Social Market Economy and against Socialist economic planning. If we now form a government jointly with the SPD, we shall be compelled to make concessions and conclude compromises which run counter to the expressed will of those who have elected us, and which will endanger the success of the Social Market Economy."

When Adenauer had finished, Dr. Pferdmenges recalls, only about half the gathering applauded. The rest remained stubbornly and disapprovingly silent. The next speaker voiced the views of this opposition. He was Peter Altmeier, Minister President of the Rhine-Palatinate, who spoke in favor of entering a coalition with the Social Democrats.

"We must bring in the Social Democrats," he declared, "and make them share the responsibility of government. We must see to it that they are firmly tied to our government, unless we are prepared to put up perpetually with an opposition bent on using every national argument in an attempt to wreck understanding and agreement with the occupying powers. Even if our government should succeed in obtaining large and substantial concessions from the Allies, the Socialists will always assert that we had obtained too little, that they would have achieved much more, and denounce us as poor advocates of the national cause! And since it will be impossible to take them at their word, they will find it easy to persuade the malcontents and get

* * *

them on their side, with the result that at the end of our legislative period we shall be facing an overwhelming opposition under Schumacher's leadership."

Again there was applause, this time from the other half of the gathering. There followed a general debate, but it produced no fresh points of view, repeating merely in a number of variants the basic arguments put forward by Adenauer and Altmeier. "Adenauer intervened several times in the debate," Dr. Pferdmenges recalls, "displaying remarkable optimism with regard to the future. 'If we remain firm now,' he declared emphatically, 'we shall reap successes which will make all criticism appear in the eyes of the people as mean and pettifogging grumbling. It is my opinion, in contrast to those gentlemen who advocate a coalition with the Social Democrats, that at the end of our four-year term of office we shall be in a very much stronger position than we are now, and that we shall have even less to fear from the opposition than we have today.' For the rest, he repeated indefatigably his basic thesis: 'The voters have decided in favor of the Social Market Economy, and to this decision we are committed.'

"This stubborn stereotyped repetition of one particular point," Dr. Pferdmenges says, "was one of Adenauer's strongest weapons in debate. He frequently succeeded with this suggestive method, and at the Rhöndorf meeting, too, the rigid consistency of his attitude did not fail to make its impression. I observed how one opponent after another fell silent and gave up. In the end, only a small group was left who clung to the coalition idea. The debate with these 'unconvertibles' Adenauer cut short by simply adjourning the meeting for supper. An excellent cold buffet was laid out on the terrace in the garden, and the wines did high credit to Adenauer's cellar. Adenauer was a most attentive host, and I noticed how he devoted himself particularly to the well-being of the coalition supporters. When the meeting was eventually resumed, everyone was in a relaxed and friendly mood."

Adenauer was quick to exploit it. Without referring again to the prickly subject of coalition, he said in a casual conversational tone:

"Now if we start from the assumption that the future government will be formed jointly by the CDU/CSU, the Free Democrats, and the German party. . . ."

It was a carefully calculated surprise move. Adenauer presented a complete and ready-made coalition as though everything had been agreed, sealed, and signed. "I could read from the various faces," Dr. Pferdmenges recalls, "that they were strenuously doing their 'coalition sums'—139 CDU plus 52 FDP plus 17 DP makes 208, that is, a majority. Not all the faces, however, looked very happy at this result, and a slight unrest could be felt in the room."

"Well, now," Adenauer repeated, this time with deliberate emphasis, "if we start from the assumption that the future government will be formed jointly by the CDU/CSU, the Free Democrats, and the German party, all that remains for us to do here is to decide on the distribution of offices—in the first place, the offices of Federal President and Federal Chancellor."

"I suggest Dr. Adenauer for Federal Chancellor," someone proposed immediately. For a brief moment Adenauer looked around the gathering. Then he said with a smile, "Well, if everyone present agrees with this view, as for myself, I've spoken to my doctor, and he has no objections."

Thus, in less than one minute, this question was settled.

Calmly and with an unmoved face Adenauer continued, "The next point is the Federal President. Being the second strongest partner in the coming government, I feel that the Free Democratic party should supply him. I therefore suggest Professor Heuss for the office of Federal President."

For a moment there was baffled silence. "Is Professor Heuss already aware of his good fortune?" someone asked. "Not so far," Adenauer replied laconically. (As a matter of fact, Professor Heuss first learned of the suggestion some time later through the press.) A representative from Bavaria objected: "As far as I know, Professor Heuss's attitude toward the Church is not exactly friendly. . . ." "But he has a very devout wife," Adenauer replied, "and that should be sufficient."

The remark aroused general hilarity. The humorous interlude had served its purpose in further mellowing the general mood, and once again Adenauer was quick to take advantage of it. Returning to the earlier controversy, he now explained once more his reasons against including the Social Democrats in the government.

"In the matter of economic structure there exists between ourselves and the Social Democrats an unbridgeable difference. There can only be either a planned economy or a Social Market Economy. There cannot be a mixture of the two. In view of this fundamental difference, even a Socialist Undersecretary of State working under a Christian Democrat Minister of Economics would be a practical impossibility. We should never get things moving at all. Besides, after this election campaign the voters would simply not understand if there were any bargaining about ministerial posts between ourselves and the Social Democrats. One's got to steer a steady course, and only if one does so will there also be a good parliamentary opposition."

By now Adenauer met with hardly any objection. A communiqué was drafted announcing the outcome of the Rhöndorf discussions in almost the same words as Adenauer had used in his address of welcome. It said:

"The elections have resulted not only in an impressive pledge to the basic ideas of the Christian Democratic conception of state and society, but also in an unequivocal approval of the Social Market Economy as opposed to Socialist economic planning. There is therefore an obligation to continue this policy in its entirety, in accordance with democratic processes, and to draw clear-cut conclusions from it for the formation of the federal government."

Thus the CDU/CSU assumed full responsibility for the course of events during the next four years. Under Adenauer's determining influence it withstood the temptations of a compromise, which undoubtedly would have led Germany along very different paths.

"The greatness of a statesman," Dr. Pferdmenges concluded his account, "should be measured not only by his positive achievements but also by what he has succeeded in preventing. If the first government of the Federal Republic had been a coalition between the Christian Democrats and the Social Democrats, this would undoubtedly have brought into being a national opposition which would not have been under the control of Parliament and which would have gone to work in a much more demagogic manner than the SPD. The consequences of such a development in the field of foreign affairs would have been catastrophic. The rise of an opposition of this type would have caused deep suspicions abroad, and these suspicions would with certainty soon have extended to the entire German people. I consider it one of Adenauer's greatest political successes to have maintained the Social Democratic party in the role of a national Opposition."

* * *

When, on October 18, 1917, Konrad Adenauer was solemnly introduced into his new office as newly elected Chief Mayor of Cologne, there sat among the audience filling the large ceremonial hall of Cologne City Hall his eldest son, Konrad, then a boy of eleven. Proudly and happily he took part in this most important hour in the life of his father, who then seemed to have reached the pinnacle of his successful career. When, thirty-two years later, Konrad Adenauer was elected first Chancellor of the Federal Republic of Germany, there sat among the crowded audience in the main chamber of the Federal Parliament Building at Bonn his youngest son, Georg, then a young man of eighteen and in his last year at school.

The day was September 15, 1949.

"Of course, we were all there, in the public gallery of the chamber," Georg Adenauer recalls. "There were Konrad and Max with their wives, Ria and her husband, Paul and Lotte, Libet and her fiancé—and myself. The house was crowded, many had had to be turned away, and behind us I heard someone murmuring, 'Just as well the old boy hasn't even more children!' We saw our father sitting on the front bench, just below the President and the Speaker's rostrum. I was terribly excited when the President of the *Bundestag*, Dr. Erich Köhler, read out the letter from the Federal President: 'I nominate deputy Dr. Konrad Adenauer for the office of Chancellor of the Federal Republic.'

"Next, the members of Parliament were called separately, by name, and one after another walked up to the boxes which had been set up below the rostrum to put in their ballot papers. This procedure took almost an hour, and was really terribly boring. All the same, one could distinctly feel the tension reigning in the chamber. When at last the endless roll call was completed, one more deputy suddenly turned up whose name had not been called. She was a lady, and she rushed forward, breathless and with whirling skirts, at the very last moment, to toss her ballot paper into the box. We learned later that she was Frau Margarethe Hütter from Stuttgart. Following the election of Professor Heuss to the office of Federal President, she had automatically moved up on the reserve list of the Free Democratic party and had only just learned that she had become a member of Parliament. Taking the next train from Stuttgart to Bonn, she had raced up in a taxi from the station, and arrived literally in the nick of time to cast her vote.

"While Frau Hütter, still breathless, slowly returned to her seat, the boxes were emptied and the count began. The Constitution required that the candidate for the Chancellorship proposed by the Federal President must obtain an absolute majority in the Lower House, and, in the event of his failure in the first ballot, further ballots must be taken. I could have wished the tellers had announced their results as they went along, but they did their work silently, only murmuring quietly among themselves, and the tension in the chamber rose to the breaking point. . . ."

At last the count was complete. Silence descended upon the House as Dr. Köhler, the President, rose to announce the result. But again there was a last-minute hitch.

"Ladies and gentlemen," Dr. Köhler said, "I shall now announce the result of the vote. But before doing so I wish to clear up one formal point. Members will recall that I explicitly instructed them to mark their ballots with either 'yes' or 'no,' and in the case of abstention to hand in blank papers. It now turns out that three ballots do not conform to this instruction but bear the name of 'Adenauer.' I request the opinion of the house as to whether these three irregularly made-out papers should be considered valid 'yes' votes."

Several members shouted, "Yes!" and Dr. Köhler said, "I hear no objection. I take it then that the House is unanimous in considering that the three ballots bearing the name of 'Adenauer' should be regarded as valid 'yes' votes within the terms of the voting procedure."

Dr. Köhler paused for a moment. Then he said:

"Ladies and gentlemen! I am now declaring the following result: 202 members have voted 'yes' as against 142 who have voted 'no'; 44 members have abstained. The absolute majority of the House, required for election, being 202, I am able to announce that this majority has been secured by the deputy Dr. Adenauer."

"So my father had actually got through with a majority of one single vote!" Georg recalled. "Many deputies burst out laughing, and there were cries from the Socialist benches which the rest of us up in the gallery could not hear distinctly. 'Ladies and gentlemen,' President Köhler now said, 'it is now my duty to ask Dr. Adenauer whether he is prepared to accept his election as Federal Chancellor.' My father rose slowly from his seat and said 'Yes'.

"Immediately afterward the session was closed, and now crowds of friends and well-wishers surrounded my father, shaking hands with him and offering their congratulations. As he stood there, tall and lean, I was reminded of Shakespeare's *Julius Caesar* which we had just read in class. It seemed to me that my father was well on the way to surrounding himself, after Caesar's prescription, with 'men that are fat.' Of course, a good many jokes were made about the circumstances of my father's election. People said he had elected himself, so to speak, with his own vote. I asked him if this was true. He admitted it without feeling in the least abashed. 'Since I was determined to accept the appointment,' he said, 'I should have felt it sheer hypocrisy not to have voted for myself!' "

Three days after his election, on the afternoon of September 20, 1949, the new Federal Chancellor presented his Cabinet to Parliament, and, with his ministers, took the oath of office. All members of the House rose from their seats as Dr. Köhler, the President of the Chamber, read out the formula of the oath as prescribed in the Constitution:

"I swear that I will devote my strength to the well-being of the German people; increase its benefits; ward off danger and damage; obey and defend the Basic Law and the Laws of the Federation; conscientiously fulfill my duties; and observe justice toward everyone."

One by one, headed by the Federal Chancellor, the new ministers went up to the President to take the oath. Clearly and distinctly Adenauer's voice rang through the House:

"I swear, so help me God!"

Thirteen times the words were repeated after him. Indeed, there were thirteen ministers in Adenauer's first Cabinet. Here and there in the House some grave shaking of heads could be observed. Not on account of the alleged unlucky number, but simply because there were thought to be too many of them. Thirteen ministers! Did the new state really need as many as that? The financial experts had recommended not more than seven or eight. Wasn't the new Cabinet organized from the start on rather too lavish a scale? And, even so, one minister seemed to be missing, the one who in a parliamentary democracy is considered normally, next to the Chief of Government and the Finance Minister, to be the most important member of the

Cabinet. It was true enough—the first government of the new German state had no Minister for Foreign Affairs.

The last of the thirteen ministers had taken the oath. The solemn ceremony was concluded. Members resumed their seats, and, as the first critical remarks were whispered between benches, President Köhler announced:

"Ladies and gentlemen, we now proceed to item four on today's agenda—an inaugural statement of policy by the federal government. I call upon the Federal Chancellor to address us."

Adenauer mounted the rostrum.

## CHAPTER XVII

WITH THE assumption of the Federal Chancellorship there begins a new period in the life of Konrad Adenauer, fundamentally different from what went before, and calling on his biographer to shift his vantage point and adjust his perspective.

Konrad Adenauer the man, the human being with a personal and private life of his own, as we have known and accompanied him up to this great turning point in his career, now disappears almost completely from our view. Only now and then, as chance permits, shall we henceforth meet him again as a family man, in the circle of his friends, with his hobbies, and in his leisure hours. All this he himself has now relegated drastically to the background of his life.

The man we must now accompany and watch at his work, day after day, year after year, from morning till evening, and often far into the night, rarely permits himself an hour away from public life. We observe a statesman of international rank, "the greatest in Germany since Bismarck," as Sir Winston Churchill has said of him who has so completely identified himself with the fortunes and affairs of his people that his own life has become all but merged in that of the nation, and has almost ceased to be a story of its own.

Henceforth the story of Konrad Adenauer, from his seventy-fourth year onward, is the story of Germany, and in telling the one we must inevitably closely follow the other.

Adenauer once remarked that he had not become a politician from passion or inclination but from "dire necessity." He described the task he assumed with the Chancellorship as that of a trustee in charge of a bankrupt enterprise who has to wind up its sad affairs as best he can, while explaining to the creditors that although they must expect nothing for the time being, he will endeavor as rapidly as possible to create fresh assets for a new and trustworthy firm. It was wrong, he added, when tackling major political issues to reckon in terms of short periods of time and expect quick results. It was necessary, above all, to be patient. "I believe patience is the strongest weapon in the armory of the defeated," he said, "and I possess a great deal of it. I can wait."

Not an obvious thing for a man of seventy-four to say! But it strikes the basic chord of his first speech as Federal Chancellor before the new Parliament in which he announces the program of his government. He makes his statement of policy soberly and factually. It is clear he is no "politician from passion." There are no brilliant turns and startling phrases, but there is forceful authority. Adenauer speaks without demagogy but by no means without a crisp and quick sense of humor, as his hecklers are soon to find out.

"Ladies and gentlemen," he begins his statement, "following the long deliberations in the Parliamentary Council and the general election, the evolution of the new Germany has taken place with great rapidity. With the formation of the federal government which was completed today, the Occupation Statute, too, has now come into force. Although the competence and jurisdiction of the Federal Parliament and federal government are restricted by this Occupation Statute, we are nevertheless entitled to rejoice over this development and greet the emergence of this nucleus of a German state with glad hearts. The progress we have made as compared with conditions since 1945, indeed with conditions under the National Socialist Reich, is great. . . ."

There is no doubt that great progress has been made. It is characteristic of Adenauer that, first of all, in this hour, he should place on record his grateful recognition of what has been achieved. "We are enjoying once more at least a relative measure of freedom and liberty, as a nation and state," he declares, "and above all the rights and privileges of the individual citizen are once more protected." One moment of remembrance of the Nazi Reich, one glance at the Soviet Zone of Germany, are enough to show how much this means.

However, even grateful acknowledgment of what has been achieved must not allow a realist politician to forget that much still remains to be done. Adenauer calls the sore points by their proper names: "The German people is still torn apart," and "it is still very far from taking its place as an equal partner among the free nations of the world." To state this bluntly at the very outset is to state, at the same time, a program of policy for the new government, and the head of this government now proceeds to outline the various ways which are to lead to these distant goals. He begins by stating the reasons which governed the formation of the government:

"My own election as Federal Chancellor, ladies and gentlemen, and the formation of this government followed logically from the pattern of political conditions which had evolved in the Bizone as a result of the policy pursued by the Frankfurt Economic Council." At this, the protocol records some "disturbances on the left," but Adenauer adheres firmly to his Rhöndorf thesis. "A coalition between the parties which have rejected a planned economy and those who advocate it would plainly have gone against the will of the majority of the electorate. In the event of a coalition between these parties, the voters would have asked with some justification why there was any need for a general election at all."

So much for the old dispute over the "great coalition." Next Adenauer turns to the question of the role of the opposition.

"It is my view," he says, "that the existence of an Opposition is a necessity of state; that the Opposition has a specific political task to perform on behalf of the state, and that genuine progress and a frame of mind accustomed to think in democratic terms can be achieved only if a Government majority and an Opposition stand facing each other fairly and squarely. It is my further view that, taking into account the unsettled state of affairs prevailing in Germany, it is far better for an Opposition, which will of course always exist, to show itself clearly in Parliament than that it should gain ground outside Parliament and beyond the reach of parliamentary checks and controls, as would be the case with a 'great coalition,' which would have left Parliament without a force able to oppose effectively."

Is the Cabinet too large? Is there "an inflation of ministers," as some had remarked? Adenauer goes on to pick up this critical point.

"I am fully aware," he says, "that at first sight the number of ministers and government departments may appear rather large. However, I must point to the fact that in present times there are a number of tasks requiring the direct attention of the state which are either entirely new and have never existed before—we need only think of the refugee problem!—or where the responsibility of the state and the volume of work involved have grown to such proportions that no ordinary, traditional government department could take them in their stride." This is true, for instance, of housing and all the economic issues raised by the rebuilding of the destroyed cities. Several government departments, on the other hand, are not intended to be permanent, but transitory; as soon as they have fulfilled their specific tasks they will disappear. Eventually only the "so-called classic government departments" will remain.

And the most "classic ministry of them all?

"It will be observed," Adenauer states drily, "that among the Federal Ministries there is no Ministry of Foreign Affairs. Nor have I felt able to accede to the wishes of those who recommended to me the establishment of a Ministry for International Relations. I have refrained from establishing such a Ministry because, under the terms of the Occupation Statute, foreign affairs, including international agreements concluded by Germany or on her behalf, remain within the province of the Allied High Commission. But the fact that we do not now possess a Ministry of Foreign Affairs should not be taken to mean that, as a result, we have renounced all activity in this field. It is a peculiar paradox of our situation that, although Germany's foreign affairs are being looked after by the High Commission, every activity of the federal government or of the Federal Parliament, even in purely home affairs, must of necessity in some way or other involve foreign relations."

How many among the four hundred members of parliament, how many among the fifty million people in the Federal Republic whose fate has now been placed in the hands of Adenauer, will have noticed that, soberly and without fanfares, indeed almost casually, he has just announced in these words the fundamental guiding principle of his entire future policy?

It may be "paradoxical" that Germany's foreign policy is conducted by the High Commission, although every German activity at home, by the government and in Parliament, "in some way or other involves foreign relations." It may be a paradox but it is the lever the Chancellor can now apply to raise Germany step by step to a level where she will "stand as an equal among the nations of the world." At this moment Adenauer is not thinking only of the Ruhr State, the Marshall Plan, and other agreements which, even now, "have involved Germany far more closely in the affairs of the outside world than ever before." He looks deeper into the wheels and gears of the great international machine.

And this is what he sees. He knows that every success achieved by the government in home affairs will lend the new state additional weight and secure for it additional confidence abroad. He knows, conversely, that every such gain of prestige abroad will in turn strengthen the reputation and increase the authority of the government at home. The chief of the new German government has clearly perceived this "law of interaction," and he has realized that, far from being a hindrance, this alleged "paradox" in fact affords him his great chance. In the unique situation in which the untried state finds itself with its untried government, there is no need for a Ministry of Foreign Affairs because for the time being foreign policy and home policy require to be conducted together; because, in a sense, they conduct each other and are, basically, one and the same thing.

Political consolidation at home, however, can be achieved at this stage, in the autumn of 1949, only in close conjunction with a consolidation of economic conditions. The new government will not be able to maintain or increase the political confidence it enjoys and needs with the German people unless it succeeds in improving the economic situation of the masses. It is for this reason that Adenauer devotes the larger part of his policy statement to the vast field of unsolved tasks at home with which his government is faced. The accomplishment of these tasks may be summed up as the "internal liberation" of Germany. It is the condition on which the "external liberation," the "achievement of full sovereignty," depends.

"The guiding star for all our work," Adenauer declares, "will be our endeavor to bring about social justice and alleviate suffering and want. The coalition parties are fully agreed that their work must be governed by a determination to act as socially, in the best and truest sense of the word, as is humanely possible."

The Federal Chancellor now takes up, singly, problem after problem, announcing in each case how his government proposes to deal with it.

"Refugees and expellees from the East will have to be distributed more evenly over the various confederate states.

"The building of new houses will be helped and furthered by the government with all the means at its disposal. But, unless we can persuade private capital to take an interest in the construction of new housing space, no solution of the housing problem is possible.

"In carrying the principle of Social Market Economy into effect it will naturally be necessary, as hitherto, to guard against a rigidly doctrinaire attitude. We shall continue to adapt ourselves, as we have adapted ourselves hitherto, to changing conditions. Compulsory measures and state controls will be abolished wherever we feel it safe to do so.

"Our entire endeavor will be to see to it that as few minds and hands are employed in the distribution and exploitation of consumer goods, and as many hands and minds as possible in their production.

"As far as its financial resources will permit, the federal government will sponsor and assist scientific research in Germany. We shall succeed in holding our own in the world's markets only if we manage to excel with outstanding achievements. A weak people, a politically weak people, is always in danger of being crowded out of economic competition with other nations unless it has something special of outstanding quality to show for itself."

But what is the largest single obstacle standing in the way of such special achievements? Adenauer makes no bones about it:

"The question of the dismantling of our industrial establishments is the perpetual preoccupation of the entire German people. There is hardly anyone in Germany who would object to the dismantling of genuine war industries. But the wholesale destruction of enormous economic assets is a matter which should not be shrugged off abroad with the remark that, once it had been so decided, there was nothing that could be done about it. There is, furthermore, a psychological aspect to the dismantling question which is of great significance. It remains incomprehensible to the large majority of the German people how it is possible that one hand may generously give economic aid while the other continues to destroy wholesale invaluable economic assets."

But not only industry must be raised to the highest possible level of efficiency and productivity. Agriculture, too, must greatly raise its production and improve the quality of its produce. "We are still importing 50 per cent of all our food requirements!" Adenauer declares. This consumes foreign currency urgently needed elsewhere.

Again, financial policy must be so conceived as to encourage saving and the accumulation of capital for investment. Still, saving the Deutsche Mark alone will not do the trick. "To enable us to regain the confidence of foreign capital," Adenauer declares, "the blocking of foreign capital assets in Germany should be rescinded as soon as possible." Such a measure is required even more urgently if foreign capital is to take a renewed interest in the German economy and if foreign credits, now desperately needed, are to become once more available. "We hope," the Chancellor adds, "that the promised reduction of occupation costs will be considerable."

Next, legislation for an "equalization of burdens" resulting from the war and its aftermath must be introduced and passed as a matter of urgency, and "the small, and smallest, sufferers from these iniquities will have to be treated with special consideration. Finally, the problem of pensions payable to civil servants expelled from Eastern Germany and to former military personnel will have to be settled by federal law."

Economic help for hard-pressed Berlin—adequate support for war widows and orphans and those wounded and incapacitated in the war—legal relations between employers and employees—the population unbalance owing to the numerical excess of women over men—care and protection of the young—civil service legislation—there is no end to the tasks and problems, and as he enumerates them the Chancellor suddenly touches on a sore and tricky point:

Denazification!

"The procedure of denazification," Adenauer declares, "has caused a great deal of harm and much misfortune and unhappiness. It is only right and just that those genuinely responsible for the crimes committed during the National Socialist period and the war should be punished with all severity. For the rest we must make an end of distinguishing in Germany between two classes of human beings—the politically acceptable and the nonacceptable, the tarnished and the clean. This distinction must disappear, and the sooner the better. The war and the chaos of the postwar years have subjected many to such cruel ordeals, and exposed them to such inordinate temptations, that there must be understanding and sympathetic consideration for many offenses and cases of misdemeanor. The federal government will therefore examine the possibility of granting an amnesty."

At the word "amnesty" the House grows restless. There is "applause on the right and in the center," and this in turn rouses the left to voice its disapproval. Adenauer continues:

"While the federal government is thus resolved, wherever it considers it warranted, to let bygones be bygones—convinced as it is that many have atoned for misdeeds which, subjectively, do not weigh very heavily—it is equally firmly resolved, on the other hand, to act upon the lessons learned from the past in its dealings with all those who are endangering the existence of the state, whether they belong to the radicals of the right or the left."

At this the parliamentary report records "laughter and heckling from the Communist party."

Adenauer: "Never mind, you aren't half as radical as you make yourselves out to be!"

General hilarity.

Communist Deputy Heinz Renner: "And you aren't half as social, either, as you would now have people believe!"

For once the general mirth is at his own expense. Calmly Adenauer allows it to ebb away, then continues, "In this connection, let me say a word about certain anti-Semitic tendencies which are once again making themselves felt among us. We deprecate these tendencies in the strongest possible terms. We consider it altogether unworthy, indeed wholly outrageous, after all that has happened under National Socialism, that there should still be people in Germany who persecute and despise the Jews for no other reason than that they are Jews!"

(There was more behind these words than a mere rhetorical proclamation of an ethical faith. Three years later, almost to a day, Adenauer put his signature to the Restitution Agreement concluded with the State of Israel, thus making peace between Germany and the Jewish world. This peacemaking move was due entirely to his own personal initiative, and Adenauer referred to it on a later occasion as "one of the rare opportunities afforded to him to assert the principle of Christianity in everyday practical politics.")

Now the Chancellor comes to the end of his speech. He speaks of Germany's prisoners of war, of her displaced persons, the arbitrarily arrested and forcibly abducted, the refugees and expellees from the Eastern provinces. And that means the crucial and controversial topics of Yalta, Potsdam, and the Oder-Neisse frontier.

"These are questions," Adenauer declares, "which for us here in Germany are very close to our hearts and which are vital questions of existence for our entire people." The Potsdam Agreement, he states emphatically, laid it down explicitly that the final settlement of the western frontier of Poland would have to wait until the Peace Conference, and he adds, "Therefore we can on no account acquiesce in the detachment of these territories subsequently carried out unilaterally by the Soviet Union and Poland. This detachment is not only a violation of the Potsdam Agreement but also contradicts the terms of the Atlantic Charter of 1941, to which the Soviet Union expressly became a party. . . . We shall not cease to press our claims for these territories by every recognized and orderly means provided by international law and procedure. . . ."

So there was going to be a foreign policy after all?

Adenauer seems to anticipate the objection. He repeats: Germany's foreign relations are being administered by the Allied High Commissioners; at the same time, while this is so, the new German state nevertheless has "close contacts" with the nations surrounding its frontiers, "some of them good, some less good." And he adds, "I should therefore be leaving a gap in this statement of policy if I made no reference to our relations with these countries."

Communist Deputy Renner: "Well, then, you'd better not forget the Saar Territory."

Adenauer: "Let me, for a start, not forget the Soviet Union!"

Renner: "I can see this part of your speech has been drafted by an expert!"

Adenauer: "Herr Renner, you are an envious man!"

After laughter and heckling have died down, Adenauer declares, "We are at all times ready to live in peace with our Eastern neighbors, especially with the Soviet Union and Poland. It is our urgent wish to see the present tensions between the Soviet Union and the Western Allies find their solutions in the course of time in a peaceful manner. . . ."

It is a long and thorny path which stretches ahead of the German people. The nation is still under the impress of the Occupation Statute, only just promulgated, and it is natural that the last point in Adenauer's declaration of policy should deal with this "new dictate of the victorious powers," as some German newspapers, notably in the remoter provinces, have chosen to call it. Here too the chief of the federal government shows an uncommon degree of insight and understanding, and a measure of optimism which in the circumstances would seem to many to border on recklessness.

"The Occupation Statute," he declares, "represents a considerable step forward as against the position we have known hitherto. However, everything will depend on the spirit in which it is applied. Of one thing I am convinced: when the time comes, after twelve months or at the latest within eighteen months, as the Occupation Statute provides, for the occupying powers to reconsider its provisions in the light of the experience they will have gained meanwhile, these powers will certainly reach the conclusion that it has become possible to extend the competence and jurisdiction of the German authorities still further. The Occupation Statute is anything but an ideal instrument—but there is no other way for the German people to regain freedom and equality. We must see to it, after the total collapse bequeathed to us by National Socialism, that we work our way up again jointly and together with the Allies. For us the only way to freedom is to endeavor, in close agreement and cooperation with the Allied High Commission, to extend step by step and little by little our liberties and the area of our independence and sovereignty."

Summing up, Adenauer draws once more a picture of the future as he sees it. It is a pledge to Europe to which "we belong in origin, tradition, and spirit." All unsolved problems still oppressing the mind of the German people, the partition of Germany and the Saar question, he visualizes as solved in the framework of a European Union in which one day Germany will march as a free nation side by side with the nations of the free world toward a better future.

The Federal Chancellor had spoken exactly eighty-two minutes. In view of the multitude of problems facing the new government, this was an uncommonly brief and concise statement of policy. Now it was the turn of Parliament itself to speak. For this first great debate the *Bundestag* gave itself plenty of time, six whole days, during which forty members, representing the various parties, rose to speak, talking altogether for twenty-six hours.

It is no exaggeration to say that during this last week in September, 1949, the entire civilized world had its eyes turned toward Bonn and followed the great debate with critical attention. Adenauer's opening speech had almost everywhere created a favorable impression, no less by its soberly measured yet forceful tone than by its well thought-out subject matter and the factual and restrained manner of its presentation. The most important question in all minds was now, how would the opposition perform? How would they conceive their task: in a positive or a negative spirit, constructively or destructively? The new parliamentary democracy in Germany had yet to make its reputation, and much depended on its first steps.

On September 22, Dr. Kurt Schumacher, leader of the opposition, rose to open the debate.

He found much to criticize in Adenauer's program. The government's statement of policy, he declared, was full of interest not only on account of what it said, but still more so on account of what it had omitted to say. The Chancellor, he said, seemed to have forgotten the workers. The term "worker" never once occurred in his whole statement. There was no mention of the trade unions either. Adenauer's whole speech, Schumacher criticized, was conceived in an "idyllic tone," giving a deliberate impression that "things weren't quite so bad, after all." In contrast to this, he, the opposition leader, had the impression that "everything was a great deal worse than the government has indicated." He found fault with the structure of the government itself. "There is no need for us to have a special ERP Minister!" he declared. "Nor do we need a special Ministry for the Eastern provinces! We should make this a department of the Ministry of the Interior and demonstrate thereby that, in the German view, relations between the Federal Republic and the Soviet Occupation Zone are entirely a matter of German home affairs."

It had been generally expected that the Social Democratic leader would attack the so-called "Frankfurt economic policy," but few had expected him to hit out with such violence. "From the basic character and the composition of this government," Schumacher declared, "there arises the great danger of this new state becoming an authoritarian state designed for the defense of property and its owners!"

What did the opposition intend to do about this? Schumacher gave the answer: "The qualities of an Opposition which enable it to contribute to the maintenance and preservation of the state are not necessarily those which will earn it the good will and benevolent approbation of the federal government or its parties. As regards the defense of property, we have here a thoroughly unsentimental Government and it will be the task of the Opposition, in representing the interests of the working population, to act in an equally unsentimental manner! The qualities of a Government, as of an Opposition, are determined by their respective achievements. The Opposition, however, must make it its principle that the Government must find its majorities for its legislation from among the Government parties. No Opposition will do justice to itself if it allows itself to be forced into the role of a 'replacement party' for the Government coalition. . . . It is equally true, on the other hand, that this Opposition would fail in its task if it were to exhaust itself in denying and rejecting the proposals made by the Government. . . . We do not conceive of ourselves merely and solely as a negation of the Government. Therefore we intend to conduct our opposition with the ultimate aim of securing, one day, in this House a parliamentary majority for a policy of socialist democracy!"

This was a clear challenge, so unequivocal, in fact, that many began to ask themselves, not only at Bonn, how Adenauer could hope to work with such an Opposition. But the "grandfather of all the foxes" was not dismayed. As one deputy remarked, he "parried Schumacher's rapier thrusts with a cotton wool buffer of unexpected conciliation." In his speech winding up the debate, on September 29, he declared:

"I greatly welcome what the representatives of the Opposition have said regarding their attitudes toward the Government and its coalition parties. . . . If the Opposition conduct their policy in the spirit and manner indicated by Herren Schumacher, Ollenhauer, and Schmid in their respective speeches—and I should not be averse to even a little more of it—this will be of the greatest significance to democratic feeling throughout the German nation. I do not hesitate to declare that any government, and in particular this government led by myself, stands to learn a great deal, and will learn a great deal, from wise and responsible opposition.

"There is one thing I would ask this House," Adenauer concluded. "I would ask you to judge the federal government by its performance. Give the federal government time to show whether it is able to achieve anything. I beg of you all, let us, in matters of decisive import to the German people, try to work together so that in these extraordinarily difficult times we may make at least some progress, in the interest of our people!"

"There is only one road to freedom—to regain our liberties little by little, step by step, through close cooperation and in agreement with the three Western occupying powers."

This had been Konrad Adenauer's thesis all along, and he had propounded it even at a time when for most Germans the aims and direction of German policy were still completely shrouded in darkness. Now fate took him at his word. As the first Chancellor of the Federal Republic, he had to tread the very road he himself had signposted as the only way to freedom.

The road was long and difficult. It began at Petersberg, one of the wooded heights of the Siebengebirge mountains which rise steeply from the Rhine Valley just south of Bonn. Shortly before World War I a large and sumptuous palacelike luxury hotel was built there. Now, visible from far away and dominating Bonn and the river valley from its wooded height, the Petersberg Hotel was the official seat of the Allied High Commission.

On September 21, 1949, two large black cars bearing German license plates drove up the steeply winding mountain road.

It was the day after the Chancellor's statement of policy in Parliament. The controversial and much discussed Occupation Statute had just come into force. The three High Commissioners, McCloy, Robertson, and François-Poncet, had planned a solemn ceremonial act. The government were to be received officially at the Petersberg, the Federal Chancellor was to introduce the members of his Cabinet, and the Occupation Statute was to be formally presented.

This ceremony did not materialize. When Adenauer heard of the plan, he asked that it should be abandoned. True, the Occupation Statute corresponded to his own wishes, but it was nevertheless confirmation "in black and white" of the fact that German sovereignty was still restricted and curtailed on all sides, and in his view this did not call for a special celebration. Adenauer intimated that he would not feel able to attend such a ceremonial act. He preferred this first official contact between the German Government and the High Commission to be as unceremonious and businesslike as possible, and for this reason deliberately did not take his entire Cabinet up to the Petersberg but was accompanied only by five of his ministers and his personal assistant Dr. Blankenhorn.

The Chancellor and his ministers were received by the three High Commissioners in the large drawing room. Protocol and etiquette had been agreed on beforehand in every detail, as had been the text of the speeches to be made, to insure that there should be no hitch or awkward moment. The three representatives of the Western Powers were standing on the large carpet in the center of the room, and the German delegation were supposed to stop short of the carpet at a certain prearranged distance, when the speeches of welcome were to be made and the members of the government introduced.

But the carefully worked-out arrangement came to nothing. The High Commissioners themselves at once flouted their own rules. François-Poncet, whose monthly turn it was to be chairman of the High Commission, immediately walked up to Adenauer with a gesture of spontaneous cordiality, and before anyone realized what had happened the solemnly established distance was no more. In well-measured words François-Poncet at once expressed the hope and expectation of the Western Powers for good and fruitful cooperation with the new German government. The Federal Chancellor in his turn introduced the members of his government.

"I have the honor to pay you an official visit today in company with some of the members of my Cabinet, thereby establishing the first contact between the government of the Federal Republic of Germany and the three High Commissioners. . . .

"A new chapter of German history of the postwar years begins. . . . A large part of the responsibility and the authority to make decisions will pass into German hands. We do not, of course, possess as yet complete freedom, since there are considerable restrictions contained in the Occupation Statute. We will do our part to bring about an atmosphere in which the Allied Powers will see their way clear to apply the Occupation Statute in a liberal and generous manner. . . . We hope the Allied Powers will, by making a corresponding use of the revision clause in the Occupation Statute, hasten the further political development of our country."

The German government, Adenauer continued, intended to give first priority in its work to the solution of its great social problems. The largest among these was the struggle against the misery and destitution of the refugees. "The drifting sands of these millions of refugees," he declared, "must be turned into solid ground" if a "serious danger to the security of the entire continent" was to be averted. The refugee problem, he insisted, was not merely a national but an international problem. It could not be solved without the help of the Western Powers.

What had the federal government to offer in return for the fulfillment of its wishes? Adenauer made it plain:

"If we are to establish a new and truly peaceful order in Europe, it is the view of the federal government that this can only be achieved by striking out in fundamentally new directions and trying new roads. In our view such new roads are discernible in the endeavors aiming at a European Federation, the first beginnings of which are now materializing at Strasbourg. We believe, however, that such a federation will be strong enough to live and survive only if it is based on close economic cooperation between the nations. The organization created on the basis of the Marshall Plan points the right direction. Yet another way of creating favorable conditions for a truly viable European Federation would be, in our view, a settlement of conditions in the Ruhr which would revise their present arbitrary and unilateral character and allow the Ruhr gradually to become the nucleus of an order embracing the basic industries of the other European countries as well.

"We are certain," Adenauer concluded, "that the narrow conception of the nation state which dominated the nineteenth and the beginning of the twentieth century has today altogether outlived its validity. From it arose nationalism in all its forms, and this brought the breakup and fragmentation of European life. If we are to find our way back to the sources of our European cultural heritage which has its fountainhead in Christian beliefs, we must succeed, first of all, in re-establishing the unity of the European way of life in all its aspects and in all its fields."

The High Commissioners were of course fully aware of the statement of policy which Adenauer had made in Parliament the previous day. Nor had they failed to observe certain "tricky points" in it. Adenauer's rejection of the Oder-Neisse frontier had been sharply and unmistakably addressed to the Allies. But no one raised so much as a murmur of objection. "There is nothing wrong with a healthy national sentiment," Sir Brian Robertson remarked. "It would be sad indeed if the Germans ceased loving their country. . . ."

At the conclusion of his address the Chancellor handed the High Commissioners a copy of the *Basic Law of the Federal Republic of Germany*. Then the formal reception dissolved into small groups, champagne was served, and informal, almost friendly, conversations took the place of the stiff ceremonial. After forty-five minutes the Germans took their leave. What had become of the Occupation Statute? Engaged in animated conversation, the High Commissioners had apparently forgotten all about it. Their German guests had already reached the cloakroom when an official of the French Foreign Ministry came hurrying after them and hastily pushed the document under Dr. Blankenhorn's arm, murmuring almost apologetically: "*N'en parlons plus*—let's not talk about it any more!"

## CHAPTER XVIII

THE Federal Republic was well set on its path. But meanwhile events of grave consequence had occurred in the eastern part of Germany.

The Soviet government had not watched developments idly but had prepared its countermove. On October 1, 1949, a week after the first reception of the federal government at the Petersberg, the Soviet government delivered a sharp note of protest to the three Western Powers. Five days later the Soviet Zone "People's Council" proclaimed itself a "Provisional People's Chamber" or parliament, put the constitution of the "German Democratic Republic" into effect, and charged former Social Democrat Otto Grotewohl with the formation of a government. On October 10, Communist Wilhelm Pieck was elected President of the new republic, and two days later Grotewohl announced his cabinet, in which the Soviet Zone CDU was represented with several portfolios.

Now Germany was well and truly split.

The Western Powers were not slow to reply. The High Commission at the Petersberg immediately issued an official statement declaring the East German state "illegal" and giving an assurance that the attitude of the Western Powers would be in no way affected by its establishment.

For Adenauer and his ministers things were not as easy as that. The establishment of a Communist republic in Eastern Germany, carried out as it was with the cooperation of non-Communist parties, could not be shrugged off by declaring it "illegal," and even less so since the East German Republic now spoke to the West in a new tone. There were no more references to the "traitors" and "quislings" at Bonn; on the contrary, the East German government declared its readiness to join in a "common struggle for freedom and unity"; and to the people of Eastern Germany the prospect of a gradual "rapproachment" between the two German governments was held out. True, the Grotewohl government emphatically affirmed the Oder-Neisse frontier, but at the same time was able to point out that in contrast with the Adenauer government it was not under the "tutelage" of an Occupation Statute and suffered from no restrictions in foreign affairs. Indeed, Grotewohl could boast, at least on paper, of a fully fledged Foreign Minister. His name was Dertinger, and he belonged to the CDU.

All this was shrewdly calculated. Clearly pointed at Adenauer, it was meant to discredit him, and with him the new government, the new parliament, the new state.

Adenauer allowed a week to pass, during which he considered the new situation in all its aspects and discussed it with his ministers. He was only too well aware of the label his own opposition were trying to fasten to him. As a Rhinelander, they said, he was not really interested in Eastern Germany but considered it only a burden and had secretly written it off altogether; isolated Berlin, they said, meant nothing to him, and free all-German elections he thought definitely undesirable since, with the illegal Social Democrats well organized "underground" in the Eastern Zone, they would inevitably result in an all-German victory for the Socialists. Adenauer was fully conscious of this whispering campaign. If he now spoke in the Federal Parliament about events in Eastern Germany it must be in a manner which would not leave the slightest doubt about his attitude. People in the Soviet Zone no less than the refugees in the West would carefully weigh and scrutinize every one of his words. This was an historic moment, and whatever he said was bound to be of importance for years to come.

On October 21, 1949, the Federal Chancellor made his statement before Parliament. He said:

"Recent events in the Eastern Zone and Berlin are characteristic of the tragic way of the German people since 1933. They underline once more with the utmost clarity the disruption of German territory into two parts—an Eastern part inhabited by 18,000,000 people living in the serfdom of a Soviet satellite state, and a Western part, with 45,000,000 inhabitants, which is not yet in full possession of its freedom but where the sovereign rights of a democratic state are passing increasingly into German hands, and where, as I wish to make clear with the greatest emphasis, people are enjoying a personal freedom and security without which we cannot conceive an existence worthy of the human race.

"There is no free will of the German people in the Soviet Zone. What is happening there now has not the support of, and is therefore not recognized as legitimate by, the population. The Federal Republic, on the other hand, is supported by the recognition and the freely expressed will of some 23,000,000 Germans who are entitled to vote. Thus the Federal Republic is, pending the achievement of German unity, the sole legitimate political national organization of the German people. It considers itself responsible for the fate of 18,000,000 Germans living in the Eastern Zone. It assures them of its faithful loyalty. The Federal Republic alone is entitled to speak on behalf of the German people. It does not recognize declarations of the Soviet Zone as binding on the German people. This applies in particular to declarations which have been made in the Soviet Zone with regard to the Oder-Neisse line. I wish to make this emphatically clear before the German people and before the whole world."

The statement was plain and clear, and it was unanimously approved by Parliament. But a statement alone was not enough. Now rapid and tangible progress had to be made, demonstrating to the Eastern Zone no less than to the West German population that the federal government was on the right road. Nothing, Adenauer felt, could furnish more solid proof than a speedy revision of Allied dismantling policy in Western Germany.

"Consider the political consequences of dismantling! A dismantling policy which leaves us no chance to achieve a decent standard of living will sow the seeds of disaster—nationalist extremism is bound to revive if people find that owing to dismantling there is no hope left for Germany. . . ."

Untiringly Adenauer hammered it home in his talks with the three High Commissioners, and eventually his persistent representations achieved their object. On November 4, 1949, a three-power conference met in Paris to reconsider the entire problem of industrial dismantling in the light of "Western Germany's integration in the European community." On the initiative of Ernest Bevin, the British Foreign Secretary, the conference decided upon a new approach to the whole issue. The dismantling program, Bevin declared, must be revised, but the time was past for decrees and ordinances to be issued unilaterally by the occupying powers. From now on things had to proceed on a basis of "give and take." Not only the Western Powers but the Federal Republic, too, was now in a position to "give" something. A new settlement would have to be freely negotiated between the Western Powers and the Federal Republic, and the Federal Republic would have to be a voluntary partner to the new agreement. Otherwise the agreement would be valueless since it would fail to create mutual trust and confidence.

These were new and most encouraging words to German ears. There remained the question of what Germany would be asked to contribute to the new agreement. The final communiqué of the Paris conference did not disclose it. It stated merely that the decisions of the Foreign Ministers were "based on the expectation that the federal government would give further evidence of its pacific intentions and of its sincere desire to associate itself with those nations devoted to the cause of democracy, justice under law, and peace." For the rest the three High Commissioners had received "certain instructions and powers" to conduct appropriate negotiations with the federal government and conclude the desired agreements.

A new phase in German postwar history had begun.

On November 15, 1949, the Chancellor felt ready to give Parliament an interim account of his negotiations with the High Commissioners, and now the outline of the issue emerged. The Western Powers, Adenauer announced, were prepared to agree to a drastic revision of the dismantling program. In return they required the Federal Republic to join the Ruhr Authority and the Council of Europe, to refrain from rearmament, and to cooperate with the Allied Security Board.

This was rather more than the Social Democratic opposition were prepared to swallow. Adenauer, they declared, had offered the Allies too much; the end of dismantling could be obtained at a cheaper price, and above all there must be no question of cooperating in the Ruhr Authority. Adenauer answered drily, "I have been informed by the Allied authorities that further proposals with regard to a stop on dismantling would serve no useful purpose as long as Germany fails to satisfy Allied security requirements by recognizing the

Ruhr Authority." Was it the view of the opposition, Adenauer asked, that Germany's wishes regarding her sovereignty must be fulfilled before she was ready to make concessions? In that case he must ask them bluntly, "Who, after all, do they think has lost the war?" There were moments, it seemed, when it was necessary to call a spade a spade.

The negotiations at the Petersberg continued.

While they were in progress, Mr. Dean Acheson, the American Secretary of State, paid a visit to Bonn and had a lengthy conversation with Adenauer which immediately gave rise to fresh rumors and speculations. Adenauer, it was said, had asked for Acheson's support against excessive French security wishes. The High Commission on their part warned against excessive optimism; negotiations were likely to be prolonged, as certain occupying powers were raising objections to German dismantling wishes.

The negotiations continued. What were they like?

On November 15, the Chancellor once again sat facing the three High Commissioners at the Petersberg conference table. For days now they had been haggling over every single industrial works, every single piece of machinery, every thousand tons of shipping space. Adenauer knew that all this was to no purpose unless his government was able to create employment. The Federal Republic had to feed more than a million and a half unemployed and over seven and a half million refugees. It must find work for them or fail in its task.

Once again U. S. High Commissioner McCloy declared, "The list of concessions granted to Germany requires, in return, German readiness to cooperate."

Once again British High Commissioner Robertson enumerated the conditions for a satisfactory settlement of the dismantling problem: acceptance of the Ruhr Statute, cooperation with the Security Board, agreement with the Allied decartelization measures. Should the Federal Parliament reject Adenauer's declaration of adherence to the Ruhr Statute, Allied willingness to grant concessions over dismantling would be correspondingly reduced.

The negotiations continued.

On November 17, the Chancellor was again at Petersberg. "Is the Federal Republic prepared to cooperate in the Security Board?" Robertson asked. Adenauer answered, "Yes." And how about the progress of democracy in Germany? Somewhat reproachfully McCloy remarked that former Nazis were known to be climbing back into leading positions in the Federal Republic. The Americans themselves, Adenauer retorted, were giving a bad example. Did they not invite former Gestapo chief Diels to go hunting with them at Nuremberg?

Indeed, it was not easy. Certainly it was not as easy as the critics seemed to imagine. At every turn one had to answer for oneself the question: who after all has lost the war? And yet preserve intact one's self-respect.

At last, on November 22, 1949, agreement was reached on all points.

What had Adenauer been able to achieve?

He had secured the removal of eighteen large industrial plants from the dismantling list—seven steel plants including the August Thyssen-Hütte, Klöckner and Bochumer Verein, and eleven chemical plants including the Bayer works at Leverkusen and the hard fought-for Chemische Werke at Bergkamen. He had saved all industrial works in Berlin which had not yet been dismantled, including the Borsig works. He had obtained a substantial relaxation of the restrictions on German shipbuilding—henceforth oceangoing ships up to twelve knots could be constructed in unlimited numbers. In addition, six oceangoing ships exceeding this limit might be built during the current year, and unrestricted repair work on foreign vessels in seven German shipyards was authorized.

These last concessions were of particular importance to Adenauer. They meant that there would be work again, at last, in the great ports of Hamburg and Bremen. These two cities were administered by Socialist mayors, and Adenauer was particularly anxious, as he confessed frankly, "to have something to offer to these gentlemen up on the coast." They at least would not now be able to claim, as Schumacher had predicted, that he was facing Parliament empty-handed.

But this was not all. There were other things of equal importance, possibly of even greater importance to Adenauer, since they promised greater freedom of movement for the Federal Republic in its foreign relations. The Federal Republic had not only become a free and equal partner in the Marshall Plan Organization but would henceforth be able to join a large number of other international organizations such as the World Bank and the World Monetary Fund, the International Labor Organization and the World Health Organization. It was furthermore authorized to establish consular offices in foreign countries—a first step toward normal diplomatic relations. And it was free to join the Council of Europe at Strasbourg.

These were the gains. What had been conceded in return?

The federal government, the official statement said, "declares its earnest determination to maintain the demilitarization of the federal territory and to endeavor by all means in its power to prevent the recreation of armed forces of any kind. To this end the federal government will cooperate fully with the High Commission in the work of the Military Security Board." Moreover, the federal government "declares its intention of applying for membership of the International Authority for the Ruhr in which, at present, the federal government is only represented by an observer. . . ."

What would the opposition say to this? There were bound to be some violent clashes, but Adenauer remained convinced that it was more advantageous for Germany to be directly, rather than indirectly, represented in the Ruhr Authority, and in any case he felt certain that the Ruhr Authority would die a natural death before long. He had never been afraid of it because he had always regarded it as a steppingstone toward a comprehensive West European economic federation.

Indeed, everything was settled at last. When Adenauer and Dr. Blankenhorn, his personal assistant, arrived at Petersberg on November 22, all that remained to do was to approve the text of the official communiqué, and sign it. Only the final communiqué! A whole day was spent over it, and this time it was Adenauer who dragged things out. But he knew why.

The meeting began at 10:38 A.M.

Sir Brian Robertson announced that the High Commission had approved the communiqué as drafted by the experts, except for a few minor alterations. But the Federal Chancellor shook his head. He desired a number of changes to be made and produced a draft of his own containing various additions and alterations. Why these new difficulties? Adenauer explained:

"I'm not only anxious to have my actions approved by a majority in Parliament. I'm even more anxious to have the support of the majority of the German people in this new move. Therefore I feel that the communiqué should be drafted in such a way as to make Mr. Bevin's words quite clear to every reader—that this definitely closes one chapter and opens an entirely new one."

He proceeded to read out his own draft. Most of his new formulas were quickly agreed to, but over the matter of the Ruhr Authority a lengthy controversy arose. Adenauer explained why he was so anxious to have his wording adopted:

"This membership of the federal government in the Ruhr Agreement is really the most difficult point in the whole business. It must be admitted that the Ruhr Agreement is a heavy thing for us to carry. All the same, the federal government is determined to take this step. . . . Besides, I have a personal reason of my own. As chairman of the CDU in the British Zone I commented publicly on the Ruhr Agreement when it was first announced, in December, 1948. It may be remembered that I criticized several of its articles but said, in essence, what really mattered was the spirit in which it was going to be worked. Although I remain essentially faithful to my basic line in now joining the Ruhr Statute, I feel nevertheless that it would be a good thing if the sentence I have just read out could be incorporated in the communiqué. . . ."

This sentence was to the effect that in the view of the federal government some of the stipulations of the Ruhr Agreement had been rendered obsolete by events, that the federal government desired their reconsideration and revision, and wished to be a partner in the negotiations to this end.

The draft communiqué was further scrutinized, point by point. On the question of dismantling there was renewed and lengthy controversy, this time with François-Poncet. Eventually the French High Commissioner sighed:

"It is a very hard task, making presents to the Germans. It is also a very thankless task."

The meeting was adjourned to enable the experts to redraft the text and the High Commissioners to consult among themselves about Adenauer's wishes for alterations. After an interval Robertson announced that Adenauer's proposal to foreshadow in the communiqué a proposed revision of the Ruhr Statute was not acceptable. Why not? Had not Adenauer declared again and again during this meeting:

"You will understand, gentlemen, that I am trying to lay this agreement open to as few critical attacks as possible."

They understood perfectly, and they appreciated it. But, explained Robertson, the inclusion of a sentence to this effect could give the impression that the Germans had made their membership in the Ruhr Authority dependent on the acceptance of conditions. That was an impression the three High Commissioners were anxious not to create, and this in turn the Chancellor would no doubt understand and appreciate. . . .

Progress was not easy. It was nearly seven o'clock. Eventually Robertson suggested leaving the text as it was but authorizing Adenauer to make a statement before Parliament in the precise terms of his proposed amendment. Would that satisfy the Chancellor? It did.

On other points it was the High Commissioners who yielded.

Robertson: "As regards dismantling, we attach the greatest importance to a formal declaration from you that you and your government pledge yourselves to insure unhindered execution of those dismantlings which remain. But in order to ease your position we are prepared to delete this sentence from the document if, in its place, you will send us a confidential note containing this assurance."

Adenauer: "I shall send such a note."

At last the end was in sight. Adenauer insisted that the closing sentence of the communiqué must end in a positive note.

"The German people must be able to feel that this agreement is part of the integration of Germany in Western Europe, as distinct from the Eastern World. . . . I must make it clear to them that this is an event of the highest political import."

He read out once more his own draft amendment. François-Poncet toned it down. Eventually a compromise formula suggested by McCloy was accepted.

The time was now 9:35 P.M. The communiqué was signed. Ten minutes later the Chancellor took his leave. He had negotiated for a full eleven hours at a stretch—stubborn, circumspect, farseeing, sincere, and in a spirit of conciliation. Would they understand this, down at Bonn? Would it be appreciated?

The following day, November 25, Sir Brian Robertson issued an official statement on behalf of the High Commission. This said:

"We have held back nothing, save on considerations of strict security. We recognize that the federal government has also made a notable contribution. . . . We are clearly not expecting that this agreement should be regarded as a steppingstone for further demands. The Occupation Statute is due for review in the autumn of next year, and the program now launched is to cover the period between now and then. . . . We hope that the constructive intent of this settlement will be recognized. In every settlement there are points which, viewed in isolation, appear unwelcome or unsatisfactory to some people. By focusing attention on individual points the picture as a whole can be seriously distorted."

Sir Brian Robertson was not alone in fearing such distortion. Adenauer, too, feared it. And his apprehension proved well-grounded when he appeared before Parliament.

"President Dr. Köhler: 'Deputy Dr. Schumacher . . . !' Loud cries of protest in the center and on the left. Members of the SPD and CDU rise from their seats and engage in heated discussion. Continuous bell-ringing from the President. Persistent uproar. President Dr. Köhler: 'Deputy Dr. Schumacher . . . !' Continued uproar and cries of 'Shame! Disgraceful!' and 'Monstrous! Get out! Throw them out!' President Dr. Köhler: 'Deputy Dr. Schumacher . . . ' Persistent disturbance. Continuous bell-ringing from the President. . . ."

Thus the official parliamentary report for the eighteenth sitting of the German Federal Parliament on November 24 and 25, 1949. It was 3:21 A.M. when President Dr. Köhler finally suspended the chaotic debate in which he was unable to get a hearing or create a semblance of orderly procedure.

The momentous debate had begun at five o'clock in the afternoon.

"I call upon the Federal Chancellor for a statement from the government," the President had announced. Adenauer rose to submit to the tense and crowded house what has since become known as the "Petersberg Agreement," preceding it by "some reflections on the method which, in my view, we should follow in our foreign policy.

"It should be realized," he said, "that in all negotiations which we Germans have to conduct with the Allies in order gradually to regain an increasing degree of authority over our own national affairs, psychological elements play a very considerable part. We cannot and must not, from the very outset, demand or expect full trust and confidence. We cannot and must not start from the assumption that there has been a sudden and complete change of mood and temper in the attitude of other nations toward Germany. We must understand that confidence can be regained only gradually, step by step, little by little. Just as it would be undignified and wrong on our part to pursue a policy of slavish submission, it would be stupid, unwise, and unavailing for us to try to assert ourselves in an overbearing manner. In particular I believe that we Germans must guard against any idea of exploiting signs of disunity among the great powers and gaining advantage from their disagreements. . . ."

What then was to be Germany's policy? It consisted in "making the necessary possible." The phrase was not Adenauer's own. It was coined by Social Democrat Carlo Schmid, and Adenauer did not quote it. But every one of his words which followed confirmed it. The Petersberg Agreement had "made the necessary possible." No more, and no less.

For the first time since the capitulation, Adenauer said, German equality of rights in negotiations had been officially recognized. "The Agreement," he explained, "has been concluded in the English, French, and German languages, and the German text has equal legal validity with the two others."

Nevertheless, the Social Democratic party had tabled a motion of no confidence in the Government. This referred especially to the proposed membership of the Federal Republic in the Ruhr Authority, the opposition challenging the constitutional right of the Chancellor to commit the Republic to this membership. His action, they maintained, was in disregard of Articles Twenty-four and Fifty-nine of the Basic Law and represented a violation of the Constitution.

Soberly and factually the Chancellor refuted this assertion: "A great deal has been said and written particularly about this question which, in my view, is altogether beside the point. I must state the following. The Ruhr Authority has been established as a result of the London Agreement. According to Article Two of this Agreement Germany is even now a member of the Ruhr Authority. At the time when the Agreement was concluded, Germany was totally deprived of all freedom of action in its own name, and was represented by the Military Governors who acted on her behalf. All Germany's rights and obligations arising from the Ruhr Authority and laid down in it exist even now. We cannot withdraw from these obligations except by force, and we are in no position to exercise force. . . ."

Constitutionally, then, the Petersberg Agreement brought no

change with regard to the Ruhr Authority. If there was a change in the position, and indeed there was a most important one, it lay elsewhere. Now, as before, Germany would have the same number of votes in the Ruhr Authority as were held by the United States, Great Britain, and France, and the three Benelux countries together—namely, three. Hitherto this vote had been cast on Germany's behalf by the Military Governors. From now on German representatives themselves were entitled to cast it direct. But to be able to do so, it was obvious that Germany must formally adhere to the Ruhr Authority or declare in some other way that she intended to fulfill her obligations arising from it.

"By making such a declaration," Adenauer said, "we assume no new obligations. For I repeat, these obligations exist even now. Nor is it correct, as has been said, that by sending a delegated representative to the Ruhr Authority we renounce certain sovereign rights. We do not at present possess these sovereign rights. We were deprived of them through Unconditional Surrender, and later by virtue of the London Agreement. Nor can there be any question of our entering into an international agreement. . . ."

And finally, since Germany was in any case a member of the Ruhr Authority, having been, as it were, "compulsorily conscripted" into it, whether she liked it or not, was it not a step forward that she could now use her own vote in order to work from the inside for a gradual transformation of the Ruhr Authority, rather than protest ineffectively against it from the outside? "The federal government," Adenauer declared, "reserves the right to table the relevant motions in the Council of the Ruhr Authority as soon as it enjoys the exercise of its vote."

Was not all this sound common sense? Did it not indeed "make the necessary possible"? The same was true of dismantling. Having read to the House the long list of plants saved from dismantling, Adenauer added:

"Now, it is not the case that all dismantling will henceforth cease altogether. A number of dismantlings—in the first place of plants originally established for specific war purposes—will continue until completed. . . . But nevertheless, the House will see from the list of plants removed from the dismantling program that we have taken a great step forward. Our own Ministry of Economics estimates that this meets our wishes to the extent of 90 per cent."

Ninety per cent! The astonishing figure was heard for the first time.

"Not all our wishes have been fulfilled," Adenauer concluded. "But justice bids us recognize that a very large part of them has been fulfilled and that, as a result, this agreement represents a very valuable and considerable success for our economic life. And in its political aspects this agreement is a very great success indeed. For the first time since the capitulation our equality of rights has been officially recognized, and for the first time we shall now re-enter the international sphere. . . ."

The Chancellor had spoken for exactly forty-five minutes. When after a short interval the sitting was resumed, the storm broke loose.

"This agreement," said Socialist Deputy Dr. Adolf Arndt, "is yet another link in the chain of attempts to exclude Parliament permanently from the conduct of national affairs, to secure victory in constitutional struggles by authoritarian '*coups de main*'!" The Chancellor, Arndt said, had endeavored, by signing this protocol, to sidestep Parliament. He had no right to agree to Germany's cooperation in the international control of the Ruhr, and he was not entitled to commit the Federal Republic to membership in the Council of Europe.

"We are here faced with an authoritarian decision over vital questions affecting the lives of millions!" Arndt exclaimed. "What we are debating here today and what is down for the vote is nothing less than the acid test of whether the Basic Law is but a scrap of paper, whether the majority will continue to ignore it and ride roughshod over it, as they have done already several times in this House, or whether we here in this House shall respect and obey the Basic Law. We had believed we were on the road toward parliamentary democracy, and now find ourselves on the way toward an unconstitutional monarchy!"

Loud laughter and catcalls from the center and the right interrupted the speaker. Angrily Dr. Arndt retorted, "Ladies and gentlemen, the day will come when you won't be at all in a laughing mood about all this. Let me assure you of one thing. We do not intend to forget that the Federal Chancellor, when he assumed his office, solemnly swore to abide by the Constitution, and, by God, Herr Chancellor, we shall be here to remind you of your oath!"

At this point Adenauer intervened in the debate. The hour was late, it was past midnight, but what Adenauer now announced to the House hit it like a bombshell and stirred the jaded minds back into the most violent controversy. The Chancellor read out a message from the German Trade Union Federation saying that the Petersberg Agreement was to be regarded as an earnest endeavor by the Allies to meet German needs and adding that, although the agreement was not in all respects satisfactory, the trade unions considered the cooperation of the federal government in the Ruhr Authority to be justified.

"But this is simply not true!" Schumacher called out. His face red with anger, the Socialist leader stared furiously at Adenauer, who met his gaze with icy composure. Now pandemonium broke out. Amid the general hubbub cries of "Lies!" and "Forgery!" could be heard from the left. Adenauer replied by reading once more the second and salient part of the trade union statement. There was no doubt that the message, published by the United Press news agency, was perfectly genuine and authentic, and it meant nothing less than that the powerful trade unions, regarded by the Social Democrats as their exclusive political preserve, were backing the Government against the Socialist Opposition.

It was a stunning blow for Kurt Schumacher but it did not end the debate which continued furiously and acrimoniously for several more hours. At last, at three o'clock in the morning, the Chancellor was able to rise for his wind-up speech. He made one last attempt to correct the distortions and adjust the perspective. But one felt clearly that he was near the end of his patience and that his sense of humor was well-nigh exhausted. He remained moderate in his tone, but his argument was now of brutal incisiveness.

"I cannot understand," he said, "what it is that keeps blurring the vision of the speakers of the Social Democratic party. The matter at issue is not at all whether we, the Government, or you yourselves consent to the establishment of the Ruhr Authority. The Opposition know perfectly well that the Ruhr Authority exists; they know that its Secretariat General exists; and they know that its administrative staff by now already numbers more than a hundred. They know all that perfectly well. And they know equally well, as does everyone in this House, that the only question at issue is this: shall we send a delegate to exercise our three votes, or are we prepared to see the whole of the dismantling program carried through inexorably to the end?"

Up to this point Adenauer had been listened to without interruption. Now the House began to get restless. Adenauer repeated:

"This is the question at issue . . ."

"No!" shouted the Social Democrats.

" . . . and I must point out—I'm unfortunately compelled to point this out following the last speech by Herr Ollenhauer—that the Social Democratic party is apparently prepared to see the whole dismantling program carried through to the end rather than——"

The parliamentary report records the reaction to these words: "Shouts of 'Very good!' and 'Hear, hear!' and applause from the Government parties. Catcalls from the left: 'Unheard of! Monstrous!' Catcalls from the right: 'Your English friends are leaving you in the lurch!' Interjection from the SPD: 'What a political tactlessness!' General unrest."

Adenauer: "This question the Opposition must face and answer——"

More shouting and interruptions.

Adenauer: " . . . this is the question which is at the heart of the matter, and nothing else: are they prepared to send a delegate to the Ruhr Authority, or are they not? And if they answer 'No,' then they know from the statements made to me by General Robertson that the dismantlings will be carried out to the end——"

These were the last words with which the Chancellor was able to make himself heard in this debate.

Schumacher called out, "This is not true!"

Cries of "Hear, hear!" and countercalls from the Government parties. More agitated interruptions from Socialist and Communist benches. The President's bell was ringing incessantly.

Communist Deputy Renner: "Where does it say so?"

Calls from the left: "Are you still a German? Are you speaking as the German Chancellor?"

Schumacher: "Federal Chancellor of the Allies!"

At these words the House lost the rest of its restraint and self-control. Pandemonium broke loose. Three times President Köhler tried to penetrate the uproar and make himself heard. In vain. Finally he shouted above the din:

"Mr. Deputy Schumacher! For this reference to the Federal Chancellor as 'Chancellor of the Allies' I herewith call you to order. I now call upon the Federal Chancellor to continue."

But the agitation was now such that there could be no question of "continuing." Into the persistent uproar Socialist Deputy Ollenhauer called out, "Herr Adenauer has provoked him, and no one else!" Amid the uproar Adenauer now left the rostrum and returned to his seat on the Government bench. CDU deputy Strauss called across to Schumacher, "You'll have to apologize now, or we shall walk out of the chamber!" Deputy Oellers proposed that the sitting be adjourned and the Council of Elders convened to consider the position. At length this was agreed to. The time was 3:21 A.M. The sitting was suspended until six o'clock.

Then, at dawn on November 25, the last scene of the drama was enacted. When the sitting was resumed, President Köhler announced that the Council of Elders had suggested to Dr. Schumacher that he should formally withdraw the "gravely offensive reference to the Federal Chancellor." If he were prepared to do this, the Federal Chancellor would be glad to have a private talk with Dr. Schumacher about the matter at issue some time during the day. Unfortunately they had not succeeded in prevailing upon Dr. Schumacher to withdraw his remark.

"Therefore," Dr. Köhler announced, "I am herewith suspending Deputy Dr. Schumacher for a gross affront to the standing orders from all deliberations of this House for a duration of twenty meeting days."

Under the influence of the nasty setback the young Parliament had suffered during this calamitous night, and the no less calamitous sharpening of the personal antagonism between Adenauer and Schumacher, the House dispersed in informal and haphazard fashion. The Socialist motion of no confidence as well as two Communist motions to the same effect were rejected unanimously without anyone being fully aware of it or taking much notice.

It was six-thirty in the morning. Adenauer drove home to Rhöndorf. How were things to go on after this? What was it Socialist Carlo Schmid, that irrepressible coiner of phrases, had said only the other day?

"What matters in politics is not to be in the right but to be proved right."

Events would show who would be proved right. Not tomorrow or the day after. But next year and the year after next. "Patience is the strongest weapon in the armory of the vanquished, and I can wait. . . ." Adenauer has said so himself, and it held good.

# CHAPTER XIX

"THE AGREEMENT reached between the Allied High Commission and Dr. Adenauer is a remarkable example of good sense and good statesmanship. It is only right that Dr. Adenauer, who has shown great skill during recent weeks, should now be given credit for his courage. Few German statesmen in the last hundred years would have signed such a declaration without even consulting their Cabinet or Parliament. If Dr. Adenauer has done well for his country, it would be churlish to deny that he has also done well for Europe. . . . Dr. Adenauer himself has unmistakably emerged as one of the leading statesmen of Europe."

Thus the London *Times* on November 25, 1949.

"More important than this, however," the paper added, "a way has been found to bring Germany back into the European family without increasing the tension between East and West. A statement by Britain, France, and the United States alone that they did not intend to rearm Germany would have hardly convinced the Soviet Union and Poland that they meant it . . . a statement by the Federal Government, on the other hand, should carry more weight. . . ."

What did this mean? What was the "declaration" or "statement" to which this weighty comment referred?

Nothing shows more clearly the different lights in which the Petersberg Agreement was viewed in Germany and abroad. For Germany the decisive points in the agreement were dismantling, the Ruhr Authority, the Council of Europe. They were the subject of debate, and Adenauer had to defend them in Parliament. No one in Germany paid much attention to Article III of the Agreement because, in German eyes, it was self-evident.

For the three other partners, however, this article was the most important section of the whole document. For in it the "Federal Government declares its earnest determination to maintain the demilitarization of the federal territory and to endeavor by all means in its power to prevent the re-creation of armed forces of any kind."

It was the unqualified acceptance of this declaration on the part of Germany which made such a strong impression in foreign countries. It was for signing this that Adenauer was congratulated upon his courage. It will be difficult to appreciate correctly Adenauer's achievement during the following years without bearing this discrepancy, this "dual light" in mind. Only by simply ignoring it could anyone go to the length of calling him "Federal Chancellor of the Allies."

Adenauer remained constantly aware of this discrepancy and took it into account. He fully realized that Germany and the rest of the world were still very far from finding themselves under a "common denominator," and that it would be a long time before they viewed dominant world problems with more or less the same eyes. Meantime he must endeavor to see things with the eyes of both sides. There was no other way to make progress.

The German public knew little or nothing of the protracted and often discouraging negotiations which preceded each decision reached at the Petersberg. All it saw were the results which the Chancellor eventually submitted to Parliament, and it often found that he had been too "lenient" or had even adopted the "point of view of the occupying powers" at the expense of German interests.

The High Commissioners on their part had but a limited idea, and the American, British, and French public an even more limited one, of the equally protracted and often discouraging negotiations which followed for Adenauer in the Cabinet, in Parliament, and elsewhere each time he returned from the Petersberg. They often complained that he was altogether too "unyielding" and would never see things from any but the "German point of view."

Adenauer knew both complaints, although understandable, to be wrong and unjustified. He felt that essentially they missed the point. What mattered to him was to find the "common denominator" and he endeavored unceasingly to bring both sides nearer to it. He tried to establish a joint vantage point from which to take a "European view" of things, and for this he labored with undaunted persistence and patience.

The short official statements issued at the conclusion of the regular Petersberg meetings told the public nothing of all these difficulties. But Adenauer the politician and statesman, Adenauer the German and the European, and not least Adenauer the human being with his virtues and weaknesses and varying shades of temperament, does not become really alive and visible unless one penetrates now and then behind the closed doors of the Petersberg conference room.

In the following chapters we shall try, whenever possible, to catch a glimpse of Adenauer moving through this secret world.

Rearmament? Armed forces?

Who, in the Germany of November, 1949, apart from a few incorrigibles, gave as much as a fleeting thought to such possibilities? People were glad to be finally rid of having to "play at soldiers," and no one was more glad about it than Konrad Adenauer. He was convinced that a genuine policy of conciliation at home and abroad would gradually produce the "common denominator" which would automatically take the wind out of the sails of the incorrigibles on the extreme right, who continued to dream of uniforms. Had anyone ventured to tell Adenauer in November, 1949, that in the end he would not be able to obtain full sovereignty, independence, and equality for the Federal Republic except by way of rearmament, he would have dismissed such a prediction as grotesque and absurd. Yet this was what eventually came to pass. Rearmament proved the only way to achieve this goal. In November, 1949, the demilitarization of the Federal Republic was the prime condition for a gradual relaxation and abolition of the occupation regime. Five years later Adenauer signed the London and Paris Protocols which granted the Federal Republic its full sovereignty and equality of rights, and the price was remilitarization.

And once again the free world paid tribute to Adenauer for the courage and determination with which he pursued his path.

This path began on November 17, 1949, in Washington.

After the Paris conference Mr. Dean Acheson, the American Secretary of State, paid a brief visit to Western Germany, and on November 13 had his first personal meeting with the Federal Chancellor. This immediately gave rise to all sorts of rumors. On November 16, the New York *Times* published a message from its correspondent at Bonn according to which the establishment of a German army of five divisions had been variously discussed during Mr. Acheson's stay in Europe. According to other reports the inclusion of German volunteers in the contingents of the occupying powers had been under consideration.

Was this possible? German opinion asked. Was it even thinkable?

Western Europe began to be nervous. In France the American rumors at once reawakened all the old fears and prejudices. M. René Teitgen, the Information Minister, declared roundly that France could never accept, under whatever conditions, a rearmament of Germany or German participation in the Atlantic Pact. "The world must realize," he said, "that France cannot remain a partner in a system of security which includes German rearmament!"

All this sounded strange and not a little uncanny in German ears. How was it that such a possibility could even be discussed? What was more, the whole world seemed to be debating excitedly the question of German rearmament, but no one, so far, had troubled to ask the Germans themselves their views on it. Certainly, no one had asked the Federal Chancellor. But this did not mean he had nothing to say on this burning topic. He had something to say, and meant to say it, too. But how? Foreign affairs and national defense—which were both concerned in this—were still "reserved fields" to which access was barred to him by the Occupation Statute.

In this situation the Americans themselves afforded Adenauer an opportunity to state his views, and he did so in a manner which he subsequently employed more than once on important occasions. What he did was to grant an interview to an important foreign newspaper. From this developed the method soon described everywhere as "Adenauer's foreign policy by interview," and severely criticized by many.

When, on December 3, 1949, the Bonn correspondent of the Cleveland *Plain Dealer* called at the Federal Chancery, it was not only with the knowledge of the American authorities but also partly suggested by them. At any rate it had been intimated to Adenauer that there was no objection to his replying to a number of questions put by the correspondent regarding German rearmament.

Adenauer seized the opportunity. The interview became a world sensation, not least in Germany itself, and gave rise to an endless tangle of misunderstanding. Apparently the American reporter had misunderstood some of the Chancellor's answers, failed to understand others completely, and had given a one-sided and sensational slant to the whole. What had Adenauer really said? Had he in fact suddenly changed his well-known and often emphasized view that he neither desired nor advocated a new German army? Were the eternally suspicious at home and abroad right, after all, in maintaining that even in this good German European there was hidden an incorrigible German nationalist, chauvinist, and militarist? From the muddled report of the American newspaper it was impossible to tell, and that was a calamity. Adenauer took steps to correct it immediately. When the Bonn correspondent of the London *Times* called on him the next day, asking him to elucidate his earlier statement, he told him:

"My attitude to this question has not changed in any way. It must be made clear once and for all that I am fundamentally opposed to the rearmament of the German Republic and therefore also to the creation of a new German *Wehrmacht.* We Germans have shed so much blood in two world wars and have also far too few people to allow us to carry through such a project. The Allies have disarmed us, and the moral and legal duty rests on them to defend us. I have always taken the view that the security of Western Germany was a matter for the occupying powers.

"If the Allies demanded that we should take part in the defense of Western Europe, I should be in favor, not of an independent *Wehrmacht,* but of a German contingent in a European force. I should be opposed to Germans being accepted into, or recruited for, a non-German contingent, or to their serving as mercenaries."

Was that clear and unequivocal? It was more than that. It was a bold advance in an altogether new direction. During the following days Adenauer returned several times to his basic argument.

"After all that has happened in recent years," he told a CDU meeting at Düsseldorf on December 8, 1949, "the German people are absolutely opposed to war. We all hope and pray that there will not be another war. But tension between East and West has sharpened of late, and if both sides take military precautions it is of course possible for something untoward to happen. In such an event Germany would face the situation disarmed and unprotected. Now Germans cannot very well be expected to serve as mercenaries in foreign armies. But in the event of a European Federation requiring a West German contribution to the common defense of Europe, Germans could in certain circumstances participate in the same way as British, French, and other nations."

This introduced a new argument into the debate.

Adenauer had said, in other words: if we are to help in the defense of Europe it is obvious that we must fully belong to Europe. Let us create a Europe in which Germany enjoys equal rights, and Germany will be willing to assume equal duties—including defense. This simple, basic argument Adenauer, faithful to his method, kept repeating over and over again for the next five years—until at last the world accepted it.

But there was another side to the problem. Adenauer explained it the following day, December 9, 1949, to a meeting of his party friends at Königswinter. "The Western Powers," he said, "talk a great deal about their security, but it should not be forgotten that Germany, too, has a claim to security." If the Western Powers were in need of security, Germany needed it no less. That was all too willingly forgotten. In his opinion the newly established so-called "People's Police" in the Soviet Zone represented nothing less than a regular army. "In their military considerations the Western Powers should not overlook the fact that Germany is not a vast and empty desert which can be conveniently used as a theater of war, but a densely populated country. The Western Allies must face the question: which danger is the greater, the danger threatening from Russia, or the prospect of a German contingent in a European army destined to defend Europe?"

Of course, there was nothing new to the Western Powers in these considerations. They were facing the question all right, but they had not yet reached a clear-cut answer. Here, as in the European question, Adenauer boldly demonstrated to them the inescapable alternative. The Federal Republic had only one potential enemy who did not wish it well and whom it had reason to fear. That was the East. The Western Powers, on the other hand, were not clear which in the last resort they should fear more—the specter of vanquished German militarism or the threat of militant communism? They were anxious to protect themselves against both. In that event a conflict, if it broke out, would be fought out on the back of Germany, and Adenauer made it clear—without putting it in these brutal terms—that in such a case no unconditional German loyalty to the West could be expected or demanded. If Germany was to opt for the West, the condition was that the West must opt for Germany.

Even in those very early days things were as clear-cut and explicit as that, although they were not expressed in these harsh, outspoken terms. It is worth remembering that the time was only December, 1949, and Adenauer had been Chancellor for scarcely three months. But then as later he approached this decisive question from quite simple moral premises. There was no need to be a military expert to reach these farseeing conclusions. Simple ethical principles sufficed.

Eventually, on December 16, the Federal Parliament concerned itself with the problem which had so unexpectedly arisen, and the debate of that day, despite some violent clashes between Adenauer and the Communists, served the useful purpose of making the attitude of government and Parliament clear to an outside world still doubtful or skeptical of German motives, and in part openly suspicious. Large sections of public opinion outside Germany were on the whole still convinced that the Germans were longing for nothing more eagerly than uniforms, decorations, tanks, and bombers, and were only waiting for an opportunity to regain all these treasures. Less than five years of "Occupation Democracy" had not been sufficient to dissuade French and British, Belgians and Dutch from this view.

Now Adenauer told the Federal Parliament:

"Even in the event of the Allies demanding in a categorical form a German contribution to European security, there can be no question whatever of an establishment of a German Army. The utmost we would be prepared to consider would be a German contingent in the framework of a European Army."

Members of all coalition parties declared unanimously that the German people "had no thought of rearmament." The Social Democratic opposition went even further, rejecting the mere consideration of the question of German rearmament as a provocation of the East and reproaching the Chancellor sharply for having raised the issue at all!

Two days after the debate in Parliament the London *Times* wrote:

"It would be a poor service to German democracy if the Western Powers were to press arms into the hands of the German people before they are ready for them and—to do them credit—before they want them.

"So far as the future is concerned much will depend on the Russians and the Germans themselves. The Russians, who have most to fear from German rearmament, have been the first to begin it by forming an armed police force in Eastern Germany. They must realize that this alone will make some degree of rearmament in West Germany necessary before the Western Powers can leave. The more they expand and strengthen the People's Police the more likely will they make the formation of a similar force in the West. Since the Russian danger is at present greater than the German danger, it is quite certain that if forced to choose the Western Powers will rearm Germany rather than submit to threats."

The Russian danger is greater than the German danger—this conclusion at which the Western world had arrived slowly and in a roundabout way was for Adenauer obvious and self-evident. Equally evident to him was that this conclusion must be exploited and made to yield a maximum of positive and constructive elements for the benefit of Europe as a whole. For once, he felt, the vanquished found himself in a position which gave him an advantage over the victor. This must not go unused.

At this point an element in Adenauer's thought and action entered the game which his friends like to call his "slyness" and "cleverness," his opponents his "calculating opportunism," and his partners in international negotiations his "blackmailing tactics," and which in any event was nothing but uncommon political intelligence. The Social Democratic opposition was quite wrong in reprimanding Adenauer for having raised the subject of rearmament at all. It was not Adenauer who had raised it. But once the debate on it had begun in Washington, London, and Paris, he perceived in it a chance for the furtherance of his own ideas. That was not only clever and astute. It was intelligent.

"Even in the event of the Allies demanding a German contribution to European security . . . " he had said. The Allies had demanded no such thing. Why then should he want to give a categorical answer to a question which had not been put? There were two reasons. Firstly, because he reckoned that sooner or later the question would in fact be put. And secondly, because in that case he saw a chance of advancing a long step toward the realization of the one idea which governed all his political thinking—the close and indissoluble integration of Western Germany in Western Europe.

For him this was not a crude attempt at blackmail in the sphere of power politics which exploited the "advantage of the vanquished": Germany will only furnish troops if the West grants full sovereignty. Such an equation was a self-evident, foregone conclusion. There was more in it than that, namely, Germany will accept this sovereignty on these conditions only if the West is at the same time prepared to revise its traditional conceptions of sovereignty and surmount the obsolete idea of the nation state in favor of an integrated Europe. It was for this reason that Adenauer, at this early stage of the debate, broached the idea of a "European Army." For it was clear to him that a European Army was unthinkable by itself as a purely military institution; it could not possibly exist in a political vacuum as in a field fenced in on all sides by economic and cultural barriers. A European Army presupposed a comprehensive European structure with a close integration in all other fields as well. This thoroughly integrated European structure was what he had at heart, and he felt that a European Army would inevitably have to result in a European Union. If this European Union could be attained by contributing German soldiers, this was a price well worth paying.

The day would come, Adenauer felt, when Germany would have a chance of compelling Europe to unite. He perceived this possibility when he spoke to the reporter of the Cleveland *Plain Dealer*. The reporter presumably did not quite grasp this, and in Germany itself as well as elsewhere, outside Germany, it took some time before people recognized the stratagem. Possibly it was sly, and even opportunist. It may well have been a gamble with high stakes. But it was not cynical. It was sound European policy.

But where, at this stage, was Europe?

On May 5, 1949, the Council of Europe in which most European countries were represented by ministers or members of parliament had constituted itself at Strasbourg. Consisting of a Committee of Ministers and a Consultative Assembly, the Council possessed neither legislative nor executive power but was nevertheless a grand forum for an exchange and debate of European political ideas. It was, it seemed, a first step toward a closer unification of Europe, and Adenauer had felt from the very beginning that Germany must participate as soon as possible in this grand debate and take an active part in its thinking and planning on a European level. Contact with Europe was what Germany needed most, and this was where it could be established.

As early as August, 1949, no less a figure than Mr. Winston Churchill had pointed out at Strasbourg that German membership in the Committee of Ministers and the Consultative Assembly was "an urgent necessity for the future of Europe." At that time a number of members of the Council of Europe had considered the "admission" of Germany as "premature." By November, general feeling toward Germany had much improved. On November 9, 1949, the permanent committee of the European Assembly recommended the admission of Germany as an "associate member," provided Germany herself applied for it, and in signing the Petersberg Agreement Adenauer committed the Federal Republic, at the explicit request of the occupying powers, to make such an application.

There was no request to which Adenauer would have responded more gladly. But now, at the beginning of 1950, he found himself faced with a severe obstacle. For the European Assembly had recommended the admission not only of Germany but, at the urgent request of France, also of the Saar Territory. In doing so it placed a barrier in Adenauer's way which compelled his own policy, the Western Powers, and all Western Europe, to take an endless and cumbersome roundabout route. Adenauer's patient and persistent endeavor to reach an understanding with France was poisoned, time and again, by the "Saar question," and the "Saar question," in its turn, from now on poisoned European relations generally for years to come.

What precisely was the "Saar question"?

In August, 1946, only few Germans had been aware of the fact that the administration of the Saar Territory had been taken over by a special French government commission which henceforth treated it separately from the rest of the French Zone of Occupation, to which Germans generally thought the Saar legally and organically belonged. But in those early postwar weeks Germans had other things to worry about and paid little attention to this French move. But when in July, 1946, French Foreign Minister Georges Bidault announced to the Paris Conference of Foreign Ministers that the Saar Territory had been detached from the French Zone of Occupation and was therefore outside the jurisdiction of the Allied Occupation authorities in Germany, people took note and began to wonder. And when in December, 1946, the French Military Governor decreed the inclusion of the Saar Territory in the French customs area and introduced passport and customs controls, French intentions became clear. Little by little the Saar Territory was being detached from Germany and made to go its own way.

From now on events moved swiftly and according to schedule. In April, 1947, the British and United States governments declared themselves in agreement with the French wish for economic integration of the Saar Territory into the French Republic. In June, 1947, a separate currency, the Saar Mark, replaced the old German Reichsmark. In October, 1947, elections for a Saar parliament were held, in December the Saar Territory formed its first separate government, and in January, 1948, a legal convention was signed between France and the Saar Territory, and the French Government Commissar was replaced by a High Commissioner.

During this whole period many voices were raised in Germany objecting to these measures. But there was nothing Germany could do. She possessed no government able to speak for the nation and had to look on powerless when in May, 1948, a "High Council" for the Saar Territory was established at Saarbrücken, and on July 15, the Saar parliament passed a law creating a separate nationality for Saarlanders. True, the Western Powers including France gave assurances that all these measures were of a provisional nature and that a final settlement would have to wait until the peace treaty with Germany. But one did not need be a German chauvinist to see that the Saar frontier bore a certain resemblance to the Oder-Neisse line. And, when France insisted on seeing the new Saar state admitted to the Council of Europe as a separate member, the Federal Republic's enthusiastic approval of the European idea cooled off very markedly. Was the Federal Republic to sit in the Council of Europe as an equal partner beside an arbitrarily detached piece of German territory? Germans refused to take kindly to such an idea.

Adenauer had no choice. He delayed the application for admission of the Federal Republic to the Council of Europe which he had promised to make. Perhaps an opportunity would offer to eliminate the obstacle. Perhaps something would turn up.

Something—or rather somebody—did turn up, on January 13, 1950. On this day, French Foreign Minister Robert Schuman, in the course of a visit to Germany, paid a call at Bonn. With him, however, on the same day arrived news from Paris that the French government was preparing a series of new agreements with the Saar Territory, providing among other things for the lease of the Saar mines for a period of fifty years. In view of the completely open international status of the Saar Territory, was the Saar government entitled to enter into such an agreement?

Adenauer decided to talk to Schuman with complete candor. As an Alsatian the French Foreign Minister once upon a time had served in the German Army. He spoke German fluently. He had even studied at Bonn. Surely, it must be possible to come to an understanding.

It proved impossible. The two statesmen had a very frank and open discussion lasting two hours which resulted in a psychological relaxation of tension but not in an actual change of position. Schuman assured Adenauer that France intended no annexation of the Saar Territory; all measures taken meantime including the lease of the mines were provisional and could be rescinded by the Peace Treaty. The German suggestion of a plebiscite in the Saar Territory he thought inopportune. "The people of the Saar," he said, "do not want a plebiscite." Adenauer on his part insisted that Germany had claims on the Saar Territory based on international law, and if there were changes in the ownership of the Saar mines, which undoubtedly were the property of the Federal Republic, the only way this could be done was in the form of an international control authority, similar to the Ruhr Authority.

At all events, the Chancellor told the French Foreign Minister that French action in the Saar made it very difficult for him and his government to obtain German popular approval for joining the Council of Europe. This greatly astonished Schuman. Did Adenauer really consider a "side issue" like the Saar more important than the creation of a united Europe? Adenauer could only shrug his shoulders. He was supposed to be a democratic chief of government. He was responsible to Parliament. Parliament was supposed to represent the people. And the German people, he had to inform his guest, after many years when no one had consulted them for their opinion, were beginning to make use of their right to object. On his desk in the Palais Schaumburg the pile of telegrams protesting, warning, and even threatening him was growing rapidly.

Petersberg, March 2, 1950.

François-Poncet: "May I ask, Mr. Federal Chancellor, whether you desire us to meet again in a week's time?"

Adenauer: "I don't know how the Saar negotiations in Paris are developing."

François-Poncet: "The Saar negotiations have been concluded. The conventions will be signed tomorrow."

Adenauer: "I have heard of these conventions and spoken to representatives of the parliamentary parties in the *Bundestag* about them.

The reaction was negative. I consider it improbable that in these circumstances a majority in favor of joining the Council of Europe could be found."

François-Poncet: "Everyone has to bear his own responsibility."

The somber mood grew steadily more somber. On the day after the somewhat tense exchange between the Federal Chancellor and the French High Commissioner, the Saar Conventions were signed in Paris. The following day, March 5, 1950, Adenauer held a press conference.

Hitherto, he declared, he had been ready to join the Council of Europe at the same time as the Saar Territory, provided always that membership of the Saar Territory would not prejudice any settlement made in the Peace Treaty. The new Paris Convention, however, by creating a "Saar Republic," had changed the situation. The Paris Convention represented a change in Germany's national frontiers and was a violation of the Potsdam Agreement. The present status of the Saar Territory, Adenauer said, was "lower than that of a protectorate" and in many respects resembled that of a colony, while in actual legal fact the Saar Territory formed part of the French Zone of Occupation and, therefore, of the Federal Republic. If such things were admissible in the West, how could anyone still raise his voice against the Oder-Neisse line?

"I regret most profoundly," Adenauer declared, "that France has insisted on making a unilateral settlement at this moment when it would have been easy, as soon as Germany had joined the Council of Europe, to find a common solution within the European framework. I implored Monsieur Schuman during his recent visit to leave the matter in abeyance until we were in the Council of Europe, or at least to consult us during the negotiations. Neither was done. This agreement is a heavy blow to the cause of French-German understanding."

Foreign Minister Schuman answered with a press statement. The West German government, he said, was just as much a provisional creation, owing its life to an Allied decision, as the Saar government, and differed in no way from it. "There can be no question of endangering a European solution. Now as before France is anxious for an understanding with Germany."

The comparison between the federal government and the Saar

government could scarcely be taken seriously. "There is no democracy in the Saar. . . ." Adenauer had declared. He chose "not to have heard" the strange comparison. Schuman's last sentence, on the other hand, turned out to have been meant sincerely. And to this Adenauer reacted swiftly and spontaneously.

In two press interviews, following shortly one after another, he suggested boldly, as Churchill had done in 1940 in the case of Britain and France, a regular union between France and the Federal Republic which would eliminate all differences over the Saar Territory. Especially in the second of these interviews, given March 21, 1950, to Kingsbury Smith, correspondent of the American International News Service, Adenauer's "foreign policy by interview" blossomed forth.

One of the most important reasons, Adenauer declared, why he considered a union between Germany and France particularly urgent at the present moment was the perpetually increasing political tension in the world.

"This tension causes me deep anxiety. It ought to cause all other statesmen equal anxiety. Some European politicians, however, seem to be blind to the existing danger. . . . I cannot help feeling that the lessons of the past have not made the world any wiser. Indeed, at times I ask myself whether the world seriously intends to benefit from the experiences of the past. If this were really the case it would have to wrestle its way through to really new and bold decisions. But the will power for this seems to be lacking today. And as a result the world tries to escape into uncertainty. . . ."

How did the Chancellor visualize a union between Germany and France, which would represent such a "bold decision," in practical terms? Adenauer reminded his interlocutor of the time of the Napoleonic wars. Here something of value could be learned from the past:

"In those days there was a multitude of small and independent German states, each keeping to itself, with its own customs barriers, its own currency, its own army. This state of affairs was overcome by the establishment of a Customs Parliament and the creation of a German Customs Union. This assured a free exchange of goods between the numerous German states. The Customs Union and the Customs Parliament were the beginning of German unification. It seems to me that a Union between France and Germany could be brought about in a similar manner. A beginning should be made with an economic and customs fusion between the two countries.

"The instrument of such a union might be a common economic parliament whose members are elected from the legislative bodies of both countries. The two governments could set up a parallel political organization which would have joint responsibility with the economic parliament. The tasks of the two bodies could be widened in the course of time to bring about the union of the two countries step by step. The Saar Conventions are an example of the way in which two countries can be merged.

"Undoubtedly it would mean a great step forward if Frenchmen and Germans could live in the same house together and sit at the same table, working together and bearing joint responsibility. The psychological effect would be immeasurable. French security claims could be satisfied and the growth of German nationalism prevented. . . . The Council of Europe, too, would greatly benefit from such a union, for its efficiency is restricted not least by the fact that no genuine understanding between France and Germany has as yet been reached. . . . In conclusion I want to emphasize once more: in a serious situation an 'escape forward' leads most surely to success!"

The proposal for a Franco-German Union was of course not an official diplomatic move and was not meant to be one. It was meant to serve as a basis for discussion. But in Germany itself it aroused new and sharp criticism of Adenauer's method of "foreign policy by interview," and the Federal Parliament showed itself increasingly sensitive to it. The Chancellor was openly rebuked in the press for ignoring the views of Parliament.

In France, too, Adenauer's method of approach was felt to be somewhat unorthodox but his friendly intentions were recognized. The idea itself, however, met with a cool reception. Franco-German relations, a French government statement declared, can find a lasting settlement only within the framework of the collective organization of Europe.

In other words, despite the Saar problem, Germany had to find a way into the Council of Europe.

Once again Adenauer took the road up to the Petersberg.

Could they not, the Federal Chancellor asked the three High Commissioners, ease his situation just a little? If, for example, Germany were invited by the Council of Europe to join instead of having to make an application? Or some kind of intimation from the Council to the effect that a German application would be welcomed? That would help considerably.

"The Saar question," the Chancellor explained, "has caused a reaction in Germany of which you gentlemen have no conception. . . . If France had not pushed the Saar question into the foreground in this form, I should not have hesitated for one moment to submit an application to Parliament for approval, and I should have obtained a majority for it. But now, in these circumstances . . ."

The argument went around in circles. François-Poncet insisted that Germany must make an application for an invitation as otherwise there would be a danger of Germany declining the invitation. That was a risk the Council of Europe was not prepared to run. Adenauer on his part declared that he must have a request for an application as otherwise the application itself might possibly be turned down by the Federal Parliament. And that was a risk he could not afford to take.

It was a most sobering and disillusioning *cul-de-sac*. Eventually the Chancellor sighed. "It seems pointless to continue the negotiations."

But for all that he was not prepared to give up. The next day, March 22, 1950, he sent a memorandum up to the Petersberg. It made three points. What he needed, the Chancellor declared, to obtain a majority in Parliament was this: (1) The Allied High Commissioners or their governments should give a written declaration that they held the entry of Germany into the Council of Europe to be desirable; (2) the Western Allies should give a formal assurance that the Saar's membership in the Council of Europe was provisional only, and that the status of the Saar should be examined and determined in the final peace settlement; and (3) Germany's status as an associate member of the Council of Europe should be only of short duration, and, pending her admission as a full member, she should be represented on the Committee of Ministers by an observer.

When this letter was disclosed to the public, world opinion was sharply divided. There were those who protested that Germany was once again "making conditions." There were others who suspected Adenauer deliberately exaggerated his difficulties over the Saar problem in order to strengthen his position. There were finally those with some insight into the true situation who asked whether it was really, after all, the general intention to bring about Adenauer's downfall? Among the latter was the Strasbourg Committee of Ministers. True, it did not greatly like being faced with "political conditions," and Adenauer's third point it had to refuse. The statute of the Council of Europe makes no provision for observers. The Federal Republic must wait for its full sovereignty. Adenauer did not press the third point, feeling that the remaining two assurances would be sufficient to help him over his parliamentary hurdle. And these two assurances he received.

Six weeks after the gloomy exchange at the Petersberg, Adenauer submitted to his cabinet a memorandum explaining the reasons in favor of joining the Council of Europe.

"It should be clear," he wrote, "that the Saar question, which has been settled without recourse to free and frank exchanges of views on the basis of mutual readiness to come to an understanding, must not be cause for us to hold back from general European cooperation, which far transcends it in importance. It is a decisive and fatal question for the German people whether it wishes to see Europe split up between the great power blocs of the United States and the Soviet Union, whether Europe is to remain divided into nation states quarreling with each other politically and working against each other economically, or whether Europe is to achieve a degree of political and economic unification which will lend it inner stability and weight of its own. Although the Council of Europe has many faults, it is yet, so far, the only way. . . . I must warn against saddling Germany with the odium of having caused the failure of the European negotiations. . . ."

The only way? So it seemed. But, at the very moment when the federal government was ready to proceed on it, a second road opened suddenly and wholly unexpectedly.

## CHAPTER XX

THE Federal Chancellor's engagement book for Tuesday, May 9, 1950, recorded: "11 AM.–Meeting of the Cabinet." The sole item on the agenda was: "Decision of the Government regarding entry of the Federal Republic into the Council of Europe."

Forty-eight hours earlier the Chancellor had circulated among the members of his Cabinet his memorandum explaining why it was desirable, in his view, that Germany should become a member of this first representative assembly of the nations of Europe. He was most anxious that the government's decision in favor of the Council of Europe should be delayed no further but finally taken this day. In two days' time, on May 11, a new conference of the three Western Foreign Ministers was due to open in London, at which the German question was once more up for discussion, and it was important, after the various vexations and irritations of recent months, that by this time the German government should have arrived at a decision demonstrating in a convincing manner its sincere intention to cooperate in the rebuilding of Europe. So as to underline the importance of the decision, the Chancellor had summoned a press conference for the same evening, which he proposed to address himself.

Such had been Adenauer's intention. But when he appeared at eight o'clock, accompanied by several of his ministers, before the assembled newspapermen, the Cabinet's decision in favor of Germany's entry into the Council of Europe had ceased to be the chief topic of the day. Something else of far greater significance, which had been the subject of agitated discussion in all the capitals of the world ever since the midday hour, had happened.

In the early forenoon, even before the Cabinet meeting, an unexpected and unannounced visitor, just arrived from Paris, had called on Dr. Blankenhorn, the Chancellor's personal assistant, at his office in the Palais Schaumburg. Revealing himself as one of Foreign Minister Robert Schuman's closest associates, he brought an urgent and strictly confidential letter from the French Foreign Minister for personal delivery to the Federal Chancellor. Asking that the letter be submitted to the Chancellor at once, he added in support of his request that a Council of Ministers was in session in Paris at this very hour and deliberating the very contents of the letter he had brought.

The letter contained what was to become known as the "Schuman Plan." It opened with this sentence: "World peace cannot be safeguarded without the making of efforts proportionate to the dangers which threaten it." A few lines further down it said: "Europe will not be made all at once, or according to a single, general plan. It will be built through concrete achievements which first create a *de facto* solidarity. The gathering together of the nations of Europe requires the elimination of the age-old opposition of France and Germany. The first concern in any action undertaken must be these two countries.

"With this aim in view, the French government proposes to take action immediately on one limited but decisive point; the French government proposes to place Franco-German production of coal and steel as a whole under a common higher authority, within the framework of an organization open to the participation of the other countries of Europe. The pooling of coal and steel production should immediately provide for the setting up of common foundations for economic developments as a first step in the federation of Europe, and will change the destinies of those regions which have long been devoted to the manufacture of munitions of war, of which they have been the most constant victims.

"The solidarity in production thus established will make it plain that any war between France and Germany becomes, not merely unthinkable, but actually impossible."

In detail the plan proposed for immediate action: the supply of coal and steel on identical terms to the French and German markets as well as to the markets of other member countries; the development in common of export to other countries, free movement of coal and steel between member countries, abolition of custom duties, and uniform transport rates.

One thing was clear immediately: if this organization became reality, the International Ruhr Authority was an antiquated institution and would be compelled to make a silent exit. But, beyond that, the foundations would be laid for a European Federation. For a European coal and steel community could just as little exist in a political vacuum as a European Army.

Schuman's emissary did not have to wait long for an answer. His letter was submitted immediately to the Chancellor, and when Dr. Blankenhorn, after a brief interval, returned from Adenauer's study, he had this message: "The Federal Chancellor welcomes Foreign Minister Schuman's initiative, and he is in complete agreement with the basic idea and the general tendency of his plan."

Adenauer's positive response became generally known almost as rapidly as the plan itself, and both were eagerly discussed everywhere. How was it possible, people asked, for the Federal Chancellor to react with such swiftness to this bold advance into unknown political territory? "Well-informed circles" pretended to know that the whole thing had been long agreed beforehand between Adenauer and Schuman, and in support of their thesis pointed to the undeniable fact that entire sentences in Schuman's letter were almost identical with various passages from Adenauer's speeches and interviews. Adenauer's press conference on the evening of May 9 was therefore awaited with considerable excitement.

To the astonishment of most of those present the Chancellor declared that Schuman's plan had been a complete surprise no less to him than to the rest of the world. "The decision of the French Cabinet in proposing to place the coal and steel industries of the two countries under a common authority, and the decision of the German Cabinet to join the Council of Europe, are a pure coincidence in time. They were not preceded by negotiations of any kind, and in particular the French proposal was not the reason for our decision to recommend to the Federal Parliament acceptance of the invitation to join the Council of Europe."

Having made this clear, Adenauer went on to make a remark which was most characteristic of his method of conducting policy. "Originally," he said, "it had been my intention, after today's Cabinet decision, to wait until the middle of June before asking Parliament to vote on this question of the Council of Europe, because I hoped that meanwhile some unforeseen event might occur which would secure general approval of this invitation in Germany. I am happy, ladies and gentlemen, to be able to inform you that this unforeseen event has in fact occurred. . . .

"The Schuman Plan," Adenauer continued, "does not contain mere phrases and empty platitudes but a series of concrete and precise proposals. I wish to emphasize in particular that it is based on complete equality of rights, and that even in cases where Germans and Frenchmen are unable to agree within the framework of their joint organization, the final decision will be made by a referee appointed jointly by both sides in common agreement. This alone is so eminently important a step forward in German-French relations that it cannot be underlined too strongly."

It was only after this that Adenauer finally got around to explaining his own Cabinet decision for which the press conference had originally been called. The Council of Europe, he said, was certainly not a completed or perfected instrument, but it was at least a hopeful beginning. It was wrong for Germany merely to ask, "Shall we get this, shall we obtain that, if we join the Council of Europe?" He believed that the question of German membership in the Council of Europe had to be viewed in a much larger context. "The Council of Europe is the first step toward a unified and united Europe," and this united Europe afforded the only chance of creating a third force capable of throwing its weight into the scales for the maintenance of peace.

Could Germany, he asked, by refusing to join the Council of Europe, take upon herself the responsibility of frustrating from the very start the evolution toward a federated Europe? Or, to put it in a positive way: "Are not we Germans, who bear so much guilt as a result of the war, under an obligation now to devote all our intellectual, moral, and economic strength to the task of making this Europe an element of peace? I believe, if the question is put in this way, there can be but one answer to it."

A week later, on May 6, 1950, the Federal Chancellor called once again at the Petersberg. The London Conference of the Foreign Ministers had ended the previous day. Adenauer had judged rightly; the Cabinet decision to join the Council of Europe had been understood the way it was intended, and the readiness with which he had responded to Schuman's initiative had created a distinctly favorable effect, not only with the Foreign Ministers in London, but also with the High Commissioners.

"We were all very happy, Mr. Federal Chancellor," said McCloy, "about the unhesitating swiftness with which you took up Monsieur Schuman's plan."

"The reason why I was able to react so quickly," answered

Adenauer, "was that in 1923, after the end of the passive resistance movement in the Ruhr, I formulated a very similar plan together with two friends and submitted it to the Reich government of the time. For this reason alone, if for no other, we shall devote all our strength to the Schuman Plan. . . ."

This time the atmosphere at the Petersberg was distinctly friendly and conciliatory. And not only at the Petersberg. The decisions of the London conference had brought considerable and tangible relief to Germany. The Foreign Ministers declared that "Germany shall re-enter progressively the community of free peoples of Europe. When that situation has been fully reached she will be liberated from controls to which she is still subject, and accorded her sovereignty to the maximum extent compatible with the basis of the occupation regime." Moreover, the task of the Allied Occupation Forces would henceforth consist not in occupying the young German Republic but in standing ready for its defense, if necessary, and a study group was to be set up immediately to review the Occupation Statute and make recommendations for its revision. Finally, and most important of all: "The Ministers assure the German people that the reunification of their country remains the ultimate object of the Western Powers' policy."

All this was contained in a document which the High Commissioners handed the Chancellor on behalf of the Foreign Ministers. And as a matter of courtesy the statement was not issued for publication until Dr. Adenauer had been given an opportunity of reading it. A small but significant gesture.

Adenauer was well satisfied. He knew that from now on things could develop very rapidly. Germany had to fulfill but one condition: she must give proof to the Western Powers through peaceful and amicable cooperation that their security was safeguarded. Once this proof was convincingly furnished, all remaining restrictions would be rapidly abolished. And the best means of giving this proof were the Council of Europe and the Schuman Plan. Not for a long time had Adenauer been so firmly convinced as he was now that he was on the right road. Skeptical and critical Dr. Schumacher had said, "The Schuman Plan is a frame. Let's wait and see what sort of a picture they're going to put in it." The outlines of the picture were beginning to emerge.

On May 25, 1950, Jean Monnet, the "Economic Organizer" of the

Schuman Plan, arrived at Bonn to discuss with Adenauer details of the next steps to be taken. Italy, Belgium, Holland, and Luxembourg, not unaware of the fact that noncooperation was likely to result in disadvantages for them, had immediately joined the Franco-German project. Thus on June 20, 1950, the first conference of the six "Schuman states" was opened in Paris. The German delegation was headed by a man hitherto totally unknown in politics—Professor Walter Hallstein, a newcomer and outsider, and a personal "discovery" of Adenauer. Diplomats and professional politicians were inclined to shake their heads over this appointment, but not for long. Professor Hallstein quickly proved his worth, and within a few months became one of Adenauer's closest associates.

Everything seemed to be well on the way. The Federal Parliament had passed the bill authorizing Germany's membership in the Council of Europe, with 220 votes against 152. In Paris Foreign Minister Schuman declared in the opening speech of the conference which bore his name, "We must be conscious of the fact that nowadays the national interest consists precisely in finding ways and means of going beyond national frontiers. . . ."

Five days later lightning struck in the Far East, shaking faraway Germany to its foundations.

Only about six months had passed since the stormy "rearmament debate" in the Federal Parliament on December 16, 1949. At that time even many of Adenauer's party friends had had no use for his concept of a European Army. During a meeting of the parliamentary CDU he had been reproached with having radically changed his attitude. Adenauer answered:

"But, gentlemen, who is going to stop me from getting a little wiser every day?"

In those December days a friend told him bluntly that the "without me mood" of the people was against him, and that as a result he was opposed by all those deputies anxious not to lose the support of their electorate. Adenauer answered him: if one day the necessity arose of arming Germany to safeguard the peace of the world, a European force was the way to prevent the resurgence of German militarism. "I am firmly convinced," he said, "that many in the

Federal Parliament who are at present speaking against it are at heart thinking the same. Let us wait and see. At worst I have said a little earlier what others are going to say a little later."

Six months later everyone in Germany had realized that the Federal Chancellor's warning words of December 16 had not been uttered irresponsibly as an "alarm and despondency" stunt. On June 25, 1950, war broke out in Korea. This armed aggression of the Communist-governed North Korea under Soviet tutelage against anti-communist, democratic South Korea was a shattering warning. The parallel with Germany stared everyone in the face. What had happened in Korea could happen any day in Germany as well.

At this time Adenauer was ill, suffering from a severe attack of pneumonia. From his sickbed he sent a note to the High Commissioners at the Petersberg asking them to make urgent representations to their governments. The Federal Republic required and demanded from the occupying powers an unequivocal and reliable guarantee of its security.

Soon afterward Adenauer left for Switzerland to convalesce. On August 11, 1950, he read in the Swiss papers: "British opposition leader Churchill suggests to Strasbourg Council of Europe immediate creation of a European Army with German participation." Turning to the German parliamentarians who had taken their seats in the Strasbourg assembly only a few weeks earlier, seventy-six year old Churchill had declared, "If Germany decides to be on our side, and I fervently hope that she will do so, I ask this assembly to assure our German friends that we shall regard their security and freedom as our own!"

Immediate formation of a European Army! Churchill's motion was adopted by the Council of Europe with eighty-nine votes against five. Under the pressure of events things now moved faster than Adenauer had expected. Still, for the moment, it was no more than a demonstration. Churchill was out of power, and the Council of Europe possessed no legislative authority. But a beginning had been made, at least in spirit, if not in fact. Meanwhile, the war in Korea raged on, and the German mood, as Adenauer was well aware, grew steadily more pessimistic. What was going to happen if "alert detachments" of the People's Police came swarming over the zonal boundary to "liberate" Western Germany? Was not the Federal Republic bound to become a second Korea, without even the certainty that the Western Powers would defend it with all the means at their disposal?

Something had to be done, Adenauer resolved. In the middle of August he was back in Bonn. One of his first official calls was at Petersberg, where meanwhile Sir Brian Robertson, the British High Commissioner, had been succeeded by Sir Ivone Kirkpatrick, a springy and nimble fifty-three-year-old professional diplomat with wide knowledge and experience of German affairs, whom Adenauer had met before. The day was August 17, 1950. Adenauer gave the three High Commissioners a comprehensive survey of the military situation in the Soviet Zone as it appeared on the basis of information available to him.

Stalin, Adenauer declared, foresaw for Western Germany much the same development as in Korea. Russia would make the Grotewohl government push the People's Police into Western Germany, and the West German population would look on passively, partly because the invading force consisted of their own compatriots but partly also because they had lost faith in the military strength of the United States.

In view of the public statements by Pieck and Grotewohl that it was the aim of the Soviet Zone to "liberate" Western Germany, Adenauer said, the federal government was shouldering an immense responsibility without possessing the means to fulfill the duties arising from it. He must ask the three Western Powers therefore to demonstrate their military strength more visibly and emphatically to the eyes of the public in Western Germany. At the same time he must request permission for the Federal Republic to create a security force of the same strength and armament as the People's Police which would be in a position to offer effective resistance to an invasion by them.

Adenauer concluded, "France, Britain, and the United States fight only for themselves, not for Germany. It is obvious, after all that has happened in the past, that Germany cannot expect other nations to defend her. Still, there is one point to consider: the third world war, should it come to pass, will presumably be won by those who hold Germany's steel production."

Adenauer's sober and cold-blooded calculation obviously impressed the three High Commissioners.

McCloy asked bluntly, "Is the Federal Chancellor in a position to raise a volunteer force of 150,000, even if the opposition is against it?"

That, as everyone knows, was the decisive question.

Again Adenauer answered with complete candor, "I could not carry through such a measure without the approval of the Social Democratic party." And he added, somewhat surprisingly, "I have already spoken to Schumacher about it, and shall shortly do so again. I have great respect for Schumacher's judgment. . . ."

This was no empty phrase. The two men were diametrically opposed in almost every respect, in their views no less than in their temperaments. But this did not prevent Adenauer from respecting not only Schumacher's judgment but also his integrity as a man.

Once again Adenauer did not rest content with verbal exchanges. A new conference of the Western Foreign Ministers was due to be held in the middle of September, in New York, and this time there was no doubt that the security of the new German state figured prominently on the agenda. Following the Petersberg conversation of August 17, Adenauer dispatched a new memorandum to the High Commission.

Bonn, August 29, 1950

His Excellency
The Chairman of the Allied High Commission
Mr. John J. McCloy
Bonn-Petersberg

Mr. High Commissioner:

I have the honor of submitting to you herewith a memorandum relating to the internal and external security of the Federal territory. I should be grateful if you would transmit this memorandum to the Foreign Ministers of the three Allied powers at an early date to enable them to make it the subject of their discussions at the forthcoming Foreign Ministers Conference in New York.

Assuring you, Mr. High Commissioner, of my sincere respect,

ADENAUER

The memorandum, six typescript pages long, summarized once more Adenauer's views of the situation. Events in the Far East, he said, had caused anxiety and a sense of insecurity among the German people; there were signs of "dangerous lethargy." Following a detailed enumeration of the Soviet forces and German People's Police units available in the Soviet Zone of Germany, including their armament and equipment, the Chancellor declared, "it must be assumed that preparations are now being made in the Eastern Zone for an enterprise which in many respects reminds one of the beginning of operations in Korea." To this must be added the existence of a Communist Fifth Column in the Federal Republic itself.

Total forces available in the Soviet Zone, Adenauer stated, were estimated at twenty-two motorized Soviet divisions including approximately 6,000 tanks, and 150,000 German People's Police. Against these, "counterforces in Western Germany amount to two American and British divisions each, plus some French units." Apart from the weak forces of the frontier police, the federal government disposed of no forces of its own.

"The Federal Chancellor has repeatedly requested a strengthening of these occupation troops, and he renews this request herewith in the most urgent manner. Only a reinforcement of Allied Occupation troops in Western Germany and a strengthening of Allied forces in Western Europe generally can make it plain to the people that the Western Powers are genuinely determined to defend Western Germany in case of need. . . . Furthermore, the Federal Chancellor has repeatedly declared his readiness, in the event of the formation of an international army in Western Europe, to make a contribution in the form of a German contingent. This makes it unequivocally clear that the Federal Chancellor rejects the idea of a remilitarization of Germany by means of creating a separate national German military force."

The memorandum went on to propose the immediate formation of a Federal Security Police Force, in adequate strength, which would be able to intervene against "open or camouflaged actions" of the Fifth Column "after the Korean pattern," in the event of "the Allies being unable, for one reason or another, to bring their own forces to bear in such an event." This Security Police could be placed under international control.

So much for the question of security. Simultaneously with this memorandum, the Chancellor sent a second letter to the High Commission, also with the request that it should be submitted to the New York conference for discussion by the Foreign Ministers. This second memorandum, considerably shorter than the first one and drawing political conclusions from it, dealt with "the reordering of relations between the Federal Republic and the Occupying Powers."

Briefly, it pointed out that political conditions had changed out of recognition since the present occupation regime, based on the Occupation Statute, had been instituted. The federal government had not only greatly consolidated its position, both politically and economically, but had also taken every possible step to integrate the Federal Republic progressively into the community of Western nations. As a result of this integration it had assumed a number of duties and commitments without enjoying a corresponding degree of freedom of action and responsibility. In the view of the federal government, the memorandum declared, it had now become "necessary to place the relationship between Germany and the occupying powers on a new basis." The state of war between Germany and the Allied powers should be ended. Military occupation should henceforth serve only the purpose of providing security against external dangers. And the Occupation Statute should be progressively replaced by a "system of treaties or contractual agreements."

If the Foreign Ministers were prepared, Adenauer concluded, to issue declarations to this effect, "they would find a very positive echo among the German people, particularly at the present moment."

# CHAPTER XXI

"GENTLEMEN, I have to inform you that immediately following today's Cabinet meeting I intend to call on the Federal President to ask him to relieve the Federal Minister of the Interior, Dr. Gustav Heinemann, of his office."

The date was October 10, 1950.

On the previous day, the Federal Chancellor told his Cabinet, there had been a personal interview between himself and Dr. Heinemann in the course of which the Minister of the Interior had handed him a memorandum outlining the reasons why, in his view, Germany should not participate in a European Army. Dr. Heinemann had added, "If you decide in favor of participating in a Western European Army, there will no longer be any room for me in the Cabinet."

The Federal Chancellor continued:

"I want to make my own attitude absolutely clear beyond any doubt. We want peace. But in my opinion one can negotiate with the Russians only from a position of strength. That is my first point. My second point is this: if we ask of the Americans, the British, and the French that they should guarantee the security of our national existence, but contribute nothing to it ourselves, no one has a right to reproach American, British, and French fathers and mothers if they say: why should our sons do something for the Germans if the Germans themselves are not prepared to make sacrifices for their own defense?"

In the autumn of 1950 this standpoint of the Federal Chancellor was by no means shared by all sections of the German people. There were important and influential circles who thought his estimate of the international situation exaggerated or even totally wrong, and who considered his policy of security which followed from it irrelevant or even downright dangerous. They felt that his policy of tying Western Germany firmly to the West was perilously one-sided and liable to lead Germany, for the third time, down the slippery slope into war and misery.

There were two main groups opposing his views. One was the Social Democrats, who feared that Adenauer's security measures might provoke precisely the kind of aggression from the East that they were intended to prevent. This school of thought was represented in the Federal Parliament, where Adenauer could argue the matter out with them. The second group was the Christian pacifists, headed by the Church President Dr. Martin Niemöller, the synod of the German Evangelical Church, and the Federal Minister of the Interior, Dr. Heinemann. This second group was not represented in Parliament as an organized unit, but in the person of the Minister of the Interior it had a prominent representative right in the government itself.

The departure of Dr. Heinemann on October 10, 1950, was the first resignation from the Adenauer Government since its formation more than a year before. It was a heavy blow to the Chancellor, not only because Dr. Heinemann had been an efficient minister, but also because his departure upset the balance between the Protestants and Roman Catholics which Adenauer was equally anxious to maintain in the government as well as within his own party, the CDU.

The conflict had begun toward the end of 1949. It broke out openly over the question of German rearmament.

On December 14, 1949, Dr. Niemöller gave a joint interview to a West German newspaper and the New York *Herald Tribune*. He told the American paper that it was Germany's duty to avoid becoming the cause of another war and to see to it that Germans would not have to fight Germans. He for his part declined to commit himself to either side. He told the German newspaper that the Federal Republic was essentially a state with a purely Catholic orientation, the federal elections had been conducted dishonestly, the Federal Republic was a "child conceived in the Vatican and born in Washington," and with the Constitution of the Bonn government Protestantism had "lost a battle."

These two interviews received wide publicity and attracted Dr. Heinemann's attention. He wrote to Niemöller, whom he had known personally for a long time, asking him for a more detailed opinion on current political problems and the consequences likely to follow from them for Germany. Niemöller responded on December 22, 1949, with a lengthy letter setting out his fundamental views.

However, the Minister of the Interior was not the only one to have noted Niemöller's views. The Chancellor, too, found them worthy of attention. On December 21 he wrote Niemöller a personal letter asking him to send the exact and authentic text of his utterances "which have attracted great attention at home and abroad." Niemöller answered on December 27. He failed to submit the authentic text of the interviews, but sent instead his own comment upon them as well as a copy of his long letter addressed to Dr. Heinemann.

In this letter Niemöller declared that the amputation of Eastern Germany, the expulsion of the East German population, and the iron curtain frontier had caused heavy loss and damage to Protestantism and it was his aim to "make people more acutely conscious of the fact that we and our brothers behind the iron curtain belong together, and that we shall not be seduced by any advantages offered by the West into recognizing the *status quo*."

In the second part of his letter Niemöller dealt with the purely political question of German reunification, stating that there would be no lasting peace as long as the partition of the German people between two mutually antagonistic groups of powers continued. The creation of two German "psuedostates" had only made the problem more difficult, since both states merely reflected this antagonism between East and West. If the four occupying powers, owing to their disunity, were unable "to bring our separated people together again," the occupation of Germany had better be intrusted to the United Nations. In that event "the iron curtain will collapse automatically, and the way will be open for a democratic and unified development of Germany."

This was undoubtedly an interesting point of view, but it was not what the Chancellor had wished to know. On January 3, 1950, Niemöller wrote again to Adenauer, this time to protest against the faulty reproduction of his interview, which, he alleged, had left out essential points and thereby created the impression that he maintained "a pro-Communist and anti-Catholic attitude." But he again omitted to send the authentic text of the interview containing his derogatory remarks about the origins of the Federal Republic.

On January 4, Adenauer asked once more for the correct text, and on January 18 for the third time. Unfortunately, he wrote, he could not conceal the fact that Niemöller's interview had caused "pained embarrassment" in Germany itself, in foreign countries, and with the High Commissioners. Niemöller answered this on a January 25. The authentic text of the interview, which had lasted for a full hour, he said, was no longer in his possession but he could confirm having made the remark "conceived in the Vatican and born in Washington"; for the rest, he said, "I must refuse to accept reprimands from you with regard to the alleged 'pained embarrassment' which this so-called interview is said to have caused with the High Commissioners." He had, Niemöller said, in the meantime had a conversation of several hours with McCloy and François-Poncet, and was "fully informed on the views of these two gentlemen."

Once again Adenauer decided "not to have heard" the rebuke, and sent no answer to the letter. The controversy subsided for a while, but revived all the more violently when on August 29, 1950, the Chancellor dispatched his two memoranda to the Petersberg for submission to the New York Conference of Foreign Ministers.

These two most important documents had not been submitted to the Cabinet for approval before being sent off. Such procedure was unusual, but there was good reason for it. Adenauer had intended to have them discussed during a Cabinet meeting on August 31, when he was suddenly informed that the American High Commissioner, who would have to take the memoranda to the conference, was leaving for New York by air on August 30. In order to make sure that they reached New York in time for the conference, he had decided to send them off without waiting for the Cabinet meeting.

Dr. Heinemann, the Minister of the Interior, took exception to this. On September 4, 1950, he had a brief interview with the Federal Chancellor in which he complained that he had not been consulted on the memorandum concerning the security of the Federal Republic, despite the fact that it dealt at length with the formation of a new German Security Police Force, which was of direct concern to his department. Heinemann offered his resignation, which Adenauer refused to accept. They agreed to have a further discussion at a later date.

Meanwhile, the New York conference, awaited in Germany with

tense expectation, cast its shadows before it. On September 6, Secretary of State Acheson stated at a press conference that it was "highly desirable to find a way in which Western Germany could participate in the defense of Western Europe." The Foreign Ministers of the three Western Powers, he said, would certainly discuss this question, and High Commissioner McCloy had said no more than the obvious when he declared "the Germans must somehow or other be given a chance to defend their own country."

Now one thing seemed clear: whatever the views of Britain and France, the United States was determined to afford the Federal Republic the opportunity of defending itself.

Was it purely accidental that on the very next day, September 7, 1950, Niemöller arrived at Bonn and paid Heinemann a visit? At all events, coming as it did at this particular moment, the visit attracted general attention, and not only Adenauer became aware of the attitude of his Minister of the Interior. He decided to scrutinize Heinemann's recent speeches and utterances a little more closely, and on September 11 he had another interview with him.

On this occasion the Minister of the Interior submitted to his chief a memorandum which expressed a highly critical attitude toward Adenauer's whole foreign policy. Heinemann charged the Federal Chancellor with acting in an authoritarian manner and disregarding the views of the Cabinet on important decisions. Adenauer answered this stricture by pointing out the unusual and unforeseen circumstances in which the memoranda of August 29 had been dispatched.

Heinemann assured Adenauer that he was in complete agreement with every step taken by the government to remind the Allies of their obligation to protect the Federal Republic. Then he continued: "But since it was once the paramount aim of the Allies to disarm us and keep us disarmed in the future, and seeing that the entire policy of the Allies during five years of occupation has been directed toward disparaging the German armed forces, destroying our capacity to defend ourselves, including the demolition of air-raid shelters and educating the German people toward an uncompromisingly antimilitary frame of mind, it is not for us to request or apply for any German participation in military measures, or even to offer such participation. This is bound to cause great confusion in the minds of the people, which in turn will seriously endanger our young democracy.

"Any activity of the Federal Republic at the present time," the Minister continued, "which goes beyond a federal police force adequate for our internal requirements must necessarily deepen the cleavage which runs through Germany and increase tension without in fact relieving the acute threat against us. If the Allies feel that they require our participation, let them approach us and tell us in binding terms what are to be the prerequisites and conditions for this German participation which they desire."

Release from Allied controls and restrictions, Heinemann said, must not be bought at the price of new entanglements, the consequences of which could not be clearly estimated or which did not spring from a free decision in accord with German interests. "If we Germans in the East and West can but muster the patience and courage to wait," Heinemann concluded, "we may hope not only to preserve our own existence but also to make a decisive contribution to the maintenance of peace."

This attitude was bound to amaze Adenauer profoundly. It was clearly incompatible with his endeavors to create a genuine partnership with the powers and nations of Western Europe. He asked Heinemann bluntly whether Niemöller's visit had been concerned with church matters or was a private one. Heinemann declared that Niemöller was a friend of his and had visited him in a private capacity. At length he said:

"God has twice dashed the weapons from our hands. We must not take them up for a third time. We must have patience and wait. In a year or eighteen months' time, we shall be able to gather the fruits of this patient waiting."

Adenauer replied that he merely intended to await the results of the New York conference. He would then return to the matter.

The conference of the Foreign Ministers in New York opened on the following day. From the very beginning it was clear that there was no unanimity with regard to a German contribution toward European defense. Foreign Secretary Ernest Bevin declared immediately, "Of course Germany must be brought back into the comity of nations, but the arming of German troops is not the way to accomplish this." And High Commissioner Kirkpatrick told the Americans, "It is quite wrong to assume that Western Germany wants to form an army. This is not so. The feeling in Germany, I think, is that they want to look after their own internal security, but there is no passionate desire to start an army again. If there were a plebiscite I think the German people would be against it. If Germany joined a Western European Army, it might be different, but it would not be very popular either."

Closeted together on the thirty-seventh floor of the Waldorf-Astoria Hotel in New York, the Foreign Ministers deliberated for ten days. All kinds of rumors trickled through to Germany. The Americans, it was said, insisted on a German contribution to the comprehensive defense organization planned by the Atlantic Pact Council. Schuman and Bevin, it was said, were against this, but Bevin had finally yielded and agreed in principle. The most Schuman was willing to concede were German "labor battalions."

Such was the position when, on September 17, 1950, the telephone rang at Palais Schaumburg in Bonn. The Federal Chancellor was wanted by New York.

"How does the Federal Chancellor visualize a German participation in the defense of Europe?" That was what the Foreign Ministers wished to know in principle, before continuing their talks.

Adenauer replied, "Please tell the Foreign Ministers that this is a matter for the Federal Parliament to decide. The Federal Parliament cannot pronounce on this question until a formal inquiry has been addressed to the federal government by the Western Allies."

Despite the perfect correctness of this answer, Adenauer continued to be reproached subsequently by Christian pacifists, Socialists, and Communists with having acted in an unparliamentary manner, and he had to defend himself time and time again against these stubbornly repeated strictures.

Two days after this telephone call, on September 19, the Foreign Ministers announced their decisions regarding Germany. They declared that they and their governments "shared the desire of the German people for the unification of Germany on a basis which respects the fundamental liberties," and that "pending the unification of Germany they considered the government of the Federal Republic as the only German government freely and legitimately constituted and therefore entitled to speak for Germany as the representative of the German people in international affairs."

Furthermore, they announced that they would "take steps to terminate the state of war with Germany" and promised to "increase and reinforce their forces in Germany" and to "treat any attack against the Federal Republic or Berlin from any quarter as an attack upon themselves." They authorized the federal government to establish a Ministry of Foreign Affairs and to enter into diplomatic relations with foreign countries, and foreshadowed a revision of the Occupation Statute and a review of the list of prohibited or restricted industries.

The Foreign Ministers did not, however, address a "formal inquiry" to the federal government regarding a German defense contribution but merely declared that they had "seriously considered" the problem of the internal and external security of the Federal Republic and were in agreement with the establishment of a police force on a federal level. Concerning Germany's external security they "fully agreed that the re-creation of a German national army would not serve the best interests of Germany or Europe," but the "questions raised by the problem of the participation of the German Federal Republic in the common defense of Europe" would be "the subject of study and exchange of views."

So far so good. Adenauer was well satisfied with this result. He let it be known that he was gratified by the "warm and friendly tone" of the New York declaration.

Three days later the Atlantic Council in New York decided upon the creation of a joint Atlantic Defense Force in Europe under the central direction of a Supreme Commander. In their final communiqué they declared laconically that Germany would "be enabled to make a contribution to the defense of Europe."

This was a vital, and indeed fateful, sentence. With it began a new phase in German history. A decision had been made in principle. Now the question was how it was to be carried out. This question, more than any other, determined Adenauer's way during the following four years and put the nerves and patience of the seventy-five-year-old Chancellor to a grim test.

The declaration of the Atlantic Council made it more than ever necessary for Adenauer to obtain clarity among the German public generally over the question of German rearmament, and more particularly in his own Cabinet. In this context the attitude of the Minister of the Interior was obviously of paramount importance. With this in view, Adenauer addressed a new letter to Dr. Heinemann on September 28, 1950. In it he explained once more his own point of view. The Soviet Union, he was convinced, would negotiate on the question of German unity only with a strong partner; a weak partner in negotiation would merely be an invitation to the Soviets to take aggressive action; and the "patient waiting" advocated by Heinemann, so far from improving the prospects, could only damage them. For the rest, it was essential that on questions of such importance the Cabinet should be unanimous in its attitude, and it was inadmissible that individual ministers should publicly pronounce widely divergent views.

A week later, on October 4, the Federal Chancellor received a letter from Church President Dr. Niemöller. Couched in very aggressive terms, it contained a number of severe accusations. Rearmament for a possible war between East and West, Niemöller declared, was being pressed forward in the Federal Republic by all available means. High-ranking officers were being commissioned, organizational staffs for the formation of German units in the framework of a European Army had been actively at work since October 1, and orders for the manufacture of arms and equipment had already been placed with German industry.

"It is widely asserted," Niemöller wrote, "that certain understandings and agreements exist between the Federal Chancellor who, according to the constitution, determines over-all direction of policy, and Mr. McCloy and possibly also the British High Commissioner, to the effect that a considerable number of German divisions are to be created forthwith as a German contribution toward a European force which is to serve the purpose of 'defense.' "

All this, the letter continued, was being done without the approval of the German people, because there was no provision for holding a plebiscite. The Constitution, Niemöller said, had been "so cleverly constructed" that it was possible to plunge the German people into another war without previously asking them for their views.

"The German Evangelical Church has never left any doubt that it is unable to pronounce in favor of remilitarization—neither in the East nor in the West. Moreover, Evangelical Christians will take practical measures to resist remilitarization in whatever form, and they will invoke the federal Constitution which gives them the right to do so. Should an amendment to the Constitution seek to deprive them of this right, we shall once again be compelled to declare that we owe greater obedience to God than to human beings.

"Within the sight and hearing of the whole German people I beg of you, Mr. Federal Chancellor, in this decisive hour not to create accomplished facts without prior and genuine consultation of the people. If for constitutional reasons such consultation is not possible in the form of a plebiscite, new elections must take place. A decision on this question by the present Federal Parliament would be tantamount to a deception of the people, since in the election of the summer of 1949, no German voter had the slightest intention of granting the German federation full powers for rearmament or participation in war. If the Western Allies require Western Germany to contribute arms and soldiers, they should issue open orders to this effect and not try to hide behind German democracy."

What was the Chancellor to answer to such a letter, which accepted all current newspaper rumors at their face value and based its own peculiar accusations and threats on them? No "agreements" or "understandings" existed. Nowhere had "accomplished facts" been created. So far the Allies had "demanded" nothing, and the Chancellor had told them plainly that in the event of such a request being made it was not he who could decide upon it but the Parliament. In his answer Adenauer confined himself to an inquiry as to whether Niemöller had written his letter on behalf of the Evangelical Churches or in his own name. Someone signing himself "Dr. Beyer, General of Infantry (retrd)" answered on Niemöller's behalf that the Church President had written his letter on his own initiative and in his own name. On the same day Adenauer received an "Open Letter," bearing thirty-seven signatures, from the brotherhoods of the Confessional Church, substantially repeating Niemöller's allegations and threatening strictures.

It was only now that Adenauer realized how deeply his own Minister of the Interior had allowed himself to become entangled in the policy inspired by Niemöller. Through Dr. Robert Lehr, a prominent CDU member of Parliament and a Protestant, he learned of the proceedings of a conference of Evangelical Church representatives which had taken place on September 26, and which had been devoted to a discussion of the problem of rearmament from a Christian point of view. Minister of the Interior Dr. Heinemann, in his capacity as chairman of the general synod of the Evangelical

Church and one of its most prominent lay leaders, had taken part in this conference and declared:

"On this issue our basic stand differs from that taken by our Catholic friends. We agree with them only on this one point: in no circumstances must the decisions which have to be taken assume the cloak of a crusade. For the rest, as regards our assessment and judgment of the rearmament issue, we are unable to follow the course of the Catholics."

These were the circumstances in which the last personal interview between the Federal Chancellor and his minister took place on October 9, 1950.

What prompted Adenauer above all was the fact that Niemöller's activity was reaching increasingly large circles of opinion, and with its arguments caused doubt and uncertainty at a moment when nothing was more urgently needed than clear and cool reflection—and that his own Minister of the Interior openly identified himself with this agitation. Adenauer was convinced that Heinemann was wrong in his views. And he was determined that in the face of impending decisions the government must be of one mind. The Heinemann crisis is important and significant above all because it shows Adenauer the man, the politician, and the chief of government in a new and highly characteristic light.

Did he not feel an impulse, after all, to disown Niemöller, or at least dissociate himself from him, Adenauer asked Heinemann? Did he really wish to identify himself with Niemöller's letter? Heinemann declared that he could not give an answer to this. He would let nothing come between himself and Niemöller.

Adenauer drew his attention to a publicly displayed poster announcing a meeting at Frankfurt, where Heinemann and Niemöller were billed together as the chief speakers. In the light of Niemöller's letter he considered it inadmissible that a federal minister should be billed with him on the same poster.

Adenauer: "As a federal minister you must free yourself from this entanglement and cancel this engagement."

Heinemann: "That I cannot bring myself to do."

Thus we come to the fateful Cabinet meeting of October 10, 1950. The Chancellor submitted the whole issue to the Cabinet. He invited Heinemann himself once more to explain his views. But the Minister of the Interior found no support with his colleagues in the Cabinet.

According to one of those present at the meeting, the Chancellor told Heinemann, "As far as I am concerned, Herr Heinemann, the decisive point is that you feel unable to cooperate in our European policy. What you are saying still leaves 2 or 3 per cent open. The federal government, however, must be 100 per cent certain where it stands."

Niemöller's letter had aroused Adenauer's wrath to a degree seldom experienced by him. He was in a mood of profound and violent agitation. Niemöller, he told the Cabinet, had openly proclaimed himself an enemy of the state to which he now denied all right of existence. "The way Niemöller is carrying on now, he's making himself guilty of high treason, pure and simple. He has written to McCloy too. I have no explanation for his behavior. A federal minister—who is responsible for internal security!—who refuses to dissociate himself from these utterances is untenable."

Later that same afternoon Adenauer wrote Heinemann a letter:

"Dear Mr. Heinemann!

Our conversation of today and the contents of the written statement you submitted to me on this occasion have deepened my conviction that our views of the factors governing the political situation of the German people are so widely divergent that fruitful cooperation between us is no longer possible. I cannot help gaining the impression that you have not been able, despite your very best intentions, to achieve the clarity of judgment and strength of resolution which a Federal Minister, and especially a Minister of the Interior, must possess in the present perilous situation. In view of the responsibility I bear toward the German people I feel reluctantly compelled, therefore, to propose to the Federal President that your offer of resignation be accepted and that he should relieve you of your ministerial post.

In the light of all the work we have accomplished together in the difficult and strenuous year which lies behind us, it has not been easy for me to come to this decision. I am anxious to express to you my sincere gratitude for the valuable services you have rendered, and you will allow me to hope that our joint work in the past will be a common bond between us in the future.

With friendly greetings,

Yours sincerely,
ADENAUER."

It was the first letter of this kind that Adenauer had been compelled to write since he became head of the government. But he felt certain that he had no choice. Later on he remarked to one of his associates:

"Just think of the responsibility Heinemann and Niemöller are taking upon themselves! If the foreign powers fail to put the question of a German defense contribution to us, the result will be a hesitant and delaying defense effort on the part of the Western Allies, and we shall get into precisely the position which Heinemann fears—Germany will become a battlefield. But if we Germans cooperate, we shall save the peace because the West will then be strong enough and Russia will not dare to attack. Once there is a German contingent in the European Army with fully equal rights we shall also be equal partners politically. Can't people see that at all?"

Heinemann was succeeded in his office by Dr. Robert Lehr. When Sir Ivone Kirkpatrick, the British High Commissioner, inquired into the background of Heinemann's dismissal, Adenauer told him:

"Heinemann takes the view that, since God has twice dashed the weapons from the hands of the Germans, they must not take them up for a third time. He feels that we must have patience and recognize the will of God in His earthly rule. Now, I don't want to go into the matter of religious devotion and faith in God as such. But when Herr Heinemann implored me to do nothing, I told him that in my view God had given us a head to think with, and arms and hands to act with."

It is only now, in the light of these words, one feels that one really gets to know Adenauer the man. For him, too, as a devout Christian, the Heinemann crisis was certainly a severe trial. But he emerged from it with a clearer head, a more precisely defined aim, and a more profound moral seriousness. He was convinced that God was watching over the destinies of mankind. But he was equally convinced that it was the duty of man to make his own decisions. To find the invisible dividing line where the "will of God in His earthly rule" is transferred to man, making him responsible to think and act for himself, that was the task of the Christian statesman as he saw it. It confronted him anew each day, and each day it required a new solution.

On October 20, 1950, a week after the settlement of the Heinemann crisis, the first annual congress of the Christian Democratic Union of

Germany took place at Goslar, in the Harz Mountains, close to the zonal border and the "iron curtain." The CDU, hitherto organized only on state level, presented itself for the first time as a great and comprehensive all-German party. The flags of the East German provinces were flying beside those of the West; the exiled CDU of the Eastern Zone was represented by a group of delegates; and a second group represented the territories beyond the Oder-Neisse line which the Grotewohl government had solemnly recognized as an "immutable frontier."

The watchword of the conference was taken from the third stanza of the *"Deutschland-Lied,"* the traditional national anthem:

"Unity and Justice and Liberty."

Six months before, during his first visit to Berlin in April, 1950, Adenauer had caused a considerable rumpus with this third stanza. At the Titania-Palast he had closed an important speech in which he pledged himself to the cause of Berlin and the German eastern territory, which was widely, though secretly, listened to in the Soviet Zone, with these words:

"We have come to recognize through suffering and misery that there is but one secure foundation on which life is worth living—freedom and the right to unity. Let us build the new Germany on the foundation of justice and unity. In asking you now to sing with me the third stanza of the *'Deutschland-Lied'* I want you to understand it as a solemn pledge that we wish to be a united, a free and a peaceful people."

The next day a storm of indignation, such as Adenauer had not unleashed since his Berne speech, broke loose throughout the world, and especially in the Allied countries. The singing of the *"Deutschland-Lied"* was considered an open provocation in which Adenauer the "incorrigible old nationalist" had once again shown his "true face." A few days later this Titania-Palast incident was discussed at the usual Petersberg conference. Sir Brian Robertson remarked that the absence of a national anthem was a grave handicap for the Federal Republic. Asking the Federal Chancellor not to misunderstand him, he said, "Of course, we know and appreciate the true meaning of the words of the *'Deutschland-Lied'*. But the undeniable fact remains that the *'Deutschland-Lied'* enjoys a bad reputation abroad."

Adenauer thereupon explained to the three High Commissioners the controversial third stanza and the story of its origin: the poet

Hoffman von Pallersleben who wrote it was a German democrat and anything but a nationalist, and the singing of the third stanza was forbidden under the Nazi regime.

"Now, if the democratic parties were to eschew the *'Deutschland-Lied',*" he went on, "they would merely hand it over to the nationalist movements who would exploit it for their own purposes and give it an even worse reputation abroad. I consider this question more important than it may appear at the moment. In my opinion one of the most important tasks of the Federal Republic must be, in contrast to the Weimar Republic, not to play into the hands of the nationalists, to avoid supplying them with material for their propaganda, and to see to it that the genuine national sentiment of the German people is channeled into the right riverbed."

Now, in October, 1950, the words "Unity and Justice and Freedom" were written demonstratively across the all-German congress of the CDU at Goslar. And here at least, close to the zonal frontier, there was no misunderstanding about their true meaning.

"We belong to the West and not to Soviet Russia," Adenauer told his listeners from all over Germany. "It will be decided even in our lifetime whether liberty, human dignity, and the way of thinking of the Christian West shall be retained for humanity, or whether the spirit of darkness and slavery and anti-Christ shall inflict its scourge for a long time on prostrate mankind. . . ."

The German people, Adenauer exclaimed, must be ready to shoulder their share of the burden of a common defense of the West against the armed threat from the East. "Security, even if it means certain burdens for the Federal Republic, is better than destruction!"

So far, Adenauer once more assured all those who had asserted the opposite, his government had accepted no obligation whatsoever with regard to German rearmament, nor had committed itself to it in any way. "Up to now nobody has asked us to enter into such a commitment. No offer has been made to us either."

The German representatives in the European Assembly, he declared, had supported the idea of a unified European Army under a unified European command and democratic control when it was mooted by Churchill, but they had rejected the idea of a separate German national army.

"The federal government, the Federal Parliament, and I myself will do everything within our power to see that militaristic thinking, which had its sharpest expression during the Nazi time, shall never in any circumstances return."

Five days later, the French Prime Minister, René Pleven, made the "offer" in a speech in the French Chamber. It was not the kind of proposal Adenauer had hoped for. But it was a beginning. The great debate on the European Defense Community had begun.

# CHAPTER XXII

THE HISTORY of the European Defense Community, if fully told, would require several large volumes. The documentary evidence for this unique political enterprise—which began with the New York conference of Foreign Ministers in 1950 and ended finally, after numberless disappointments and setbacks carrying it to the verge of failure, in May, 1955, with the deposition of the ratified Paris Treaties at the Palais Schaumburg—fills not only the archives at Bonn but the files of the Foreign Ministries of the entire Western World.

It is impossible to recount here this immensely complicated historical process in all its detail. On the other hand, it represents a chapter of such paramount importance in the life of Konrad Adenauer that it is equally impossible to dismiss it with a few summary paragraphs. For the personality of Adenauer between his seventy-fifth and eightieth years emerges nowhere more forcefully and impressively than from the infinitely involved story of the political and military unification of Western Europe.

Nothing was nearer to Adenauer's heart during these years than this unification. For nothing else did he work so untiringly, devoting to it all his experience, influence, and prestige, and investing in it everything he possessed in the way of political, parliamentary, and purely human capital. His unwavering belief in the correctness of the basic idea and his determination to make no concession on the principle itself while agreeing to every acceptable compromise which would facilitate its execution have contributed more than anything else to making this great conception a reality.

In the autumn of 1950 it was clear to all concerned with the security of the Western World, the powers of the Atlantic Pact as well as the Federal Republic, that no defense organization like NATO, then in the early stages of its construction, was possible without German participation. One of NATO's foremost tasks was the protection of the Federal Republic. A defense of Europe based on the Rhine instead of the Elbe meant an attempted suicide for the Atlantic

Powers, and certain self-murder for the Federal Republic. Up to this point all concerned were in agreement. But here the differences began.

The United States government was convinced that Congress would agree to a weighty American contribution to NATO in troops and materials only if the Federal Republic, for its part, took a share of the burden commensurate with its means. For this reason Secretary of State Acheson, at the New York conference, demanded a measure of German rearmament and the inclusion of the Federal Republic in the Atlantic defense system as a matter of principle.

The rest of the Atlantic Powers, especially Germany's former opponents in the war, regarded this demand with considerable skepticism. Realizing, however, that NATO stood or fell with an American contribution of overwhelming weight, and that such a contribution was to be obtained only at the price of German participation, they finally yielded to the American request.

To Adenauer it seemed that the American demand was entirely justified, not only in material respects but above all morally. If American soldiers were to defend the Ruhr territory, German soldiers were in duty bound to help them, as soon as they were invited to do so. On the other hand, he fully appreciated British and French fears with regard to a resurgence of German militarism. He was as much aware of this danger as were Bevin and Schuman, and disliked the prospect no less than they. He was not willing, therefore, to agree to German rearmament except within the framework of an integrated European Defense force. This he considered not only a military necessity but also highly desirable from a political point of view. He felt certain that military cooperation within a European Army, in the same way as economic integration within the Schuman Plan, was bound sooner or later to bring about political unification. And this political integration, a United States of Europe, was his real and ultimate goal. However, there was one indispensable prerequisite for such integration: it required a genuinely free and sovereign German partner, enjoying equal rights, released from all tutelage, and acting on its own independent resolve. During the long and protracted negotiations over the European Defense Community, or EDC as it came to be called, Adenauer never yielded an inch of this basic condition.

For Foreign Minister Robert Schuman and Defense Minister Jules

Moch the New York NATO conference had been a nasty surprise. They had had no inkling that the question of German rearmament would be raised by the United States in so precise and urgent a manner. What was more, they had been convinced that the British government would reject German rearmament as unconditionally as they did themselves. Now they were suddenly faced with Acheson's demand which appeared to them very much in the nature of an ultimatum, and found to their horror that Bevin had left them in the lurch. Schuman and Moch discovered that they were an outvoted minority in the Atlantic Council, and they knew that they would risk their own downfall in the French National Assembly if they supported the American request.

It thus became necessary for them to bar the road to further discussion of the American plan in the Defense Committee of NATO, and to do so as quickly as possible. The Pleven government must submit an alternative scheme which was acceptable to their own coalition and had prospects of approval by the National Assembly, while at the same time meeting the American demand for a German contribution. Foreign Minister Schuman had already pointed the direction in which such a scheme must be sought. The only acceptable solution would be a military version of the Schuman Plan.

This was worked out and drafted without delay and submitted to the National Assembly by the French Prime Minister, René Pleven, on October 24, 1950, only a few days ahead of the meeting of the NATO defense committee. The so-called "Pleven Plan" for the creation of a European Army was approved by the French Parliament with 343 votes against 225.

At first sight the Pleven Plan seemed to correspond fairly precisely to what Adenauer had in mind. The French government, Pleven declared, refused to consider any form of German rearmament that did not fit into the European framework he outlined. "Any system that would lead, either immediately or in the future, directly or indirectly, with or without conditions, to the creation of a German Army would renew suspicion and distrust. The constitution of German divisions, of a German War Ministry and General Staff, would inevitably lead sooner or later to the reconstruction of a national army and to the resurrection of German militarism."

All this was very much in tune with Adenauer's own ideas. But the Pleven Plan itself, although providing for "a complete fusion as far as possible of the human and material elements under a single political and military European authority," in its detailed provisions fell far short of this high-flown conception. It proposed the creation of a European Army composed of the "smallest possible national units," i.e., battalions, which was to be under the authority of a European Minister of Defense. This Minister of Defense, in his turn, was to be responsible to a European Defense Council, which again was to be subject to an international political authority such as a European Parliament or the European Assembly at Strasbourg. The German contingents were not to be incorporated in the European Army until after the signing of the Schuman Plan.

Adenauer felt immediately that this was not the way. He was plainly disappointed by the French proposals, and expressed his opinion in a statement couched deliberately in very decided terms:

"If the Federal Republic is to put a contingent at the disposal of an American-European army, it will do so only on a footing of complete equality with all other contingents. That is our condition, without which we shall in no circumstances cooperate."

The French plan, Adenauer said, contained good ideas but much time would be required to give effect to them, and it was doubtful whether so much time could be spared.

France's eleven partners in the Atlantic Pact were of the same opinion and rejected the Pleven Plan as unworkable. The entire, vastly complicated superstructure of political control, they felt, had nothing to do with the defense tasks of the Atlantic Treaty Organization and was bound to cause endless delay in the creation of a European defense organization. Besides, a European Army composed of the "smallest possible units" was generally considered impractical from a military point of view.

But at all events France had succeeded in throwing the Defense Committee of NATO out of gear. Faced with the Pleven Plan, the committee was unable to reach agreement on the German defense contribution and referred the entire problem to the Deputy Foreign Ministers in London. "The French are trying to arm Germany without arming the Germans," one Minister commented. "That is absurd and will never work. Besides, it is not for the Atlantic Council to enforce the signature of the Schuman Plan."

For Adenauer all this resulted in an increasingly difficult situation. The whole world was by now discussing the "German divisions," numerous committees were considering ways and means by which Germany could be enabled to make her "defense contribution," but Germany herself was represented at none of these meetings and deliberations. The indispensable request had still not been made and could not be made as long as France had not come to an understanding with the rest of the Atlantic Powers and there was no agreement on precisely what Germany should be requested to do. The entire international discussion proceeded over the head of the Federal Chancellor, and German popular opinion began to become restive.

Adenauer tried to steady the restless mood. "We are not offering ourselves," he said in a speech at Stuttgart, "but neither must we, by making all sorts of speeches, preclude ourselves from being asked!" While outside Germany the first voices were heard declaring that it would be unwise to count one's chickens before they were hatched and that it was well within the powers of the Federal Parliament to reject the Schuman Plan as well as the defense contribution, a fact people were inclined to overlook, inside Germany Dr. Schumacher and Pastor Niemöller met at Darmstadt and discussed for seven hours the possibilities of a common platform regarding the question of rearmament.

All this portended nothing good. It increased popular confusion and was grist for the mill of the defeatists. Adenauer realized that he could wait no longer. With or without a request from the Allies, his government must take up a clear and unequivocal position in the Parliament, to steady disorientated public opinion. After a discussion with François-Poncet, who assured him that he had misunderstood the Pleven Plan and that the Federal Republic would naturally be an equal partner, the Chancellor decided to raise the whole matter in the foreign affairs debate of the Federal Parliament on November 8, 1950, with a government statement of policy.

Adenauer began by stating that "so far we have not been asked to make a defense contribution, and we have not offered to make one. The German people must realize, however, that the Western Powers cannot very well be expected to assume the defense of Germany if Germany herself is not prepared to contribute to it. For every German in his sound senses it must be a compelling moral duty to defend his own homeland."

There were, however, two basic prerequisites for Germany's

participation in such a defense front. In the first place, the strength of this defense front must be adequate to render any Russian aggression impossible; and secondly, the German Federal Republic must enjoy complete equality not only of duties but also of rights, with the other powers taking part. "I believe," the Chancellor declared, "that by forming such a united front we shall also eventually achieve reunification with our brothers and sisters in the Eastern Zone."

The debate which followed showed that the fundamental views of Adenauer and Schumacher did not differ nearly as widely as had been generally believed. The Socialist leader was just as little inclined as the Chancellor to look idly on in the event of a Communist aggression, and it appeared indeed that his logical mind had little use for Niemöller's cloudy idealism. He, too, insisted on "equal risk and equal sacrifice." But there was one important difference. Schumacher demanded that the Federal Republic postpone its decision until the Western Powers had appeared in full strength. Adenauer answered that it was morally inadmissible for the Federal Republic to join the protective front only when it was clear that it incurred neither risk nor danger in so doing.

This fundamental difference of opinion was to manifest itself again and again during the following months and years. It dominated the entire defense controversy between the Government and the Opposition, between Adenauer and Schumacher, from first to last. Adenauer did not think, as he told one of his confidants, that further attempts to persuade Schumacher into a change of mind would have much effect, since, "in view of Dr. Schumacher's character and temperament, every renewed attempt would only stiffen his attitude and make him even more certain of the correctness of his own views." All the same, Adenauer did not believe that the Social Democrats would say no, once the issue was put to a final vote.

The debate of November 8, 1950, was a milestone in the development of the rearmament issue. Adenauer had chosen the moment for his statement with shrewd political instinct. Now public opinion, inside as well as outside Germany, knew where it was. Especially the outside world realized that Germany's conditions for participating in the defense of Western Europe were likely to be considerably more stringent than had apparently been expected, and, more important still, that German readiness for rearmament was by no means a foregone conclusion.

"I should like to say a few words about the psychological attitude of the German people toward this issue," Adenauer told the three High Commissioners at their next Petersberg meeting on November 16. "Apparently the rest of the world is astonished to find that the prospect of German military formations is not joyfully welcomed by the German people. Duncan Sandys, Churchill's son-in-law, has stated openly in the House of Commons that the idea of a European Army should be supported because it insured that after the end of the present difficulties the Germans would not establish an independent national army of their own. In my view reflections of this kind entirely miss the point. No one in Germany, except a relatively small group of ex-officers, desires a restoration of the former army. As for myself, I would not lift a finger for it. The new brigades will not form a class by themselves. They must feel themselves representative of the people as a whole, and they will be subject to civilian authority."

No, the real problem was elsewhere. The Chancellor pointed it out with great frankness. He revealed a far deeper insight into the thoughts and feelings of the German people than one would have assumed with so reticent and withdrawn a man.

"It is the inner, mental attitude of the German people which causes me anxiety," he remarked. "After all they have gone through, the German people have gradually reached a point where, with all their love and appreciation of liberty, they are unwilling to make sacrifices for the sake of liberty, and prefer others to sacrifice themselves. As a purely human attitude this is perhaps understandable, but . . ."

Not only the nationalist propaganda of the Communists, Adenauer explained, was trying to exploit this attitude during the present elections for the state parliaments. The Socialists were doing the same thing, and they advanced two main arguments. First: "It is surely a good thing to sacrifice everything for freedom, but you aren't free at all, and therefore it isn't worth your while doing anything for it." And secondly: "At bottom, the Western Allies do not seriously mean to defend Western Germany, but merely want to use the German troops for delaying actions and for the protection of their own withdrawal."

Faced with such irresponsible propaganda, Adenauer pointed out, the Government parties were at a disadvantage because, in the present state of affairs, "they do not know whether a request for a defense contribution will even be made to them," since there is no agreement on this point among the Atlantic Powers.

"I beg of you, gentlemen," Adenauer told the High Commissioners, "not to regard what I am going to tell you now as in the nature either of a condition or a demand. As far as I personally am concerned, I am determined to stick to my point of view, even if you should turn down all my suggestions. But I consider it necessary to do something now to effect a psychological reorientation among the majority of the German people."

What should be done? Above all, Adenauer said, the Western Powers must come to a clear decision regarding the defense contribution, and so "make an end of the present state of semidarkness." They should reinforce their troops in Germany, to make it clear to the German people that their own destiny was in fact tied to that of Germany. They should, as the Chancellor had repeatedly requested, replace the obsolete Occupation Statute by a system of contractual agreements. They should stop the remainder of the industrial dismantling program, for "this is simply incomprehensible to the people." They should swiftly wind up the war crimes trials still pending, grant further relief in the field of prohibited and restricted industries—there were many possibilities.

"I am asking your governments," the Chancellor urged, "to enable me to inform and enlighten the German people, correctly and truthfully. . . ."

A fortnight later, on December 1, 1950, the Chancellor repeated his arguments at the Petersberg, with unusual urgency. There was good cause for this. His fears had come true. The state parliament elections in Württemberg-Baden, Hesse, and Bavaria had resulted in serious losses for the CDU. Everywhere the Social Democrats had gained first place. Schumacher's slogan, "The Basic Law is the constitution of a state without an army," had apparently made a considerable impression upon the confused electorate.

Adenauer was now compelled to ask himself: what was it the Atlantic Powers really wanted? Did they want a German defense contribution, or did they not? And if they wanted it, why did they go out of their way to tie the hands of the only government which could—perhaps—get it for them? This time Adenauer was resolved to speak bluntly. He went immediately to the heart of the matter:

"Gentlemen, I'm speaking to you with all the respect I owe you, but also with all the candor I owe the entire situation. We are now in December. For more than three months the Western Allies and the Atlantic Pact Powers have been negotiating and arguing back and forth as to whether or not Germany should be asked to make a contribution. During all this time the Federal Republic has received no official information whatsoever but is reduced to what it can glean from the newspapers. This places the federal government in an utterly impossible position. It is more than embarrassing for us to have to reply to questioners: sorry, I know no more than you do; I only know what is in the papers. The prestige of the federal government has suffered greatly from all this. It is quite impossible to allow this state of affairs to continue. . . ."

Once again the Chancellor urged the occupying powers to issue an official declaration to the effect that the Occupation Statute would be replaced by a system of bilateral security treaties. "I feel the situation is ripe for an announcement that the word 'Occupation Statute,' which has a very ugly ring in our ears, is about to disappear. . . ."

On behalf of the High Commissioners McCloy replied that it was not possible to replace the Occupation Statute by a security pact in "so short a space of time." But all the same, Adenauer's request would be duly forwarded to their governments. "I feel we must all assume a more positive attitude," McCloy said. "There are moments when it is downright ridiculous that we should be haggling over all sorts of conditions and completely lose sight of our paramount aim. . . ."

That was precisely how Adenauer felt. One of his paramount aims was, and remained, an understanding with France, and this suffered the most from the present difficulties. Work on the Schuman Plan, so hopefully begun, was progressing very slowly and laboriously—the industrialists of the Ruhr were discovering more and more "hairs in the Schuman soup"—and now these delays over the defense contribution owing to French procrastination and indecision!

"It pains me particularly," he told François-Poncet, "that I have to remain silent when people openly assert that all my endeavors to reach an understanding with the French have ended in failure. . . ."

François-Poncet: "Schuman has done what he could. But rapprochement between Germany and France is not a flat race but a handicap race, and one mustn't be discouraged and balked by every hurdle."

A week later, on December 7, 1950, the Atlantic Powers at long last reached agreement among themselves about the German defense contribution. What emerged was the so-called "Spofford Plan," and this turned out to be a compromise between the original American conception and the Pleven Plan.

Under the Spofford Plan France agreed to immediate preparations for the creation of an Atlantic defense force including German units, while the other members of the Atlantic Pact agreed that France should go ahead with her attempts to form a European Army within the framework of the Atlantic defense system. France furthermore abandoned her original plan for a complicated political superstructure as an indispensable prerequisite for the formation of German military units, and waived her stipulation that the recruiting of German units should be made dependent on the prior signature of the Schuman Plan. Next, the French government agreed that the German units should take the form of "combat teams" of about 6,000 men, but maintained its original opposition to the creation of a German general staff and a Ministry of War. Finally the French government announced that it would shortly issue invitations to a conference in Paris which would discuss the practical realization of the European Army, on the assumption that the Schuman treaty for a coal and steel pool would by then have been set up.

Was this a solution? It was a solution only in so far as the Americans had made it clear that the nomination of a supreme commander for the Atlantic forces depended on the settlement of the German rearmament issue, and the appointment of General Eisenhower as supreme commander could now take place. For the rest, the compromise of the Spofford Plan meant simply that there would be two separate Western European defense forces—the continental Pleven Army, whose real purpose was to "keep Germany under control," and the Atlantic defense force proper, consisting of the United States, Canada, Great Britain—who had declined to join the European Army—and those NATO states on the European continent who did not wish to join Pleven's European Army. For the time being the German units would remain suspended somewhere in a vacuum between these two organizations until they were eventually incorporated in the European Army—provided that the European Army materialized. A meeting of the NATO Council was summoned for December 18, at Brussels, to approve the Spofford Plan. And at some time or other an invitation to take part in the Pleven conference in Paris could be expected to reach Bonn.

This was not at all what Adenauer had had in mind. But how was he to obtain a hearing before the Brussels conference met and things took a course unfavorable for Germany? Once more he had recourse to a press interview. On December 11, 1950, he told Kingsbury Smith of the International News Service that he had no doubt that the Spofford Plan would be rejected by the federal government, the Federal Parliament, and the German public.

"In saying this I have no intention of interfering with the negotiations of the Atlantic powers," Adenauer declared. "But I am anxious to prevent such a plan from being formally submitted to us. If this were the case we should find ourselves in the unhappy position of having to reject it." He was quite willing, the Chancellor continued, to leave the question of integrating the German units into the Atlantic army to the discretion of the American supreme commander, provided that France and the other Western Allies granted the principle of full equality of status for the German military forces, especially regarding command authority and armament and equipment.

Germany did not insist on equality in numbers within the Atlantic Army, Adenauer declared. That was not how the term "equality" should be understood. "Figures are not decisive. If our contribution in manpower is fixed at one tenth of the total strength of the Atlantic Army, we shan't grumble. But in respect of weapons and command authority we must have full equality. This is indispensable, or there will be an inevitable impression that our troops are being used merely as cannon fodder. Without heavy equipment of their own the Germans would have no chance of defending themselves, and without a command of their own they would feel like second-class soldiers. In all probability this would achieve precisely the opposite of what France desires. It would be difficult to keep such discontented combat troops under control.

"I'm not a soldier," Adenauer said, "but I know how a soldier feels. I believe, furthermore, that from a military standpoint, too, the French scheme is not practicable. I cannot imagine that France is really afraid of 150,000 German soldiers. It would be utterly foolish to think that this small force would invade France, with Russia at its back and Western Europe and the United States on France's side!"

Agreement about a German contribution could now be quickly reached, the Chancellor said, if the High Commissioners were authorized to negotiate direct with the federal government.

"How do you imagine the German people feel," the Chancellor asked, "when they hear of negotiations in Washington, Paris, and London, in the course of which their fate is being discussed, and in which they have no part whatsoever? One thing is certain: the German people will not simply do as the other nations decide and decree. I have spoken frankly, and revealed the most secret recesses of my heart. For it is my most urgent desire to obtain clarity in this matter."

Whatever the objections to it might have been, the "foreign policy by interview" was undoubtedly effective. At the end of the next Petersberg conference, on December 14, 1940, the American High Commissioner remarked, "And now, Mr. Federal Chancellor, I would ask you to give no more interviews before the end of the Brussels conference—just in order to avoid misunderstandings."

Translated from the friendly and confidential, and at the same time official and diplomatic, language which the Petersberg meetings had evolved in the course of time, this meant simply: We have understood you, and now please show some understanding for us!

The Chancellor asked the three High Commissioners to prevail upon the Brussels conference not to take decisions which in all probability would be rejected by the German people. He suggested that the High Commissioners should obtain authority from their Foreign Ministers to commence direct negotiations with the federal government on the entire complex issue of the German defense contribution.

Adenauer: "I feel, gentlemen, that you can regard this as a proof of confidence."

François-Poncet reassured the Chancellor that the Brussels conference had no intention of "dictating" a solution, but that the proposals of the conference would be discussed with the federal government. He added, "The Federal Chancellor has told us that he has confidence in us. I can tell him that this confidence is justified."

Adenauer: "That is not what I said!"

François-Poncet: "But I say it."

Adenauer: "I did not say that I had confidence in you."

François-Poncet: "But surely you did say: 'I have confidence'?"

Adenauer: "No. I said: 'Please regard my request to entrust you with the negotiations as a proof of confidence.' "

François-Poncet: "I must regretfully state that you have immediately withdrawn your declaration that your confidence in us was well deserved."

Adenauer: "No. I didn't say that either."

Is it just chaff and banter, or are they serious? Is it ironical hair-splitting, or genuine, deep-seated animosity? It is hard to say with these sudden acerbities which were still liable to flare up unexpectedly during the Petersberg meetings. Despite mutual respect for each other's "cleverness," the Chancellor and the French Ambassador still found it difficult to strike a common note, and these short but sharp animosities show in a flash how sensitive both sides still were, despite all the common ground between them.

On one occasion Adenauer remarked with a humorous sigh, "The trouble is, you gentlemen understand English, and I understand German. I've understood the interpreter."

It wasn't easy. But a way out of the *cul-de-sac* was in sight.

The Brussels conference did not disappoint the Federal Chancellor. There was no question of a "dictate," but rather the contrary: it was decided to proceed in exactly the manner suggested by Adenauer. The three Foreign Ministers, their statement said, "authorized their repective High Commissioners, in discussions with the government of the Federal Republic, further to explore this problem on the basis of the Council's proposals, as well as any change in the present occupation arrangements which might logically attend a German defense contribution."

This was a distinct success for the Federal Chancellor. His firm attitude in matters of principle had proved itself. Now, regarding its practical application he was ready, as always, to make any concession likely to serve the common purpose. At the Petersberg meeting of December 21, 1950, François-Poncet declared that, with regard to military equality, they had always considered this as obvious and understood. "We never harbored any idea of turning the Germans into cannon fodder." McCloy, too, emphasized that there was complete agreement on the basic principle of equality, namely, that arms and equipment must be the same and that "German soldiers will face the enemy with the same equipment as the soldiers of other nations."

The Chancellor stated that he was in agreement with the Brussels decisions, for two reasons: they served the preservation of peace, in view of the danger threatening from the East, and they served the integration of Europe. Since he himself was "not an expert on military matters," he suggested the setting up of a joint commission to explore these aspects, on which Germany would be represented by Theodor Blank, undersecretary in charge of Security, and former generals Adolf Heusinger and Hans Speidel. This proposal was accepted.

The political aspect of the matter proved more difficult.

"A German defense contribution would create a new political situation," François-Poncet declared. "The present occupation regime would have to be adapted to this new development. The Federal Chancellor has requested that the Occupation Statute be replaced by a contractual settlement. The occupying powers take the view that the essential principle which provides their presence in Germany with a legal basis cannot be modified for the time being. This reservation apart, the occupying powers are willing to see the present arrangement replaced by a system of treaties."

Of course Adenauer had never expected the Occupation Statute to be abolished overnight by a stroke of the pen. He fully agreed to its gradual and progressive dismantling. But what did François-Poncet's statement mean? What else could it mean but that the principle of occupation must remain unshaken? At this point the old and experienced jurist in Adenauer pricked up his ears, and again there occurred one of the brief "storms in the Petersberg tea cup." This time it was roused by McCloy, who declared that the Allies' title to their presence in Germany could not be based on a contractual agreement because the question of Allied presence in Berlin was closely connected with it. "We must be clear about one thing," McCloy said. "Once we're out of Berlin, we're out of Europe altogether. In this respect we must not, and will not, commit ourselves at the present moment. A contract or treaty can always be invalidated by either side giving notice. . . ."

Did not this mean that it was intended to maintain the occupation for many years to come? With "complete frankness and in all seriousness" Adenauer replied, on principle, "Unconditional surrender of a country does not give the power to which it is made the right to keep such a country occupied for an indefinite period. I ask that this entire problem be once more closely investigated. Otherwise, I fear that participation of the Federal Republic in the defense of Europe will be impossible. I must point to the danger of this measure being rejected by the Federal Parliament. I am accountable to other people, too, for the negotiations we are conducting here. If I were to tell these people that the American High Commissioner had informed me that it was impossible to replace the Occupation Statute by contractual agreements because Germany might give notice to these treaties, you cannot imagine the effect this would have."

François-Poncet: "Mr. Federal Chancellor, why don't you go by what I've told you? The idea of the Ministers at Brussels was to have contractual agreements in all those instances where it is possible . . ." The French High Commissioner, a man much given to picturesque language, tried to make his meaning clear with the help of a metaphor: "Occupation law has grown like a tree from the roots of unconditional surrender. We must begin by cutting down the branches before trying to pull out the roots!"

Adenauer the gardener replied like a shot, "If you cut branches off a tree with strong roots, it will soon grow new ones!" Then he continued in complete seriousness, "May I say the following, to be quite clear and definite: if it is impossible to replace the Occupation Statute by contractual agreements while the present tension with the Soviet Union exists, I am under an obligation to the Parliament and the German people to tell them so with complete frankness. I recognize that you are unable to abolish the principle of occupation at the present moment. . . ."

Kirkpatrick: "I have the impression that all this is just one great misunderstanding. If the Chancellor were to write down his views we should probably be able to agree with him at once."

Adenauer: "If the remark of the American High Commissioner, to the effect that a transition from the Statute to a treaty was impossible because Germany might give notice to the treaty, could be regarded as not having been made. . . ."

Kirkpatrick: "It was you who first said it. This annoyed Mr. McCloy a little, and he answered, perhaps a trifle rashly, that the same thing might happen on the part of Germany. . . ."

Adenauer: "I thank you for this explanation. I am most anxious to be absolutely clear about this point. Therefore I may perhaps be permitted to put a question to our chairman—but I should like to add at once that if you prefer not to answer it now, I shall fully understand. My question is this: do the Western Allies possess the right, as long as the occupation regime continues, to suspend the Basic Law?"

François-Poncet: Allow me to answer by putting a counterquestion: do you intend to violate the Basic Law?"

Adenauer: "One further question. Are you entitled, as long as the principle of occupation is maintained, to promulgate a new Occupation Statute?"

Kirkpatrick: "Only in the form of treaties concluded with you."

Adenauer: "That means that the principle of occupation is circumscribed and narrowed down by the treaties?"

Kirkpatrick: "Yes, that is so."

Adenauer: "If that is the general view, we are already much closer to one another."

François-Poncet: "It is clear that with the concluding of the treaties the Occupation Statute will gradually shrink and wither away."

Adenauer: "That is the decisive point. . . . I must be absolutely open and honest with my own people, as I must be with you. That is why I feel I must express my doubts and misgivings such as these with complete frankness. I believe that these discussions have helped us to get very much closer together. . . ."

Adenauer was right. Looking back, it can be said that this was the decisive Petersberg meeting. Henceforth, the Federal Republic was heard and consulted in all matters affecting its internal or external status. It ceased being merely an object of international politics and began to take an active part in shaping them. This transition was largely Adenauer's work. His candor and frankness, at times almost brusque, which did not hesitate to cause a minor annoyance if this could help to eliminate a major quarrel, had managed to create an atmosphere of genuine trust which was the prerequisite for the return of Germany into the comity of free nations.

## CHAPTER XXIII

"HERR DR. BÖCKLER," the private secretary announced. Adenauer immediately rose behind his desk and with an outstretched hand came forward to greet the stocky, broad-shouldered man with the impressive features who entered his office.

The former Chief Mayor of Cologne and the former Cologne Municipal Councilor had known each other for nearly a quarter of a century, and during this time had had more than one sharp brush with one another. Hans Böckler, who began life as a metal worker, had been a Social Democrat and active trade unionist since his early youth, and in the Cologne city parliament the shrewdly thoughtful yet temperamental labor leader was often among Adenauer's most severe critics. But despite their fundamental differences of political outlook the two men had always felt genuine respect for one another. Born in the same year, 1875, they both accomplished their major achievements in the eighth decade of their lives: while Adenauer led the German people out of total political collapse, Böckler rescued the German trade union movement from the chaos of utter defeat. The year 1949 in which Adenauer became Federal Chancellor saw Böckler elected chairman of the first postwar German Trade Union Congress. Now, in January, 1951, the *Deutscher Gewerkshafts-bund*, or D.G.B. as it was generally called, had a membership of nearly six million and ranked among the largest and most powerful labor organizations in the world. This was very largely Hans Böckler's achievement.

But respect for each other's achievement was not the only tie between the two men. They knew and appreciated the fact that each, in his own field, was selflessly working for the best of the nation as a whole, and they knew one another to be realistic in the pursuit of their aims, averse alike to doctrinaire stubbornness and the chase after cheap popularity within the narrow confines of party politics. Thus Adenauer had never forgotten that it was Böckler who, in the critical days of the Petersberg Agreement, had the courage to oppose the decision of the Socialist party and support the first international agreement concluded by the young Federal Republic, which put an end to industrial dismantling and preserved and restored the livelihood of hundreds of thousands of German workers. Conversely, Böckler the trade unionist was well aware that Socialist propaganda depicting Adenauer as an incorrigible reactionary and "handmaid of capitalism" was far from the truth, and that the man now facing him possessed sympathy and understanding for the position of the workers and sincerely endeavored to bring about social equality and peace.

It was this conviction which had prompted Böckler to request a personal interview with the Federal Chancellor and which had brought him to his office in the Palais Schaumburg in this critical hour. For the storm signals were up in the Federal Republic, and the trade union leader was trying in a last-minute talk with the head of the government, to reach an agreement and avert the worst.

A few days before the iron and steel workers had decided to go on strike on February 1, 1951. In these industries 230,000 workers had given notice that they would down tools, and if they carried out their intention the blast furnaces of the Ruhr would have to be extinguished. Worse still, 600,000 coal miners had threatened to join the strike, and this at a moment when the country was suffering from an acute shortage of coal. There was no doubt that this strike in the heavy industries would cripple the whole economy of the country and certainly set production back many months.

What was the issue? It was defined in the German term *Mitbestimmungsrecht*, meaning broadly the workers' right to partnership in the management of industry—in this particular case in coal-mining and the iron and steel industries.

It was not a new demand. The claim of German workers to joint responsibility in industrial management dated back to the days of the Weimar Republic, and in 1947 the British military government had in fact conceded to the workers in the major industrial enterprises of the Ruhr a right to share in the working and business management of their plants. The primary objective of the occupying powers in doing this was presumably political; the measure was seen as a way of preventing German heavy industry from ever again becoming an instrument of German rearmament. For the German worker, however, it had a larger and deeper significance, since it brought the fulfillment of a demand the trade unions had raised against the employers for more than a generation. But now, in January, 1951, a crossroads had been reached. The vast combines of West German heavy industry, having been broken up and decartelized by the occupying powers, were about to be passed back into the hands of German management, and the question was whether the trade unions could maintain their newly gained position or whether the rights conceded to them by the Allies would now be lost again. In order to forestall such a retrograde development the German Trade Union Congress requested on behalf of its members that the rights granted to the workers of the coal and iron industries by the occupying powers should now be reaffirmed by specific German legislation passed by the German Federal Parliament, and that in doing so, the principle of *Mitbestimmungsrecht*, or copartnership, should be extended to other branches of industry, notably the railways, docks and shipyards, and the chemical industries.

Böckler had already made this demand in 1950, and leading industrialists had promised its fulfillment, but subsequently hesitated to make good their promises. These delaying tactics had eventually brought about the threat to strike, and the threat was not an empty one. Both the coal miners and the metal workers union possessed sufficient funds to maintain their organized members during a strike of several months' duration.

This then was the situation in which Böckler, at "five minutes to twelve," as he had said himself, called on the Chancellor. Now they sat facing each other in the large, bright and airy room with its low, yellow-covered easy chairs, its pictures and soft carpets, and their discussion was no more stiffly official than the distinctly private and personal atmosphere of the room.

Hans Böckler was at this time an old and ailing man battling valiantly against mortal illness, but when Adenauer, in sincere sympathy, inquired after his health, he brushed the question aside with a few noncommittal words and went straight to the heart of the matter. "You know the purpose of my visit—to talk to you about the *Mitbestimmungsrecht* and the impending strike. You will remember, Mr. Federal Chancellor, what I told you shortly after the outbreak of the Korean War. Things might have taken a different turn in Korea, I said, if the South Koreans had not held on so stubbornly to the privileges of the large landowners and obsolete vested class interests. We here in Germany are threatened by the same danger unless the government gets down to tackling the long-promised economic reforms. The only thing which will effectively protect us against Communism is an economic order in tune with the requirements of our time."

"And you know, dear Herr Böckler," Adenauer answered, "that I agreed with you when we talked about Korea. I fully share your opinion that we must have a sensible and reasonable modern economic structure. The only question is, how are we going to get it? I'm sure we're not going to get it through a strike. It is simply not permissible, on any grounds, to paralyze the entire economy in order to force Parliament to adopt this or that piece of legislation."

"Not at all!" Böckler contradicted. "Strike measures have always been recognized as legitimate weapons of struggle in a democratic state. Of course the worker is entitled to refuse to work in an economic system which makes him the object of the employer's arbitrary measures and deprives him of every possibility of exercising an influence on the conduct of the economy, and thus on the shaping of his own conditions of life."

"I take it then," said Adenauer sharply, "that you're advocating the strike in order to compel Parliament to pass a specific act of legislation?"

Böckler shook his head. "If that were the case, I shouldn't be sitting here talking to you."

"Then what are you planning to do? How are you going to restore calm and order among your agitated people?"

Böckler was by no means at a loss what to do. He had his plan ready. "It seems to me," he explained, "that the best thing would be for employers and employees to get together under your chairmanship. They should thrash the matter out among themselves and come to an agreement. For a start, let's leave out the various ministries and the Federal Parliament. I'm firmly convinced that those directly concerned will agree much more quickly if the political parties don't interfere. Their first thought in any social conflict is always how to exploit it for their party propaganda."

Without lengthy reflection, Adenauer accepted Böckler's proposal in principle. Next they discussed how it should be carried out in practice. Eventually it was agreed that the Chancellor would first invite representatives of the employers' association for a discussion under his chairmanship; next he would preside over a corresponding meeting with the representatives of the trade unions; and finally there were to be joint conferences with representatives of both sides. Jointly they would have to formulate proposals acceptable to both parties, which the government would undertake to frame as a draft bill and submit to Parliament. Once employers and trade unions had reached agreement, Adenauer and Böckler reckoned, Parliament was most unlikely to reject such a bill.

But one thing I'm bound to tell you, Herr Böckler," Adenauer remarked at the end of their talk. "If you're now getting your *Mitbestimmungsrecht,* there can be no more talk about socializing the basic industries. It's either one thing or the other!"

Böckler pricked up his ears. Then he smiled. "But your own Ahlen Program, Mr. Federal Chancellor," he said, "the social program of the CDU, promises the socialization of the basic industries: 51 per cent of the shares to be transferred to state ownership. Now is that in your program, or isn't it?"

For a brief moment Adenauer seemed at a loss what to answer. Then he said earnestly, "Quite right, Herr Böckler. But here is the point. If the Federal Republic, or any one of the states, or a local community, possesses the majority in any enterprise, control is automatically vested in either the Federal Parliament, the state parliament or the local council concerned, and those responsible are the government or the mayor, as the case may be. But once the workers and the trade unions take a share in the management of the basic industries, no government and no mayor can any longer assume responsibility. It's either copartnership or socialization. You can't have both."

Noticing a skeptical expression on Böckler's face, Adenauer continued his argument. He did not conceal the fact that, personally, he found copartnership a more sympathetic and acceptable form of economic democracy than socialization, because the latter always carried with it the danger of making the working man dependent on the state which, in its capacity of employer, adds economic power to political power, concentrating and fusing both in the same hands. Was not the sad role played by the trade unions in totalitarian states, whether National Socialist or Communist, a grave warning in this direction?

Böckler remained silent. Had the Chancellor's argument convinced him or did he continue to regard copartnership merely as a steppingstone toward socialization which, after all, remained one of the principal tenets of the Socialist party program? Whatever his thoughts may have been at this moment, he was certainly not willing to jeopardize what had just been won by entering a fresh dispute.

The two men took leave of each other in as friendly and cordial a manner as they had greeted one another.

"Well, there you are, Herr Böckler," Adenauer said, at the door. "You see, you could have had all this without threatening a strike. I should have been in favor of such a settlement even if you had not caused us the bother of 230,000 strike notices in the metal industries. . . ."

Once the "Big Two" had reached agreement, things moved rapidly. Within a few days, on January 17, 1951, the employers were conferring with the Chancellor; on January 19 both sides assembled at the round table. In this joint meeting under Adenauer's chairmanship the two federal ministers directly concerned—Professor Erhard, the Minister of Economics, and Labor Minister Anton Storch—also took part. As soon as agreement was reached, the Chancellor submitted the results to the Cabinet, who were waiting in an adjoining room. The Cabinet approved the proposed measure with a large majority, and decided to submit a corresponding draft bill to both houses of parliament.

But all this did not mean that the great strike was finally averted. The threat remained. A solution had to be found by February 1, 1951, or it would be put into effect. Nor did everyone in the government coalition agree with Adenauer's method of procedure. The Free Democratic party, for instance, declared that strike notices must be withdrawn before negotiations could take place, and they had the support of the Christian trade unionists in the CDU, who opposed the strike.

However, on February 14, the "law for the copartnership of employees in the management of the coal and iron industries" was submitted to the Federal Parliament for a first reading. Its main provisions were these. The *Aufsichtrat,* or supervisory board, of each major enterprise in these two industries was henceforth to consist of eleven members, five of whom were to represent the shareholders and five the workers, while the eleventh man had to be chosen jointly and must obtain not less than three votes from either side. Of the workers' representatives two must be directly employed in the enterprise concerned, two more must be trade unionists, while the fifth had to be an independent who must not be actively engaged either in the branch of industry concerned or in the trade unions. The *Vorstand,* or board of management, in turn was to consist of three directors, one of whom was to be in charge of labor and must be a trade union or workers' nominee. The supervisory board was to have a number of rights and powers, applying equally in each major firm in the steel and mining industries, and including the right to scrutinize all the firm's books, accounts, and details of policy as well as authority to remove, by a two-thirds majority, any member of the board of management.

"A great step forward!" declared Böckler.

"A great step indeed, but into dark and unexplored territory!" declared the parties of the political right who opposed the new bill in the Parliament.

Adenauer himself did not hesitate to criticize the trade unions sharply for their threat to call a strike on political grounds. "In a democratic state," he declared in Parliament when the bill was read for a first time, "there can be no such thing as a strike against a constitutional legislative body. The final decision must always be with the legislative assembly. But notwithstanding the attendant circumstances, I am of the opinion that this bill is a great step forward on the road to social peace and contentment."

Even while Adenauer spoke those words in the Chamber, Hans Böckler, after a severe heart attack, fought with his last strength for his life in a Cologne hospital. Forty-eight hours later, a week before his seventy-sixth birthday, he gave up the struggle. All government buildings in Bonn and every factory throughout the length and breadth of the Federal Republic hoisted their flags at half-mast. At the memorial services for the great trade union leader the Federal Chancellor took his place beside Professor Heuss, the Federal President, and the leader of the opposition, Dr. Schumacher.

The new law was discussed no less passionately in Germany's neighboring states than in the Federal Republic itself. In Socialist-governed Britain there was a good deal of astonishment at seeing this measure brought in by a Federal Chancellor generally considered thoroughly "reactionary," and many who had hitherto regarded

Adenauer with unconcealed suspicion now saw him in a new and somewhat different light. In the United States opinion was decidedly critical. An American trade delegation which happened to be in Bonn at that time declared roundly that this new arrangement would considerably hinder the investment of foreign capital, of which the mining and iron industries in particular stood in urgent need.

The most negative response came from France. In the middle of March, 1951, when the bill had reached the committee stage, François-Poncet told Adenauer that the measure would drastically change the industrial structure of Western Germany at precisely the moment when the Schuman Plan was at last ready for signature. Ten days later the governments of Belgium, the Netherlands and Luxembourg made official representations to the same effect. Adenauer, they declared, was imperiling the Schuman Plan. François-Poncet tried to have the whole issue discussed by the Allied High Commission, with a view to securing a revision of the draft bill before it was finally passed and became law. Adenauer refused to consider such a move, and the British High Commissioner, Sir Ivone Kirkpatrick, supported him. The Allied High Commission, Kirkpatrick declared, could intervene only if it could be shown that the proposed German industrial reform was detrimental to the security of the occupying powers. This was plainly not the case, and there were no legal grounds, therefore, which entitled the occupying powers to interfere with the conduct of German governmental policy.

On April 10, 1951, the *Mitbestimmungsgesetz*, as it was generally called, was submitted to the Federal Parliament in its final shape for a third reading and adoption. It was an agitated sitting, and a strangely contradictory one.

"We are not prepared," declared the spokesman of the German party, "to hand to a trade union hierarchy instruments of power which they can employ to the detriment of industry and the entire German people!"

"This whole law is unconstitutional!" exclaimed the spokesman of the Free Democratic party. "Even if it is passed, it will remain null and void because it was conceived and drafted under the pressure of a threatened strike. We shall reject this bill because it is a measure of the class struggle!"

Now the odd and perplexing thing about these two voices was that they belonged to two parties which were members of the

Government coalition bloc. Indeed, they were essential elements of this coalition, their representatives were ministers in the Cabinet and normally Adenauer relied on them for his majority. Yet, although his two partners in the coalition had come out against the bill, its safe passage was insured. For once Adenauer enjoyed the full support of the official Socialist Opposition.

It was a strange and unaccustomed process. Clause after clause, Adenauer and Schumacher, CDU and SPD, voted jointly against the two government parties of the right wing of the coalition. It seemed to put the cohesion of the Government to a severe test, and more than one member in the House began to wonder whether the Government would not break apart under the strain. Adenauer himself, however, seemed untouched by such apprehensions. Calm and composed, he sat in his place on the Government bench, and with equal calm and composure he eventually rose to speak.

"The workers," he said, "have in the past made sensible and reasonable use of their copartnership rights in the Ruhr. The trade unions have, during the past few years, shown a positive and constructive attitude toward the state, and in difficult situations have acted with wisdom and moderation. The fact that this bill makes special and separate arrangements for the mining and iron industries seems to be justified in view of the severe and continuous tensions which have existed in past decades between employers and workers, especially in the heavy industries."

It seemed clear that the Chancellor was determined to hold fast to the line of policy laid down between him and the late Hans Böckler in their momentous interview. He relied on the trade unions to maintain their positive and constructive attitude toward the state and its institutions. For him there was more at stake at this moment than an internal German industrial reform. What was at stake was the future economic structure of Europe. If the French felt that the trade unions' right to copartnership endangered the Schuman Plan, he could and would answer them that, without the cooperation and against the will of the German trade unions, the Schuman Plan could never become a reality.

It was getting late on this night of April 10, 1951. The sitting dragged on, as clause after clause of the bill was taken and put to the vote. Now and then the members on the Government bench were casting anxious glances at their watches. The Chancellor had to be at the airport early the next morning. He was expected in Paris at midday for the solemn ceremony of signing the six-power treaty establishing the European Coal and Steel Community.

Adenauer was anxious to have the Copartnership Bill safely passed before he flew to Paris. Now, as before, the Social Democrats were implacably opposed to the Schuman Plan, but the Trade Union Congress had come out clearly and unequivocally in favor of this first step toward a European economic union, and it was most important to keep this valuable ally in a good humor.

Toward ten o'clock there were signs of crisis. The debate seemed to have lost its sense of purpose, and was drifting in all directions. Differences had arisen between the strange allies, CDU and SPD. There was a danger of the bill being thrown out after all. At this point Adenauer intervened. He suggested a suspension of the debate on this controversial clause, so that the differences might be ironed out in "small committee." The House itself could meanwhile continue with other work.

Negotiations in "small committee" lasted for two hours. Then the difficulties were resolved, and agreement was reached. At the stroke of midnight the final vote was taken, and the bill was passed. Henceforth the German worker could justly say that he enjoyed more rights and carried more responsibility than the worker of any other country in the world. But another and no less urgent problem was still waiting to be solved.

PERSONAL!

Lübeck, January 16, 1952

The Federal Chancellor
Dr. Konrad Adenauer
Bonn

> . . . month after month passes, year after year, and apart from a few meaningless platitudes we expellees have received nothing to relieve our misery and destitution. Are we to bear alone the consequences of the war? Is it not enough that we have lost our entire families, our homeland, our livelihood and everything we possessed, and that the currency reform devoured our last few reserves? Must we, on top of all this, now also die from starvation? Is this ridiculous "immediate help program" really meant to compensate us for the terrible blows of fate we have suffered?

> As a devout Christian I am beginning to doubt whether the many assurances given by Christians about a just equalization of burdens and the elimination of the grossest social discrepancies are really meant seriously and sincerely . . . I hope very much, Herr Federal Chancellor, that you will now intervene to bring the equalization of burdens to an acceptable conclusion . . . Should my son be compelled, against his will and mine, to become a soldier, all he would have to defend would be his own poverty and the poverty of his parents, and neither is worth defending . . .

This was but one among several hundreds of letters, addressed personally to Adenauer, which arrived day after day at the Palais Schaumburg. They came from all parts of the Federal Republic, from Schleswig-Holstein, Westphalia, and Bavaria, from the large cities and from unknown little villages, and their writers were men and women, old people and young, expellees, political refugees, sufferers from war damage of all kinds. But they all spoke the same language, and told the same story.

Obviously the Chancellor himself could not read all these innumerable letters, some of them many pages long, let alone answer them personally. All he could do was to pass them on to the Ministries and departments concerned. On one thing, however, he insisted: that every one of them should be read carefully and that none remained unanswered. Although it was not possible, in many cases, to help these petitioners immediately and in the manner they hoped or expected, he felt that they were at least entitled, without exception, to know what the position was. Thus, again and again, Finance Minister Dr. Fritz Schaeffer, answered:

> ". . . In reply to your letter forwarded to me by the Federal Chancellery, I am able to inform you that final settlement of all war damage claims will be effected within the framework of the proposed scheme for the equalization of war burdens. At present the draft equalization bill is still before the Federal Parliament for consideration and approval. The special parliamentary committee concerned with the equalization of war burdens has meantime concluded the third reading of the draft bill, and the accomplishment of this large and complicated task may now be expected in the near future. I wish to assure you that everything is being done to complete this legislative work as speedily as possible."

Such was the official information up to the beginning of April, 1952. To accept it patiently was not easy for a petitioner who had by then been waiting for a full seven years for the state to grant his claims for compensation and help him build a new existence from the wreckage of the war. And behind everyone who sat down to write a letter there stood a host of silent millions who wrote no letters but bore the same fate.

The magnitude of the problem can be demonstrated only with the help of figures. Before World War II there had lived in the territory of the present Federal Republic approximately 30,000,000 people. Now there were nearly 48,000,000. Into a space which amounted to 52.3 per cent of the former Reich territory, 71 per cent of the population of 1939 had been compressed. Among them were 8,000,000 people who had been expelled from the East German provinces annexed by Poland and the Soviet Union, the Sudeten area of Czechoslovakia, Hungary, Rumania and Yugoslavia, as well as nearly two million refugees from the Soviet Zone of occupation. To these must be added a monthly influx of between 30,000 and 35,000 refugees from the Soviet Zone who found life behind the iron curtain intolerable and fled to the West. All in all: 10,000,000 people! Every fifth inhabitant of the Federal Republic was a homeless and dispossessed "expellee," and more than one-third of the unemployed in the Federal territory were refugees.

On January 24, 1950, unemployment in the Federal Republic stood at 1,750,000; by February 19 it had risen to over 2,000,000. At the end of the year over-all employment had increased by more than 1,000,000, and yet the unemployment figure had not changed substantially. Industrial capacity and productivity were expanding rapidly, but they could not keep pace with the steady influx of people from Eastern Germany seeking work in the West. However fast the economy expanded it was impossible to absorb them all, and absorb them as fast as they arrived. There remained an army of millions of hungry and desperate people who represented an enormous potential danger to internal social peace and the security of the state.

"Don't you think, Mr. Federal Chancellor," François-Poncet asked at a Petersberg meeting in February, 1950, "that these refugees from the East are being deliberately driven out in order to create insoluble problems here in the West?"

Adenauer: "That was Stalin's idea even at Potsdam."

François-Poncet: "We are witnessing a process of de-Germanization which is obviously deliberate and intentional. The federal government is being compelled to increase continuously its expenditure in support of the refugees. I can see the moment approaching when you will have to close the frontiers."

Adenauer: "We cannot and must not close the frontiers against the German refugees."

Robertson: "We fully appreciate the position of the Federal Chancellor if he were compelled to close the frontiers now. On the other hand, we are firmly convinced that these expulsions represent a carefully planned maneuver on the part of the Soviets to throw the West German economy into disorder. I feel we should instruct the Federal Chancellor, after all, not to allow these people to come in."

Adenauer: "I must refuse to accept responsibility for such a move. In any case, this is only the execution of an agreement which was concluded between the Allies."

McCloy: "It will be remembered that, at the time, we instructed the federal government that they must accept all non-German refugees. In view of this we cannot now demand that they should turn back Germans at the frontiers of the Federal Republic."

François-Poncet: "Our original instruction dates back to a time when the extent of this stream of refugees could not be foreseen. One must always be permitted to change one's opinion. One must avoid resembling a pedant who goes on giving instructions to a child about to drown in a river. The High Commissioners are under the impression that the federal government is not dealing with the unemployment problem with the necessary urgency and dispatch."

Adenauer: "If despite all our endeavors the unemployment figures continue to rise, this is not because the number of employed is decreasing, but because of the steady new influx from the East."

McCloy: "Do you anticipate a gradual decrease in the stream of refugees from Poland?"

Adenauer: "Unfortunately, we Germans have no influence upon these developments."

Again and again, whenever opportunity offered, Adenauer made it clear: the refugee problem was created by the Allies; the Allies were at least partly responsible for its consequences and must assume their share in this responsibility; and a real solution was possible only if the whole free world helped as much as it could. At the same time, however, he made it equally clear: the world will help us only if we ourselves call upon all our resources and make a beginning with a determined effort of "self-help." The first step toward this must be to distribute the burdens, sacrifices and losses of the war and post-war period evenly over the whole population. There must be some restoration of balance between those who have lost all, or most of their possessions, and those fortunate enough to have lost very little or nothing at all.

This first step was what came to be called *Lastenausgleich*, or equalization of burdens.

The sum total of loss and damage caused to the German people by the war and post-war events was estimated at 213,000 million German marks (approximately $50,735,000,000). To distribute this burden even over the entire German people and raise this astronomical sum by means of taxes, rates and various levies, would have meant the total collapse of the entire German economy. Other ways and means must be found, and the best way seemed to be for those who had suffered loss or damage to call direct on those whose assets had remained intact and ask them to help to balance things up. The idea seemed simple and obvious enough. The difficulty was, how to carry it out. For in 1951 the total German national income amounted to approximately 90 billion marks, and this meant right from the start that the claims and expectations of those hoping for compensation must be drastically reduced. The question now was: where should these cuts begin and where should they end?

The government's draft bill provided for a levy of 50 per cent on all capital assets to be contributed to a joint equalization fund. It was clear, however, that an immediate full payment of this levy must result in economic and financial ruin for practically all of those required to contribute. CDU Deputy Johannes Kunz, one of the spiritual fathers of the bill, gave a drastic illustration of the likely consequences of such procedure. "Imagine a soldier who has lost both legs in the war returning home and demanding of his uninjured neighbor that he give him one of his legs. You would get precisely the same effect as with an immediate equalization of burdens—you would have two cripples instead of one."

The obvious thing to do was to pay off the debt on the installment plan. This again caused prolonged controversy. How large should the installments be, and over what period should they be spread? The representatives of the refugee organizations insisted that, in order to have any effect at all, payments must not be spread over more than five or ten years at the most. The representatives of property who were required to pay the levy were unwilling to consider anything under fifty years. The long and acrimonious argument ran straight across political party lines and split every single party in Parliament into two or more opposing camps. Eventually, after endless negotiation, thirty years was agreed as an acceptable compromise.

Adenauer rarely intervened in these controversies between the experts and various interested parties. But he kept a close watch on the development of the bill, and, although fully realizing the difficulties of drafting such a bill, he soon began to press for greater speed.

He had good reasons for urging the legislators to complete their work. The issue was not purely an economic one but was beginning to assume a political aspect as well. There was growing and vociferous unrest among the refugees, and there was a very real danger of many of them drifting into political extremism. Feeling that they could not rely on the government to help them in their plight, the refugees began to look to the radical parties of the extreme right, and even to the Communists, for support. The increasing radicalization of the refugees was becoming a serious political problem.

Moreover, as time went on, dissatisfaction was not confined to the refugees. As soon as the main provisions of the draft bill became known, trade and industry loudly voiced their anger with the government, and a new flood of letters of complaint poured onto the Chancellor's desk. "If private enterprise is driven into debt by this legislation," one of these letters said, "the day will come when it can no longer fulfill its function. You cannot slaughter a cow in order to eat it and yet go on milking it!"

Finally, there was a last but most important point. Unless the Parliament succeeded in passing the equalization bill before the end of the current period of legislation, there was a danger of millions of discontented and disaffected refugees deserting the government parties and voting for the Socialists in the next election. There were many signs even now of the Social Democratic party exploiting the slowness of the legislature over the equalization bill for their propaganda ends.

For all these reasons Adenauer kept pressing, pushing and urging the legislators to complete their work. In the end he achieved his aim. On May 15, 1952, the Equalization of War Burdens Bill was read for a third time and passed by the Parliament, and on August 14, 1952, it came into effect. It provided for a 5 per cent levy on all capital assets which had not suffered from the war, distributed over thirty years and payable with compound interest in quarterly installments.

What did this mean in practice?

Adenauer explained it when, during his American visit in the spring of 1953, he spoke to an audience of American politicians and industrialists. There had been many doubting voices in the American press, which had frequently criticized the attitude of the German people toward the refugees. Adenauer told them:

"Even before this new law was passed, in the period between 1945 and 1952, we raised by one means or another approximately 50 billion German marks for the support and rehabilitation of the refugees. Now, under the new law, some three billion marks will flow regularly into the equalization of burdens fund for the benefit of refugees and expellees. This amounts to a drastic and far-reaching redistribution of the national income of the German people in the course of which everyone who owns anything is forced to hand half his property over to those who have nothing at all."

## CHAPTER XXIV

THREE great enterprises designed to lead Germany back into the community of free nations had now been set in motion, and at the same time the foundations for the economic, political, and military integration of the new Europe had been laid. All three matured but slowly and were accompanied in their progress by many setbacks and disappointments.

Most rapid progress was made in the economic field. Early in March, 1951, Professor Hallstein, the leader of the German delegation, was able to inform the Chancellor from Paris that after nine months' labor the draft treaty for the establishment of the "European Coal and Steel Community" had at last been initialed by the delegates of the six member states.

More difficult was the second problem, namely, the achievement of full sovereignty for the Federal Republic. It was true that the Western Powers, under persistent pressure from Adenauer, had eventually agreed to a revision of the Occupation Statute, and the revised statute, promulgated by the three High Commissioners on March 6, 1951, marked a great step forward on the road to German national freedom. But it was equally true that it had been largely overtaken by events. It was not surprising, therefore, that a few weeks later Adenauer again approached the High Commissioners with proposals for a further revision of the Occupation Statute. This time, however, he aimed at a last and final revision: the Occupation Statute, he urged, should be replaced by a treaty to be freely negotiated between the Federal Republic and the three Western Powers. This project became known as the *Deutschland-Vertrag* or "German Contract."

Greatest of all, however—indeed, almost insuperable—seemed the difficulties standing in the way of the German Defense Contribution. Here, in respect of its military security, the Federal Republic was still farthest from its goal. True, again following Adenauer's urgent representations, the New York Conference of Foreign Ministers had declared in September, 1950, that the three Western Powers would "treat any attack against the Federal Republic or Berlin, from any quarter, as an attack upon themselves," and the Atlantic Council, in its final communiqué, had stated its intention that "Germany shall be enabled to make a contribution to the defense of Europe." But even the first steps taken toward this aim were a severe disappointment for the Germans. The plan submitted by the French Prime Minister René Pleven to the National Assembly on October 24, 1950, provided that the German contingents in a future European army would be subjected to special requirements and regulations, and these were generally felt in Germany to amount to outright discrimination.

Despite his annoyance over the French attitude, Adenauer did did not hesitate to accept the invitation to take part in the Pleven Plan Conference when it reached him at Bonn on January 26, 1951. Charging Professor Hallstein with representing the Federal Republic at this new conference, as well as in the Schuman Plan negotiations which proceeded concurrently in Paris, he instructed him nevertheless to state clearly: "Although the federal government does not approve the Pleven Plan, it is prepared to accept it as a basis for negotiation."

Adenauer had his special reasons for showing this immediate readiness, which earned him the angry displeasure of many an affronted old German soldier. The Soviet Union had at once answered the announcement of the Pleven Plan by suggesting a new four-power conference on Germany, and after prolonged preliminary negotiations it had been agreed to hold a preparatory meeting in Paris early in March, 1951, which was to prepare the ground for a conference of the four Foreign Ministers. There could be little doubt about the object of the Russian move: it aimed at loosening the ties between Germany and the Western World and pushing Germany back into the Potsdam vacuum. In view of this threatening danger, Adenauer felt that it would have been suicidal to refuse the French invitation, even though negotiations began under distinctly unfavorable auspices.

Adenauer took one further step. Once before, in an hour of national distress in December, 1948, when the Ruhr Statute was issued from London threatening the life of the entire German economy, he had turned to his old adversary Kurt Schumacher in an attempt to find common ground with him. He had traveled to Hanover, but Schumacher had refused even to see him. Despite this humiliating experience, deeply wounding to a man with so pronounced a sense of personal dignity, Adenauer now turned for a second time to the leader of the Social Democratic party. The chance of creating a front of national unity in this situation of suspense between the Pleven Plan and the Russian threat prompted him to forget what had gone before and to disregard all personal feelings. On February 10, 1951, he sent Schumacher a memorandum entitled "Reflections on the present situation" and explaining, under eight principal heads, the basic points of his foreign policy, on which he invited the opposition leader's comments. But in a long letter containing little more than a repetition of all the arguments currently used by the Socialists in their propaganda, Schumacher declined to discuss Adenauer's views.

Now no further purpose could be served by further discussion. Evidently the gap which had opened between the head of the Government and the leader of the Opposition was not to be bridged even in this hour of distress. Yet an astonishing fact remained, and deserves to be noted. Of all the Socialist parties throughout the Western World, the German Social Democratic party was the only one, in 1951, to reject outright a German defense contribution. Even the British Labor Party, despite grave misgivings and much resistance among its own ranks, finally gave it its blessing.

"We have agreed in principle to German rearmament. . . . It is so easy to get excited by a word on this, and it is so easy to pass resolutions without thinking out exactly what they mean. I have a lot sent to me from various people protesting against German rearmament. Yet if I asked those people if they were prepared to go and defend Germany while she did nothing, they would do nothing either. It is easy to protest against rearmament in the abstract without considering what is the real position in the world today. . . . It is useless to discuss the question of German rearmament in isolation. It must be discussed in the wider context. . . ."

These words were spoken on February 12, 1951, the day of Schumacher's negative reply, by Prime Minister Clement Attlee in the House of Commons. They might well have been Adenauer's.

The treaties establishing the "European Coal and Steel Community" were due to be signed in solemn ceremony in Paris on April 12,

September, 1949: on the entry into office of the first government of the Federal Republic of Germany, the Federal Chancellor accepts the congratulations of the Allied High Commissioners. *From the left:* John J. McCloy (United States), the Federal Chancellor, Sir Brian Robertson (Great Britain), André François-Poncet (France)

*Acme Photo*

The Federal Chancellor with Federal President Theodor Heuss (*right*)

*Wide World Photo*

French Foreign Minister Robert Schuman (*left*) greets the Federal Chancellor in Paris, November, 1951

*Wide World Photo*

Konrad Adenauer with his daughter Lotte and his youngest son, Georg, in his home at Rhöndorf

*Wide World Photo*

Konrad Adenauer with the late Kurt Schumacher (*left*), leader of the Social Democratic party (*International News Photo*)

The Federal Chancellor with Prime Minist Winston Churchill of Great Britain at N 10 Downing Street (*Wide World Photo*)

The entire Federal Parliament rises to its feet on September 27, 1951, as a sign of its sympathy for Jewish victims of Nazi wrongs (*Wide World Photo*)

A dedicated gardener

*Wide World*

1951, by the Foreign Ministers of the six contracting states. One of them was Konrad Adenauer, who a month before, on March 15, had officially assumed the duties and title of Federal Minister for Foreign Affairs. There had been criticism of this dual capacity, and the Federal Chancellor had been told that the new German Foreign Office was not the kind of department which could be administered as a side-show. Adenauer had replied that this was a provisional arrangement, meant to last only until the treaties establishing Germany's full sovereignty were signed. The provisional arrangement was destined to last for a full four years.

In the early morning of April 11 the special aircraft of the French High Commissioner took off from Wahn airport, near Cologne, to take Adenauer to Paris. François-Poncet accompanied him to the French capital.

The night before, in the Parliament, Schumacher had fired one more heavy broadside against the Chancellor's entire policy. The Pleven Plan, Schumacher had said, treated the Germans as "second-class human beings and first-class blood donors." Only the worst and most unreliable type of mercenary in Germany would voluntarily enlist in such a European Army, and these were precisely the types who would at once desert to the Russians. Regarding the Schuman Plan, the opposition leader said the Chancellor had failed to inform Parliament on the nature of its detailed provisions, nor had he troubled to obtain the provisional authority of Parliament for the signing of any treaty. If Adenauer now went to Paris, he was doing so as "a businessman without authority or power of attorney."

"You know," remarked Adenauer pensively to François-Poncet as the aircraft crossed the German frontier, "as long as twenty-five years ago I had this very same idea. An understanding between Germany and France will become possible only if the heavy industries of the two countries are merged. . . ."

And what had Schumacher said the day before? "The Schuman Plan is not only unfair to Germany; it is, moreover, an economic absurdity without the participation of Britain and Scandinavia. I warn you not to misuse the word 'European' in connection with a plan which embraces only this southwest corner of Europe which is the breeding ground of capitalism, clericalism, and cartels."

Indeed, it was but a small corner of Europe. During the flight Adenauer had occasionally glanced at his watch: seven minutes to cross to Luxembourg, twenty minutes to fly across Belgium, thirty minutes later Paris appeared below. It was a small space, but in it beat the heart of Europe.

"It is only when one sits in an airplane," the Chancellor remarked to François-Poncet, "that one becomes fully aware of how closely our countries belong together. . . ."

The reception at Orly airport was simple and unceremonious. Adenauer was the first member of a German government to visit Paris since the end of the war. Comment in the French press had been reserved but friendly, except for the Communists, who had been conducting a violent campaign against the visit. So as to lend no unnecessary weapon to their propaganda, Foreign Minister Schuman had refrained from meeting Adenauer personally at the airport, but had sent his *chef de cabinet* Bourbon-Busset and Jean Monnet to welcome him. Addressing them, Adenauer said:

"It is not without emotion that I step onto French soil, for this is the first official visit to a foreign country that I have undertaken as Federal Chancellor and Federal Minister of Foreign Affairs. There is a profound meaning in this. It is with deliberate intention that my first official visit abroad is to the French capital. In doing so I wish to demonstrate that I consider German-French relations the basic issue of any European solution."

The Chancellor and his staff were staying at the Hotel Crillon, in the heart of the city, with their windows looking out on the wide sweep of the Place de la Concorde and across the river Seine to the pillared façade of the French Chamber of Deputies. Little did Adenauer anticipate the succession of surprises waiting for him behind those imposing columns; there was nothing to tell him at this moment that during the next few years it would be here that his political fate would be at stake in a high gamble, putting his patience and staying power to an unparalleled test of endurance.

On this day, however—April 11, 1951—he was full of hope and confidence. The European Coal and Steel Community was safe. The Pleven Plan Conference was at work this very hour. And not far from it, at the Palais Rose, the Four Power Conference was in its fifth week, trying unsuccessfully to agree on an agenda. Adenauer had felt from the very start that it had no great chance of success, and he was not going to be surprised if it adjourned without result;

there would be no agreement at the expense of the Federal Republic.

The pearl gray April sky above Paris was brightening up when, before midday, the Chancellor paid his official courtesy call on the President of the Republic, Vincent Auriol. In front of the Elysée Palace, the Garde Républicaine in their shining cuirassier breast-plates saluted him with drawn swords as he arrived. A traditional ceremony, no more. Yet every trifle counted on the long road toward full international recognition, and it seemed no small thing that the German Federal Chancellor was greeted with the respectful decorum due the head of a sovereign state.

The following day work began in earnest at the Quai d'Orsay, the French Foreign Ministry, under Robert Schuman's chairmanship. Six Foreign Ministers had come together to put the finishing touches to the Schuman Plan Treaty, men whom Adenauer was frequently to meet again during the following months and years—Count Carlo Sforza from Italy, Dr. Kirk Stikker from the Netherlands, Paul van Zeeland from Belgium, and Joseph Bech from Luxembourg. Their experts had left them a number of tricky problems which had to be solved before the treaty could be finally signed.

Decisions had still to be taken about the seat, composition, number of members, and powers of the High Authority for Coal and Steel; on the Council of Ministers and the common assembly; the number of votes allowed each country; the method of voting; the language in which the work of the common institutions would be performed; and the powers of the chairman of the High Authority. It was a sizeable agenda, and they hoped to dispose of it before the end of the week. One question, which for Adenauer was by far the trickiest and most delicate, did not figure on the agenda, yet it would be impossible for him to face the Federal Parliament without a reasonably satisfactory answer to it. This problem was the Saar.

True, as soon as the High Authority had become a fact, many of the economic issues arising from the present status of the Saar would disappear automatically. There remained the political issues, especially the question whether the economic inclusion of the Saar Territory in the Coal and Steel Community would prejudice its eventual and final international status. This question fell outside the scope of the conference, and Adenauer had to clarify it with Schuman direct.

As they had done eighteen months ago when the French Foreign Minister had visited the Federal capital, the two men withdrew after the official conference, and over a private and informal dinner had a heart-to-heart talk. As they had done at Bonn, they talked German together, which Schuman spoke faultlessly and without accent. Now, as before, they discussed the eternal bone of contention which again and again poisoned Franco-German relations.

"France," Schuman assured his guest, "will safeguard the interests of the Saar Territory in the European community in the same way as those of Monaco."

"That is not sufficient," answered Adenauer.

The Social Democratic opposition at home asserted in their propaganda against the Schuman Plan that the signing of the treaty would amount to nothing less than tacit recognition of the final detachment of the Saar and its national independence. What Adenauer needed was an unequivocal statement from the French that this was definitely not so. Schuman appreciated this, but how was it to be done? A way had to be found which was acceptable to both French and German parliaments. Adenauer was not the only one to have to contend with a parliamentary opposition.

There was not much free time left between conference sittings and political discussions, but what there was Adenauer used to "have a good look at Paris," strolling alone down the great boulevards, mingling freely with the crowd, and looking with much interest at the shop windows. The French "security man" detailed to accompany the Chancellor on his walks and responsible for his personal protection complained with a sigh that he was "turning gray with worry" because "*Monsieur le Chancelier*" refused to listen to his advice and "simply walked off on his own." Before long, the tall gentleman in the black overcoat and gray woolen scarf, carrying a rolled umbrella, became a popular and familiar figure. People recognized him and stopped wherever he showed himself, and soon he was surrounded by reporters and press photographers. He made no attempt to evade them; on the contrary, they found him always willing to have his picture taken or to answer their questions. His friendliness toward the press and general "approachability" soon became known and contributed much to his popularity. This was clearly felt when he was the guest of the Foreign Press Association of Paris at a luncheon given in his honor on April 13.

His speech on this important occasion had been well prepared beforehand, and when he arrived at the luncheon he noticed that his hosts had had the courteous foresight to distribute a French translation of his German address among the guests. When the moment came for him to speak, Adenauer rose and took up his prepared script. But having read out the first few lines, he suddenly put it down again, and after a moment's hesitation said:

"Well, ladies and gentlemen, you all know my speech anyway, since you have copies of it before you, and therefore I might as well say something else. . . ."

Before his audience had recovered from their baffled laughter, he continued:

"You will understand that this visit to Paris fills me with emotion. Even a sober and realistic man like myself, who has come to know the disappointments of public life, cannot but feel hopeful for the fate of our old continent when he considers the prospects and vistas now opening up before us. In this ancient city of Paris which has so often been the scene of far-reaching decisions, there now begins within the sight of us all a new chapter in the history of Europe.

"Let me emphasize here that I do not set much store by the fleeting transitoriness of high-flown enthusiasm engendered by big words and fine phrases. Rather do I believe that the skepticism shown nowadays by almost all European nations after the bitter lessons of the past is almost a vital necessity if we are to get away from mere empty rhetoric and down to the practical realization of the projects on which we have set our hearts. . . .

"Henceforth war between France and Germany is not only unthinkable but materially impossible. The conclusion of the treaty for the European Coal and Steel Community marks above all, solemnly and irrevocably, the closing of a past in which these two peoples, animated by suspicion, jealousy, and selfishness, found themselves again and again facing each other with arms in their hands. . . .

"I believe," Adenauer said, "that the solution now found could and should do far more than reconcile France and Germany. All Europe, indeed, the whole world, should benefit from it. For it is not the purpose of our joint enterprise to shut Europe off from the rest of the world and thus transfer selfishness, as it were, from the national to the continental plane.

"The common economic sphere which is now forming and the possibilities of mutual exchange in all fields which it offers will preserve the young generation from falling prey to false prophets. People whose thoughts and feelings are still at present largely governed by suspicion, envy of their competitors, and other resentments will become neighbors and friends. In our mind's eye we can visualize even today, as a not too distant goal, the union of the European peoples who love liberty and justice in one house which they jointly own and whose old and time-honored name is Europe. This truly new Europe, this common parental home of all Europeans, will henceforth be the strong room in which Christian Occidental tradition is safely kept and preserved, a well of spiritual strength, and a place for peaceful work. It will defend itself against anyone threatening its peace and its liberty, but it will be the enemy of no one. . . ."

A moment of tense silence followed by a sudden burst of enthusiastic applause told Adenauer that he had struck the right chord. His words had come from his heart, and that was how they had been understood. Later that afternoon when he returned to the Hotel Crillon he found a letter waiting for him. It seemed unusually heavy, and when he opened the envelope a weighty object fell out—a French *Croix de Guerre* from World War I. It was accompanied by a letter in French, seven pages long and signed "Simone Patouilles, student in Paris." the letter said:

*Monsieur le Chancelier,*

I have the great honor to write to you as a Frenchwoman from Paris who, in common with many others in our old city, has been immensely happy to welcome Your Excellency in our ancient capital. To me your visit is the symbol of a first true and real step on the road to peace and salvation, not only for Germany, your fatherland, but also for France and for all nations who are conscious of the joint heritage we have a solemn duty to defend. . . .

My father died of the consequences of the 1914-1918 war which he fought from the first day to the last. . . . I ask you, *Monsieur le Chancelier,* to accept this *Croix de Guerre* of a French soldier which belonged to my father and which I enclose in this letter, and to keep it as a modest token of remembrance of your important and significant visit to Paris in April, 1951. It is a humble gesture of hope for a true and genuine reconciliation between our two peoples who have suffered so much at one another's hands. . . .

Adenauer had not much time to spare in those few days for private and personal matters. But he replied immediately:

Dear Miss Patouilles,

It is with profound emotion that I have received your letter and the *Croix de Guerre* of your late father. I should like to feel that your gift is a token and symbol heralding the genuine friendship above all of the young generation of our two peoples. Please accept my heartfelt thanks for it.

Yours,

KONRAD ADENAUER

A few days later Adenauer asked Simone Patouilles to come and see him for a personal talk, and upon his return to Bonn arranged for the French student to be granted a scholarship for one year at the University of Munich.

The conference made slower progress than had been expected. More and more amendments and modifications had to be incorporated in the text of the draft treaty. At long last, on April 17, all outstanding issues seemed settled—except one. The Foreign Ministers still had to agree on the seat of the High Authority. Van Zeeland suggested Liege; Stikker, The Hague; Sforza, Turin; and Bech, Luxembourg. Foreign Minister Schuman surprised the conference with yet another suggestion: Saarbrücken! The Saar Territory, he proposed, should be given a "political statute," to be adopted with the concurrence of the Saar population, and until that time Strasbourg might become the provisional seat of the High Authority.

This proposal found Adenauer totally unprepared. He knew that, if it was accepted, the European Coal and Steel Community had no earthly chance of being approved by the Federal Parliament. It was a most awkward and unpleasant moment for him. He replied at once by putting a number of precise questions. What, in any case, was the present national status of the Saar Territory? How was the agreement of the Saar population to be obtained? Would there be a plebiscite? If so, was there going to be full freedom of political opinion and association? Would the pro-German parties be allowed to take part? And what was the "political statute" for the Saar Territory to look like?

Foreign Minister Schuman decided to adjourn the meeting. It was midday. Until one o'clock the language question was discussed once more in plenary session. After lunch the Foreign Ministers alone resumed their deliberations while the staffs waited in the various anterooms. Hour after hour passed, and they were still waiting. Toward midnight exhaustion and fatigue were general. But there was still no result. Occasionally a Minister emerged from the conference to report on the state of negotiations. No agreement had yet been reached. . . .

At four o'clock in the morning Adenauer left the conference to return to his hotel. As he emerged he said to Hallstein and Blankenhorn, his lieutenants, who were waiting outside, "This has been the most hideous meeting I have ever attended. . . ."

An hour later, at five o'clock, agreement was reached. Luxembourg was chosen as the provisional seat of the High Authority.

And the Saar?

When the six Foreign Ministers met again, on the afternoon of April 18, at the Salon de l'Horloge of the Quai d'Orsay for the solemn signing of the treaty, this problem too had been solved. Following Adenauer's suggestion, official letters were exchanged between the two governments and published simultaneously with the text of the treaty. In his letter addressed to Schuman Adenauer repeated his declaration which he had made before, that "the final settlement of the Saar status can only be effected by the peace treaty or an equivalent treaty, and that the signature by the federal government of the Schuman Treaty does not imply recognition of the present position in the Saar." In conclusion the letter requested Schuman to confirm in writing that the French government was in agreement with this view. Schuman's letter in reply contained the desired information.

In a second letter Schuman informed the Chancellor that in the view of the French government "the powers and functions at present vested in the International Ruhr Authority must progressively become invalid as they are being taken over by the High Authority of the European Coal and Steel community." The French government intended, the letter said, to take the necessary diplomatic steps to secure the agreement both of the powers signatory of the London agreement and of the other occupying powers to the requisite revision of the Ruhr Statute. Thus, to all intents and purposes, sentence of death had been pronounced on the Ruhr Authority.

The Foreign Ministers had to place their signatures to the Schuman Treaty on blank sheets of paper. There had been so many amendments and modifications of the treaty text that the French state printing office had been unable to catch up, and the printed treaty was not ready in time. Only the last sheet with the closing paragraph of the treaty was available, and this was signed in alphabetical order. Germany—Allemagne—headed the list, and Adenauer signed first.

In the eyes of the world Adenauer had won a great and resounding political success, and as such the signing of the Schuman Treaty was acclaimed. But the Chancellor knew that his struggle was still far from over. True, there had been one piece of good news from Bonn. The Free Democratic party, which had been very critical of the Schuman Plan, mainly on account of its implications for the Saar, had made it known that it unreservedly approved of the treaty in its final version. With that, ratification of the treaty by the Parliament was secure. But in this particular instance, when it was a question of the unification of Europe, Adenauer was hoping for more than just an ordinary, adequate parliamentary majority. The Paris negotiations, he felt, had gone far toward disposing of Schumacher's objections and reservations. Might it not be possible, after all, he reflected, to create a united front in Germany and range all major parties, including the Social Democrats, behind the European idea?

On July 12, 1951, the Federal Chancellor submitted the bill ratifying the Schuman Treaty to Parliament for a first reading. Once more he enumerated in detail all the reasons in favor of ratification. But Schumacher refrained from taking part in the debate. In his place Carlo Schmid spoke for the Socialist party, and he rejected the Schuman Plan "in its present form."

This conditional refusal nevertheless left the door ajar. There seemed a chance of the Socialist party being prepared, in certain circumstances, not to insist on its rigidly negative attitude. It was just a chance, to put it no higher, but Adenauer was determined not to ignore even the slightest possibility, however remote, of obtaining all-party unity over the European issue. Eventually, on December

17, 1951, he had a lengthy private talk with Schumacher. The general tone and atmosphere were unusually friendly, but at the end Schumacher announced that the attitude of his party was "in every respect unchanged."

The great three-day debate, in which the second and third readings of the Schuman Plan were taken in one continuous run up to the final vote, finally opened on January 9, 1952. It maintained, as one foreign correspondent found, "the best standard of parliamentary dignity," and to many German observers it presented one of the most moving chapters in the life of the young German Parliament. Certainly, the purely human element played a large part in it. Again and again the seventy-six-year-old Chancellor intervened, pleading, exhorting, begging, and warning, in a last passionate attempt to win his opponents for the great political concept of the Schuman Plan.

"Everything great bears within it a hazard, and the creation of a new Europe is not a venture free from risk," he said. "But if the step is not taken, if the Coal and Steel Community is not constituted, there will be, as far as can be foreseen, no hope left to Europe and no hope for a lasting economic and political recovery. If the present attempts were to fail, it could not be seriously presumed that the governments of Europe would get together again in due course to try again. The disappointment over the failure would paralyze all such attempts. The youth of the European nations would lose all hope for a better future. America, which regards the Schuman Plan as the touchstone of Europe's ability to overcome its internal quarrels, would turn away in deep disappointment. The international situation, which at present, despite its serious aspects, gives room for hope, would radically deteriorate.

"A beginning must be made here and now. Our peoples, Europe, and the world await it. All confidence not only in us but in Europe depends on this beginning. The decision which you therefore have to make is in truth a decision for or against Europe. The federal government begs of you all, irrespective of party, to do as the representative assemblies of France and the Netherlands have already done, and to decide in favor of Europe. It depends on your 'yea' whether European unity becomes a reality. I beg of you, ladies and gentlemen, to let your decision be worthy of the hour!"

In the late night hours of January 11, 1952, during the third reading and shortly before the final vote, Adenauer intervened once more in the debate. The deputy leader of the Social Democratic party, Erich Ollenhauer, had just ended a long speech with the words, "We say no!" Now the Chancellor made one last attempt.

"I regret that Herr Ollenhauer should have spoken as he did," Adenauer said. "What is the use of a Platonic declaration of love for Europe and the community of nations if one fails to use the opportunity to show that one genuinely wants Europe, and is a sincere friend of the community of nations, and instead goes on to say things which are bound to offend the other nations and governments with whom, after all, we have to work? Let me say one thing in this connection. I have the impression, generally speaking, that members opposite are not in the least aware of what the outside world really and truly looks like. Is it possible that human memory should be so short? Have people here in Germany completely forgotten that this war was unleashed by German National Socialists, and that they brought about the immense misery and agony from which the world still suffers today? And if one has such a past as we have, and other nations —let us make no mistake about that!—are filled with deep suspicions toward the German people, can one, I ask, proclaim from the rostrum of the German Federal Parliament that it is for others to give first proof of their European attitude, and declare that not until we have such proof shall we ratify this treaty?

"Ladies and gentlemen, believe me, I am not saying this in order to hurt your feelings. I speak from deep and genuine anxiety. People outside will be bound to say: isn't this just another example of that peculiar German attitude which always looks for guilt and responsibility in others, which always demands and is never willing to give? Ah, ladies and gentlemen, we are living in confused times. I could paint you all sorts of very odd and strange pictures. In all the other countries of the Schuman Plan the Socialist parties and the trade unions are voting in favor of it, but with us the Social Democrats are against it and the trade unions are for it! Has there ever been a like confusion of minds? In the face of this, one can only shake one's head in wonderment. . . .

"The Social Democratic opposition, more than anyone else, should by rights say 'Yes' from a glad heart. Even if you feel doubts and reservations about this article or that in the treaty—good God, don't I feel them too? But there comes a moment when, for a change, one must be able to forget and take a new road. I envy the Anglo-Saxon nations for the way in which, in Britain and the United States, Government and Opposition work together on the great issues of foreign affairs. This is truly the test of a mature democracy which takes the view that on national issues party interest must take second place after the interests of the community as a whole. . . ."

Once more, in a last appeal, Adenauer pointed out that, for the first time since the war, the Schuman Plan would lead Germany out of its isolation among the nations of the world:

"First we were the dreaded enemies; then we were the objects of occupation; and tomorrow we shall be the partner of the others. Two and a half years ago, when we first met in this house, no one would have thought in his wildest dreams that such a thing was even remotely possible. Believe me, after this war which has raged across the world, in this atmosphere which the aftermath of the war has created in the world, there is only one way of making progress in politics, and that is step by step, slowly, with unflagging patience. It is really so—I have convinced myself of this. Material issues and points of view play, of course, a large part in foreign affairs, but a much larger part still is played by the psychological climate; a much more important part is played by the conviction, to speak in concrete terms, that the German people are a peaceful people, a people who want a community of nations and are anxious to live in peace, friendship, and freedom with all other free peoples of the world.

"And now, gentlemen of the Social Democratic party, since the chapter we have discussed during these last few days is now being closed, I address to you once more as the German Federal Chancellor and as a fellow German the earnest and most heartfelt plea: let us try to walk this road together in a joint effort to raise Germany to its full stature, and do not, I beg you, expose yourselves to the danger—for I'm fully aware that the Social Democratic party includes many valuable people——"

Interruption from Socialist Deputy Arndt: "It is not for you to pass judgment on that!"

Adenauer: "Believe me, Herr Arndt, I wasn't referring to you! This interruption, although it came from a single individual, is really most characteristic. I am in utter seriousness when I say that the Social Democratic party contains valuable forces whom we need for the reconstruction of the German nation. Therefore, I beg of you: reconsider the entire situation once more in this light. We on our part shall do our best to get on with things. But I feel that you, on your part, could with advantage do the same, in your own interest, so that it shall not be said in later years: everything that was achieved for Germany during these historic years, and everything still to be achieved in 1952, had to be won in a struggle against a great party at home!"

The appeal remained in vain. The Schuman Plan was approved by the Parliament on January 11, 1952, against the votes of the Social Democrats, Communists, and a few Independents. The Government emerged from the division with a majority of eighty-nine.

The entire democratic world welcomed the decision. Hundreds of telegrams congratulating Adenauer poured into Bonn during the week end. "Europe is born, long live Europe!" cabled Jean Monnet. "A triumph for Adenauer," declared Robert Schuman. But for Adenauer himself there remained a taste of bitterness in the cup of joy: a large part of his people stood aside from this decision for Europe, and was to remain standing aside.

# CHAPTER XXV

On Thursday, March 27, 1952, toward five o'clock in the afternoon, two schoolboys walking along Bayerstrasse in Munich were approached by a stranger who handed them a medium-sized parcel and a tip of three marks, asking them to post the parcel for him at the post office in the nearby railway station. The man, who was about thirty years old and of somewhat neglected outward appearance, then disappeared in the crowd. The parcel was addressed to "Dr. Konrad Adenauer, Federal Chancellery, Bonn," and the sender was given as "Dr. Berghof, Frankfurt on Main."

The two schoolboys were Werner Breitschopp, aged twelve, and Bruno Beyersdorf, aged thirteen. Feeling that there was something wrong with the parcel, they walked across to the streetcar stop at Stachus and asked the official in charge what they should do with it. Stationmaster Beck was suspicious and informed the traffic policeman, who in turn called a police car. This took the schoolboys and their parcel to police headquarters in Ettstrasse.

Here police vice-president Weitman sent for Karl Reichert, a forty-five-year-old explosives expert of the Munich fire department, who took the suspicious parcel down to the air-raid shelter of the building where, in the presence of three policemen, he investigated it carefully. When it was clear that the string with which the parcel was tied up was not connected, as had been assumed, with a detonator inside, Reichert cautiously tore the wrapping off the four corners of the parcel. What emerged was a stiff blue cardboard case containing a book. Reichert now untied the string and took the case from its wrapping. The spine of the book showed that it was Volume L-Z of the *Little Brockhaus*, a well-known German encyclopedia.

One of the policemen said, "I'm sure there's something wrong with this. Why should anyone want to send Adenauer a single volume of a dictionary?" Reichert bent over the cardboard case and carefully pulled the volume from it. At that moment there was a loud detonation, the cellar was lit by a sheet of yellow flame, and an enormous blast threw everything into confusion. An ambulance took Reichert to the hospital. The infernal machine had torn off both his hands and inflicted grave injuries on his face, arms, and legs. He died four hours later.

Telegrams poured into Bonn from all parts of the world, from among others Churchill, Eden, de Gasperi, and the three High Commissioners, congratulating Adenauer upon his miraculous escape from an attempt on his life. Adenauer invited the two Munich schoolboys to visit him at Bonn. They arrived with their mothers on the following Tuesday, and in the Green Drawing Room of the Palais Schaumburg Adenauer treated them to cocoa and apricot tart and made them tell him their adventure with the fateful parcel. Then he pulled a gold wrist watch from each of his trouser pockets and presented them to his young rescuers. "If you like," he said, "I'll have them engraved for you. In that case leave them here with me, and I'll send them on to you." The two boys agreed, but after they had left one of them said, "God knows if we'll ever get them back again." They did get them back, suitably engraved with their names and the words: "As a souvenir, Bonn, 1.4.52. Adenauer." Later Bruno Beyersdorf said, "This Herr Dr. Adenauer was very nice to us, like a father. What I liked best about him was that he wasn't at all haughty or stuck up. With him you can talk just as you always do."

The police offered a reward of 15,000 marks and searched all over the Federal Republic for the "man with the parcel." Hundreds of suspects were arrested, interrogated, and released again. The unknown man was not among them.

But on Monday, March 31, 1952, several French newspapers received carbon copies of a typewritten letter in faulty French, posted in Geneva on March 29. This letter, whose authors described themselves as "Organization of Jewish Partisans," said:

"On March 27 our comrades carried out their first mission on German territory. A book filled with explosives was sent to Dr. Konrad Adenauer, the Chancellor of the nation of assassins. Owing to an accident, this bomb exploded in the hands of Herr Adenauer's policeman, who opened the book. We are at war with the nation of murderers, a war until the end of time. . . .

"The German people," the letter continued, "who have murdered six million Jews in cold blood, now wish to obtain forgiveness from our people on the deceptive pretense of restoring to us part of the property they've stolen from us. They are trying to deceive our people and the entire world by conducting negotiations with 'representatives of the Jewish people,' thinking that in this way they are showing repentance and are worthy of our trust.

"The Germans should know that there is no excuse for their crimes, and that there never will be. There is not enough money in the world to make us forget their crimes. No act of reparation or restoration can ever cleanse them of their sins. The Jewish people will never permit the return of Germany to the family of nations. . . ."

This wildly threatening anonymous letter was brought to the knowledge of the Federal Chancellor. He made no comment upon it. Undersecretary of State Dr. Lenz said that even if the letter did in fact come from an organization of Jewish terrorists—and there was no indication whatsoever that it did—such circles had nothing to do with the Jewish people and must not be identified with them. And a spokesman of the World Jewish Congress in London declared that an organization such as that mentioned in the Geneva letter did not exist.

When about two years later the present biographer visited the Chancellor at his house in Rhöndorf, Dr. Adenauer showed him a book. It was a precious edition of the Old Testament, showing on its silver binding the embossed symbols of the twelve Jewish tribes. "This book," the Chancellor remarked with an inscrutable smile, "reminds me of a political event to which I like to think back. It was one of the rare occasions when the translation of a Christian idea into terms of practical reality was achieved without distortion."

It was clear what he meant. He was referring to a document called, "Paper No. 4141 of the Federal German Parliament." Its full official designation was "Law for the ratification of the Agreement concluded on September 10, 1952, between the Federal Republic of Germany and the State of Israel."

The story of "Paper No. 4141" is told at first hand by Dr. Nahum Goldmann, President of the World Jewish Congress. The following contains his own account.

"The preliminaries," said Dr. Goldmann, "were not exactly promising. The story began on March 12, 1951, when the government of Israel transmitted through its ambassadors identical notes to the three Western Powers and the Soviet Union. . . ."

This note was a lengthy document, divided into ten main points and containing a horrible balance-sheet of the sufferings endured by the Jews in Hitler's Germany. Three out of every four European Jews had been murdered in Germany and German-occupied territories. The loss of Jewish property through confiscation, robbery, and the destruction perpetrated during the so-called "crystal night" in November, 1938, amounted to six billion dollars. Although it was impossible, the note declared, to atone for crimes of such dimensions through material reparations, the Allied powers were nevertheless requested to prevail upon the Federal Republic to lend some assistance to the State of Israel in its hard and difficult task of development. Ever since 1933, the note pointed out in support of this request, Palestine had been compelled to receive an unending stream of hundreds of thousands of homeless and destitute Jewish refugees from Germany and the German-occupied countries of Central Europe, who had been a tremendous and unbearable charge upon the young Jewish state, which was desperately struggling to maintain its existence. A large proportion of these people hunted and expelled by Hitler were old, sick, or infirm and, owing to the privations they had endured, no longer able to work; they could not help in building up the new country but must nevertheless be supported and were, through no fault of their own, still living in the most miserable conditions.

"The Jewish people have borne all this bravely," the note declared. "It is therefore in no way unreasonable for us to ask the German people, in view of the hardships of this situation, to give the surviving Jews what they need in order to restore them to normal conditions of life. We believe, seeing that we have suffered most from the Nazi regime, that we are well entitled to make such a request, legally as well as morally. It is our view that unless these conditions are accepted, Germany cannot be rehabilitated. . . ."

The tone of this note was decidedly sharp.

"It expressed all the implacable and deeply felt anger of the Jews over what had been done to them in Hitler Germany," Nahum Goldmann remarked. "It was because of this deeply felt and very understandable resentment that no attempt was made at first to establish direct contact with the Federal Republic and that the request was addressed to the Allied occupying powers. The note had a mixed and not altogether favorable reception with the three Western Powers. Although the moral justification for the Jewish complaint was recognized, it seemed to rest on somewhat doubtful foundations in international law."

At this juncture the Federal Chancellor took a hand. Although the note of the Israeli government had not been addressed to him, Adenauer had been informed of it through the German diplomatic representatives in Paris, London, and Washington. It would have been perfectly possible for him to ignore it, but he decided to take cognizance of it and instructed his personal assistant, Dr. Blankenhorn, who happened to be in London at that time, to establish contact with Jewish circles there. The satisfaction of private claims for restitution lodged by individual German Jews had always been, in Adenauer's view, a matter of course. Now Dr. Blankenhorn was to find out how, beyond this, in the opinion of responsible Jewish circles, a larger and more comprehensive restitution or compensation on a national basis could be put into effect.

Blankenhorn discussed the matter in London with representatives of the World Jewish Congress, notably with Dr. Barou. The Jewish proposal was this: before official negotiations with the Federal Republic could be entered upon, the Chancellor should make a declaration before Parliament which would make it clear that Germany assumed responsibility for what had been done to the Jewish people by the Nazi regime. This declaration should contain, furthermore, a definite promise that the material damage caused would be repaired, as well as an undertaking that representatives of the Jewish people and of the State of Israel would be officially invited to formal discussions of the matter. Dr. Blankenhorn transmitted these proposals to Bonn, and the Chancellor accepted them.

However, promising as it seemed, this was but a first step. The very next move already endangered the mutual trust just won. When the Chancellor went to Paris, in April, 1951, he took the opportunity of negotiating personally with Mr. Maurice Fischer, the Israeli ambassador to France, and Dr. Horowitz, secretary general of the Israeli Ministry of Finance. He received both gentlemen privately and unofficially in his apartment at the Hotel Crillon, fully prepared to hear their case and to meet them as far as possible. Maurice Fischer and Dr. Horowitz, however, seemed to misjudge the psychological situation, while placing a very one-sided interpretation on the legal aspect of the issue. Starting from an unqualified assumption that the Jewish demands represented a legally valid claim of the State of Israel against the Federal Republic, they used the occasion for reproaching Adenauer once again with a long list of misdeeds perpetrated by the Hitler regime.

The Chancellor listened calmly to both and promised to consider the whole complex issue carefully. But the fact remained that the interview, in which Dr. Blankenhorn had taken part as a silent witness, had been distinctly painful and embarrassing. All the same, Adenauer was fair enough to concede that in view of the past one must have understanding for this particular Jewish attitude.

"It says much for the Chancellor's strength of character," Nahum Goldmann commented, "that he did not allow this episode to influence him. At any rate, his next step showed that he himself, and the German Federal Parliament, were genuinely willing and anxious to rise above unworthy political resentment. This was made clear to the whole world by the inspiring session of the Federal Parliament on September 27, 1951."

Dr. Hermann Ehlers, President of the Federal Parliament: "Ladies and gentlemen! I herewith open the one hundred and sixty-fifth sitting of the Federal Parliament. Item Number One on our agenda today reads: Submission of a statement by the federal government. I call upon the Federal Chancellor to speak."

Federal Chancellor Dr. Adenauer: "I have the honor to submit to the House on behalf of the federal government the following statement:

"In recent times public opinion abroad has on various occasions given attention to the attitude displayed by the Federal Republic toward the Jews. Here and there doubts have been raised as to whether in this important matter our new state is guided by principles which take into account the terrible crimes of a past epoch and is capable of placing the relationship of the Jews to the German people on a new and sound basis. . . ."

The attitude of the Federal Republic, Adenauer continued, was clearly laid down by the Basic Law, Article III of which declared that all human beings were equal in the eyes of the law, and no one must suffer disadvantage or enjoy preference on account of his sex, his extraction, his race, his language, his homeland and origin, or his religious or political beliefs. It was in this spirit that the federal government had put its signature to the Human Rights Convention drafted by the Council of Europe.

"But these rules and maxims of law cannot become effective unless the ethical attitude from which they spring becomes the common property of, and is shared by, the entire people. We are therefore faced with a problem of education. . . . The federal government will see to it that the spirit of human and religious tolerance is not only formally acknowledged by the entire German people, and especially among Germany's youth, but that it is also translated into reality in their innermost attitude and through practical deeds. . . . In order to insure that this educational task is not hindered or disturbed, the federal government has resolved to combat those circles who continue to engage in anti-Semitic incitement with rigorous and unforgiving prosecution and punishment!"

Many who had listened to Adenauer up to this point may have asked themselves what the Chancellor was driving at with this statement. But Adenauer knew why he was proceeding in this fashion. He had always liked to feel himself as a fatherly teacher and educator, not only toward his own children but toward the entire German people. It was a difficult and not always a gratifying task, and it frequently earned him the reproach of being a "schoolmaster and moralizing sermonizer." But he felt clearly that Germany could take this great step of reconciliation abroad only if she also demonstrated her change of heart toward the Third Reich plainly and convincingly at home. He continued:

"The federal government, and with it the great majority of the German people, are conscious of the immeasurable suffering brought upon the Jews in Germany and the occupied territories during the National Socialist period. The great majority of the German people have abhorred these crimes perpetrated against the Jews and have taken no part in them. There were many among the German people during the time of National Socialism who, at great risk to themselves, from religious motives, compelled by their consciences, and from a sense of shame at the defilement of the German name, have come to the aid of their Jewish fellow citizens.

"Nevertheless, the fact remains that unspeakable crimes were committed in the name of the German people which call for moral and material restitution, and this obligation concerns cases of loss and damage suffered by individual Jews as well as cases of Jewish property for which individual claimants no longer exist today. In this sphere the first steps have been taken.

"But a great deal still remains to be done. The federal government will see to an early completion of restitutory legislation, and its just and fair application and execution. Part of such Jewish property as can be identified has been restored; further restitutions will follow. Regarding the total amount of restitution and compensation involved, which in view of the immense destruction of Jewish assets through National Socialism is a very considerable problem, the limits which have been set to German capacity by the bitter necessity of our having to support great numbers of war victims and refugees must be taken into account.

"The federal government is ready to work out in conjunction with representatives of Jewry and the State of Israel which has given shelter and refuge to so many homeless Jewish refugees a solution of the problem of material restitution and compensation, and thus to clear the way toward a spiritual healing of this immense suffering. The federal government is convinced that the spirit of true humanity must again become a living and fruitful force, and it regards it as the foremost duty of the German people to serve this spirit with all its strength."

The House willingly echoed the note Adenauer had struck. Members felt that if this was a "moralizing sermon," it was for once most appropriate. There were no objections, no interruptions, not even from the Communists and the groups of the extreme right who refrained from joining in the general applause. There was no debate, but merely a series of brief declarations of approval from the various parties.

First to speak, for the Social Democrats, was old Paul Loebe, senior president of the Federal Parliament and "Father of the House," who as far back as 1919 had been Vice-President of the Weimar National Assembly and, for twelve years afterward, from 1920 until 1932, President of the German Reichstag. This son of a carpenter and himself a former typesetter, almost of the same age as Adenauer, reminded the House of the great contribution German Jewry had made to the intellectual, social, and economic life of Germany and Europe as a whole. Recalling Felix Mendelssohn-Bartholdy, Heinrich Heine, and Walther Rathenau, and the many German Nobel Prize winners of Jewish extraction, he said:

"We feel indissoluble ties especially with those Jews who, like ourselves, were born as Germans, and we can neither forget nor ignore their contribution to our common history. Every German is therefore called upon to repair the injustices wrought upon the Jews in our midst, to combat the pestilence of racial hatred and overcome it through humble respect for our fellow humans. The terrible enormity of the injustice which the Federal Chancellor has pointed out demands sacrifices of us. More than ever before must we prove by active deeds that this restitution is the standard by which the renewal of law and justice in Germany must be measured. It is in this frame of mind that we are endeavoring to make peace with Israel."

The Father of the House was followed by the spokesmen of the other parties, with the exception of the Communists and the right-wing extremists, who apparently had nothing to contribute on this subject. The shortest speech was that of the spokesman of the Bavarian party, who uttered exactly one sentence: "The standpoint of my party is this—whoever is pledged in loyalty to the constitutional state upholding law and justice must approve, welcome, and support the statement of the Federal Chancellor." Things could hardly have been expressed with greater brevity. President Dr. Ehlers proposed that, "as a sign that they are united in their sympathy for the victims and in their willingness to accept and make amends for the consequences of past happenings," members should rise from their seats. The House rose and observed one minute of silence.

This was more than a political gesture. It was a moral demonstration of good will, and as such Adenauer's declaration was understood and appreciated throughout the world.

"What happened on that day in the German Federal Parliament," Nahum Goldmann recalled, "was a novel departure in political history. In contrast with customary political practice, which always seeks to justify its own point of view and to make moral demands only on its opponent, the German people in this instance, through their authorized representatives, freely and of their own accord acknowledged their guilt of past events and assumed responsibility for them.

"This suddenly opened an entirely new dimension in politics.

"It must be said, however," Dr. Goldmann continued, "that at first this declaration of the Federal Parliament failed to produce any tangible results. For us Jews who were willing to grasp Germany's outstretched hand of conciliation, this was a severe disappointment. It was therefore altogether understandable and pardonable if increasing irritation and nervousness on the part of Israel eventually found vent in a new note, again addressed to the Allied powers.

"In its general tenor this note of November 30, 1951, was very different from its predecessor. Although it once more denounced the crimes committed by the Nazis against European Jewry, it did so in sober and factual terms. The estimate of the total value of Jewish assets confiscated, plundered, and destroyed by Hitler Germany was the same as before—six billion dollars—but the demand for actual restitution was limited to one and a half billion, while it was explicitly pointed out that this represented a very large gap between what had been taken and what would be restored.

"In support of this demand, the note referred once more to the heavy economic burden placed on the State of Israel, which had accepted approximately half-a-million destitute refugees, the greater part of whom were incapacitated and unable to work for their own support. For the rest, the note expressly objected to having these claims classified as reparations. It took the view that German restitution to Israel represented a claim *sui generis*, and that therefore Jewish claims must be satisfied outside and apart from any general reparations settlement. In view of the notable economic recovery of the Federal Republic, the note pointed out, such an indemnity was a perfectly bearable burden, and reparations claims made by the victorious Allies need not be affected by it."

Since this note was again addressed not to the Federal Republic but to the Allied powers, the federal government was not in a position to comment on it directly. All the same, Adenauer did not wish to leave matters as they were, and once again immediately intervened.

"I was enormously impressed by his way of taking every problem he encountered by the horns," Nahum Goldmann remarked. "Generally speaking human beings are inclined to avoid and evade unpleasantness as long as possible, and in my experience this inclination is especially marked in politicians. Not so with Adenauer. He sent word through Dr. Blankenhorn that he was going to England on a state visit at the beginning of December and would like to meet me on this occasion."

This meeting took place on December 6, 1951, at Claridge's Hotel in London.

"It was then," Dr. Goldmann said, "that I saw the German Federal Chancellor for the first time, and I must confess that among all the politicians I have met in the past twenty years, including Churchill,

Roosevelt, Truman, and other great names, this tall and lean old gentleman was one of my most interesting partners in conversation. He walked up to me, held out his hand in spontaneous cordiality, and said, 'We politicians rarely have an opportunity to do something that really accords with the wishes of our hearts. But let me assure you that I'm profoundly anxious to repair the injustices inflicted upon the Jews. Let us jointly do our best so that the past may be buried and we can hope for a new relationship between Germans and Jews.'

"At this moment," Goldmann recalled, "I felt that I was facing a man through whom the voice of humanity spoke directly to my heart. As a rule moralists do not play a particularly happy role in politics, as we all know. A good politician is more often than not of rather doubtful moral stature, and the moral character in politics is, to put it politely, almost invariably hopelessly naive. Only twice in my life have I met men in whom political sagacity and moral principles were truly matched and balanced. One was Franklin D. Roosevelt, the other Konrad Adenauer.

"In the face of such a man there was no need for tricks or feints of any sort. I analyzed the Jewish situation for him and asked him to appreciate what it meant for me, as a representative of the Jewish people and of Israel, even to meet the head of the German government, after all the sufferings the Nazis had inflicted upon the Jewish people. I told him that I had organized the Conference on Jewish Material Claims against Germany, in which all important Jewish organizations throughout the world were represented; that I had prevailed upon the conference to authorize me to speak to the Federal Chancellor; and that I had taken this step because I felt—particularly after his statement in the Parliament—that he was a man who would understand that this problem of restoration and compensation was not just an ordinary political issue but a moral question of the first order.

"I told the Federal Chancellor, 'Either this problem is treated as a moral issue, and a truly great gesture is made by you on behalf of the new Germany, or it is better not to engage in such talks at all, because they can only end in failure and are bound to poison German-Jewish relations still further. All matters of detail, as to how and when payments should be made, can be worked out by our experts. But in order to make it easier for the Jewish people, whose public opinion is by no means unanimously supporting me, to understand the meaning and purpose of our negotiations, you, Mr. Federal Chancellor, as the representative of the new Germany, should demonstrate by a bold and courageous gesture that these negotiations are being conducted in a spirit of generosity commensurate with the magnitude of the problem. I hope to be able to leave you today with an assurance that you accept the claim of the State of Israel for one billion dollars as a basis for our negotiations. I know that you can answer me that you must first consult your colleagues in the government, or the party leaders. But having sat opposite you in this room for the past half hour, I'm convinced, Mr. Federal Chancellor, that you are a man who will not hesitate to make bold decisions if his conscience sanctions them.'

"Adenauer looked me straight in the face and said, 'I share your view that this is primarily a moral problem. I also understand your difficulties with public opinion in Israel. I believe that the German people must do something truly great if they are to build a bridge to the Jewish people. I am aware of the sacrifices Israel has made in order to shelter half-a-million refugees, and I feel that it is our duty to help. I am therefore ready to accept the claim of one billion dollars as a basis for future talks. I shall send you a letter confirming this before the day is out.' "

This letter, dated December 6, 1951, and drafted by Adenauer personally, has rightly become a famous historic document. It reads:

London, December 6, 1951

Dr. Nahum Goldmann
Chairman of the
Conference on Jewish Material Claims against Germany
London

Dear Dr. Goldmann,

With reference to the statement made by the federal government on September 27, 1951, before the Federal Parliament, in which it declared its readiness to enter into negotiations with representatives of the Jewish people and Israel regarding restitution and indemnification for loss and damage caused by the Nazi regime, I wish to inform you that the federal government considers the moment to have arrived for such negotiations to begin. I shall be obliged if, in your capacity as chairman of the Conference on Jewish Material Claims against

Germany, you will inform this conference as well as the government of Israel of this readiness.

I should like to add that the federal government views the problem of restitution and indemnification primarily as a moral obligation, and considers the German people in honor bound to do everything possible to repair the injustice inflicted upon the Jewish people. In this connection the federal government would welcome an opportunity to make a contribution to the building of the State of Israel by supplying goods and services. The federal government is prepared to accept the claims made by the State of Israel in their note of March 12, 1951, as a basis for these negotiations.

Yours faithfully,

ADENAUER

The simple, unadorned, matter-of-fact language of this letter did not reveal the far-reaching import of the decision lying behind it. It was one of the characteristic "solitary moves" Adenauer liked to make in decisive moments, which had often before earned him bitter reproaches from the opposition and severe strictures from his own supporters.

"In order to appreciate what had happened," Nahum Goldmann continued, "it must be remembered that the German Federal Chancellor, without authority of any kind, had entered into an obligation on behalf of the federal government which, in view of its size and scope, was bound to be a very considerable burden upon the federal budget. For, although the Chancellor had avoided naming a specific figure, acceptance of the Israeli claim for one billion dollars as a basis for negotiation nevertheless represented a certain commitment and a moral engagement. It was a spontaneous decision, born of the immediate situation, which Adenauer's intuition had grasped correctly: it was either now or never. Feeling instinctively that the next German step was due, he did not hesitate to take it—not from cool political calculation but under compulsion from his conscience. When did it ever happen in private life, let alone in politics, that the debtor in a legally somewhat doubtful and contestable claim almost encouraged the creditor to press it? That is precisely what Adenauer did.

"The echo of this brief letter was tremendous. Leading articles in newspapers the world over praised this extraordinary and unusual moral step. Still, the reaction was not everywhere favorable. Serious disapproval was voiced in Germany as well as in Israel."

As was to be expected in the Federal Republic, representatives of trade and commerce, bankers, and industrialists called on the Chancellor and reproachfully pointed out to him the immeasurable and unforeseeable burdens with which he had charged the German people by his voluntary acceptance of a claim which rested on very debatable legal foundations. Finance Minister Dr. Schaeffer was deeply worried, his budget being already so overburdened by occupation costs, reparations, and the support of millions of refugees that a large additional claim of this kind could easily and fatally upset its painfully achieved balance.

There were political considerations as well. The Arab States protested, declaring that a state of war existed between them and Israel, and Germany would render herself guilty of violating her neutrality by assisting their enemy. The Arab States threatened to boycott German goods, and their threat was not without its echo in the German press and in German commercial and manufacturing circles. The Arabs, these circles declared, had always been pro-German, they had been the only asset German diplomacy had possessed after the collapse, and now this traditional friendship was being jeopardized at the risk of economic and financial losses which might easily far exceed any indemnity payable to Israel.

"In Israel, too," Dr. Goldmann recalled, "enthusiasm was by no means unqualified when the agreement with Germany became known. There was a very sizable group of irreconcilables who were not prepared, as some of our papers wrote, 'to give the Germans an opportunity of buying themselves free with blood money from the historic guilt of National Socialism.' They told us that even on the basis of an indemnity of six billion dollars, which had been mentioned in the note of November 30, 1951 and assuming that six million Jews had been murdered by the Hitler regime, the cash value of an individual Jewish life amounted to a mere thousand German marks! Adenauer, however, pursued his path undeterred by such considerations and calculations. For him the issue concerned the fulfillment of an ethical duty in which material considerations had to take second place. At that time it became clear, with the Germans as with us, that there was in fact such a thing as a common front of men of good will which runs through and across all peoples."

At this point the story is taken up by Dr. Felix Shinnar, leader of the Israeli Delegation to Germany, who played an important part in the next phase.

"Again it was Adenauer who got things moving," Dr. Shinnar said. "Following his initiative, a German delegation led by Professor Franz Böhm and Dr. Otto Küster, a legal expert, met an Israeli delegation, of which Dr. Josephtal, Dr. Avener, and myself were members, at The Hague at the end of March. Our meetings took place at the former castle of Wassenar, now converted into an hotel, situated in an enormous park and surrounded by idyllic lakes. At first the psychological climate was distinctly favorable, but despite a promising beginning negotiations did not proceed as propitiously as had been expected."

There were a number of reasons for this. For one thing, the German delegation was not in a position to enter into definite commitments with regard to the amounts to be pledged and the manner and terms of payment. It was obliged to point out that the authority of the federal government over the transfer of currency to foreign countries was severely restricted by the Occupation Statute and other restraints, and that the sum total of the Federal Republic's other commitments placed certain limits to its capacity to help Israel. Finally, they had to insist that payment obligations toward Israel must be coordinated, in some way or other, with the final settlement of Germany's external debts. Negotiations for such a settlement, shortly to begin in London, made it difficult, if not impossible, to grant preferential treatment to Israel without annoying the rest of Germany's creditors.

"We had started our talks on the basis of the original Israeli claim," Dr. Shinnar said. "We reckoned that between 1933 and the end of 1951 the State of Israel had accepted approximately 540,000 immigrants from Germany and German-occupied territories, of which 115,000 had come from Germany and Austria and some 158,000 from Poland and the Baltic States. We had assessed the minimum required by each Jewish refugee to start a new existence at 7,000 German marks, and in this way had arrived at a total of 3,500 million marks, of which 500 million were to be allotted to Jewish refugees who had settled outside Israel. So far so good. But when it became a question of making this calculation the basis of a draft treaty, the Germans raised objections and made reservations.

"We ran into some very stormy discussions," Dr. Shinnar recalled.

"Bitter words were spoken on both sides which would have been better left unsaid. The two German delegates were by no means in an enviable position. We fully realized that it wasn't they who offered resistance. They were caught between the demands of their own conscience and the directives laid down by Dr. Hermann Abs, the well-known German banker who had been entrusted by the federal government with conducting the London debt settlement negotiations, and who viewed the entire problem with the eyes of a financial expert. Naturally, he was fully entitled to do so, but our own negotiations were now in danger of slipping off the high moral plane on which they had begun.

"The Israeli delegation were bitterly disappointed when they realized that owing to German restrictions and reservations the conclusion of an agreement could not even be considered as long as the problem of German debts had not been finally settled in London. Such a settlement might take years to reach, whereas the plight of the refugees in hard-pressed Israel was a burning problem demanding a rapid solution.

"At all events, the first part of the Hague conference ended in failure."

It was Dr. Nahum Goldmann who now resumed the account.

"It really looked as if the great moral event of a German-Jewish reconciliation was to get bogged down before it had properly gotten under way. At that time I addressed myself direct to the German Federal Chancellor in a lengthy and private letter, and again I was not disappointed. Adenauer invited me to visit him at Bonn. I saw him several times during the following months, and we had our decisive meeting at Bonn on June 10, 1952. It was then that agreement was reached in principle; the sum total of Germany's contribution was fixed at 3,000 million marks for Israel, plus 500 million for the Claims Conference to help Jewish victims of Nazi persecution outside Israel.

"The main difficulty in these negotiations was the manner of payment. Germany was offering goods and products, whereas Israel asked that one third of the total should be paid in foreign currency. Germany was unable to accept this demand, since at that time she possessed no foreign currency. Eventually a solution was found: Germany was to supply not only her own manufactured goods but also products of foreign origin, notably oil—a vital requirement in

Israel—which could be paid for from German export surplus in Britain.

"I well remember the decisive meeting on the afternoon of June 10, 1952," Dr. Goldmann recalled. "There were two amusing little incidents which seemed to me highly characteristic of Adenauer. Among various other products, the German economists had offered to supply us with Danish butter. I answered that Israel was not yet in a position to afford butter and had to make do with margarine. Adenauer turned spontaneously toward his assistants, saying, 'Now you can see, gentlemen, how bravely this small people is fighting for its life and how necessary it is that we should assist Israel.' Next Dr. Abs suggested that negotiations should be adjourned and the drafting of our agreement postponed until later because he had to fly to London that same night and still had to pack his bags. With a smile Adenauer said to him, 'You'd better stay here and draft the text of the agreement. I'll have a car sent to your house to fetch your things.'"

Thus, on June 10, 1952, at Bonn, everything was settled within a few hours which weeks of negotiations at The Hague had not been able to achieve.

"We Jews," Nahum Goldmann remarked, "give the entire credit for this to Adenauer, and there is no doubt that to many of us the German Federal Chancellor is today the most popular statesman of the West."

All essential points had been agreed. The sum total of German deliveries was finally fixed at 3,000 million marks for the State of Israel, 450 million for the Jewish refugees settled outside Israel, and 50 million for those who, although no longer belonging to the Jewish religious community, had been persecuted in the Third Reich on account of their racial origin. Dates and methods of payment had been agreed, and all that remained was to put the draft agreement into proper legal terms.

This was done during the following weeks, and on September 10, 1952, three months to the day after the Bonn meeting, the agreement was signed in Luxembourg by the German Chancellor and Mr. Moshe Sharett, the Israeli Foreign Minister. The signing took place at eight o'clock in the morning, at the Luxembourg City Hall, the unusually early hour having been chosen deliberately because both partners felt that this was a diplomatic act of deep ethical significance in which their innermost convictions were concerned, and that it would be inappropriate to turn it into a public spectacle. The signing took place in silence. Foreign Minister Sharett had brought a statement, drafted in Jerusalem and containing once more all the old charges against Hitler Germany, but decided not to read it out.

"After the solemn act," Nahum Goldmann said, "the leaders of the delegations met for a prolonged private talk in one of the reception rooms of the large, rambling City Hall. And here, in intimate, personal conversation, they voiced their true feelings. It is a pity that such utterances, which mean so much more than the big phrases of public statements, penetrate so seldom to the outside world. Adenauer said, 'I'm no friend of high-sounding words, but I will say that today, as we were sitting together at this long table, I was deeply moved and impressed by the significance of this act.' And when Foreign Minister Sharett was later asked by a Jewish chauvinist in what language the negotiations had been conducted, he answered, 'We conversed in the language of Goethe.' "

Subsequently, the language of Goethe was not spoken, or even understood everywhere. In Jerusalem as well as in Bonn the men who had championed this attempt at reconciliation had their difficulties with their opponents on the extreme right and the extreme left.

In Israel, the Herut, the parliamentary section of the former terrorists, and the left-wing Socialist Mapam violently opposed the agreement. Serious disorders and street battles occurred in Jerusalem as early as March, 1952, and during the debate on the agreement in the Israeli Parliament extremists attacked the parliament building, smashing its windows with stones and throwing tear-gas bombs. The session was concluded only with difficulty, and the agreement finally approved against much resistance and opposition.

In the Federal Republic things took a less stormy course, but here, too, approval was not unanimous. When, on March 4, 1953, the Federal Chancellor moved the first reading of "Paper No 4141," he pointed out with some emphasis that the federal government was "now confirming through practical deeds the solemnly promised closure of a chapter which to every German must be the saddest in our entire history. The name of our fatherland," he declared, "must regain the respect which corresponds with the historic achievements of the German people in the cultural and economic fields."

The contributions which the Federal Republic had undertaken to make, Adenauer explained, were not in the nature of reparations.

The State of Israel had not come into existence until 1948, and Germany had conducted no warlike operations against it from which claims for reparations could arise. The government had concluded this agreement "not in fulfillment of a legally valid claim made by the State of Israel but in fulfillment of a moral obligation of the German people as represented by the Federal Republic."

The protests of the Arab League, Adenauer declared, must not deter Germany from fulfilling this moral obligation. The federal government had "taken precautions against the misuse of the agreement, as for instance through the delivery of arms, munitions, or other war materials." Experts in international law differed widely in their opinion as to whether a state of war did actually still exist between Israel and the Arab League, and in no circumstances could the agreement be regarded as a breach of neutrality.

"In approving the agreement now submitted to you," Adenauer declared in conclusion, "we desire to take up a clear, unequivocal standpoint which permits no misunderstanding or misinterpretation. After all that has happened in the past, we shall show patience, and for the rest shall have to trust to the effects of our readiness to make the restitution, and to the healing powers of time."

When the law approving the agreement was read for a second and third time on March 18, 1953, it was seen that by no means all members of the Parliament shared the Chancellor's point of view. The Christian Democrats and Social Democrats approved the agreement without reservation. The spokesman of the Free Democrats, the second largest party in the government coalition, declared that his party was not unanimous and its members would be allowed a free vote so that "each may decide according to his conscience." The German party, pleading "justified constraint of conscience," declined to follow the leader of their own coalition, and the Communists as well as the German Reich party, on the extreme left, rejected the agreement.

The final division produced a curious result. Of the 358 members present and entitled to vote, 238 voted for and 34 against, and there were 86 abstentions. The coalition partners of the CDU had deserted the Chancellor, but the Social Democrats, his major opponents, had rallied in support of him and helped to make his great conception a reality.

* * *

Representatives of Great Britain, France, the United States and the Federal Republic of Germany after the signing of the German Contract at Bonn, May 26, 1952. *Left to right:* Eden, Schuman, Acheson, and Adenauer

*Wide World Photo*

Federal Chancellor Adenauer at the Tomb of the Unknown Soldier in Arlington National Cemetery, April, 1953. Major General F. K. Wright stands beside the Federal Chancellor

*Wide World Photo*

*Wide World Phot*

The Federal Chancellor is greeted by President Eisenhower as they meet at the White House in June, 1955. With them are Dr. James B. Conant, U. S. Ambassador to the Federal Republic of Germany (*second from left*), and Secretary of State John Foster Dulles.

The Federal Chancellor receives the honorary degree of Doctor of Laws from President A. Whitney Griswold of Yale University, June, 1956

*Wide World Photo*

"We Jews," Nahum Goldmann concluded his account, "find it hard to forget the evil inflicted upon us. But we never forget the good done to us. We invited Professor Böhm, the leader of the German delegation at the Hague, with his family to be our guests on a visit to Israel. And to the Federal Chancellor I presented on behalf of the Israeli government a copy of the Old Testament in binding of embossed silver. . . ."

Nahum Goldmann paused, then added:

"One last point must be mentioned which is not generally known. The stranger who, on March 27, 1952, handed the two Munich schoolboys the parcel addressed to the Chancellor was in fact a Jewish fanatic who wished to protest against the negotiations then in progress. But when the investigations of the Federal criminal police had at last established the man's identity, the Chancellor intervened and asked that this fact should not be published in the German press. Adenauer is reported to have said on this occasion, 'As far as I am concerned, this is the deed of a lunatic. Just as every decent German refuses to be identified with the mad outrages of sadistic Gestapo men, I must refuse to blame the Jewish people for the insane fanaticism of an individual for no other reason than that this individual happens to be a Jew.'

"With these words," Nahum Goldmann said, "the Federal Chancellor has erected a monument for himself in the hearts of all those to whom humanity is still a living reality."

## CHAPTER XXVI

AFTER the conclusion of the Schuman Plan Treaty, two main issues continued to dominate the exchanges between Germany and the Western occupying powers. They were the so-called *Deutschland-Vertrag or* "German Contract" which was to replace the Allied Occupation Statute by a system of contractual agreements between the Federal Republic and the Western Powers, and the German contribution to the European defense. In the course of the numerous discussions which had taken place on these two topics between the Chancellor and the three High Commissioners since the outbreak of the Korean War, a gradual change of mood and outlook had manifested itself on the part of the Western democracies, which found clear expression in the decisions of the New York Conference of Foreign Ministers, announced on September 14, 1951.

"The three Foreign Ministers declare," the statement said, "that their governments aim at the inclusion of a democratic Germany, on a basis of equality, in a continental European community. . . ." This integration would "completely transform the relationship between the three Western Powers and the Federal Republic" by placing these relations "on as broad a contractual basis as possible, in the light of German participation in Western defense. . . . Such integration would be inconsistent with the retention in the future of an occupation status or of the power to interfere in the Federal Republic's domestic affairs.

"The Ministers believe," the statement continued, "that the agreements now to be reached with the federal government should provide the basis for its relationship to their countries until a peace settlement with a unified Germany becomes possible. . . ." The Western Powers intend to retain "in the common interest, certain special rights, but only in relation to the stationing of armed forces in Germany and the protection of the security of these forces, as well as to questions affecting Berlin and Germany as a whole, including the eventual peace settlement and the peaceful reunification of Germany."

The High Commissioners would "proceed to negotiations with the federal government as rapidly as possible."

Adenauer was well satisfied with these results. Now at last the careful synchronization of his own policy with the development pursued by the Allies was gradually beginning to bear fruit. The Western Powers seemed at last resolved to open a new chapter. Personal contacts between the three High Commissioners and the Federal Chancellor, despite occasional differences, had become increasingly cordial. The stiff formalities of the Petersberg meetings had lapsed in favor of more intimate contacts, and their discussions now took place in turn at the private residences of the three High Commissioners: at Mehlem where McCloy presided, or at Castle Ernich or Castle Röttgen, where François-Poncet and Sir Ivone Kirkpatrick respectively were the hosts. Their conversations, which in the beginning at the Petersberg had often been rather in the nature of a trial before a court of law with Adenauer acting as Counsel for the Defense on behalf of an accused Germany, now assumed a personal tone and friendly warmth in which each partner sought sympathy and understanding for his own difficulties—and usually found it.

Even existing factual differences, as long as they did not touch on questions of principle, could often now be resolved with a humorous remark and disappear amid general laughter. The atmosphere had sensibly improved. The prospects for a swift conclusion of the "Contractual Agreement" seemed good. Then suddenly came a severe disappointment.

When François-Poncet, on September 24, 1951, at Castle Ernich, submitted the Allied draft for the proposed German Contract, Adenauer felt immediately that it was impossible! The principle of equality which had been proclaimed in the Washington declaration had obviously not been upheld in this draft. How could one speak of freedom in foreign affairs when a "Conference of Ambassadors" was to be established, with authority to intervene in German foreign policy on the basis of majority decisions; when, in other words, a controlling organization was established which was bound to create the impression in Germany that the High Commission continued to exist and function merely under another name? The idea of equality within the European Army had apparently not been considered at all. Germany was to build no aircraft, produce no heavy weapons, and conduct no atomic research.

"Our negotiations," the Chancellor explained, "start from the assumption that the replacement of the Occupation Statute will proceed simultaneously with the German defense contribution. These two agreements are coupled; they are conditional upon one another. But a German defense contribution requires a different basis from what is provided in this Allied draft. If you create a European Army in which several nations participate, it is quite impossible to impose prohibitions on one partner which do not apply to the rest. A community containing a partner enjoying so little confidence is an impossibility. No Federal German Government will ever put its signature to such a treaty!"

The discussion ranged back and forth. The Chancellor maintained his objections: "The moment has come when a decision has to be made one way or another, for or against integration. If Germany is not integrated now, this entire plan has to be abandoned for good. I can imagine that my attitude strikes you as immodest, even arrogant. But I would ask the High Commissioners for once to put themselves in my place!"

This reference to his difficulties with the opposition at home was only too well justified. "The whole conception is wrong!" Schumacher had exclaimed in reply to the Washington decisions. "Sixteen cripples don't add up to one athlete!" And a little later he had added sarcastically, "The Federal Chancellor spends his time winning unreal political victories instead of concentrating on his main task—the social consolidation of the Federal Republic. This is the only really effective protection against Communism."

A week later, on October 1, 1951, the discussion was resumed at Castle Röttgen, residence of the British High Commissioner. Again Adenauer declared, "I must point out once more, with all due emphasis, that the Allied draft of the German Contract is not in accord with the Washington declaration of the Foreign Ministers!"

What was the issue? The Chancellor demanded that in return for a German defense contribution the Allies should completely relinquish the supreme authority of government which they had assumed through "unconditional surrender," and that henceforth such rights as they were to enjoy in Germany must spring solely from a freely negotiated treaty. He visualized a treaty of security and mutual military assistance between Germany and the Allies, with the presence of Allied troops in Germany based on an agreement similar to that which authorized the stationing of American troops in Britain and France.

Against this the Allies took the view that as long as there was no peace treaty with Germany they must retain supreme governmental authority, since this was the basis of their relationship with the fourth ally, the Soviet Union. For this reason, Allied troops must remain in Germany as "conquerors" as a matter of principle, and the Allies must reserve the right, to be embodied in a "general clause," to reassume supreme governmental authority at any time, if and when the security of their forces required it.

These were sharply opposed views. All that could be done for the moment was to set out the differences fairly and clearly. By November 1, 1951, a document had at last been drafted showing the German and Allied drafts of the German Contract side by side and pointing out their divergences. This document was to be submitted to the Foreign Ministers for their decision. Their new conference began on November 22, in Paris. But this time the Foreign Ministers of the United States, Britain, and France were not conferring alone. There was a "fourth man." The three Western Powers had invited the Federal Chancellor to come to Paris and consider the draft treaty jointly with them.

There was genuine and urgent anxiety to reach agreement. As a result considerable concessions were made by the three Western Foreign Ministers, and several important points in the Allied draft were amended. Only two questions remained open: the future status of the Allied forces in Germany, and the production of armaments in the Federal Republic. There was agreement that in view of the exposed geographical situation of Western Germany certain types of armaments should not be manufactured in the federal territory. Only details remained to be settled. These were to be discussed further by the experts and embodied later in additional protocols or "conventions." The Paris Treaty, it was agreed, should not be signed or published until these conventions were ready as well. American Secretary of State Acheson, pressing for rapid action, asked that the entire body of treaties and agreements, including the "coupled" treaty for the establishment of a European Defense Community, be completed within ninety days. He was anxious to obtain ratification of the treaties by Congress before the beginning of the impending American presidential election campaign, to prevent them from being turned into an election issue.

As he flew back to Bonn, Adenauer was convinced that the ship would be safely in port by the beginning of January. For the rest he hoped that the results he brought back from Paris would also satisfy the opposition at home. Much had been achieved: the Occupation Statute was to be abolished, the High Commission was no to be replaced by a Conference of Ambassadors, and the imposition of occupation costs would cease. Instead, Germany was to make a voluntary contribution to the defense of the West. German sovereignty was to be restored, and the Federal Republic was to receive a renewed guarantee of its security from the Western Powers.

"What is being done now," Adenauer told his critics, "is in truth the best that human agencies can achieve to prevent Germany from becoming a theater of war again. The German Contract restores to us our freedom, to an extent we would not have dared to hope for a year or even six months ago!"

London, Monday, December 3, 1951.

Driving rain, pouring down ceaselessly upon Northolt airport, greeted the private aircraft of British High Commissioner Sir Ivone Kirkpatrick as it finally touched down. The machine was three hours late, engine trouble having delayed the take-off at Bonn, and the flag of the Federal Republic, hoisted beside the R.A.F. ensign over the airport building, hung limp and sodden. A guard of honor mounted by the Royal Air Force was drenched to the skin, but presented with faultless smartness as the tall, lean figure of the seventy-six-year-old Federal Chancellor emerged from the airport.

Adenauer behaved with fortitude as he stood for long minutes, hat in hand, in the pouring rain, exchanging courtesies with those who had come to welcome him on British soil, among them Mr. Anthony Nutting, parliamentary Undersecretary for Foreign Affairs. "I am very grateful to the British government," Adenauer replied, "for having invited me, and it is my cordial hope that the talks I shall have here will contribute to peace and understanding all over the world. I am certain that the German people will appreciate the honor of my being asked to visit London." At last the civilities were over, and the Chancellor was born away by the large black Daimler which the British government had placed at his disposal for the duration of his visit, "his stern and corrugated face," as one London paper wrote, "still visible through the streaming windows of his car as it sped toward London."

It was Adenauer's first visit to London, and the second state visit he had made that year. Earlier, in June, he had visited Rome for conversations with Alcide de Gasperi, the Italian Prime Minister, and a private audience with the Pope. This journey had given rise to much oracular speculation, and Socialist newspapers in England and elsewhere, speaking of a "triumvirate de Gasperi-Schuman-Adenauer," suspected a "Roman Catholic alliance which, after the pattern of Metternich's Holy Alliance, was to deliver all Europe into the hands of reactionary clerical despotism." In truth, however, the journey to Rome, as far as Adenauer was concerned, served precisely the same purpose as that which had now brought him to London.

London impressed Adenauer immensely, and he observed its ways with a shrewd eye. As his car took him to Claridge's Hotel, he was particularly struck by the silent smoothness with which the vast seas of traffic flowed all round him, the patient lines waiting at the bus stops in the rain, the absence of haste and hurry, of ill-mannered pushing and scuffling. This was obviously a quiet, disciplined, and serious city, and that suited him. The two cream-colored rooms of Suite No. 101-2, which had been reserved for him, were richly decorated with pink, red, and white carnations, called "Marion," "Cardinal," and "Purity," and Adenauer the gardener and lover of flowers was delighted. Someone told him that there was a new English rose called "Peace." He would like to have a sample of it, he said, "for my garden at Rhöndorf."

The welcome extended to the Federal Chancellor by the British press on the following morning was somewhat less cordial, without, however, being unfriendly. The Liberal Manchester *Guardian* said, "Dr. Adenauer must have come to London with mixed feelings. It is just six years since the British authorities dismissed him from office as Mayor of Cologne. . . . The truth is that both Dr. Adenauer and British official opinion have greatly changed since the dark days of 1945. He is not, as he was, acutely distrustful of British policy and disinclined to cooperate. The British on their side see that he has not moved so far toward autocratic conservatism as they once expected, and they admire his achievements. . . . But it would be wrong to conceal the doubts and differences which still exist. Probably the greatest among them is Dr. Adenauer's continuing suspicion of Mr. Churchill, and especially of Mr. Churchill's policy toward Russia. . . . Dr. Adenauer is said to be obsessed with the fear of a new 'Yalta.' It is as well that he and Mr. Churchill should together clear their minds on the matter."

This "clearing of minds" was not long delayed. It took place at lunchtime on the following day.

Downing Street is a short and narrow little street, and the 300-odd people who had collected there waiting for the Federal Chancellor to arrive gave the impression of a large and unusually noisy crowd. As Adenauer stepped from his car, a group of young men threw handfuls of leaflets in the air, saying, "No arms for the Nazis," and there were shouts of "Adenauer, go home!" and "Heil Hitler!" Adenauer appeared surprised at the demonstration, which was the most unfriendly he had so far experienced in any foreign country. But he was soon enlightened: these same young people occasionally showered the same sort of leaflet from the gallery of the House of Commons onto Churchill and Eden; they represented no one but themselves; in England everyone was entitled to voice his own opinion; but slander and disturbances were dealt with by the police. So it was. Later that same day four men appeared at Bow Street Police Station on a charge of "using insulting words and behavior."

It seemed almost as if Churchill was anxious to offset the tactlessness of the youthful demonstrators, for he welcomed his guest from Germany with a warmth and cordiality which went considerably beyond normal diplomatic civilities. With his very first words he reminded Adenauer that they had met before, in 1948, at the Congress of Europe, at The Hague. He even recalled the exact locality of their first encounter: it was the Knights Hall or Heinsius Room, the same room where Churchill's ancestor, John, Duke of Marlborough, conferred with the Grand Pensioner.

A large number of ministers and members of parliament of all parties, including the opposition leaders, had been invited to meet the Chancellor at lunch, and it was not until these guests had left that discussion began in earnest between Churchill, Eden, and Adenauer, with Sir Ivone Kirkpatrick acting as interpreter. Adenauer immediately attacked what seemed to him the central problem in British-German relations: the position of Great Britain with regard to European integration. He frankly admitted his disappointment at a remark made to him by Mr. Herbert Morrison, the then British Foreign Secretary, when he visited him at Bonn. England was anxious, Morrison had said, to be "a good neighbor." "I'm rather disturbed at the thought," Adenauer said, "that the Europeans are no more than just good neighbors for the English."

Churchill: "Neighbors of Europe but not in Europe."

Adenauer: "It seems to me that it would be sufficient if Britain were to declare clearly and unmistakably where her sympathies lie."

Churchill: "England's task is to maintain the balance. Germany is stronger than France, and France is haunted by fear of a German attack. In such an event we should place ourselves on the side of France, although I do not anticipate that such an event will occur."

Adenauer: "One mustn't even utter such a thought! I beg of you to have confidence in Germany. The Germans incline toward extremes. Often their approach is too theoretical. But we have paid dearly for our lessons. Today Germany is a shapeless mass which has to be remolded. What matters is whether this is done by good or bad hands."

Churchill: "It is not possible completely to eradicate all national sentiment. Germany and France must be friends and walk together. Great Britain will do everything she can to contribute to this German-French friendship. Germany is stronger than France—and the equilibrium is established with the help of England."

Adenauer: "Please do not overrate Germany. We too have our weaknesses."

Churchill: "I know. You have nine million refugees. What you have achieved commands the highest admiration."

Now the Chancellor attacked the "sore spot," his nightmare of a new "Yalta." At what price did Churchill seek an understanding with Russia? Was Germany to be the price? That was the question which troubled many Germans. Adenauer approached the delicate subject cautiously, by pointing out that people outside Germany had scarcely a conception of the extent to which the Soviet Union was trying to undermine the Federal Republic. Did they realize that the Communist party in Western Germany had twenty million marks to spend each month on its propaganda activity?

Eden: "Germany need not fear, now or ever, that we shall sell her to the Soviet Union. Britain will only act in accord with the Federal Republic."

Churchill: "That is correct. We shall not betray you. If the West is strong enough, the Soviet Union may possibly yield and agree to a reunification of Germany. But we would never consider coming to an understanding with the Soviets at the expense of Germany. Only a false friendship could spring from such a betrayal."

Adenauer: "We may therefore count on the support of Britain?"

Churchill: "We stand by our word. But why did the Soviet Union behave so foolishly, why on earth? You may have full confidence in England. We shall conclude no bargains behind your back. All peoples without exception are longing greatly for peace. But their fear of the Soviet Union is just as great. The door must be left open for an understanding. But not at Germany's expense. If the Federal Republic stands by the West, the United States and Great Britain will honor that stand."

Next Churchill inquired into Germany's internal situation. Adenauer answered that the federal government was firmly in control of developments: "We shall not tolerate a repetition of the events of 1930-1933. It would be wrong, too, to take Herr Schumacher too seriously. He is a nationalist on a Marxist basis. Our greatest danger is the refugee problem."

Churchill: "What can be done about it?"

Adenauer: "This danger can only be fought effectively with the help of America. The building of houses and a stepping up of industrial production are the best remedies. There is always a danger of the refugees turning to radical extremism while their claims remain unsatisfied. Another danger is the attitude taken by the young people under thirty-five toward the state. They refuse to cooperate because they have gone through too much. The more firmly the Federal Republic is integrated in Europe as an equal partner, the more attractive it will become for the younger generation."

Churchill: "Youth always needs a symbol. Are you a Prussian? The Prussians are villains. I am afraid of them."

Adenauer (laughing): "I'm not a Prussian; but Schumacher is."

Churchill: "If we fail to agree, we shall all be destroyed. But if we stick together we shall, God willing, get through. If nevertheless we go down, at least we shall have nothing to reproach ourselves with. . . ."

On that note the historic conversation, reproduced here from a record preserved at Bonn, came to an end. It was nearly four o'clock when Adenauer left, and there was a crowd of about 200 outside No. 10 Downing Street, but there was no demonstration.

The first part of Adenauer's mission in England had been completed: he had received clear-cut answers to what he wanted to know. Now came the second part: he had to give the British equally clear-cut answers to their questions. He had a double opportunity to do this, and made full use of it. The first occasion was an address on "The Position of the Federal Republic in the European Community," which he gave at the invitation of the British group of the Inter-Parliamentary Union before a large gathering of members of both Houses of Parliament in the Grand Committee Room of the House of Commons. The second was a speech on "Germany amid the Problems of Our Time," made at a dinner given in his honor by the Royal Institute of International Affairs.

"The Federal Republic today is a borderland of the Western World," Adenauer told the British parliamentarians. "In a war between the two great groups of powers, our country would inevitably become a battlefield. Naturally, we seek a way to prevent this terrible fate from overcoming us. The neutralization of Germany is sometimes proposed to us as one such way out, both by people with honest convictions and by people with powers of political calculation. The word 'neutrality' sounds tempting. . . . We in Europe, however, both inside and outside Germany, should not abandon ourselves to any illusions.

"The neutralization of the Federal Republic would have a practical value only if it were a genuine and armed neutrality; in other words, if the Federal Republic, on the strength of an adequate defense power, could resist any attempt at armed aggression with some chance of success—armed to the teeth, that is, like Switzerland! But this is not the case. An unarmed, neutralized Germany, on the other hand, constantly alarmed as to the developments the future might bring, would sooner or later inevitably be drawn into the maelstrom of the Eastern bloc. This would mean the end of Germany's membership in the European community, and would be followed by the downfall of the other free nations of Europe as well."

At the end of his speech many questions were put to the Chancellor.

"What guarantee can Germany give that she will remain in the Western camp?" one member of Parliament inquired.

Adenauer: "The guarantee is contained in the fact that we know what it means to go along with the East!"

"What is becoming of the plan for a European Army?"

Adenauer, with a calming gesture: "Do not let yourselves be disturbed by temporary setbacks or crises. The European Army will come, in a few weeks, or a few months, or at worst in a few years."

During the five days of his visit the Chancellor got through a truly enormous program. There was an unceasing succession of conferences, receptions, luncheon and dinner engagements, including lengthy and thorough visits to Westminster Abbey, the British Museum, and the National Gallery, and a whole day spent at Oxford. Here, at Balliol College, Adenauer came upon something unexpected: on the College's 1939-1945 war memorial he discovered the name of his own nephew. C. A. M. Adenauer was a student at the college in 1928-1929, and his name was here inscribed, although he gave his life on the side of the enemy.

A strange country, Adenauer felt. During the banquet given in honor of the German Chancellor by Mr. Eden, the Foreign Secretary, his host unexpectedly stopped short in the middle of his address, asking Herbert Morrison, the deputy leader of the opposition, to carry on in his place. And Morrison, who had been Eden's predecessor at the Foreign Office, without a moment's hesitation took up the thread and concluded the speech. So this sort of thing was possible, too, between a Government and an Opposition, Adenauer thought with slight wonderment.

Finally, on the last day of his visit, the Chancellor was received by the King at Buckingham Palace. The King had barely recovered from a recent protracted illness, but insisted on interrupting his convalescence at Sandringham and traveling to London especially to see the Federal Chancellor. With lively interest, and showing himself well informed, George VI inquired after conditions in Germany and dwelt at some length on the problem of German equality. Adenauer was not to see the King again. When he came to London on his next visit, it was to attend his funeral.

The last item on the program, on the eve of his departure, was a press conference. By now Adenauer looked and was tired, but still his answers to questions put to him by newspapermen of all nations were anything but fatigued. One German newspaper correspondent asked point-blank whether the Federal Republic would ask to join the Atlantic Pact if she were not invited to do so. The answer came, surprisingly, in Italian: *"Chi va piano, va sano. . . ."* He who goes slowly, goes safely. He did not complete the proverb. An Italian newspaperman did it for him, murmuring audibly *". . . E va lontano."* And goes far.

Of Acheson's ninety days, sixty had passed, but work on the additional protocols or conventions, instead of decreasing, seemed to be growing steadily in volume and complexity. At the same time, in Paris, the draft treaty for the European Defense Community had swollen to a tome of several hundred pages, and the more questions of detail were solved through lengthy negotiation, the more seemed to crop up. The Atlantic Council was due to meet in Lisbon at the end of February, to coordinate and synchronize the North Atlantic Treaty Organization (NATO) and the European Defense Community (EDC), to enable General Eisenhower, the Supreme Commander, to start work at last, but the EDC and German Treaties were "coupled," and neither was anywhere near readiness.

Now even Adenauer was seized by impatience. On January 24, 1952, he addressed a polite but decidedly forceful letter to Sir Ivone Kirkpatrick, the British High Commissioner.

> Mr. High Commissioner!
>
> . . . I consider it indispensable, for general political reasons, that the target set for the Lisbon meeting should be kept. Allow me to say in complete frankness that in my view one of the chief obstacles preventing us from achieving final results in good time consists in the fact that on the Allied side undue weight and importance is attached to many secondary issues, which, in comparison with the great tasks we have to complete together, is not their due.
>
> If the goal for which we are working jointly in these negotia-

> tions—namely, the safeguarding of the free world against the threat from the East, and the building of a peaceful, cooperative European-Atlantic community including Germany—is earnestly meant to be achieved, this will be possible only through generous and farseeing decisions. The psychological impact which our treaty must have upon the German people, and which is absolutely essential if the Germans are to become reliable and valuable members of the defense community of the West, may easily be impaired if the additional protocols are weighed down by irksome and essentially unnecessary ballast which is bound to arouse all kinds of resentment. . . .

Adenauer knew why he was urging speed. Early in February the opposition forced upon him a two-day debate on defense, from which he emerged with a vote of confidence of no more than forty-eight—his smallest majority so far. And even this scanty mandate authorizing him to continue the negotiations with the Allies he was able to obtain only by accepting a whole series of resolutions pressed upon him by his partners in the coalition and containing demands upon the Allies considerably more stringent than his own.

Could people in Paris, London, and Washington not see where they were pushing him? Their dilatory policy almost compelled him to adopt a nationalist line. Or were they intent upon his downfall? Since the vote on the ratification of the Schuman Plan, his majority in the Federal Parliament had shrunk to half its original size. Were they going to delay matters until it had disappeared altogether? Did they believe that it would be easier to come to an agreement with Dr. Schumacher as Federal Chancellor?

What indeed was in the Allied mind? Adenauer decided to obtain clarity by speaking openly to the three Foreign Ministers. Opportunity to do so was soon at hand. King George VI had died on February 6, 1952, and Acheson and Schuman had arranged with Eden to hold a preliminary NATO conference, in preparation for the Lisbon meeting. According to strict protocol, it would have been the duty of the Federal President, Professor Heuss, to represent the Federal Republic at the funeral. Adenauer insisted that he must go in his stead.

It was his second visit to London within a space of two months. Again he drove to Buckingham Palace, this time to pay his respects to the new Queen. The solemnities of the state funeral, at which the farthest corners of the Empire and Commonwealth were represented, made a profound and lasting impression on him. On his return to Bonn he said to a friend, "When you have witnessed the whole world mourning the dead king, you cannot help feeling that all this talk about the disintegration of the British Empire is just so much ridiculous twaddle."

The political hopes which had brought Adenauer to London proved to be justified. The "Big Three" took advantage of Adenauer's presence and invited him to join them in their talks. For two days this impromptu "Four Power Conference" worked without pause from morning till night. Point after point, item after item, all the questions still open were tackled, from the financial contribution to the production of armaments and the security controls. It was over this last problem of safeguards for Allied security that Adenauer raised his first objection. He felt that the pledge Germany was asked to give in a formal declaration "went a little far."

"What all this boils down to," he said, not without a slight undertone of reproach, "is that we are requested three times running to promise this, that, and a third thing as proof of our good intentions. Now, please do not misunderstand me if I say that it must be a strange partner who is required, upon entering the partnership, to declare three times over that he is a decent fellow and harbors nothing but honest intentions. Surely everybody is perfectly well aware that no agreement and no declaration is worth anything unless it is backed up by honest intentions and good will. But if you keep asking one of the partners over and over again to give proof of his good will, this makes a very poor impression. I've just been to see Mr. Churchill, and he said something to me, in a different context, which is very true: generosity creates confidence. Everything the federal government is now asked to do and say is already contained in the EDC treaty. . . ."

In short, Adenauer pleaded, could not the three Foreign Ministers help him to fulfill the wishes of the Allies in such a way as not to cause him unsurmountable political obstacles at home? But he was not the only one to have to contend with an opposition at home which was bent on weighing carefully every single one of his words. Foreign Minister Schuman was plagued by the same anxieties.

"The French Parliament," Schuman explained, "has authorized us with a majority of no more than forty votes to continue the negotiations. We are therefore dependent upon the support of the Socialists.

But the trouble is that during the most recent divisions there were far more deserters from the Socialist camp than at earlier votes. For this reason I want to appeal to my three colleagues most cordially to support my policy with all their strength. . . ."

It was difficult to find a formula which would allow for all these complexities. There was, for instance, the question of the German police force.

Adenauer: "I really cannot understand why you should worry so much about a German police force which hasn't even got arms! I beg of you to bear in mind the actual position: now and for many years to come heavily armed American and British divisions as well as EDC forces will be stationed in Germany. How can anyone in these circumstances be afraid of a bunch of unarmed policemen? If we go on arguing this point very much longer, I shall return home convinced that in reality we are very much stronger than I had ever thought we were!"

General hilarity. At Eden's suggestion, the triple assurance of Germany's "peaceful intentions" was deleted from the draft. It was hard work. Next came the most tricky point of all: the list of arms whose manufacture was to be prohibited on account of the strategically exposed geographical position of the Federal Republic. Adenauer suggested that these technical questions should be referred to the military experts in Paris. Eden and Schuman desired an immediate settlement.

Schuman: "It is a well known fact that as a rule Foreign Ministers find it easier to agree than soldiers."

Adenauer: "On the contrary, I always find that the military settle their differences much more swiftly than Foreign Ministers. May I take another look at this list? I feel that many of the terms used here are not at all clear. What is meant, for instance, by 'chemical weapons,' and what is the difference between long-range and guided missiles? What are smaller coastal vessels? How large are they permitted to be? As regards aircraft production, I am prepared to send a letter to the governments concerned giving an assurance that the federal government has no intention of manufacturing civil aircraft but wishes to purchase them. . . ."

Eden: "That would satisfy me."

Schuman: "But such an assurance can be withdrawn at any time—of course, not by you, Mr. Federal Chancellor——"

Adenauer: "For the love of God, can't you have just a little confidence? The manufacture of civil aircraft is so costly, unless you produce military aircraft at the same time, that my successor would have to be totally insane to contemplate such a thing! On the other hand, this treaty here is concluded for fifty years, and I really cannot give an undertaking that we shall not build any aircraft during the next half century. . . ."

At a later stage in the discussions the Chancellor returned once more to the list of weapons.

Adenauer: "I really must take exception to the vagueness and lack of precision in this list. Are we really not allowed to have any gunpowder factories? The stuff is needed for all sorts of nonmilitary purposes, for instance, in the mining industry. I also find it illogical that we should be permitted to produce heavy tanks, on which we are not at all keen, but no gun barrels of more than 10.5 centimeters. I'm very much afraid that this is a case for the proverb, 'He who bears the cross can bless himself. . . .' "

Schuman: "Although the exchange of views we are having here is rather painful, it is also extremely useful."

At length agreement was also reached on the controversial list.

Eden: "Now all that remains is to decide where the further negotiations are to take place. I suggest Bonn."

Schuman: "I'm in favor of Paris."

Adenauer: "It makes no difference to me."

Eden: "Well, now, please—where do we start? It shouldn't be necessary to discuss that at great length!"

Adenauer: "The best plan would be to start in Paris and then go on to Bonn."

Schuman: "But one always ends up by agreeing in Paris."

Eden: "All right, then, let's start in Bonn."

At the end of the conference a colorless and uninformative official communiqué was issued. No newspaper reader anywhere in the world could gain from it even an approximate idea of what such a conference was actually like. Certainly no one could find in it as much as a hint of the part which the German Federal Chancellor had played in these London discussions.

## CHAPTER XXVII

WITH ALL major differences between Adenauer and the three Western Foreign Ministers resolved at their London conference, it had been expected that the two treaties would now be speedily completed, signed, and ratified. But this expectation proved false. Adenauer had no sooner returned to Bonn than his talks with the High Commissioners on details of the draft treaties were resumed, but these talks dragged on over many weeks and even months, and on some occasions lasted from the early morning until late into the night. The official record shows, for example, that the meeting of May 16, 1952, lasted for a full seventeen hours; that of May 19, for ten.

Often the argument seemed merely to concern petty details, but they were details, nevertheless, of decisive significance for the spirit of the future European community. Thus the Chancellor requested the deletion of Article 6 of the treaty concerning the stationing of Allied forces in Germany. This article stipulated that there must be no discrimination against persons cooperating with the Allied powers in Germany on the score of "collaboration."

Adenauer: "Just think what a painful impression such a clause must make in a treaty of friendship!"

McCloy: "All right, then. This is now the one hundred and twenty-second concession the Allies have made to the Germans."

Occasionally there was a spark of humor, too, such as when Adenauer remarked, "I read in the foreign press that I am using blackmailing tactics and that I am trying to walk in Bismarck's shoes. I can assure you, gentlemen, that those boots are much too big for me."

Only rarely did the supreme goal of all these negotiations emerge from the depths of haggling over paragraphs, as when Adenauer said, "As far as I am concerned, the European Defense Community is infinitely more important than the German Contract. The German Contract merely draws a sponge across the past. But the European Army opens the road to the future. For me the European Defense Community is a matter of fundamental belief!"

Parallel with the talks between the Chancellor and the High Commissioners, the experts plodded on with their work. While in Paris the military experts were working on the EDC treaties, the legal experts at Mehlem, near Bonn, were struggling with the German Contract, now officially called "Treaty between the Three Western Powers and the Federal Republic." In both places the experts worked slowly and thoroughly, unperturbed by the politicians, who were anxiously and impatiently peering over their shoulders and urging greater speed. Eventually, on April 22, 1952, it was decided to take drastic action. The experts were to be locked up in their offices at Mehlem and not to be let out until they had definitely and finally cleared up all remaining points.

Adenauer: "Is there anywhere the experts can sleep at Mehlem?"

Kirkpatrick: "Most experts sleep at the conference table."

Even so—the end gradually came in sight. On May 9, 1952, Paris reported the completion of the draft EDC treaties, and a week later the legal minds at Mehlem followed suit.

During all this time Adenauer had devoted his entire attention unremittingly to the one great task, the completion of the great body of treaties, and had scarcely looked aside. But now, as completion approached, voices which he could not ignore penetrated to him from the outside world. They were not pleasant voices.

There was Schumacher, the opposition leader, who declared, "Whoever signs this Treaty will be called to account for it! Anyone approving this Treaty ceases to be a German!" There was the Soviet Zone government, who threatened that it would find itself compelled to create armed forces of its own for its protection. There was Edouard Herriot, President of the French National Assembly, who warningly told the French public, "I have great fear of German rearmament!"

If it was not easy, in the face of such resistance, to retain belief in the correctness of one's course, it was even harder to maintain one's enthusiasm for the work in hand. But Adenauer was determined not to allow such reflections to depress him. May 26, 1952, was fixed as the date for signing the German Treaty at Bonn, and on the following day the EDC treaties were to be signed in Paris by the Foreign Ministers of the nations concerned. It is not without emotion that one reads of the lively eagerness with which the Chancellor devoted himself personally to the preparations for this important day. There is a huge pile of papers at Bonn, assembled by the Chief of Protocol and consisting of nothing but the program of receptions and other ceremonial occasions for this one day, May 26, down to the minutest details, and on nearly every sheet of this vast mass of minutes, drafts, proposals, and interoffice memoranda of the Chancellery there are Adenauer's own notes, observations, and remarks in the margin. Nothing escapes his attention. He checks the list of invited guests and makes alterations; he scrutinizes the seating order at the official banquet and changes it; he takes a careful look at the menu, dislikes it, and orders a different sequence of dishes. Here, in his loving attention to the niceties of ceremonial detail, we see this dry and reserved man from a new angle. He had set his heart on this day. The signing of the treaties, he felt, was the crowning of his political work; he was looking forward eagerly to the day, and was anxious to make it a truly festive celebration.

The three Western Foreign Ministers reached Bonn on the afternoon of Friday, May 23. There were still some finishing touches to be put on the treaties, and this work was to begin the following morning. Suddenly a bombshell burst in Paris. Late on the night of May 23, when Schuman had already reached Bonn, the French Cabinet held a five-hour meeting, at the end of which it resolved that it could not submit the treaties to the National Assembly for ratification unless further safeguards against a possible withdrawal of Germany from the European Defense Community were inserted. Foreign Minister Schuman was instructed to submit these new French demands to his colleagues at Bonn on the following day. The most important among them was a joint Anglo-American guarantee, to be given to France, against the possibility of a German withdrawal from the EDC at a later stage.

For Adenauer this was a profoundly depressing moment. Despite all the proof he had given of his sincere intention to come to an understanding, France was obviously still unable to rid herself of her traditional misgivings and suspicions. What was the use of Schuman assuring him that there was complete confidence in him personally, but that they must safeguard themselves against his successor? All Adenauer could reply was, "Make the EDC treaties a reality, and that will be your best safeguard against my successor."

Throughout the Saturday morning Acheson, Eden, and Schuman negotiated among themselves, and there was much frantic telephoning between Bonn, Washington, London, and Paris. It was not until the afternoon that Adenauer was invited to join in the discussion. And now it was he who felt obliged to raise objections.

The two great treaties, he pointed out, did not exist independently of each other, but were coupled; the German Contract owed its origin to the necessity of creating the political basis of German equality on which the EDC treaty was to rest. The two treaties could only come into force simultaneously, and as a consequence the Federal Republic would not have its sovereignty restored until all its partners in the European Defense Community had ratified the EDC treaty. Until that had happened, Germany must wait, and this, Adenauer pointed out, might lead to grave complications.

Secretary of State Acheson answered that the best way to avoid such complications was for all concerned to ratify the treaties as quickly as possible. That was true enough, but it did not relieve the Chancellor of his anxiety. He was certain that Britain and the United States would ratify the German Contract without delay. But Britain and the United States were not partners to the EDC treaty. What would happen if France delayed ratification, or in the end even refused to ratify the EDC? In view of what had just happened in Paris such a development was not altogether unthinkable.

About one thing the Chancellor was quite clear in his own mind: the Federal Republic could not wait for its sovereignty until the last of the EDC partners had ratified the treaty. He asked for an assurance from the occupying powers that in the event of the ratification of the EDC treaty being considerably delayed, certain provisions of the German Contract would come into force meanwhile and irrespective of it. To this Schuman objected vigorously, fearing, no doubt, further complications in the French Parliament. Eventually, however, the three Foreign Ministers agreed in principle, and Adenauer received written assurance that in such an event the Western Powers would call a joint conference with the Federal Republic to consider the question of putting the German Contract into effect independently of the EDC treaty.

By midday on Sunday, May 25, complete agreement was at last reached, and even the thorny question of an amnesty for war criminals had been settled. But Foreign Minister Schuman was still waiting for the final word from his government. At last, on Sunday night, after a further meeting of the French Cabinet, Paris announced that they were now ready to sign. Britain and the United States had issued a joint declaration: "If any action from whatever quarter threatens the integrity or unity of the European Defense Community, the two Governments will regard this as a threat to their own security." Britain and the United States pledged themselves, furthermore, to "maintain in Europe such forces as are necessary for the defense of the NATO area and the safeguarding of the integrity of the EDC." This pledge, in which Germany was not explicitly mentioned, answered the French requirement.

Now at last the road was clear.

On Monday, May 26, 1952, at 10 A.M. the German Contract was solemnly signed in the "Federal Council" or Upper House of the Federal Parliament—the same chamber, now somewhat transformed and adapted, in which three years earlier the Parliamentary Council had deliberated upon the Basic Law. The four Foreign Ministers took their seats at a long table covered with silver-gray velvet in the center of the hall, while three rows of chairs along the side of the hall were occupied by guests invited to witness the ceremony. Only the Social Democrats were absent. Having declared this May 26 "Germany's Black Day," they had declined to attend.

There was complete silence in the hall—so complete indeed that the rain could be heard pouring down outside—when the Chancellor, amid the buzzing of film cameras and the flashlights of the photographers, rose to welcome his guests:

"After long and sometimes difficult labor, this treaty is now ready for signature and submission to the parliaments of our different countries which will have to pronounce final judgments on it. This contract will bring freedom back to our country, to Germany. . . ."

The Contract was a large volume bound in parchment and resting on a separate table nearby. Its contents confirmed in black and white what the Chancellor had said. The Occupation Statute would be abolished. The Allied High Commission would be dissolved. The three Western Powers would henceforth be represented by their ambassadors. Their forces stationed in federal territory were occupation troops no longer but troops of the Atlantic Powers, allied to Germany and entrusted jointly with the European Army with the protection of the Federal Republic. Occupation costs would be done away with. Instead, the Federal Republic would make a monthly financial contribution of 850,000,000 German marks to be distributed between NATO and the EDC and to be reassessed on June 30, 1953. Only a few indispensable restrictions had remained. The former occupying powers retained the right of reassuming supreme governmental authority in Germany in the event of an armed aggression against the Federal Republic or an internal emergency endangering the security of their forces, but they might do so only if the Federal Republic and the EDC were unable to meet such an emergency. Finally, Berlin continued to remain under the direct protection of the three Western Powers.

That, in short, was the essence of the Contract.

"But," continued Adenauer, "the total value of this agreement cannot be fully appreciated as long as it is considered in isolation. It has to be viewed and judged in conjunction with the treaty establishing the European Defense Community, which is to be signed in Paris tomorrow. The whole, taken together, will bring Germany not only freedom but peace as well. Moreover, we are convinced that it will lead to the reunification of Germany in freedom. At this hour we Germans remember especially our brothers in the East. We send them our greetings, and we give them the assurance of our deepest conviction that what we are doing here is the first step toward reunification in freedom and peace. The work as a whole, which will be completed in Paris tomorrow, marks the beginning of a new epoch in the history of Europe."

Foreign Minister Schuman replied on behalf of the three Western Powers: "The texts which we are now about to sign are the fruits of the persistence of purpose of those who have molded the new and bold ideas with which we are dealing here—the persistence of purpose of a man like yourself, Mr. Federal Chancellor, who, despite the incomprehension of many, leads his people toward a new destiny; and the persistence of purpose also of this people which now resumes its place among the nations. . . ."

On the same afternoon the three Foreign Ministers and the Federal Chancellor flew to Paris, where, on the following morning, Tuesday, May 27, 1952, the EDC treaties were solemnly signed in the Salon de l'Horloge of the Quai d'Orsay. The six Foreign Ministers of Belgium, France, Germany, Holland, Luxembourg, and Italy confirmed with their signatures that henceforth any aggression against any one of the signatories would be regarded as an aggression against all of them.

The Foreign Ministers of Britain and the United States were present as "godparents" to this new European Community, but their presence was of more than symbolic significance. After the signing of the treaty, Eden, Acheson, and Schuman in turn put their signatures to the security guarantee demanded by France, and once this was done Eden and the six EDC Foreign Ministers on their part signed a guarantee agreement between Britain and the European Defense Community. In this Great Britain undertook, for the duration of her membership of NATO, to come to the assistance of the EDC or any of its partners, should they become victims of an aggression in Europe.

Now, it seemed, everything was doubly and trebly joined and tied. In all, more than 400 signatures had been applied to the multitude of related documents. The procedure took several hours to complete. By the time all was safely signed and sealed, everyone was exhausted. And yet the real struggle had scarcely begun.

Adenauer was fully aware that his long and tough struggle with his partners in the treaties was but a prelude to the no less tough and exhausting battle he must now wage to secure approval from the German people and its elected representatives for what had been achieved. Again speed was essential. The United States Senate had promptly ratified the German Contract, and Adenauer feared a cooling off of American sympathies unless the Federal Parliament swiftly followed suit. Besides, he knew that the five other partners in the EDC Treaty had unofficially agreed among themselves to wait until Germany had taken the first step before they themselves ratified. He was anxious to take this first step without delay.

But now a series of obstacles arose.

On June 20, 1952, the *Bundesrat* or Upper House of the Federal Parliament declared that ratification of the treaties by the elected Chamber alone would not suffice, but that approval by the Upper House, was, in this case, indispensable. This unexpected interference on the part of the second chamber did not only portend delay. It also introduced a dangerous element of uncertainty about the final outcome. The Upper House was strongly dominated by the Social Democrats, and the Chancellor could not with certainty rely on obtaining a majority.

A second complication followed. The Social Democratic party had maintained all along that there was no provision in the Constitution for the creation of armed forces in the Federal Republic, and that therefore the EDC treaty entailed a change in the Constitution. Adenauer had consistently disputed this view, but now the Social Democratic party applied to the Federal Supreme Court at Karlsruhe for a ruling on this matter. If the Supreme Court confirmed the Socialist interpretation of the Constitution, the treaties required two-thirds majorities in both houses of Parliament, and such majorities the Chancellor knew he could never hope to muster. In that event the treaties were doomed.

The second complication gave rise to a third. The Socialist application to the Supreme Court for a ruling aroused doubts in the mind of the Federal President, and he in his turn asked the Supreme Court for legal advice on whether he would be acting constitutionally in signing the treaties after they had passed through Parliament.

All this made it clear to Adenauer that it was simply no longer possible to pass the necessary legislation through all its parliamentary stages before the House adjourned for its long summer recess, and that final ratification would have to wait until the autumn. It was equally clear to him, however, that he would be merely playing into the hands of the opposition if he waited for the Karlsruhe Court to announce its findings. He decided therefore to go ahead and submit the draft ratification bills to the Federal Parliament for a first reading on July 9, 1952.

When this day came, millions of German listeners sat glued to their radio sets. For the second time in the existence of the new German Parliament, an entire sitting was being broadcast from beginning to end by all German transmitters. A first experiment of this kind had been made five months earlier, on the occasion of the Schuman Plan debate. It was a new departure in the history of parliamentary custom, and not without its dangers and pitfalls, but on these two exceptional occasions it was certainly justified.

For with these so-called "Western Treaties," as with the Schuman Plan Treaty, such large, fundamental, and far-reaching decisions were involved that not even the humblest citizen must be allowed to feel that he was left in ignorance while matters of the gravest import were decided behind his back. Every citizen should be enabled, as the debate proceeded, to form his own opinion on the merits of the case. Indeed, the fact that the Chancellor addressed on this day not only the 400 members of Parliament but, beyond them, nearly

50,000,000 Germans throughout the Federal Republic and many thousands of others secretly listening to him in the Soviet Zone lent his great speech a special note of its own. This became apparent in his very first sentences.

"At the present moment," Adenauer said, "we owe the German people, and the world at large, a clear-cut statement of our views with regard to the fundamental principles underlying these treaties. The German people must see for themselves, and must see clearly, what is at stake, to enable them to form their own judgment on the standpoint taken up by the federal government and the Federal Parliament. They will give their final verdict in the general election next year. I am awaiting this verdict with calm, indeed with confidence, because I know that the German people, in their great majority, endorse the course we have taken.

"In my view," Adenauer continued, "the question we must ask ourselves in reaching our final decision is this: do these agreements permit us to reach the goals we have set ourselves, and do they take the Federal Republic appreciably nearer to them, or is there another and better road by which these goals can be reached more speedily and with greater certainty? If you cannot see such an alternative road, and if conscientious examination shows that the course taken with these treaties will carry us nearer to our goal, then you must have the courage to say 'Yes' and decide in favor of them!"

This was a second challenge to the opposition. Did they know of another and better way? If so, what was it? If not, could they take the responsibility for blocking the present course?

"Theoretically speaking," Adenauer told the deputies, "the choice before you is this: first, acceptance of the treaties and thus union with the West; secondly, rejection of the treaties in order to obtain union with the East or the neutralization of Germany; thirdly, deferment of a decision with a view to starting new negotiations."

Clearly, the greatest temptation for all those hesitating honestly and sincerely to take the responsibility for either acceptance or rejection was contained in the third course. For this reason Adenauer explained its implications with particular emphasis:

"You will have to examine very conscientiously whether a deferment of the decision for the purpose of fresh negotiations is at all possible, and whether it is compatible with German national interests. For my own part I will say at once that any deferment of a decision for which there exist no good and cogent reasons will always be tantamount to an evasion. In the present international situation this is simply not possible. Once the governments of eight nations, after long and painful labor, have reached agreement, it is simply not feasible for individual partners in the agreement to sit on the fence and adopt a policy of wait and see. The world moves on. We cannot arrest its movement. Delay which is not justified by substantial reasons is nothing but disguised rejection, and that is how it would be interpreted by our partners."

What were the likely consequences of rejection, whether "genuine" or "concealed," Adenauer asked.

"In the first place, one thing is absolutely certain," he declared bluntly. "There will be no new negotiations on the same basis in order to obtain this or that modification of this or that clause." Another consequence of rejection, however, would be even graver. "Rejection of these treaties by the Federal Republic would mean that the policy pursued hitherto by the Western Powers with regard to the Federal Republic had become a total and unmitigated fiasco, and such a fiasco would mean, by implication, a diplomatic success for the Soviet Union which would inflate Soviet self-assurance to unbearable proportions. The international diplomatic situation would no doubt shift in favor of the Soviet Union. The failure of their present German policy, in conjunction with the diplomatic advantages gained by the Soviet Union as a result of it, would most probably cause the Western Powers to reappraise most thoroughly their entire policy toward Germany, Europe, and the Soviet Union. I regard it as clearly possible that, as a result of such a shift in the diplomatic emphasis, the Soviet demand for a neutralization of Germany, which they have repeatedly made in their notes, would have a good chance of succeeding."

And what was the probable result of this?

"The Occupation Statute would remain in force," Adenauer said. "The trust and confidence we have been able to win up to now with the Western Powers and throughout the world would be lost again, owing to our uncertain attitude. The Occupation Statute would no doubt be applied much more stringently than at present. Should the Soviet Union succeed in its demands for the neutralization of Germany, the integration of Europe would become impossible, because Western Europe cannot be created without Germany. As a result of the situation thus produced in Western Europe, the Federal Republic would be drawn, in one way or another, into the Soviet sphere of influence. We would then experience the same development as in the satellite states. All Germany would become a satellite state, and the hope of the Eastern Zone that our political work here will eventually achieve their peaceful reunion with us would remain unfulfilled."

Was there another and better way? What was the attitude of the Socialist opposition toward the choice Adenauer had pointed out?

When Professor Carlo Schmid, knowledgeable, intelligent, and a highly versatile orator, mounted the rostrum to put the case for the Social Democratic opposition, many expected that now at last a clearly thought-out, consistent Socialist alternative program would be submitted. But after his very first sentence it became clear that this expectation was ill founded.

"If the Western Powers are now giving Germany a security guarantee," Carlo Schmid declared, "they are doing so not least for the sake of their own safety."

True enough, but what was so objectionable about that? Was it not obvious and perfectly natural that any genuinely profitable contract must contain advantages for both partners? Indeed, it had taken immense labor to make it clear to the Western Powers, in the first place, that their own security was bound up with that of Germany.

It was not that the Socialists had no counter proposals to make. They had. They asked that another Four Power Conference be called before a final decision in favor of the Western Treaties was taken. And what was to happen if this conference, like its predecessors, produced no result? Carlo Schmid answered, "If it becomes clear at this conference that the Russians do not want a unified Germany under acceptable conditions, a new situation would arise and this would cause us to think again. Should it then become necessary to conclude treaties with the West—and it may well become necessary—they would at any rate have to be treaties not burdened with heavy mortgages such as these."

Mortgages! What a word in this context! For three years now, ever since his first pilgrimage up to the Petersberg, Adenauer had tried to make it clear to the German people that these mortgages were the heritages of the war unleashed by Hitler, and that the only way to get rid of them was to clear them little by little, installment by installment. Adenauer refrained from answering this particular argument which seemed to brush all his immense labors aside as an unimportant trifle. In his stead CDU deputy Franz Josef Strauss exclaimed:

"You gentlemen of the Social Democratic party cannot very well expect of Dr. Adenauer that with these treaties he should, on top of everything else, posthumously win the war seven years after it has ended!"

It seemed clear to the House, after this, that the Socialist opposition had no practical alternative to offer. With a large majority, which included the Socialists, the Parliament referred the treaties to the various parliamentary committees for detailed consideration. There were seven of them, and as soon as they had completed their work, the treaties would be read a second and third time and finally voted upon. This was to take place on September 3 and 5. The first hurdle had been taken, and on July 27 the Chancellor traveled to the Bürgenstock, in Switzerland, for a vacation. No one doubted that the Western Treaties would be ratified in September with an adequate majority. Unless, of course, the Supreme Court ruled that they required an amendment to the Constitution. . . .

While Adenauer was away, several important events occurred.

On July 30, 1952, the Supreme Court at Karlsruhe rejected the plea of the Socialist party to declare the treaties unconstitutional. Dr. Höpker-Aschoff, the President of the Court and one of the main architects of the Constitution, stated that the Court was not competent to rule on the constitutional character or otherwise of draft bills which had not yet become law, and it was not authorized to intervene in the legislative work of Parliament with an anticipatory veto. In other words, the Supreme Court could pronounce on a breach of the Constitution only after it had—possibly—occurred, but it could not anticipate and prevent it.

Two days after this verdict the British House of Commons ratified the German Contract and the guarantee treaty with the EDC. Among the Western Powers only France was still outstanding.

A third event of major significance occurred on August 22, when Adenauer's great opponent at home, Kurt Schumacher, died suddenly at the age of fifty-five. Adenauer was deeply shocked by the news, which reached him in Switzerland. He had always felt great respect for the uncompromising strength of character of this fanatical man, and had always given him high credit for his iron resistance to the Hitler regime and the resolute manner in which he had fought off Russian blandishments and attempts to entice the Social Democrats into the Communist camp. At times he had set great store by Schumacher's judgment, and he had at no time doubted his genuine patriotism. "Despite many differences which divided us in our political concepts, we were yet united in our common goal, to do everything possible for the benefit and well-being of our people." That was the message Adenauer sent from Switzerland, and it was no hollow phrase.

Still—Schumacher's successor in the leadership of the Socialist party seemed to open up new possibilities. Erich Ollenhauer was a cooler, more moderate, and less temperamental man. Might it not be possible to work out with him a basis for a nonpartisan foreign policy? Adenauer greatly hoped for some such understanding, but even his first interview with Ollenhauer, on September 18, 1952, showed that with regard to the Western Treaties there was no hope for a common line of policy.

This was a severe disappointment, and it was not the only one the Chancellor had to face on his return from his vacation. The parliamentary committees deliberating on the texts of the treaties and draft bills were obviously being hampered by Socialist delaying tactics, and were making no progress in their work. There was now no prospect whatever of the second and third readings taking place in September, and as October and November came around it was still impossible to see how soon the committees would be ready.

Meanwhile unfavorable news came from France. Two prominent politicians, Edouard Herriot and Edouard Daladier, publicly voiced grave doubts and reservations about the EDC treaty. Ollenhauer immediately went to the support of this French opposition by declaring, "If the government enforces ratification of the Western Treaties against the express wishes of the Social Democratic party, we shall fight from the first day onward for their radical revision by new negotiations on a new basis!" That was grist to the mill of the French opponents of the EDC, and they in turn caused Adenauer's stock to slump at home. In the elections for the state parliament of North Rhine-Westphalia on November 10, 1952, the CDU suffered a defeat and the Socialists emerged, though with a narrow margin, as the strongest party. A week later the Government was outvoted in Parliament on a motion by the Chancellor to fix the second and third readings of the Western Treaty Laws for November 26 and 28. In their anger at the French, who had refused to admit the pro-German parties in the Saar to the impending elections, some twenty members of the coalition parties refused to support the Chancellor, thus leaving him in a minority of thirteen. It was the first sizeable defeat Adenauer had suffered in the Parliament.

In the course of the following week Adenauer succeeded in restoring unity among his supporters, and in a trial of strength on November 27, managed to coax the Federal Parliament into accepting December 3, 1952, as the date for the ratification debate, his majority having risen to a comfortable sixty.

Throughout Germany, December 3, 1952, was generally felt to be a "day of destiny." There was high tension in Bonn. The entire area surrounding the parliament building and all streets leading to it had been cordoned off by the police with barbed-wire fences. Four hundred police, armed with rubber truncheons and so-called "water cannon," had been brought in from outside to deal with threatened Communist disturbances. Actually several busloads of Communist sympathizers, brought up from the Ruhr, made an attempt to penetrate to the parliament building, but failed to get past the police barriers. Instead, Communist deputies inside Parliament did their utmost to discredit the Adenauer government with the millions who were once again following the debate on their radio sets. All through Adenauer's two-hour opening speech the President's bell never ceased ringing. The Chancellor was rarely able to utter two or three consecutive sentences without being interrupted by furious catcalls and abusive interjections.

Once again the Chancellor marshaled every available argument to persuade the opposition to change its mind, warning, begging, pleading with, and imploring them. Turning to the Social Democrats in particular he said:

"I may be permitted to ask members of the Social Democratic party to tell us in a clear and unequivocal manner which way and which method they would adopt, and above all what goal they are aiming at, what goal they wish to reach. For in the last resort it is not the way and not the method which count, but the ultimate goal.

So far, however, the Social Democratic party have not revealed their secrets to us. They have outlined neither their way nor their method, and they have not defined their goal in comprehensible language. Ladies and gentlemen, you think just as realistically as I do, and in your heart of hearts you know perfectly well that I am right!

"Well, then, ladies and gentlemen, as things stand now the position is that he who rejects the European Defense Community thereby rejects Europe as a whole. He who rejects Europe will assuredly deliver up the peoples of Western Europe, and in particular the German people, to the bondage of Bolshevism. He who rejects Europe abandons the Christian and humane way of life of Western Europe. He who rejects Europe digs the grave of the German people because he deprives them of their one and only chance to pursue their lives in a way worthy of them and dear to them and in that freedom which is founded on Christian principles. I cannot think that this is what the Social Democratic opposition wants. And if it isn't, I would ask them for once, on this one occasion when the destiny of the whole German people is at stake, to rise above considerations of party policy!"

At this the House was thrown into pandemonium. The parliamentary record notes: "Lively applause from the Government parties —calls from the SPD: 'You ought to be ashamed of yourself!'—SPD Deputy Dr. Menzel: 'This is sheer infamy!'—more shouts from SPD: 'Is this supposed to be worthy of a Federal Chancellor?'—Persistent interruptions from the left—Bell-ringing from the presidential chair!"

Unperturbed by the tumult and shouting, Adenauer continued his speech, concluding with these words:

"I beg of you, ladies and gentlemen of the opposition, I beg you cordially and urgently to examine these treaties as thoroughly as you wish, examine them as rigorously and critically as you must, but please bear in mind one thing. Bear in mind what is at stake. The entire German people on both sides of the iron curtain must know what the issue is. What is at stake is their freedom, their lives, the future of their children and of generations yet unborn. I appeal to the entire German people to be conscious of the significance of this decision and to remain conscious of it. The question you have to answer involves the destiny of all Germany. We are faced with the choice between slavery and freedom. We choose freedom!"

After this last, passionate appeal a majority in favor of the treaties seemed assured. The division concluding the second reading was to take place in the late hours of December 4, and the third reading and final vote were to follow the next day.

But now something wholly unexpected happened.

On the afternoon of December 4 it was rumored in the lobbies that the Chancellor had decided to postpone the third reading because constitutional difficulties had arisen. The coalition parties were thrown into the utmost confusion and uncertainty until, late in the evening, Dr. Heinrich von Brentano, the chairman of the parliamentary CDU, rose to confirm the rumors. The combined CDU/CSU moved the adjournment of the third reading to give the Government an opportunity to lodge a plaint against the Social Democratic party with the Supreme Court at Karlsruhe! Despite the general consternation caused by this announcement, the second reading was duly completed, with the Government obtaining a majority for the German and EDC Treaties of fifty-two and fifty-one votes respectively.

But what had happened? That was what everyone was anxious to know. What had prompted Adenauer to hazard once more the victory which was already in his grasp? The answer was for most members a complete surprise.

It will be remembered that the Federal President, Professor Heuss, had asked the Supreme Court for legal advice as to whether he would be acting within the constitution if he put his signature to the two treaties once they had been ratified by Parliament. It was true that the Supreme Court had rejected the plea of the Socialist party to find that the treaties were unconstitutional and required a two-thirds majority for ratification, on the score that the Court could not pronounce upon draft bills but only upon completed legislation. Now it was clear that this ruling did not finally settle the issue but merely postponed it, for there could be no doubt that the Socialist party would renew their plea as soon as Parliament had passed this legislation, and this would cast doubt on the constitutional validity of the vote of approval. It was understandable in these circumstances that the Federal President wished to be quite clear whether he ought to sign so disputed a piece of legislation.

Now it was said that in the middle of the debate on the second reading Adenauer received word from Karlsruhe that the legal opinion which the Federal President had requested of the Supreme Court would in all probability "not confirm the view held by the Government." If this turned out to be correct, it meant that the Federal President would decline to sign the treaties until the constitutional validity of the parliamentary vote of approval was definitely confirmed!

What was to be the next move? The political battlefield was suddenly transferred from the parliamentary debating chamber to the courtroom. But Adenauer, who had not studied and practiced law for nothing, did not hesitate to take up the struggle in this new field, and he opened it with a masterly stroke. On behalf of the government coalition he requested the Supreme Court to prohibit the Social Democratic party from asserting that ratification of the two treaties required a two-thirds majority—an assertion which was unproved since the Supreme Court itself had so far refrained from pronouncing on it.

The German public failed to grasp the legal significance of this move, and there were many who misunderstood and misinterpreted it, and as a result criticized Adenauer for trying to involve the Judiciary in the political party game. "The plaint of the SPD was rejected," these indignant voices declared, "because the Supreme Court pronounced itself unauthorized to interfere in pending legislation, and now Adenauer tries to force the judges at Karlsruhe to deviate from this ruling for the benefit of the government! This means a violation of the elementary principle of equality of all in the eyes of the law!" It sounded plausible enough, and the Chancellor had to endure a good deal of stinging criticism. All the same, these reproaches missed the essential point of his move. The two plaints, the Socialist party's and that of the Coalition, were not comparable. The Socialist plaint had been a litigation of a political party against the law, and this the Court had rightly declined to entertain. Adenauer's plaint, on the other hand, was not directed against pending legislation but was a litigation by one political party, or group of parties, against another party, and this deprived the judges of escape on the grounds that they must not interfere with the Legislative Assembly.

To the ordinary public the whole thing looked very much like legal splitting of hairs, and they could scarcely be blamed for finding it a little unworthy. For Adenauer, however, much more was at stake than the scoring of legal points. He was determined to secure ratification of the two treaties as speedily as possible, knowing that at this juncture only one political danger threatened—procrastination and delay. This could be fatal, and it was in order to avoid it, or cut it short, that he had gone to Karlsruhe.

The Supreme Court, however, had a mind of its own. Obviously annoyed by the manner in which it had been dragged into a political party squabble, it decided to restore its authority with a bold stroke. On December 8, 1952, the Court announced that the legal advice sought by the Federal President would, when given, taken precedence over any ruling issued on the plaint of the coalition parties and must be considered binding in all further plaints brought by government or opposition parties with regard to the Western Treaties.

Adenauer immediately retaliated by disputing the validity of the Court's decision: the Federal President, he declared, had not sought a "ruling" but merely "advice," and such advice could not possibly constitute a binding precedent over a ruling such as was sought by the coalition parties. Simultaneously with this legal move he made a political one, in the hope of cutting through the Gordian knot and thus averting the major constitutional crisis which now threatened. He called on Professor Heuss, and in a long discussion, at which no witnesses were present, they considered the political aspects of the legal tangle. The result of this interview was that the Federal President agreed to withdraw his own request for legal advice.

In a short broadcast speech the following day, Professor Heuss explained to a baffled and puzzled nation the reasons which had prompted him to take this step. He had, he said, wanted a "piece of advice from the Supreme Court, and not a definite ruling." However, in view of the decision of the Supreme Court, to turn this "advice" into a legal precedent and to make it binding for all future rulings relating to the same issue, there was now a danger of the Supreme Court—which was, after all, the guardian of the Constitution—becoming involved in political responsibilities. And that must not be allowed to happen. For this reason, and this alone, he had withdrawn his request. For the rest, he must deny most emphatically that he had acted under pressure from the Chancellor as was being widely alleged. "I'm in the habit of making my own decisions," Professor Heuss declared, "and no one can relieve me of this responsibility before history and my own conscience."

As was to be expected, the Social Democratic party rose in wrath.

Despite the Federal President's statement, it continued to charge the Chancellor with having "exerted massive pressure upon the President." The "constitutional foundations of the new state have been shaken," they declared, "and the democratic form of government is in serious peril." Ollenhauer announced that he would table a motion of no confidence in the Government and demand new elections before a third reading of the treaties was taken. Adenauer was not intimidated by this. In a broadcast speech on December 17, he reaffirmed that he was "determined, now as before, to secure ratification of the Western Treaties as quickly as possible, and would not allow himself to be in any way deterred by stormy scenes in Parliament or idle talk about an alleged constitutional crisis."

The air had been cleared considerably, and all that remained now was to await the outcome of the plaint of the coalition parties at Karlsruhe. As soon as this arrived, the third reading of the treaties could take place.

But at this point, early in January, 1953, calamitous news came once again from Paris: the French government had fallen, Robert Schuman had quitted the Quai d'Orsay, Georges Bidault had succeeded him. And the new French Prime Minister, Réne Mayer, announced in his statement of policy before the Chamber that he was unable to accept the EDC Treaty in its present form. France would have to ask for further security guarantees from Germany, and these would have to be embodied in supplementary protocols.

This was a heavy blow indeed. A man of less strength of character might well have succumbed to it and finally given up. Adenauer received the evil news with complete composure, as though he had long been prepared for it. The EDC Treaty, he told the press, was not a dead but a living and dynamic organism, and naturally it could be developed further through additional protocols. But first of all it must be ratified.

The legal pundits at Karlsruhe, however, took their time. At the beginning of February, 1953, John Foster Dulles, the new United States Secretary of State, arrived in Bonn and declared roundly that the United States was dissatisfied with the progress made in Europe. Unless there were sure indications by April 1 that the treaties would be ratified, serious difficulties must be anticipated in Congress over the granting of further American aid to Europe. As far as Adenauer was concerned, this merely confirmed his own views. But there was no way in which he could speed things up at Karlsruhe.

At long last, on March 8, 1953, the Supreme Court gave its ruling, in the form of a 150-page dissertation, the upshot of which was that the Government was right and the Socialist Opposition wrong: it was not permissible for a party to obstruct the passage of a bill through Parliament because it considered it unconstitutional.

Now the road was clear. On March 19, 1953, the two treaties were submitted to the Parliament for a third reading. This time the Chancellor had his supporters firmly behind him. Compared with the riotous progress of the December debate, the atmosphere in the House was calm and sober. The German Contract was approved with a majority of sixty-two, the EDC Treaty with a majority of fifty-nine. The second chamber duly ratified the treaties two months later, on May 15, 1953, and once this was done the Federal President no longer hesitated to append his signature.

Of the eight years which Adenauer had once said he needed to put the German people on the right road, nearly four had passed, and the moment was approaching when the nation would decide, in the second federal elections, what it thought of the results at "half time."

## CHAPTER XXVIII

AMID the life of unceasing political struggle which Adenauer had led without respite ever since 1945, his journey to the United States in April, 1953, was something like a restful oasis. Naturally, the visit was not a private one. The original invitation had been issued by President Harry S. Truman several months earlier and had been renewed by his successor, General Dwight D. Eisenhower, and it was an official state visit in the fullest sense of the word. The thirteen days which Adenauer, now in his seventy-eighth year, spent in the United States and Canada were filled with an uninterrupted series of visits, conferences, receptions, and speeches. After it was over, American statisticians computed admiringly that the Federal Chancellor had spoken 288,000 words during his stay, shaken 2,500 hands on a single evening, and traveled nearly 10,000 miles across the American continent. Yet he always looked back on this first American journey, which was to be followed by several others in subsequent years, as a singular spell of calm and rest. The inordinate strain of his whirlwind tour, he felt, was relieved, indeed overcome, by the climate of "mutual well-wishing and genuine sympathy" in which he found himself. "We were simply among friends," he said later, after his return to Germany, and this was an unusual thing for a man who normally uses the word "friendship" sparingly to say.

The crossing of the Atlantic was stormy. The sixteen companions and members of his staff, including his daughter Lotte, who had set out with him from Le Havre on April 2, 1953, in the new liner *United States*, felt anything but cheerful. Adenauer alone seemed wholly unaffected by the persistently "unstable situation," taking his strolls along the decks every day in the best of humor, chatting with the captain, inspecting the ship, and inquiring after the latest radio news from home. Then again he would wrap himself firmly in thick blankets, stretch out in his deck chair, and settle down comfortably with a detective novel, a favorite form of relaxation of many years' standing.

Even before the *United States* reached harbor the first Americans came aboard—a host of reporters and photographers, accompanying the American High Commissioner in Germany, James B. Conant, and his predecessor in office, John J. McCloy, who had come out to welcome the Chancellor. In their presence Adenauer gave his first American press conference, on board ship.

"Upon my arrival in the United States," Adenauer said, "I feel above all one thing—gratitude toward the American people. We Germans thank you from the bottom of our hearts for the many acts of help and kindness you have shown to us after our defeat. I think very rarely in past history has a victorious people extended a helping hand toward the vanquished as you have done. This spirit of helpfulness has manifested itself in all conceivable ways, from human being to human being, from organization to organization, through decisions of Congress and through measures taken by the government. This has raised the spirit of the German people and given us new confidence. It has proved to the German people that in the life of nations force and selfishness are not the only motive powers.

"Let me add one more reflection. Those in responsible positions, and American public opinion, have realized in an exemplary way the truth that power and wealth impose obligations toward others. The American people have not only realized this truth, they have acted accordingly. In the history of our own time, which contains so many dark pages, it will be recorded in golden letters that the United States, faithful to its traditions and on the basis of its strength, has assumed the defense of freedom in the world."

This was meant to be more than a formal compliment to the host country. Adenauer genuinely felt this sense of gratitude toward America, and often expressed it spontaneously in official as well as private conversation. But to express the gratitude of the German people toward the United States was surely not the only purpose of the journey? When the *United States* reached her berth early the next morning, the Chancellor was besieged by newspapermen who fired a barrage of questions at him.

"What do you think of the new Soviet peace moves?" one reporter wanted to know.

"I shall be a good deal wiser after I've been to Washington," Adenauer answered. "Then I'll be able to reply to your question."

The official state visit to Washington did not begin until the following day. Adenauer's first day on American soil, in New York, was still "private." He was the first German Chancellor in office ever to visit the United States, and the German flag was flying beside the Stars and Stripes, for the first time in more than ten years, from the Waldorf-Astoria Hotel, where he was staying. He had no sooner arrived than he started on his "private" program, and his first call was in his own hotel, on ex-President Herbert Hoover. Adenauer went to thank this great humanitarian on behalf of Germany for the immense efforts he had made, following his two visits to Germany after the war, to organize relief work and save tens of thousands of German children and youths from starvation.

Next, the Metropolitan Museum, where Adenauer spent the rest of the morning contemplating the treasures of painting which had found their way from the old world into the new. From there, out to Greenwich, Connecticut, where an old friend awaited him for lunch: D. N. Heinemann, who nearly twenty years ago, in 1934, helped the hunted ex-Mayor of Cologne in his dire straits. Heinemann, who possessed a unique private collection of Goethe and Napoleon letters, was anxious to show his treasures to his friend, and they soon lost themselves in a long and animated conversation on these two great men.

In the evening Adenauer was back in town for a dinner party McCloy had organized in his honor at the Union Club, where a large number of prominent New York citizens had gathered to meet him, among them Governor Thomas E. Dewey, John D. Rockefeller, Jr., eighty-year-old Bernard Baruch, Cardinal Spellman, and, not least, an old acquaintance of recent and yet seemingly already historic days—General Lucius D. Clay.

That was Adenauer's first "entirely private" day in the United States. He had set the pace, and he kept it up.

Washington, April 7, 1953.

President Eisenhower's private aircraft, the "Columbine," had carried the Chancellor through a radiant spring morning in seventy-five minutes from New York to Washington. A red carpet had been duly laid down on the runway as he touched down, an honor normally bestowed only upon chiefs of governments of fully sovereign states.

Vice-President Nixon, Secretary of State Dulles, Secretary of the Treasury Humphrey, Defense Secretary Wilson—half the American Cabinet were present to welcome him to the capital.

"We are witnessing the birth of a new Europe," the Secretary of State said, "and we are encouraged by the fact that the large majority of the German people are ready to unite their fate with the rest of the free nations. American hopes for the realization of unity and strength in Europe are largely due to the contribution which you, Mr. Federal Chancellor, have made in the movement toward these objectives. The whole world can be grateful that you and your country have given the lead to Europe at this critical time."

Next, Vice-President Nixon assured the Chancellor that Americans were aware of the "tremendous contributions" made by millions of Germans who had emigrated to the United States and added to America's culture and progress. Indeed, there was a tradition of German-American friendship, and one of the names that immediately came to mind was that of Friedrich Wilhelm von Steuben, the German general who created the army with which George Washington won independence for America.

Adenauer answered briefly but succinctly: "I wish to give you this pledge: the German nation will be a loyal and willing partner of the United States, which is leading the world toward peace and freedom. I make this solemn declaration. The German people are on the side of freedom. The German people are on the side of right and justice for all nations." And turning to Vice-President Nixon, he added, "You just mentioned Baron Steuben. I wish to thank you for the generous manner in which you have paid tribute to the friendship between America and Germany, without mentioning the last few decades. . . ."

The Chancellor was visibly moved by the cordiality of the welcome. It was informal, without solemn guards of honor and military bands playing. After the somewhat stiff ceremonial in France, Italy, and England, he now met with men who managed to lend the official occasion a personal and almost intimate character. The white, airy city of Washington was at its very best as Adenauer drove in from the airport to Blair House, the government's official guest house, opposite the White House, where he was to stay. Thousands of Washington's famous cherry trees were in full bloom. Not far from Blair House, as Adenauer had learned, stood the statue of General Steuben. The following day the Chancellor went across to lay a wreath there.

Within two hours of his arrival the Federal Chancellor called at the White House, where President Eisenhower came out to welcome him. It was just two years since they had last met, when Eisenhower, then Supreme Commander of NATO, had paid an official visit to Bonn. At the end of their two-hour talk on that occasion, the General, who scarcely six years earlier had accepted unconditional surrender from Hitler's generals, had declared that he was firmly convinced of Germany's sincere readiness to fight for freedom. History had indeed moved fast within very recent memory.

Adenauer the lover and collector of paintings had not remained unaware of the fact that the new President of the United States, like the British Prime Minister, was an amateur painter, and he had brought as a present "The Adoration of the Magi," by an unknown South German master of the sixteenth century. Eisenhower, on his part, held a return gift ready: some English school copybooks of Carl Schurz, the famous German-American who, after the revolution of 1848, fled from his native Baden to America, where he rose to become Secretary of the Interior.

Adenauer's first visit to the White House lasted just over one hour. The meeting took place in the Cabinet room, at a long table with the Americans along one side, the Germans on the other, and Adenauer occupying the Vice-President's chair, facing the President. The conversation was Adenauer's and Eisenhower's alone. No one else spoke. The rest just listened. And then they were not even allowed to listen when Eisenhower, Adenauer, and Dulles finally withdrew for half an hour's private conversation. What was said, no one learned. When he finally emerged, the Chancellor merely declared that complete agreement had been reached in principle, and no doubt there would be agreement on details also. For the rest, the President and himself had agreed to treat their talk as strictly confidential.

Now the official program ran its course, at the traditional Adenauer pace. At three o'clock in the afternoon the Chancellor called at the State Department for a talk with Secretary of State Dulles; at five he was once more looking at pictures, this time in the National Gallery; at seven he was the guest of the President of Georgetown University, to receive an honorary doctor's degree. Georgetown is the oldest Roman Catholic University in the United States, and the honorary degree it bestowed on the Chancellor was the sixth he had collected in the course of his life. Four of them, the doctorates *honoris causa* of political science, law, medicine, and philosophy, had been conferred upon him successively by the University of his native Cologne, and the fifth was a law degree from the University of Maryland.

The following morning, after a brief visit to Mount Vernon, George Washington's historic country home, Adenauer drove out to Arlington, the national cemetery. Here, in an immense park amid trees and lawns, 80,000 American soldiers have been put to rest in long rows, with nothing but small stone slabs showing their names. In the center of this vast cemetery stands a monument, bearing on its pedestal this inscription: "Here rests in honored glory an American soldier known but to God."

A battery of guns fired a salute as the column of cars turned into the cemetery. General Wright, commanding officer of the Washington Military District, welcomed the Chancellor on the steps of the Custis-Lee Mansion. Three young American soldiers were drawn up, the middle one carrying the German flag.

At one side of the bright, sunlit Arlington Memorial Amphitheater, a wide flight of stairs led down to an open square. Stairs and square were lined with detachments of all branches of the United States armed forces forming a guard of honor while the Chancellor, followed at a short distance by the three flag-bearers, descended the stairs and walked bareheaded across the square toward the memorial of the Unknown Soldier. As he placed a large wreath of red roses, inscribed "The Federal Chancellor," at the foot of the memorial, a military band struck up the "*Deutschland-Lied*," followed immediately by the national anthem. Soon afterward the German cars rolled out again, and once more the batteries fired their salute.

It had lasted only a few minutes in all, but whenever Adenauer later dwelt on his impressions of his first American journey, he always mentioned the solemn ceremony at Arlington as one of its most unforgettable moments. "It was one of the most beautiful and most moving things I have ever experienced," he said. "I felt then as though in this hour our own dead German soldiers had their honor restored to them."

Adenauer spent three days in Washington, and the remainder of these three days, too, was filled to bursting point with a multitude of engagements. On the evening of the third day, April 9, 1953, an official communiqué was issued from the White House summarizing the political harvest of the state visit in eleven points.

"The United States government," this declaration said, "joins with the Federal German government in asking the Soviet government to give proof of the good faith of its recent peace moves by permitting genuinely free elections in the Soviet-occupied zone of Germany and by releasing the hundreds of thousands of deported German civilians and prisoners of war still in Soviet hands. . . . There can be no lasting solution of the German problem short of a reunification of Germany by peaceful means and on a free and democratic basis, and the present treaties, ratification of which will restore Germany's sovereignty, are a means toward this end."

This was the overture from which, as a French newspaper remarked somewhat bitingly, "Adenauer's trumpet voice" could be clearly heard. But the remainder of the agreement was no less "music for German ears": there was to be American help for Berlin and the refugees from the Eastern Zone; the status of war criminals still in United States custody was to be re-examined; trade relations between the United States and the Federal Republic were to be normalized; confiscated German prewar property was to be returned, and the question of confiscated German industrial and scientific patents to be reconsidered; help was to be given in equipping the German military contingents in the European Defense Community, and American arms contracts were to be placed with German industry; some 350 small vessels taken from Germany after the war were to be returned, and there was a special agreement on the promotion of cultural exchanges between the two countries.

Yet the most important result of the Washington talks did not find direct expression even in the official communiqué. What was said and agreed between Eisenhower and Adenauer in their private talk remained secret. But those with ears to hear were nevertheless able to detect one or two significant hints in the statement Adenauer made at his final press conference, despite its cautious wording. As Adenauer announced triumphantly, "In the future nothing in international politics will be done over Germany's head!" it seemed clear that the Washington visit, which had begun in the shadow of a new Soviet "peace offensive," had relieved the Chancellor of his nightmare of a "new Potsdam." There seemed little reason to doubt that Eisenhower, like Churchill before him, had given the Federal Chancellor an assurance that the United States, like Britain, would not seek to obtain an understanding with the Soviet Union behind Germany's back and at Germany's expense.

After his Washington success Adenauer might well have returned home satisfied and with a good clear conscience. That he did not do so, but instead followed it up with a most strenuous eight-day lightning trip across the American continent to the West Coast and to Canada proved, as one American newspaperman said, that he possessed a "most unusually sharp instinct for publicity." State visits were normally and traditionally confined to the East Coast, and never before had a European chief of government penetrated beyond Washington to the West.

Adenauer flew straight across the American continent to San Francisco, where he addressed a gathering of 700 prominent representatives of the political, industrial, and economic world at the Commonwealth Club. Then to Chicago, where the large colony of Americans of German descent gave him an enthusiastic welcome, and on, via New York and Boston, to Harvard University at Cambridge, Massachusetts. Harvard was the spiritual home of James B. Conant, who had relinquished his post as the University's President in order to serve his country as High Commissioner in Germany, and Conant had insisted that Adenauer must pay it a visit, however brief. Adenauer deeply appreciated this and expressed it in his address to the students and teachers of the University:

"American universities have played a leading part in the great effort of putting Europe back on its feet after the severe ordeals of World War II. The helping hand you offered us, and especially Germany, has meant a great deal to us. Your latest gift which you have presented to us—and I am sure that you found it the hardest to part with—was President Conant, who gave up his prominent position as head of this university in order to tackle the thorny problems which fall to the lot of the American High Commissioner in Germany. And, while I am thanking you for all you have done to help restore good relations between our two countries, allow me also to recall with gratitude the open-minded generosity with which, during the dark period of the Nazi tyranny, you offered refuge to hundreds of German scholars and scientists, among them one of my predecessors in the equally thorny office of German Chancellor."

There was no need for Adenauer to mention the name. Everyone present knew that he was referring to Dr. Heinrich Brüning, and there was no one who did not take this loyal reference, just because it remained unspoken, for what it was—a gesture of genuine conciliation.

From Boston, that same afternoon, Adenauer traveled on to Canada, for a dinner party at which he was the guest of the Canadian Prime Minister St. Laurent, a brief conference with the Canadian government on problems of European defense, a press reception at the parliament building in Ottawa, and yet another honorary doctor's degree from the university of that city. By the time this honor had been conferred upon him, time was so advanced that the Chancellor was unable to make his prepared speech to the students of the university but had to limit himself to a brief impromptu address. Outside, an aircraft of the Royal Canadian Air Force was waiting, its engines running, to take him back to Boston, where he changed to the scheduled Stratocruiser of Pan-American Airways which took him straight to—Hamburg.

The journey across the American continent had taken sixteen days in all, with an average of one thousand miles' travel each day. "The strain of his journey was unexampled," one American newspaper said, "but equally unexampled was its success." Sixty million Americans, it was estimated, had seen the German Federal Chancellor on their television screens. Five hundred American radio stations had devoted a daily average of ten minutes to news broadcasts on the Chancellor's visit. More than five thousand newspaper articles had been written about him, and over one thousand different photographs were published in the papers. And some 15,000 movie theaters all over the United States had shown newsreels of his visit.

It was a balance sheet of success such as, apart from Winston Churchill, no European statesman had yet been able to achieve in the United States, and it was a success from which the entire German people benefited. "Adenauer's immense vitality," one American weekly magazine summed up the visit, "is the best proof of the unbroken vital strength of the German people."

There was a particular reason for Adenauer to fly straight back, not to Bonn, but to the city of Hamburg. As he arrived, the annual party conference of the Christian Democratic Union had just opened there under the chairmanship of Dr. Ehlers, the President of the Federal Parliament. It was the last party conference before the general elections due to take place later that summer, and naturally the CDU concentrated the entire limelight of their election campaign on the person of Adenauer, whose successful mission to the United States was now redounding to his credit with the German public in general.

But now, on June 17, 1953, an event occurred which like a blinding flash of lightning revealed the true situation of eighteen million Germans behind the iron curtain. All of a sudden the people of the Eastern Zone rose in revolt against the Soviet system. It was a rebellion of desperate impotence against the brutality of a Communist dictatorship, which was soon crushed, after bloody street fighting, under the fire of Russian tanks and machine guns. But henceforth the world knew what to think of the "people's democracy" in Eastern Germany.

Adenauer at once flew to Berlin to attend the solemn memorial service for the victims of the June 17 rebellion. There, standing beside the coffins, he gave this pledge:

"The German people behind the iron curtain call upon us not to forget them. We swear here in this solemn hour that we are not forgetting them. We shall not rest, and this vow I make upon behalf of the whole German nation, until they too have regained their freedom, until the whole of Germany is reunited in peace and freedom!"

Nor did Adenauer allow matters to rest there. He immediately despatched telegrams to Eisenhower, Churchill, and René Mayer, requesting assurances that the Western Powers were in earnest about reuniting Germany. On July 1, 1953, he was able to inform the Parliament of the Allied response to his call for help. "All three statesmen," he said, "have pledged themselves in complete agreement to the reunification of Germany in freedom and peace, and have declared that they intend to follow the policy outlined in their note to the Soviet government of September 23, 1952. This policy can be summarized as follows: free elections throughout the whole of Germany; formation of a free all-German government; conclusion of a peace treaty freely negotiated with that government; settlement of all territorial issues through this peace treaty; and safeguards for the freedom of action of an all-German Parliament and an all-German government."

Henceforth Adenauer's German policy could be reduced to a very simple formula: full sovereignty for the Federal Republic to enable it, by virtue of this sovereignty, to help East Germany to regain its right of self-determination. Long before most Germans, Adenauer had realized that, once the Federal Republic had ceased to be the "plaything of the powers," the whole of Germany would no longer be one either.

# CHAPTER XXIX

"HONORED assembly! My dear party friends!"

"Yesterday, Friday, I drove through Heidelberg, and I recalled that it was there, on July 21, 1949, exactly four years ago, that I opened the election campaign of the Christian Democratic Union. When I reached home last night I sent for the text of the speech I made on that day, as well as for the statement of policy I made as Federal Chancellor before the first Federal Parliament, on September 20, 1949. And having these two papers before me, I conducted an investigation of my conscience—whether we of the Christian Democratic Union had, or had not, fulfilled the promises we made during the first election campaign and in our policy declaration."

"For I believe that in this second election, which is now before us, every party must above all render account to the German people of what it has achieved during these past four years. On this, and not on vague party promises, the electorate will base its judgment on September 6. We of the Christian Democratic party can today stand before the German people with gratitude to God that He should have allowed us to achieve a measure of success for them so vast that it seems almost incredible. We should never have been able to achieve this unless God had given us His blessing. . . ."

With these words Adenauer began his great election speech at Dortmund, on July 26, 1953, which opened the election campaign for the CDU. His very first sentences already contained the basic theme which ran like a thread through the entire campaign from its first day to the last. In the name of his party, and in the name of the government which rested on this party, Adenauer simply rendered account, soberly, clearly, and factually, of the results of the past four years. There was no other theme in his speeches. Again and again he would say:

"I shall have to trouble you with a few figures, my friends. I have tried to marshal these figures in such a way that they do not appear too boring. But when one draws up a balance sheet, when one gives an account of one's stewardship, one must be able to express this in clear, hard figures. Words are often deceptive. But figures are impartial and stand up to scrutiny. . . ."

Then he would give such figures, always skillfully juxtaposing what had been promised in 1949 and what had been achieved by 1953. The juxtaposition told its own story and told it very well. Four years before, in his statement of policy, the Chancellor had promised to increase agricultural production. It had risen from 58 per cent of the prewar level to 111 per cent. He had promised to raise the exchange value of the new German currency. Whereas in 1940 100 German marks stood at the rate of 17 U.S. dollars, they now represented the equivalent of 22½ dollars. He had promised to improve the general standard of living, and now even trade unionists freely admitted that it had in fact risen by 20 to 25 per cent.

On other occasions Adenauer changed his tactics, comparing his own achievements with the promises made by his opponents and critics during the 1949 election campaign: "The Social Democratic speakers then declared that if they came to power they would build 750,000 dwellings, or possibly even a million, by the end of 1952." Drily he added, "During the same period we built a million and a half, and in the course of this year shall reach the two million mark.

"The German Trades Union Congress," Adenauer went on, "accuses us of having done nothing to combat unemployment. Well, we have succeeded in providing employment for an additional two and a half millions, and, despite the steady influx of refugees from the East, we have reduced unemployment to some 900,000. And this figure includes at least 500,000 sick and elderly people no longer fully employable, or even totally unemployable."

Against this the Social Democrats found it hard to make an impression. It was difficult, in view of these figures, the correctness of which could not be disputed, to make out a case for the failure of the economic and social policy of the government without incurring ridicule, and the opposition therefore shifted their ground and directed their main attack against Adenauer's foreign policy. "Schuman's gone—de Gasperi's gone—Adenauer will soon be gone too—and then the whole European bogey will be gone!" Thus ran one of their favorite slogans. Adenauer replied bitingly that it was plainly childish to assume that the necessity of European unification was indissolubly tied to the names of two or three particular men. And when the Socialists mocked him for his "Little Europe," from which Britain and Scandinavia were missing, he answered, "This Little Europe has a population larger than that of the United States, and its industrial potential is equivalent to that of America. Isn't that sufficient for a start?"

But there were other charges brought against the Chancellor and designed to discredit him in the eyes of the electorate. One of the more dangerous among them was the assertion that in his heart of hearts Adenauer was really an opponent of German reunification, and his public utterances and pledges on this vital matter should not be taken at their face value because they were not meant seriously but were just so much hypocrisy. At the beginning of the campaign this was not openly proclaimed from the hustings, but the whispering campaign set on foot instead was all the more intensive and damaging. Thus it was said that Adenauer's deep-rooted attachment to his native Rhineland had made him "anti-Prussian"; that he felt a profound antipathy against Berlin; that he was incapable of any understanding for the people of Eastern Germany and that in the last resort their fate meant nothing to him. There were others who maintained that his Catholicism created an unbridgeable gap between himself and the Protestant sections of the German people, determining his entire political concept and aiming at a predominantly Roman Catholic German State. There were others again who asserted that Adenauer did not want German reunification because this meant free all-German elections, and the "old fox" knew perfectly well that in such elections the CDU would be beaten, and the Social Democratic party emerge as the strongest party in Germany.

Adenauer was fully aware of this whispering campaign and did not take it lightly. In his election speeches he referred repeatedly and pointedly to the issue of German reunification. On one occasion he recalled his statement before the Federal Parliament in which he had said:

"I should at any time prefer a free united Germany, with the Socialists as the strongest party, to a Federal Republic separated from the Soviet Zone, with the CDU as the strongest party. In this issue the fatherland and the nation really stand above party issues, and the statesman begins where the party politician ends. Regarding the all-German issue, there is no such thing as a CDU policy or a Catholic policy. This exists just as little as a Socialist policy or a Protestant policy could exist in this respect!"

On another occasion he recalled to his audience the numerous attempts the federal government had made to achieve progress in the matter of reunification. It was, as he read it out, a depressingly long list of vain endeavors, every one of which had come up against silence or a stubborn Russian "No" and failed.

Finally, at a third election meeting, Adenauer played a trump card. He read the text of the letter he had written to the three Western heads of government under the impact of the events of June 17 in Eastern Germany. This letter, dated June 22, 1953, and addressed to Secretary of State Dulles as Chairman of the Washington Conference, ran as follows:

> The conference of Foreign Ministers will be dealing primarily with the German question. I shall be obliged if you will submit to the conference the following proposal of the Federal Government:
>
> 1. A Four Power Conference dealing with the question of Germany should meet not later than this autumn.
> 2. This conference should have as a basis for its discussions the Five Point Program approved by the Federal German Parliament on June 10, 1953.
> 3. The European Defense Community should be made the basis and starting point for a security system taking into account the security requirements of all European nations including those of the Russian people. This system should be integrated into the system of general disarmament and security within the framework of the United Nations, as suggested by President Eisenhower on April 16, 1953.

Having read out this letter, Adenauer added:

"I charged Dr. Blankenhorn with taking this letter to Washington. This was a difficult mission for him, for it is always unpleasant to have to intrude upon a meeting to which one has not been invited. I can assure you that even our best friends were taken slightly aback when he turned up in Washington, for this was a conference of the three Western Powers in which Germany had not been asked to participate. Still, they did not close their minds to the fact that it was our fate, after all, which was being discussed, and I am profoundly grateful to Mr. Dulles, the American Secretary of State, for having submitted my letter to the conference without delay. Eventually the conference issued a communiqué which took our proposals into account in every respect. We shall, therefore, have a four-power conference on Germany, provided the Soviet Union agrees. And the initiative for holding such a conference—I wish to tell you quite explicitly—came from me and not from Herr Ollenhauer. . . ."

The Social Democrats did not leave this unanswered. Barely a week before the election they came out officially in favor of a neutral, reunited Germany which would be debarred from entering any alliances and whose security would be safeguarded by a four-power system of mutual guarantees. And finally, three days before the polling day, the opposition openly accused Adenauer of not being interested in German reunification. An official Socialist election statement said:

"It is the whole nature and character of the Chancellor that he is rooted in the West and has no understanding for the East—the far side of the Elbe. To him Berlin is a pagan city, and Königsberg is more alien to his whole mental outlook than anything in the West. It is a disaster for Germany that it should be governed by a Chancellor who regards everything lying beyond the Elbe as no more than colonial territory."

Adenauer reacted swiftly to this. Concerning the Socialist policy of neutrality, he declared, "Those who feel they must find fault with the treaties we have concluded with the Western Powers should consider above all that we have succeeded, with these treaties, in getting three of the four powers which have to decide Germany's fate on our side!" And the charge that to him Eastern Germany was merely colonial territory he dismissed with one sentence: "I should like nothing better than to be able to conduct an election campaign in the Eastern Sector of Berlin and in the Eastern Zone of Germany, because I'm firmly convinced that the people there share our views and not those of the Social Democrats. . . ."

This swift reaction to every new charge or challenge brought by his opponents and to every new turn in the development of the situation at home or abroad was very characteristic of Adenauer's method of conducting his campaign. During this period of five weeks, from the end of July until early September, 1953, he made no fewer than thirty-three full-length election speeches, most of them lasting for two hours or more. No two of them were identical or even alike. Invariably references to the latest events were worked in. Each time he had new quotations, new facts, new figures to offer. No sooner had a political opponent anywhere made an ill-considered remark or stated his facts incorrectly than Adenauer promptly took up the point at his next meeting, answering, correcting, returning the challenge. Going through the mass of these election speeches one finds that invariably they are most carefully and conscientiously adapted to the circumstances and conditions of the particular locality where they were made, taking into account not only the needs and requirements of the particular town or region where he happened to be speaking, but emphasizing at the same time their specific achievements and underlining their successes in particular fields. Thus, in order to demonstrate the increase in German productivity, Adenauer was careful, when speaking for instance at Brunswick, to quote detailed and precise figures about developments in the motor industry; but when speaking on the same subject at Bremen and Kiel he would exchange them for corresponding facts and figures relating to shipbuilding and the merchant navy—facts and figures which were all designed to prove the same thing but which, in each instance, every one of his listeners could check against his own experience and find correct.

It was undoubtedly this conscientious and painstaking method of "rendering account of his stewardship" to which Adenauer, now in his seventy-eighth year, largely owed the impact of his campaign.

Sunday, September 6, 1953, was a radiantly beautiful summer day. Accompanied by his daughter Lotte, Adenauer first attended Mass and then went to his local polling station at Rhöndorf to cast his vote. Once again he was the CDU candidate for the Bonn constituency, and looked forward to the result with complete confidence. He was in an excellent mood, and after the enormous strain of the past weeks spent the day quietly in the family circle. And in contrast to most politicians, who spent the night at their radio sets waiting for results to come in, he retired to bed at his usual hour.

Toward three o'clock in the morning it became clear that the Christian Democratic Union would emerge as the strongest party. Adenauer had asked to be roused at six-thirty. But at five Secretary of State Dr. Lenz could no longer restrain himself and telephoned from Bonn to give the Chancellor news of his victory. Adenauer answered laconically, "Thank you very much, Herr Lenz." A little later there was another telephone call from Bonn. This time it was

Herr Felix von Eckardt, chief of the Government Press and Information Office, giving the final result. Later, he said how disconcerted he was when Adenauer merely answered, "Thank you very much, Herr von Eckardt," and hung up.

The magnitude of the CDU's success was a surprise even to the party managers. The CDU had obtained an absolute majority in the new Parliament and its lead over the SPD had increased from eight to ninety-four seats.

Comparison with the results of 1949 showed that interest had increased considerably in the intervening four years. The total poll had risen from 78.5 to 86.2 per cent. Of the 28,500,000 votes cast, 12,500,000 had gone to the CDU and just under 8,000,000 to the SPD. The Communist party had suffered a crushing defeat, losing more than half their former vote and all their seats in the Federal Parliament. The German Reich party, one of the small parties of the extreme right, had been wiped out. The Refugee party had achieved a mere twenty-seven seats. The Free Democrats and the German party, the two partners of the CDU in the coalition, had more or less held their own. But the decisive feature was that Adenauer's party had won an absolute majority. Of the total of 487 seats in the new parliament, the CDU had gained 244, and the Government parties jointly commanded 307.

The whole Western World was plainly surprised by the size of the victory and greeted it with unconcealed pleasure and satisfaction. It was felt everywhere that the result amounted to nothing less than a plebiscite in favor of the European Defense Community and Adenauer's European policy as a whole. The New York *Times* declared roundly, "The Kremlin has lost. Western Germany is the cornerstone of the new European order. . . ." And the Manchester *Guardian* commented, "Of Dr. Adenauer it used to be said that he was a one-man Cabinet. Of yesterday's election results it might well be said that they were a one-man triumph. Dr. Adenauer's personality, his record in office, and his immensely energetic campaigning have brought him victory. His success has been greater than ever he can have honestly expected. He deserved it. . . ." The echo from France was rather more subdued, the newspaper *Le Monde* interpreting the reaction of the French people thus: "Of the three great champions of European integration, only Adenauer is left, and he is stronger than ever. From this realization it is but one step to the conclusion that henceforth the Washington government will rely more and more on Western Germany, and less and less on France and Italy."

This large and unexpected increase in strength which had fallen to his party now opened new possibilities for Adenauer. The Government coalition possessed an overwhelming majority in the new House, but even more than that lay within its grasp. The leaders of the Refugee party, contrary to Adenauer's original fears, had resisted Socialist advances and offers to make common cause with them and had come out in support of the European Defense Community. This was an important gain. Together with the Refugee party mandates the Government could now in fact muster the necessary two-thirds majority in the House in case this was needed for passing an amendment to the Constitution. It was clear, however, that the Chancellor could only rely on the Refugee party's support with any degree of certainty if he gave this young party a share in governmental responsibility. There was a good case for broadening the basis of the coalition, and Adenauer resolved to seize what was within his grasp.

For the moment, however, he decided to relax, and accompanied by his daughter Lotte took a three weeks' vacation in the Black Forest. His ship had safely reached port, and he could permit himself to leave the bridge for a short spell of rest. In Bonn, however, things did not stand still meanwhile. There was frantic bargaining and haggling among the new coalition parties over the distribution of portfolios in what was going to be the second Adenauer administration. Claims and counterclaims were put in, each partner claiming to have had a major share in the victory. Adenauer watched it all with an amused and wistful smile from his Black Forest retreat.

The new Federal Parliament met on October 6, 1953, for its first sitting, and three days later, on October 9, Dr. Ehlers, its reelected Speaker, submitted the Federal President's recommendation to elect the leader of the Christian Democratic Union, Dr. Konrad Adenauer, Federal Chancellor. There were many who at this moment remembered the tense atmosphere of the election four years ago when Adenauer just barely managed to scrape through with a majority of one. This time it was very different. There was no tension at all. The result was a foregone conclusion. Adenauer obtained 304 votes and was elected for his second term of office.

The formation of the new government proved more difficult. On October 20, 1953, when Adenauer presented his new Cabinet, it was found, to Finance Minister Dr. Schaeffer's intense displeasure, that it comprised no fewer than nineteen ministers, two of whom belonged to the new partner, the Refugee party. That, however, had been the price of their support, and Adenauer had not hesitated to pay it.

The detailed statement of policy on behalf of the Government, in which Adenauer outlined his program for the next four years, was acknowledged by the Opposition with respectful silence. There were no interjections, no disturbances.

Three major problems, the Chancellor declared, remained to be solved—German sovereignty, German reunification, and the integration of the whole of Germany with the rest of Europe. His government, he said, would endeavor to solve these problems by faithfully adhering to the German Contract, by joining the European Defense Community, and by working for the closest possible relations with neighboring France.

"In my view," Adenauer declared, "there exists no problem, however difficult and complicated, for which the methods of negotiation will not find an infinitely more durable solution than the methods of force and violence from which, as our own past has amply taught us, only new conflicts are born."

Adenauer uttered these concluding words in a tone of sober confidence which seemed to permit no doubt that his optimism was fully justified. He was at the height of his influence, prestige, and authority, in Germany and in the world.

Twelve months later his work lay shattered at his feet. The smashing blow was struck by France. His most bitter disappointment as well as his greatest triumph were still before him.

## CHAPTER XXX

August 30, 1954.

Two years and three months had passed since the historic day at Bonn in May, 1952, when Adenauer and the Foreign Ministers of the three Western Powers put their signatures to the German Contract, the treaty which was to give the Federal Republic full sovereignty and equality of status in the comity of nations. Nearly a year and a half had passed since the Federal Parliament had taken the lead among the six European parliaments by being first to ratify the treaty establishing the European Defense Community. And still Germany was waiting for her sovereignty; still the Occupation Statute was in force; still the High Commissioners officiated as before; still the Chancellor was pleading for patience and confidence.

The Netherlands, Belgium, and Luxembourg had ratified the treaties. Italy had at last taken the initial step of submitting them to Parliament. Only in France, where the concept of the European Army had been born, the treaties had not so far even been presented to the National Assembly. French governments had come and gone, and none of them had dared, in twenty-seven months, to confront the National Assembly with the necessity of making a decision.

A year ago Adenauer had entered the election campaign under the banner of the European idea, and the German electorate had given him an overwhelming mandate for continuing on his chosen path. These twelve months of waiting, during which the ultimate goal seemed to move steadily further away into the remote distance, had put the patience of the seventy-eight-year-old Chancellor to a severe test of endurance, while the confidence of his supporters in the correctness of his course had undergone a trial no less hard.

Now at long last there seemed an end to waiting and uncertainty. On this day, August 30, 1954, the French National Assembly was to vote on the first reading of the treaties on which depended the fate not only of Germany but of all Europe. But still no one could know what the decision would be.



* * *

For a German it had been difficult to follow the zigzag course French policy had pursued through recent years until this day in August, 1954, or to understand its restlessness, the ever more rapid succession of governments, and above all the pervading lack of resolution, manifesting itself on the one hand in more and more additional demands, and on the other delaying tactics which, in the shape of new objections, doubts, discussions, and conferences, aimed at avoiding an ultimate decision altogether.

In his London conversation with Churchill, Adenauer had once remarked, "Today Germany is a shapeless mass which has to be molded. But everything depends on the hands which mold it." Well, he had molded it. Firmly convinced that no people can exist and maintain itself in the political field without belief in an ideal, he had given the Germans this new belief, the belief in a Christian Europe. This belief had taken root, mainly among the younger generation, and the last elections had confirmed it.

In France this development had been watched with misgivings and suspicion. There was a distinct feeling that the Germans were "using the European backstairs to regain a position of predominance." That was how the election result was widely interpreted, and Adenauer understood this suspicion. Until now he had succeeded in keeping the nationalist elements in the Federal Republic away from political influence, and the voters had supported him in this by practically eliminating the smaller parties and extremist splinter groups. But the support of his own voters was not enough. He needed the support of the free world, and in particular the assistance of France. He was fully aware of the ravages wrought by German militarism on the French body politic, and therefore bore the irritating seesaw of French postwar politics with a degree of patience and forbearance which frequently earned him the charge of weakness and spinelessness from his own people. He was willing to put up with all this as long as the great ultimate goal remained in sight—Europe.

The Pleven government was succeeded by the Pinay government, and when Pinay in his turn fell at the end of 1952, the new French Prime Minister René Mayer secured the support of the Gaullists by giving an undertaking to enter into negotiations with France's partners in the EDC with a view to obtaining additional protocols to the EDC treaty. The purpose of these amendments was to safeguard "the integrity of the French Army and the French Union," in other words, the French colonial empire. At the same time he undertook not to submit the EDC treaty for ratification unless and until a Franco-German agreement on a European Statute for the Saar had been concluded.

This opened a new phase. Henceforth the fate of the EDC treaty was dominated by the *conditions préalables,* the conditions which France insisted must be fulfilled before ratification of the treaty itself could be taken in hand. The apparent impossibility of reaching agreement over the Saar furnished further excuses for delaying the ratification of the EDC treaty. Yet another argument was supplied to the French advocates of delay by the Four Power Conference with the Soviet Union, which, upon Churchill's initiative, was summoned to Berlin at the end of January, 1954. "We must not ratify the EDC pact," it was now said in Paris, "as long as there is still a chance of reaching agreement with the Russians on a common German policy." When the Berlin conference ended in failure on February 18, 1954, the road seemed clear at last. But again the Laniel government did not find it possible to take the final step and ask the National Assembly to ratify.

Britain and the United States now took a hand by offering France a number of concessions designed to help her in reaching her difficult decision. Foreign Secretary Eden announced that Britain was ready to place one of her divisions under EDC, and President Eisenhower promised that American forces would remain stationed in Europe as long as the threat of aggression lasted.

On June 4, Secretary of State Dulles let it be known that he was in favor of discontinuing all military aid to France and Italy until these two countries had ratified the EDC treaty. On June 9, the Foreign Affairs Committee of the French National Assembly rejected the EDC treaty by twenty-four votes to eighteen, and three days later the Laniel government resigned.

Now a new man appeared on the scene: Pierre Mendès-France. At the age of forty-seven he was the youngest Prime Minister France had ever had, and before he reached the highest office he had been, at the age of twenty-five, the youngest deputy in the National Assembly, and at thirty-one the youngest undersecretary in the Blum Government. The Second World War had interrupted the rapid rise of this uncommonly gifted and energetic politician. Arrested by the

Vichy government, he managed to escape, joined the French underground resistance movement, and eventually made his way to England, where he joined forces with de Gaulle and became his adviser on economic affairs, and eventually de Gaulle's Minister of Economics in the provisional Algiers government. Returning to Paris as soon as the capital was liberated, he founded his own newspaper, *L'Express,* and once again became a deputy to the National Assembly. Although a Radical Socialist, it soon became clear that he was not prepared to follow blindly the rigid course pursued by his party chief Herriot.

Evidence of Mendès-France's strong-willed and single-minded personality was soon at hand when he succeeded Joseph Laniel as French Prime Minister and surprised friends and opponents alike with a "program of immediacy," setting a series of short-term "deadlines" for the rapid settlement of the most urgent outstanding issues. He would end the war in Indo-China within four weeks, he told the Assembly, and, should he fail in this, he would resign. Following this he undertook to grapple in the same energetic manner with France's two other major problems, economic reform and the EDC treaties.

Adenauer, who, like everyone else, gladly welcomed any sign of political consolidation and stability in France, was perfectly ready to cooperate with the new Prime Minister. But things had not stood still in Germany while France had tarried and procrastinated, and there was a new development to be taken into account. Under insistent pressure from public opinion, Adenauer had meantime requested the three Western Powers to consider releasing the German Contract from its automatic coupling to the EDC Treaty and to implement the conventions restoring German sovereignty independently and irrespective of French ratification of the EDC Treaty. This seemed a not unwarranted request, and Adenauer's attitude met with full understanding from Britain and the United States.

But, despite this urgent request to the Western Powers, Adenauer did not conceal that he would greatly prefer the "normal course," namely, the simultaneous coming into force of both treaties, if it could be achieved. It is in this light that the broadcast interview which he gave to the well-known German publicist Ernst Friedländer on July 1, 1954, and which subsequently raised a good deal of political dust, must be understood. In this interview Adenauer addressed himself directly to Mendès-France, suggesting to him that he should now finally submit the two treaties to the National Assembly and leave the discussion of possible modifications and amendments until a later date.

"I do not by any means take the view that the EDC Treaty is dead," the Chancellor declared, "even if people say so a hundred times over. I still believe the European Defense Community to be the only possible practical solution. Of course, it is possible to visualize various alternatives, but none of them is nearly as good. No alternative to the EDC is possible or feasible without the creation of a German national army. The German people, however, do not want a national army. We realize quite clearly that such a national army would inevitably awaken new fears and new suspicions in France. It would indeed be a political paradox if France, of all nations, were to compel us through her procrastination to create a German national army which she herself fears more than anyone else."

Adenauer's assertion that the creation of a German national army represented the only possible alternative to the European Defense Community was not the first indication of this kind France had received. Four days earlier Eisenhower and Churchill had issued a considerably sharper warning to France from Washington. Nevertheless, French public opinion concentrated its furious indignation exclusively upon Adenauer. It was "unbearable," it was said, "that a German should employ such language toward France."

The Chancellor was not unduly irritated by this reaction. On the contrary, he tried to build a bridge for France. In an interview he gave to the French newspaper *Aurore* he promised that he would "interpret the EDC Treaty, once it was ratified, as generously and liberally as possible, in order to meet France and dispel her misgivings." But in spite of these assurances, Mendès-France came to the conclusion that the EDC treaty in its present form had no prospect of being ratified by the National Assembly. He therefore drafted a long list of modifications to be submitted to a conference of the six EDC states, which was to meet at Brussels on August 19, 1954.

The Mendès-France memorandum contained no fewer than sixty points, practically every one of which amounted to a revocation of the spirit of the European community.

All supranational provisions of the EDC Treaty were to be suspended for eight years. That sounded the death knell of the political integration of Western Europe. Next, France was to be permitted to withdraw from the EDC as soon as either German reunification was achieved or British and American troops left the continent of Europe. That spelled the end of military integration. Finally, the EDC was to comprise only 'covering troops," which meant that no German troops would be stationed on French territory. That made nonsense of equality of status.

When the main points of the French memorandum became generally known, through an indiscretion of the French press several days before the Brussels conference, anger and indignation throughout Western Germany were genuine and deeply felt. One West German paper commented sarcastically, "The only thing missing is a provision that German soldiers must hand in their rifles every evening."

Adenauer traveled to Brussels with a heavy heart. He had not yet met the new French Prime Minister, and they saw each other face to face for the first time on the morning of August 9, 1954, when the conference delegates were received in audience by King Baudouin. Half an hour later they sat facing each other at the conference table without having previously exchanged a single word.

It was a truly tragic situation. It was clear that all six ministers desired nothing more urgently than to avoid a failure of the conference. But it was equally clear to at least five of them that the French memorandum offered no basis for an understanding.

Mendès-France's opening speech, in which he explained his proposals, far from giving any hope deepened the gloom of the pessimistic gathering. If the treaty were submitted to the National Assembly in its present form—"and this," said Mendès-France, "would be by far the easiest way out for me"—its rejection was an absolute certainty. "My government would fall, to be replaced in all probability by a Popular Front administration. This would plunge the entire NATO defense structure into a serious crisis. The Communists would have achieved a great success, and we should have gained nothing."

Despite all attempts by Paul Henri Spaak, the Belgian Foreign Minister, to find a compromise formula, the conference broke down on August 22, 1954. For the first time in modern history France found herself completely isolated. Italy and the three Benelux countries had left no doubt that they agreed with the German point of view. In common with Adenauer, they were convinced that the majority of the French proposals were unacceptable because they ran contrary to the fundamental concept of the EDC treaty and made nonsense of the idea which had originally inspired it.

Adenauer traveled back to Bühlerhöhe, in the Black Forest, to continue his interrupted summer holiday. He felt profoundly and utterly depressed. The great plan whose prime object had been to bring about a final reconciliation between France and Germany had achieved the precise opposite: at no time since the end of the war had relations between the two nations been more tense than now.

What next? Adenauer reflected. There was only one hope left. It was just conceivable that the drastic failure of the Brussels conference might at the very last moment induce the French National Assembly to think again when Mendès-France submitted the EDC treaty in its present form to the Chamber on August 27. It was a faint chance, no more.

The debate in the French Chamber had now been going on for three days. Mendès-France himself had withdrawn to a "neutral" position, in which he was not committed, and had refrained even from making the treaty an issue of confidence. And now, on this day, August 30, 1954, the Federal Chancellor sat on the small balcony of his apartment in the Bühlerhöhe sanatorium, waiting for the decision. With him, millions in Germany and France sat waiting at their radio sets.

Shortly after nine o'clock in the evening the telephone rang at Bühlerhöhe. The German Embassy in Paris asked to speak to the private secretary of the Federal Chancellor. When Adenauer was handed the ambassador's message, he cast one brief glance at it and without a word withdrew to his bedroom.

With 319 votes against 264 the French National Assembly had decided to remove the EDC treaty from its agenda. It had not voted against it. It had not rejected it. It had simply decided not to debate it at all, either now or ever.

The European Defense Community was dead.

At first sight the step taken by the French Parliament seemed totally incomprehensible. It just did not seem to make sense. The EDC Treaty, the German Contract, the additional protocols, the treaty between Great Britain and the six EDC states—the entire vast structure at one fell swoop had been swept off the table and into the wastepaper basket! It seemed incredible but it was true.

What had happened? Of the 319 votes cast against a continuation of the debate, 99 were those of the Communist deputies, who immediately rose from their seats and started singing the "*Marseillaise.*" Their chorus was speedily reinforced by the Gaullists and other deputies of the extreme right. It was as Adenauer had predicted: Communists and Nationalists had joined forces and brought the attempt at European integration to nought.

There could have been no more shameful and humiliating end. This was the greatest and most shattering disappointment Adenauer had suffered in all his long political career. Scarcely a year after his immense triumph at the polls everything he stood for and had worked for had been ground into dust.

It is not normally Adenauer's way to display anger or disappointment in public. "I'm not going to do my opponents the favor of letting them know that they've hit me," he once remarked during the election campaign. This time, however, he proceeded differently. And since he has always been opposed, as a matter of principle, to emotional appeals in politics, one can only assume that in this instance, too, he proceeded deliberately, knowing full well what he was doing, without being carried away by his feelings. He obviously intended to let the French know the full extent of the damage they had caused, and to bring home to them the shattering disappointment they had inflicted upon millions in Germany who had supported the European idea honestly and in good faith.

That was undoubtedly the mood in which John Freeman, the special correspondent of the London *Times,* found the Chancellor when he called upon him at Bühlerhöhe, and it was the mood Adenauer was anxious to express. He seized the opportunity. He was not angry, he explained later, but "anxious to let off steam." Of all the famous and sometimes controversial Adenauer interviews, the one which appeared in the *Times* of September 4, 1954, became the most famous and the most sensational.

"I cannot say too strongly or too often," Adenauer said, "that a situation of much gravity has been created by the French National Assembly's rejection of the EDC Treaty. The idea that German policy is being directed toward the isolation of France is sheer nonsense. Now, as before, it is my firm conviction that the tranquillity and security of Europe depend essentially on a good understanding between France and Germany. The idea that there was at Brussels a common front against France, that there could be any intention of humiliating France, is quite absurd.

"I regret to have to say," Adenauer continued, "that Mendès-France wanted to destroy the EDC. Consider the manner in which the issue was decided in the National Assembly. What is important to note is that Mendès-France has no majority behind him."

The good will which Germany had shown and the desire to go forward together with France in friendship and fellowship had been grievously disappointed.

"What are the Germans saying now?" Adenauer asked. "They are saying something like this: 'Stresemann negotiated with Briand, Brüning negotiated with Daladier, and Adenauer negotiated with Schuman—all to no purpose. Must we now assume that the French do not wish for this understanding between our two countries?' Just think now of the younger generation of Germans. I think I can fairly claim that we have displaced the old conception of narrow nationalism with the European idea. If the European idea is now wrecked by the action of France, will not that mean a return in Germany to an exaggerated nationalism? I do not mean a return to the Nazism of Hitler, but a return certainly to some form of nationalism. If Germany is rebuffed by the West and wooed by the East, do you not think that a new nationalism will look to the Soviet Union? This is a great danger. This new nationalism will not come all at once. You remember how long it took for Nazism to develop. The new nationalism will take years to evolve, but do not let us underrate its beginnings. It is quite clear to me that the Russians will be only too happy to encourage a German nationalism looking to the East."

It was not least for these reasons, Adenauer said, that he deplored developments in France. "If some French circles think that, with the help of Russia, they can play a decisive role in Germany, then they are making the same mistake as Benes. I do not regard France as lost to the West, and I still hope that she will recover her greatness, and that the European Defense Community will yet come into being. I do not for a moment underrate the difficulties in France, but I am persuaded that the European idea stands, and will stand. We require patience and discretion. The conception of Europe cannot be killed by a procedural discussion in the French National Assembly with the help of a hundred Communists."

But what next? What could be done to counter the disappointment which the French decision had caused among the German people?

"There is only one answer," Adenauer said. "The Federal Republic must now obtain its full sovereignty. The Occupation Statute cannot be sustained nine years after the war. And implicit in sovereignty is the right of self-defense. We are not asking for the right of rearmament as such, but only as a part of our sovereignty. Nor are we asking for rearmament unlimited and without shackles. We shall exercise the right to rearm in the light of European policy."

Two days after this conversation, the Chancellor repeated his demands in a broadcast speech: "The Federal Republic must receive its full sovereignty without further delay. As soon as it enjoys this sovereignty, it will be ready to negotiate with the Western Powers for the conclusion of new treaties."

The *Times* interview as well as the broadcast speech caused deep displeasure in France. Adenauer regretted this but felt that it could not be helped. His words had been addressed primarily to the German people, and beyond them to Britain and the United States. They were meant as a signal: I'm still on the bridge, and I'm not changing my course.

The signal was picked up and understood. At this most critical moment in his fortunes Adenauer found that the years of patient striving for the confidence of the West had not been in vain, and that this confidence now represented a thoroughly concrete political asset. This time Britain took a hand, and took it swiftly. Even before the fateful Brussels conference, on July 12, 1954, Churchill had stated in the House of Commons:

"We feel that we are bound to act in good faith toward Germany in accordance with the treaties we have signed and ratified, and also that those concerned in these decisions owe this to Dr. Adenauer, who, during a score of long and weary months of delay and uncertainty, has never shrunk from facing unpopularity in his own country in order to keep his word and range Germany definitely with the free world. . . ."

Within a few days after the disaster of the EDC treaties, the British government suggested to all interested powers the early summoning of a conference in London to consider the new situation created by the failure of the EDC and if possible find an alternative solution. On September 11, Mr. Eden, the Foreign Secretary, set out by air on a lightning trip to Brussels, Bonn, Rome, and Paris, to obtain a first-hand impression of the views of the various governments and to see whether there was enough common ground to serve as a basis of negotiation for the proposed London conference.

Eden did not confine himself to vague consultations. He brought a plan with him. This suggested briefly that for the time being all projects for a political integration of Europe should be set aside, that the German Contract should be put into force forthwith and the Federal Republic accepted as a sovereign state with its own national army into the North Atlantic Treaty Organization. In order to create the necessary safeguards against a German preponderance in the new setup, on which European NATO members and former partners in EDC would insist, Eden proposed to extend the so-called Brussels Treaty, concluded in 1948 between Britain, France, and the Benelux countries, to include the Federal Republic and Italy and to adapt it to the new conditions.

The plan was simple and to the point, and its execution seemed to present no insuperable difficulties. True, it abandoned, at least for the time being, the political ideas which had been the basis of the original European Army concept, and to this Adenauer had to resign himself. But against this stood the fact that it created a basis for practical cooperation between the European nations from which eventually the genuine trust and confidence might spring which the EDC had not enjoyed, and this was a hope Adenauer refused to give up. It was a pragmatic approach to which Adenauer was by no means unreceptive.

The Nine Power Conference, consisting of the six former EDC nations, to whom Britain, the United States, and Canada had added themselves, met in London on September 9, 1954, under Eden's chairmanship. Once more Britain took the initiative. At an early stage in the talks Eden announced that Britain would commit herself to keeping the full strength of her present NATO forces on the European continent for the duration of the new defense pact: four divisions and one tactical air force would remain firmly stationed in Europe for half a century. This was a revolutionary step, and a completely new departure in British foreign and military policy; but there was a string attached to it. With a glance at Mendés-France, Eden told the conference that Britain was willing to enter into this commitment on the condition and assumption that the conference would also reach agreement on all other outstanding issues. In the event of failure or only partial agreement, the British government would consider itself committed to nothing.

On the following day, October 3, 1954, agreement was reached.

The nine Foreign Ministers signed a series of preliminary draft agreements to be embodied in a new treaty. They provided for the end of the occupation regime in Germany, the restoration of Western Germany's full sovereignty, the rearmament of the Federal Republic within the framework of the North Atlantic Pact, and the inclusion of Germany and Italy in the mutual security and assistance system of the Brussels Pact.

"Western European Union" had come into existence.

Adenauer flew back to Bonn that same afternoon. The day was the twenty-fifth anniversary of the death of Gustav Stresemann, who had spent himself in trying to achieve an understanding with the Western Powers. Now, it seemed, this tragic shadow had at last been banished.

Three weeks later Adenauer was in Paris.

The experts had incorporated the London agreements in a series of treaties, and these were now ready for signature. The NATO Council, meeting at the same time, approved the membership of the Federal Republic as soon as the new treaties had been ratified by all parliaments concerned.

These new treaties, it must be admitted, had one flaw which could not be overlooked. For the sake of agreement, France and Germany had accepted the creation of an independent German national army and a separate German general staff. Both had been desperately feared by France, and both Adenauer had striven desperately to avoid. Both had now become a fact. Had Adenauer been the inveterate German nationalist for which many Frenchmen continued to take him, he might have felt gratified by this development; indeed, he might have felt that it served France right that her stubborn resistance should have produced precisely the result which was most contrary to her wishes. As it was, Adenauer harbored no such thoughts. Then as later he never concealed his view that the NATO solution was but a second best, and that it must be regarded as no more than a milestone on the road to the ultimate goal to which he remained pledged—the integration of Europe.

However, there was, as always, a last-minute stumbling block. It was not a new difficulty; indeed, it was a very old one. Once again the Saar problem stood in the way. Mendès-France declared that he must refuse to sign the new treaties as long as no agreement had been reached between Germany and France on the Saar. The bombshell burst during a dinner which Eden gave to the assembled Foreign Ministers at the British Embassy. What was to be done? The banquet was no sooner over than Eden opened the doors to the adjoining library and invited Adenauer and Mendès-France to step inside. Then he closed the doors behind them and set himself to wait outside. He waited until three o'clock in the morning. Then the two men emerged, tired and worn, and quietly slipped out of the Embassy.

The following afternoon Adenauer and Mendès-France also signed, along with the rest of the Western European treaties, the new agreement on the Saar—the fruit of their long night's discussion. It contained one decisive concession on the part of France which was of paramount importance to Adenauer. Pending a German peace settlement, the Saar Territory was to be given a statute within the Western European Union, but the Saarlanders themselves were granted the right to hold a plebiscite in which to decide freely whether to accept or reject it.

Everyone was aware of the responsibility Adenauer took upon himself in agreeing to this, and the risk it would cause him to run at home. He was giving a very large hostage to fortune, and no man was more aware of this than Mendès-France. And now this "adventurer of reason," as one French newspaper had called him, having fought hard and long, set himself to demonstrate that trust and confidence were not, after all, misplaced.

The barrage against Mendès-France opened almost at once. On the day the Paris Treaties were signed there arrived promptly—as always when the unification of Europe came within sight—a Soviet note addressed to the three Western Powers suggesting a Four Power Conference to discuss the restoration of German unity. On November 13, 1954, there followed a second note, this time proposing a European Security Conference. On December 9, shortly before the first reading of the Paris Treaties in the Federal Parliament, there arrived a third. This time the Soviet Union refused categorically all further discussion of German reunification once the decision to rearm Germany had been taken. And on December 15, a few days before the beginning of the ratification debate in the French Chamber, Moscow denounced the Franco-Soviet Treaty of 1944.

It was a veritable diplomatic hailstorm which poured down jointly on France and Germany, and its combination of threats and blandishments, overtures and ultimata, placed both Adenauer and Mendès-France in a perilous position. But this time Mendès-France, the "man without a majority," stood his ground. He flatly refused to take part in any Four Power Conference as long as the Paris Treaties were not ratified. With a last desperate effort, mobilizing every ally he could find and throwing in every ounce of authority at his command, he finally secured ratification of the Treaties on December 30, 1954. His majority was twenty-seven. Five weeks later he was driven from office, and resigned.

Adenauer sincerely regretted the dismissal of this resourceful and capable statesman. He had come to know and appreciate his qualities, and he had reason to feel grateful to him. The great task had at last been accomplished, and Mendès-France had had a large share in it.

Two weeks later the Federal Parliament approved the Paris Treaties, and on May 5, 1955, the ratification documents were deposited at Bonn in solemn ceremony.

At the stroke of noon on May 5, 1955, the three Allied High Commissioners presented themselves at the Palais Schaumburg, the Federal Chancellor's official residence.

"Since I am the only one of us three," said François-Poncet, "who was present at the birth of the Allied High Commission and who has taken part in its work without interruption for five and a half years, it now falls to me to pronounce the funeral sermon."

After this introduction the French High Commissioner took a formal document from his brief case and solemnly read out:

"The Occupation Statute is abolished. The Allied High Commissioners in the Federal Republic are dissolved. This proclamation comes into force on May 5, 1955, at twelve noon."

Three hours later, to the strains of the "*Deutschland-Lied,*" flags were hoisted on all government buildings throughout the Federal Republic. In front of the Palais Schaumburg a detachment of Frontier Police presented arms. The Federal Chancellor stepped out among the large crowd which had gathered before the Chancellery.

He hoisted the flag, and then read to the assembled people the federal government's own proclamation:

"Today, almost ten years after the military and political collapse of National Socialism, the era of occupation ends in the Federal Republic. It is with profound satisfaction that the federal government is able to declare: we are once more a free and independent state. What has long been preparing on the basis of trust and confidence has now become a fact valid in international law: a free nation ourselves, we are taking our place among the free nations of the world, bound to the former occupation powers in a genuine partnership.

"Together with the federal government, fifty million free citizens of the Federal Republic are at this hour thinking in brotherly love of millions of other Germans who are still forced to dwell, separated from us, in thraldom and lawlessness. We call to them: you are part of us and we belong to you. Our joy at having regained our freedom will be overshadowed as long as this freedom is denied to you. You may forever rely on us, for, together with the free world, we shall not rest until you too have regained your human rights and live peacefully united with us in one state and as one nation.

"In this hour, too, we think of the many Germans who still have to endure the hard fate of prisoners of war. We shall strain every nerve to insure that for them as well the hour of freedom will strike soon. Freedom imposes obligations. For us here at home there is only one road—the road of the constitutional state of law and order, of democracy and social justice. There is for us only one place in the world—side by side with the free nations. Our goal is a free and united Germany in a free and united Europe."

The crowd had listened in silence, deeply stirred. When Adenauer had ended a young woman came forward and without a word handed him a bunch of red roses.

# EPILOGUE

"THE Federal Chancellor is expecting you in the garden," the police guard told me at the gate in Zennigsweg.

Slowly I climbed the long and steep flight of stone steps leading up to the house. It was a beautiful, sunny Sunday afternoon in the late summer of 1955. I had completed my work, and I had come for a final talk, to express my thanks for the help and encouragement given, and to take my leave.

The last chapter in this book is of course not the last chapter in the life of Konrad Adenauer. The end of this long career is not yet. But whatever new events and experiences may yet add themselves to the long chain I have tried to unroll, they will not materially change the picture of the man as it has emerged from these pages, and they can do little to alter the historic significance of his work. His portrait is clear, and his achievement stands. He has led the German people out of the greatest defeat in history; he has restored not only its material well-being, but also its courage to live and its self-confidence; and he has regained for this people who, a bare ten years ago, was still a pariah among the nations of the earth, the confidence and respect of the free world. The great and ultimate goal of all his political striving still lies veiled in the distant future, but, if it is ever reached, the tall figure of Konrad Adenauer will certainly be found standing among the fathers of this new Christian Occident.

Not so long ago, during the London Nine Power Conference, the Chancellor is said to have told an old friend late one night, "I am worried by the thought of what will become of Germany when I am no longer here. . . ." I was reminded of this when I sat down beside him on his garden bench. Now in his eightieth year, Adenauer looked tired, it was true, and his words would sound arrogant were it not that the majority of Germans felt them to be the truth. Indeed, what is to happen when he decides to retire? Once again, as in Bismarck's day, German political destiny is held by one pair of hands and one pair of eyes. Will his successors, whoever they may be, observe the same virtues of patience and prudence, modesty and self-abnegation which he has so visibly embodied in his political as well as his private life? Adenauer has set a new and high example among German men of politics. Are there others willing and able to follow it?

"What of the future, Mr. Federal Chancellor?" I asked at length.

He gave me a somewhat puzzled look, and then dismissed the question. "I have long given up the habit of trying to work out all future possibilities down to the last point of detail. The world, after all, is in perpetual movement. . . ."

He paused, thought for a moment, and then went on:

"One thing, however, I think one can say. The struggles which have shaken the world during the past years cannot be compared to the wars of nations during the past centuries. Those wars aimed almost invariably at the extension of areas of national sovereignty. I don't think the future will see much of that type of war. The great struggles of our time, through which we live now, are not concerned with territorial dominion but with the clash of different and opposed ways of life—between democracy, which is ultimately founded upon the Christian concept of individual freedom, and a conception of the world in which the freedom of the individual is subordinated to a collective whole. These collective concepts, whether they are called National Socialism or Communism, are invariably rooted in materialism and therefore must inevitably lead to the totalitarian state.

"This struggle has now spread over the entire globe. Europe, and in particular Germany, are placed at the focal point of this conflict. It is a struggle which will continue for many more years, and in my view the world will not finally achieve peace and freedom unless the concept based on Christian principles emerges victorious."

"Are you then rejecting the idea of coexistence between democracy and Communism?" I asked, somewhat perturbed.

Almost indignantly Adenauer shook his head.

"There are things which reach beyond the realm of everyday politics," he said. "Of course I wish to establish tolerable relations with the Russians. If I had no such wish, why should I take the trouble to travel all the way to Moscow? No, there is much more involved in this question than that; it is essentially a conflict between Christianity and materialism. That is what the struggle is about, and this conflict also exists within the democracies. The modern technical world in which we live, with its movies, radio, and television, favors development toward a mass society, and this 'man of the masses' will always incline toward materialism. To counterbalance this we need, in all countries, Christian parties which not only permeate political, social, and economic life with a Christian spirit, but over and above that aim at creating the essential conditions for a Christian existence of the individual.

"Among these conditions are a modest measure of property which will relieve the working man of his fear of starvation and misery; an adequate home for the family where the children can grow up in healthy surroundings, in fresh air, light, plenty of sunshine, and enough space to move in; another condition is sufficient leisure and free time, for any true personality needs calm and unhurried rest in order to develop. And there must above all be a Christian education of the young.

"For the great struggle between Christianity and materialism is fought out in the soul of youth. Unless we succeed in persuading the individual young person to conceive of himself as a Christian personality with a duty to account for his life to God, we shall have worked in vain.

"I know that it is a long road, and many will have to tread it before the promised land will come into sight. We're not promising a paradise on earth. Man's fortune and happiness will always be in the hands of God. But we firmly believe that along our road greater chances of happiness can be found than in the world of Communism. That gives us the strength to act as we do, always hoping, of course, that the best among those who come after us will take up the torch and carry it further, once it has fallen from our hands."

*INDEX*

# INDEX

# A

# B

# C

# D



# E



# F

# H

# I



# J



# K

# L



# M



# N

# O



# P

## Q



## R

# T



# U



# V



# W

# Y



# Z